JOHN COIT SPOONER
Defender of Presidents

by Dorothy Ganfield Fowler

PROFESSOR OF HISTORY
HUNTER COLLEGE OF THE CITY OF NEW YORK

University Publishers   New York

TO MY MOTHER

Mrs. William Arthur Ganfield

Preface

IN 1957 a committee of United States senators selected a Wisconsin senator as one of the five "outstanding" senators in American history. The one chosen was Robert M. La Follette. John Coit Spooner was not even included in the list from which the five were selected. Yet Spooner, while he was in the United States Senate, had considerably more influence on legislation and on the policies of the federal government than his insurgent colleague. But Spooner was a conservative; he co-operated with the administrations in power and was overshadowed by President Theodore Roosevelt. La Follette, on the other hand, was always a rebel. He continually disagreed with those in authority and proclaimed economic and political ideas which at that time were considered very radical, but which since then have received more or less general acceptance. Not only did

Spooner suffer from a shift in public opinion, which no longer respected the principles for which he stood, but he was also a victim of the propaganda of the progressives in Wisconsin, who were intent on portraying him as the tool of the "interests" or on erasing his name from the annals of Wisconsin history.

My attention was first called to Spooner when I was working on my doctoral dissertation at the University of Wisconsin, under the auspices of Professor Frederic L. Paxson. He suggested that it would be interesting to discover if Spooner was an original thinker or primarily a pleader who merely argued the case for which he was briefed, so that he became the effective mouthpiece of his group. At that time I wished to write a biography of the former Stalwart Senator, but could not obtain permission to examine Spooner's correspondence. In 1945, however, Charles and Philip Spooner, the two remaining sons of the former Senator, gave me unqualified permission to use the Spooner papers. I never met the sons, since they died shortly after that. Mrs. Charles Spooner and her daughter, Miss Dorothy Spooner, were very co-operative. They let me consult Mrs. John Coit Spooner's diaries and related to me their own recollections of the former Senator.

So many librarians have aided me in my research that I should like to pay tribute to them as a professional group. I particularly wish to thank the librarians in the Manuscript Division of The Library of Congress, in the American History and Manuscript divisions of the New York Public Library, and in the Manuscript and Newspaper divisions of the Wisconsin State Historical Society Library.

I want also to acknowledge with thanks the grant-in-aid from the Social Science Research Council, which enabled me to travel from Boston to Des Moines in search of letters that might throw light on Spooner's activities.

Finally, a word of thanks to my husband, Emmett Fowler, for his patience during the many years in which I worked to try to reanimate the former Senator from Wisconsin.

D. G. F.

Contents

John Coit Spooner: DEFENDER OF PRESIDENTS

1 : *Ancestry, Education, and Military Service (1843-1870)*

"MY GREAT GRANDFATHER'S NAME I DO NOT KNOW"*

COMMENTATORS writing shortly after the turn of the twentieth century were in general agreement that the United States Senate was at the time the most powerful branch of the public administration, and that it was dominated by an inner circle of which John Coit Spooner was a member.

Beyond that, however, there was little unanimity of opinion on the subject of Spooner. On the one hand, journalists such as Walter Wellman acclaimed him as a brilliant statesman devoting his talents to the service of his country; on the other, the muckraker David Graham Phillips saw him as the tool of special interests. "It is within bounds to say," wrote the former eulogistically,

that no important measure reaches the statute-books, or even the calendar of the Senate, without having the hallmark of the

* Spooner to H. L. Alden, March 21, 1903, in Spooner Papers.

active and sympathetic mind of Mr. Spooner stamped upon it in greater or less degree. . . . If we now add that Mr. Spooner's counsel is as eagerly sought at the White House as it is in the Senate, and as often accepted, we shall begin to understand the unique position which the Wisconsin Senator holds in the American government.[1]

Phillips, however, claimed that the depiction of Spooner as the "ideal Senator" was a myth created by the "merger" on behalf of the "interests." He wrote:

Many of our foremost newspapers, Republican, Democratic, and independent, have been assuring us for the past few years that Spooner is a great statesman, an honor to his state, his country, and his era. But they have cited no acts of signal or even modest public service in the one direction in which a statesman could serve the people—in correcting conditions that have built up a plutocracy in a single generation, that have reduced the average American family's income to a scant six hundred dollars a year, and have driven our children by the hundreds of thousands to hard labor in mines and factories.[2]

Which was the real Spooner? Was he the great statesman his admirers called him or one of the "enemies of the Republic," as the muckrakers dubbed him?

John Coit Spooner was born in a small Indiana town on January 6, 1843. Coit was his mother's maiden name and John was a favorite given name in her family. It was a John Coit who had come from Glamorganshire, Wales, in the 1630's to settle in Salem, Massachusetts.[3] The first Spooners to come to America were the widow Ann and her sons William and Thomas. Ann Peck Spooner had been the

---

[1] Walter Wellman, "Spooner of Wisconsin: A Sketch of the Present Leader of the Senate," *Review of Reviews,* 26 (August, 1902), 167–70.

[2] David Graham Phillips, "Chief Spokesman of 'the Merger,'" *Cosmopolitan Magazine,* 41 (June, 1906), 123–32.

[3] Frederick William Chapman, *The Coit Family,* p. 13.

ward of William Brewster, who had shepherded the little group of Separatists (the Scrooby congregation) when they left England in 1608 in search of religious freedom. They had settled in Amsterdam, Holland, and then moved to Leyden, where John Spooner, of Colchester, Essexshire, a widower of nine months, met and married Ann Peck in December, 1616.[4] The Spooners did not come over on the *Mayflower* but remained in Leyden when William Brewster and others of his congregation sailed for America on that famous ship. It was early in 1637 that Ann Spooner, then a widow, and her two sons arrived in Massachusetts. She and Thomas settled in Salem.

William, then about seventeen, indentured himself for six years to John Coombs, a prosperous resident of Plymouth, who contracted to "give the said Willm Spooner one comely suit of apparell for holy days, and one suite for working days, and twelve bushells of Indian Wheate, and a good serviceable muskett, bandoleers, and sword fitt for service." William was evidently a faithful servant, for he was entrusted not only with the administration of his master's estate but with the custody of the children during Mr. Coombs's absence in England.

After his term of indenture had expired, William Spooner acquired some land and became one of the respected members of the community. In 1654 he became a freeman of Plymouth, a status that presupposed a "sober, peaceful conversation, orthodoxy in the fundamentals of religion and a ratable estate of twenty pounds." In 1660 he moved to the new settlement at Acushnet in the Dartmouth Purchase (now New Bedford, Massachusetts), where

4 Morton Dexter, "Members of the Pilgrim Company in Leyden," *Proceedings of the Massachusetts Historical Society* (April, 1903), pp. 167–84; George F. Willison, *Saints and Strangers*, pp. 54, 81–83, 88.

he built the first mill in the purchase. He married twice; his second wife, mother of Samuel, who was John's ancestor, was Hannah Pratt, daughter of Joshua and Bathsheba Pratt, who had come over on the *Anna* in 1623. When William died in 1684, he bequeathed to Samuel a house and the "seat of land belonging to it," which amounted to forty acres. The Spooners continued to live around New Bedford. They were members of the Congregational church, well thought of in the town, and most of them at some time in their lives held a local public office, frequently that of constable.[5]

The Coits were an even more prominent colonial American family. One of their most distinguished members was the Reverend Joseph Coit (1673–1750), grandson of the first American Coit (John) and son of Deacon Joseph, a well-to-do shipbuilder in New London, Connecticut. The Reverend Joseph Coit was a graduate of Harvard College and received his master's degree at the first commencement of Yale College in 1702. A man of great independence, he declined a pastorate at Norwich because he disagreed with members of the church on points of theology. He finally accepted a regular appointment as pastor of the church in Plainfield, Connecticut, where he remained for almost fifty years.[6]

[5] Thomas Spooner, *Records of William Spooner*, pp. 13–17, 25; *The National Cyclopedia of American Biography*, 16:33, confuses this first William with his grandson. The latter was the oldest of the eleven children of Samuel Spooner and Experience Wing, and lived from 1689 to 1750 and married Mercy Delano. They had seven children, among them Nathaniel (1716–1799), who married Hannah Blackwell. The youngest of their four children was Philip (1756–1820).

[6] Chapman, *Coit Family*, p. 21. His annual salary as pastor was at first forty pounds and finally was raised to ninety. When he died he left a large estate, including three Negro slaves.

Both the Coits and the Spooners were "patriots" during the struggle with England. Philip Spooner, who was only twenty at the outbreak of the Revolution, served in the army but did not distinguish himself. He was described as a quiet, retiring, honest, diligent, and thrifty person.[7] Samuel Coit (1708–1792), eldest son of the Reverend Joseph Coit and Experience Wheeler, had commanded a regiment in the French and Indian War and had risen to the rank of colonel. He was prominent in his community; had represented Preston in the Connecticut General Assembly for six terms, had been moderator of the town meeting which protested the Boston Port Bill in 1774, and a member of his town's committee of correspondence. During the War of Independence he sat as a judge on the bench of the county court and a maritime court.[8]

This was Spooner's heritage—ancestors whose lives had been closely woven into the fabric of New England's colonial history. Spooner, however, interested in his own contribution to America, was not a man to pay tribute to distinguished forebears; in fact, he was almost completely ignorant of his genealogy. When asked about his ancestors, he could only say, "My grandfather's name on my mother's side was Roger Coit. He was from Plainfield, Connecticut. His father's name I do not know. My grandfather on my father's side was Charles Spooner. I think he was born in New Bedford, Massachusetts, where my father was born. My great grandfather's name I do not know." [9] Spooner's

7 Spooner, *Records*, p. 179.
8 Chapman, *Coit Family*, p. 32.
9 Spooner to H. L. Alden, March 21, 1903, in Spooner Papers in The Library of Congress. Roger Coit (1786–1856) was the grandson of Colonel Samuel Coit and the youngest of the nine children of John Coit and Mehetabel Tyler Coit.

paternal grandfather had joined the westward trek of the early nineteenth century. After leaving New England he had made short sojourns at Mansfield, Marietta, and Cincinnati, Ohio, and in 1829 had finally settled with his family in Lawrenceburg, Indiana. John's father, Philip Loring Spooner (1811–1887), had studied law in the office of George H. Dunn, congressman from 1837 to 1839, and after his admission to the bar had returned East to marry Lydia Lord Coit (1814–1881) on September 11, 1839.[10]

There in Lawrenceburg, John Coit Spooner was born on January 6, 1843, and there he spent the first sixteen years of his life. The town is on the north bank of the Ohio River, twenty-one miles below Cincinnati and two miles below the Big Miami, which marks the eastern limit of the state. Situated in the center of rich bottom land, it was for a time a prosperous and growing community. Its population had more than trebled between the time of the Spooners' arrival and John's birth. Its growth did not continue at that rate, however, and by 1859, when the Philip Spooners decided to leave, its population was only four thousand; there were then six churches, ten schools, five hotels, two mills, three distilleries, two breweries, and eight lawyers.

Two of the lawyers were Spooners. John's father had built up a good law practice both in Lawrenceburg and Cincinnati and ranked as one of the foremost attorneys in Indiana. John's uncle Benjamin J. Spooner, after his return from the Mexican War, had been admitted to the bar and became prosecuting attorney for Dearborn County.

10 Spooner, *Records,* p. 179. Charles Spooner (1784–1853) was the son of Philip Spooner and Lydia Baker. See *Reports of Cases Argued and Determined in the Supreme Court of the State of Wisconsin,* 72:xxvii–xxxvii (1888), and *Wisconsin State Journal,* November 3, 1887.

He was prominent in the Whig party and later active in the new Republican party.[11]

John had a comparatively uneventful childhood. He was small for his age, had curly red hair, which he wore rather long, and somewhat girlish features. He was surrounded by a large and devoted family. His sister Mary was a year older than he, and his brothers Philip and Roger were four and six years his junior, respectively. Besides his immediate family there were many Spooner relatives, among them John's paternal grandfather who lived with them until John was ten. His mother's father, Roger Coit, who after sixty-six years in Connecticut, where he had been high sheriff of Windham County, caught the western fever, lived near them for a short time in Cincinnati before moving to Michigan.

Since there was no Congregational church in Lawrenceburg, the faith in which Lydia Coit Spooner had been reared, the Spooners attended the First Presbyterian Church, which had been the first pastorate of the famous Henry Ward Beecher, who had only recently left. Mrs. Spooner became a very devout member of the church but her husband, though he attended services, never formally joined nor did John ever do so. These years in Lawrenceburg evidently made little impression on John, for only twice does he make any mention of them in his voluminous correspondence. He spoke once of attending the Lawrenceburg Institute, one of the two secondary schools in the town. His keenest recollection was of the first Republican

11 *History of Dearborn and Ohio Counties, Indiana,* pp. 156, 241, 251, 259–60. During the Civil War Benjamin Spooner rose to the rank of major general and was presented with a magnificent sword, which was one of Senator Spooner's prized mementos.

speech he ever heard, one delivered by Anson Burlingame, of Massachusetts, during the campaign of 1856. "I listened to [it] at the home of my boyhood, on the banks of the Ohio river, at Lawrenceburg, Indiana, in sight of the Kentucky hills." [12]

When John was sixteen his family moved to Madison, Wisconsin, where his father became reporter for the Wisconsin Supreme Court. John entered the Madison High School to prepare for the university; all that he remembered of it was that it had a vigorous debating society.[13] In August, 1860, he enrolled in the University of Wisconsin. At that time it was just a small college. There were but three buildings, the third, University Hall (later named Bascom), having been completed just that year. There were only five professors. Tuition was five dollars per term, with three terms a year. Since Spooner lived at home, at the corner of Carroll and Wilson Streets, near Lake Monona, he had to pay, in addition, one dollar for the use of the public rooms. John enrolled in the classical course for which there were twenty-nine students registered. The curriculum consisted of many courses in mathematics, Latin and Greek, several in philosophy and ethics, and a few in English literature and rhetoric. A course in French and one in German were required, but Spooner was never able to speak either language. The few lectures in international law, constitutional law, and political economy probably interested him the most, for he had already decided to follow in his father's footsteps and become a lawyer.[14]

---

12 *Ibid.,* pp. 273, 278; Spooner to O. F. Roberts, February 9, 1885; to W. E. Riley, April 16, 1893, in Spooner Papers.

13 Spooner to William H. Beach, February 18, 1888, in Spooner Papers.

14 *Catalogue,* University of Wisconsin, 1862, pp. x, xi, xiv, xv.

In later years it was not his studies that John remembered but his debating club, the Hesperian Society, which he joined immediately on entering the university. Forty years later, in sending a donation of $50, he wrote: "I derived more pleasure and benefit from my training in that Society than almost anything else in my college life." [15] The society's clubroom was on the fourth floor of the new University Hall. The Board of Regents had appropriated $130 for outfitting the hall and the members contributed out of their own meager resources the funds for matting on the floor, a kerosene lamp, and a "library," to which John contributed a book shortly after he became a member. A picture of Daniel Webster addressing the United States Senate, which the club purchased on the installment plan, completed the furnishings of the quarters.[16]

Mr. Spooner—the young men were very formal in their meetings—enjoyed debate; every Friday he attended the meetings and almost every other week was a member of the debating team, which usually won. These college boys took the meetings very seriously, although occasionally one or two of them were penalized by the censor for loud whispering. Only once did John have to pay the ten-cent fine. They worked hard in preparation for the debates. With confidence they disposed of such legal and constitutional questions as: that the signs of the times indicated the downfall of the American Republic; that the constitution of England, rather than that of the United States, was better suited to secure the ends of good government; that capital

15 Spooner to O. G. Libby, March 30, 1901, in Spooner Papers.
16 Merle Curti and Vernon Carstensen, *The University of Wisconsin: A History, 1848–1925,* I, 424–25; Hesperian Society Records, pp. 76, 136, 139, 146, 180, in the State Historical Society of Wisconsin, Madison.

punishment ought to be reinstated in Wisconsin. A great number of the subjects for debate dealt with historical events. It is probably here that John gained most of his early knowledge of history, for he had only two history courses, both in his freshman year. Only one of the debate topics dealt with the college curriculum, and that was one which still arouses discussion among college students: *Resolved,* That students in college ought to direct their studies with reference to a profession. John championed the cause of the liberal arts.[17]

On that momentous day of April 12, 1861, when Fort Sumter was fired on, the topic debated before the Hesperian Society was: *Resolved,* That the United States ought to coerce the seceding states. The members of the society decided in favor of the team supporting the negative. They learned soon afterward that hostilities had begun in Charleston, South Carolina, that morning at four. At the next Friday meeting the debate was interrupted by the entrance of three members who had enlisted immediately after President Lincoln had issued his first call for volunteers; they were greeted with great applause. After the debate the three volunteers expressed their feelings in regard to the cause for which they were going to fight, and the society solemnly passed a resolution commending their action.[18]

More and more war filled the minds of these college boys. Neglected were the historical questions. They debated more immediate issues: Was the arrest of Mason and Slidell on board the *Trent* in accordance with the principles of international law? Should the government of the

17 Hesperian Society Records, p. 217; Bill of Exercises contains the records of the debates.

18 Hesperian Society Records, p. 127; Harvey Reid, "Diary of Harvey Reid," *Wisconsin Magazine of History,* 1 (September, 1917), 46.

United States proclaim emancipation as a military necessity? Was the draft constitutional? At the annual anni-
versary exercises in May, 1862, after the usual Bible reading, recitations, orations, and toasts, John Spooner, as
president of the Hesperian Society, gave his toast. It was to
"Hesperians Departed." Already the ranks of the society
had been badly depleted as members left to join the fighting forces. At every call for volunteers John tried to enlist,
but his mother refused to give her consent. His father
urged him to remain in college at least until he was twenty-
one. Finally, in the spring of 1864, one month before he
was to be graduated, he cast aside his schoolbooks and enlisted, regardless of the consequences. On May 27 he attended his last meeting of the Hesperian Society.[19] Years
later a school friend, congratulating Senator Spooner after
one of his encounters with Senator Pettigrew, wrote: "Do
you know John it brought all back so vividly some of our
old debate scenes in the State University especially that last
night just before you left for the 100 day service. I can see
you now standing on that platform facing old Schrieber &
giving it to him warm." [20]

John Spooner and his classmates had answered the call
for one-hundred-day men, which the governor had issued
on May 4, a call that pretty well emptied the university of
men. It was fortunate that the Normal Department had
been established in 1863 and women had been admitted

[19] Hesperian Society Records, pp. 184–85, 304–5. See also James Lambert
High, "University of Wisconsin During the Civil War," in *The Great
Chancellor and Other Papers*, pp. 217–35. The Board of Regents bestowed
the degrees on five seniors, four of whom had enlisted. Spooner received
the Ph.B. degree, which means that he had not completed all the ancient
language requirements for the B.A. See Minutes of the Regents of the University of Wisconsin, Vol. B., June 28, 1864.

[20] E. W. Christie to Spooner, May 26, 1900, in Spooner Papers.

for the first time. The university men, under the command of Captain Charles H. Allen, head of the Normal Department, made up Company D of the Fortieth Regiment. Wrote the chronicler of the regiment:

They were young men mostly, and Greek testaments and all manner of classic books were common in their tents. . . . It was the ambition and boast of the University boys that they were Privates. . . . There were no equal number of commissioned folk in the regiment more capable, nor more worthy of holding any commission, than all of these, who advocated that "a private station claims most honor" in the 100 day service.[21]

John had been offered a clerkship in the regiment but he insisted on serving in the ranks, much to the distress of his mother and sister; they did not think it right that he should be a private. For a month they drilled assiduously at Camp Randall, opposite the university. On June 14, singing "John Brown's knapsack is strapped upon his back," they left Madison. They reached Memphis, Tennessee, at nine o'clock Sunday morning, June 19, and marched to their camping grounds, about two miles from the levee on Pigeon Roost Road. They had no tents and slept on the ground. John was more comfortable than most, for he had brought along a rubber blanket. It was a very unhealthy locality, hot and wet, and many of the boys became ill.[22]

21 *Wisconsin State Journal*, May 4, 16, 21, 1864; Julius Converse Chandler, *Annals of the Fortieth*, p. 9.

22 Roger to Spooner, May 19; Mary to Spooner, July 3; P. L. Spooner to J. Spooner, July 13; Mrs. Spooner to Mary, June 10, 1864, in Spooner Papers. The biographical sketch in D. I. Nelke, *The Columbian Biographical Dictionary and Portrait Gallery of the Representative Men of the United States. Wisconsin Volume*, p. 128, says John Spooner borrowed three hundred dollars from a local bank in order to pay the expenses of raising the company and then proposed that they all remain privates.

They were in a quiet sector, where the monotony of camp was broken only occasionally by an order for a detail to stand guard along the Memphis and Charleston Railroad. An amusing story was sent to the home town paper by one of Spooner's comrades. A woman, with two hundred dollars concealed on her person, had tried to slip through the lines. She was driving an old mule, was caught and arrested.

Capt. Allen sent her back under the charge of Private S., who is well known in Madison. S. mounted into the establishment and endeavored to get up locomotion. Mule was obstinate and would not proceed; the "lady" commenced reviling "Lincoln's minion" in whose possession she was. S. became impatient; proceeded to active measures, and applied the point of his bayonet to the incarnate obstinacy in harness before him. Mule forgot his dignity, and proceeded to a vigorous kicking, which threatened to demolish the entire establishment. It was a long time before quiet was restored, but I refrain from further particulars in order that S. may have an opportunity of relating his own adventures.[23]

The only fighting this company saw was when a detachment of Forrest's cavalry attacked Memphis. The Fortieth was ordered to support a Missouri battery which was engaged with the enemy. During the skirmish they lay down about a hundred rods from the rebel lines to support the artillery behind them, and later pursued the enemy about two miles.[24] Spooner always regretted that he had seen no

[23] *Wisconsin State Journal,* August 20, 1864; Roger to Spooner, August 8, 1864, in Spooner Papers.

[24] Edwin B. Quiner, *Military History of Wisconsin,* pp. 855–59; U. S. War Department, *War of the Rebellion: Official Records of the Union and Confederate Armies,* Series 1, Vol. 39, Part I, p. 469; Part II, p. 332. Statistics on the Fortieth Regiment: original strength, 776; mustered out, 763; lost by death and disease, 13.

real action, and later refused to join any veteran organization because he felt he had done nothing to deserve membership.[25]

As his term of service drew to a close, John's family looked forward longingly to the day of his return. These one-hundred-day men were not subject to the draft, for they were in service when the draft in Wisconsin took place. Special inducements, however, were offered to get them to volunteer for one, two, or three years. Spooner was torn between two loyalties. He felt he should re-enlist if his country needed him, and yet both his mother and father objected. He was devoted to his parents and usually did as they wished. They had always presented him to his sister and brothers, especially to Roger, as a model son. They now begged him not to remain in the army one more day than was necessary. His mother pointed out what a "noble" man his uncle was, for he had hired a substitute for $900 but had received back $800. His father wrote that he was resigning as reporter for the supreme court and was going to open his own law office and was looking forward to the day John would have finished his studies and become his partner. He hoped the day would be soon.[26]

[25] Spooner to J. V. Quarles, March 4, 1890, in Spooner Papers: "The truth is Joe., that while I was in the army a little over three months as a private soldier, and a little over a year as a Captain, my army service, in which I did faithfully what was given me to do, was entirely inglorious, and I have never felt that I had any right to march in times of peace with those who fought in time of war. I never was in a battle; I have never claimed the slightest consideration as a soldier; I have declined constantly invitations to the Loyal Legion and other military banquets here and in the east for this reason. . . . I may be wrong about it, but in these days, when I see so many men active as soldiers, who were not so active from 1861 to 1865, I instinctively hold back."

[26] Letters to Spooner from his father, July 2, August 9; from his mother, August 18, 1864, in Spooner Papers.

John did not re-enlist immediately but returned home on September 15 and was mustered out the next day. While he was recuperating from an illness he had acquired in the army, he obtained a job as assistant state librarian. In the spring, when the governor issued a call for the organization of the Fiftieth Regiment, he volunteered immediately and was made captain of Company A. Under his command the first four companies of the regiment left Madison for St. Louis, Missouri, on March 25, 1865, and were stationed at Benton Barracks.[27] Since the war ended shortly after their arrival, they were assigned the task of disarming and disbanding rebels and bushwhackers in Missouri. On August 12 the regiment was ordered to leave immediately by boat for Fort Rice, Dakota Territory. A commission had been appointed to treat with the Indians on the upper Missouri and the regiment was sent there to preserve peace during the negotiations. The Indians were quiet and all the army had to do was prevent the Sioux from returning to Minnesota, from whence they had been removed after their uprising in 1862.[28]

The nine months (August 31, 1865–May 31, 1866) Spooner spent in that desolate region made a great impression on him. Thirty years later he wrote one of his companions: "I often think over our frontier soldiering. It seems sometimes a long, long while ago, and again it seems but yesterday. It was a happy thought on the part of my Father to give me the two volumes of Blackstone, which I read and studied hard up among the Indians at Fort Rice.

[27] Quiner, *Military History*, p. 188; *Wisconsin State Journal*, February 17, March 4, 11, 25, 1864.
[28] *War of Rebellion Records*, Series 1, vol. 48, Part I, p. 1285; Part II, pp. 197, 214–15, 268, 335, 1179; *Roster of Wisconsin Volunteers, War of Rebellion*, II, 869. See Muster Roll, in Spooner Papers.

There wasn't much else to do." [29] In later years his favorite gift to aspiring young lawyers was a set of Blackstone, accompanied with the advice: "I expect to see you master Blackstone, and when you shall have mastered Blackstone you will be master fundamentally of the science of law." [30] It was during this time that Spooner acquired his fondness for riding and hunting and in later years when he needed relaxation he went for a few weeks' hunting trip in the West. These months on the frontier provided him with much firsthand information on the Indians and on Dakota Territory, which he was later to use with considerable effect on the floor of the Senate.

Spooner spent the first few months after he and his company were mustered out, on June 12, 1866, winding up army business. Clothing and camp and garrison equipment had to be returned.[31] Many of his men found themselves in difficulty with the military authorities; several had been charged with desertion because they had overstayed a leave. Almost 20 per cent of the members of the Fiftieth Regiment had deserted while they were stationed in Dakota Territory. Spooner, however, maintained that his men had not deserted; that they had been told to remain at home until they received other orders and these they had not received. He prepared an argument on their cases and presented it to the military court. He was able to get several of them honorably discharged. Others of his regiment had claims for back pay; these claims he presented to the appro-

29 Spooner to O. M. Dering, January 23, 1897. See Spooner to J. Cohor, September 10, 1866, in Spooner Papers. It was at this time that he joined the Masonic order but he was never active in the organization.

30 Spooner to A. Collins, November 3, 1899, *ibid.*

31 Spooner to M. C. Meigs, June 24, 1866, *ibid.; Wisconsin State Journal,* June 9, 13, 1866.

priate military authorities, but he warned the men not to expect a quick decision, for government red tape "winds its slow length along." Spooner aided members of his regiment in their pleas for exemption from civil processes and helped parents of deceased soldiers to obtain pensions. At the end of the summer, much to his surprise, he was given a brevet majorship.[32]

That fall John Spooner made his first excursion into politics. The death of President Lincoln and the policies of President Johnson had split the Republican party into two factions—the Radicals, who supported Congress, and the Union Republicans, the administration wing. Spooner was one of the organizers of the Republican Union Club and was a delegate from the Fourth Ward of Madison to the county convention that nominated the candidates for local offices, among them Willett S. Main for sheriff. The *Wisconsin State Journal* claimed that few rendered more efficient service to the Union Republican's cause during the campaign than John Spooner. After the election he was appointed private and military secretary to Governor Lucius Fairchild. Spooner was commissioned colonel by the governor and thereafter was generally known by that title.[33]

Spooner's secretarial position gave him not only an income of two thousand dollars a year but also lessons in

[32] Spooner to H. McDermott, August 15; to Lieutenant Boner, July 11, 31; to C. H. Cooley, August 31; to J. Cohor, July 7, August 20, September 10; to A. B. Neal, July 7, 1866, in Spooner Papers. Quiner, *Military History*, p. 867, gives these statistics on the Fiftieth Regiment: original strength, 942; gained by recruits, 16; loss by death, 28; discharged, 127; deserted, 141.

[33] *Wisconsin State Journal*, September 20, October 3, November 8, 15, 1866, February 1, 1867.

practical politics. He became acquainted with the men who controlled the Republican party, a group known as the "Madison Regency." At the head of it was Elisha W. Keyes, mayor and postmaster at Madison. He was assisted by David Atwood, editor of the *Wisconsin State Journal,* and Congressman Benjamin F. Hopkins. They had supported President Johnson in the 1866 Congressional election, but since then the President had become increasingly unpopular. Their official friends in Washington were divided; Postmaster General Alexander W. Randall, the distributor of patronage, and Senator James R. Doolittle supported the President, but Senator Howe had joined the Radicals. Governor Fairchild urged party unity; he was a candidate for re-election in 1867 and feared a split in the party might bring about his defeat.[34] Spooner acted as the governor's political scout, sounding out party leaders in various sections of the state. One of his trips took him to the St. Croix region, which later was to be his home for many years.[35]

Spooner returned from his political jaunt in northwestern Wisconsin in time to attend the concert given by Annie Main, daughter of Alfred Main, one of the early settlers of Madison. John was well acquainted with her brother Willett Main, the sheriff, for they had been associated in the campaign of 1866, but he barely knew Annie. When he entered college she had been away at the Albany Female Academy, and since his return from the army she had been singing professionally in Chicago. She had been in Madison in January to sing at the Baptist Festival, for the Mains

[34] Helen J. Williams and Harry Williams, "Wisconsin Republicans and Reconstruction," *Wisconsin Magazine of History,* 23 (September, 1939), 17–39.
[35] Spooner to L. Fairchild, May 1, August 12, 1867, in Fairchild Papers in State Historical Society of Wisconsin.

were devout members of that church. It was August when she returned to give her concert. According to her brother, she took the large audience by storm. Evidently she also captivated John Spooner. For a year he courted her. Whenever Annie was home for a visit, he spent much of his spare time at the Main farm; it was quite a walk but shorter in the winter, only four miles, for then he could walk or skate across the end of Lake Monona. He had some difficulty persuading her to give up her musical career for marriage, but finally, at two o'clock, on September 10, 1868, at the Main home, they were married. They went to St. Paul for their wedding trip, and on their return settled at the Main farm.[36]

John Spooner had finished his law studies and had been admitted to the bar of the circuit court of Dane County and to the state supreme court in 1867. He had resigned his position as secretary to the governor in March, 1868, but had remained a member of his military staff.[37] He had been appointed assistant attorney general by Attorney General Barlow at a salary of one thousand dollars a year. He appeared not only in the local police court but also in the state supreme court in cases involving forgeries, robberies, gambling, and sale of intoxicating liquor.[38] One of his

36 Willett S. Main, Diary, January 28, August 30, December 7, 1867, February 1, September 10, 1868, in State Historical Society of Wisconsin; *Wisconsin State Journal,* February 1, 1867, July 5, 1902.

37 Spooner to W. E. Webster, December 2, 1895, in Spooner Papers; L. Fairchild to Spooner, March 27, 1868, in Fairchild Papers: "You have before you a bright career for which you are well fitted, having been blessed with capacity far above the average of men, and with the will and industry necessary to success in life. Of your future success in your profession I have no doubt, and I hope to live to see the day when you shall have reached the topmost round of any life ladder you choose to climb."

38 *Wisconsin Blue Book,* 1870. 23 Wisconsin 634 (*State* v. *Miller*); 24 Wis. 43 (*McEntee* v. *State*), 60 (*State* v. *Hartfiel*), 145 (*Griswold* v. *State*); 26 Wis. 423 (*Gallagher* v. *State*).

cases in the police court involved Roger Spooner, who had been shot in the arm. His brother was attending the university preparing to become a lawyer. He was a brilliant student but had been badly spoiled, and even at that early age was getting into scrapes out of which his oldest brother had to extricate him.[39]

Assistant Attorney General Spooner's first appearance before the state supreme court was during the February, 1869, term. Elisha W. Keyes was the lawyer for the plaintiff. Spooner argued that successive utterances of forged drafts, even if only a single minute elapsed between the commission of each forgery, constituted separate offenses and the plaintiff was therefore liable for each forgery. He won the case.[40] The most notable case in which he appeared as assistant attorney general was one concerning the taxation of national banks. His father was retained as counsel. The Spooners argued that a tax levied on shares of stock of national banks was similar to the tax levied on the capital of state banks and therefore was not discriminatory against national banks. He cited the famous *McCulloch* v. *Maryland* decision in which Chief Justice Marshall had stated that national banks could be taxed by a state if the tax were not one levied merely against banks chartered by the federal government. He won the case although his adversaries were the well-known S. U. Pinney and J. C. Gregory.[41]

John Spooner had also joined the law firm of Spooner and Lamb. His father Judge Spooner (once judge of Dane County court) was one of the state's leading authorities on

39 Willett Main, Diary, August 23, 24, 25, 26, 1869.
40 23 Wis. 587 (*Barton* v. *State*).
41 25 Wis. 112 (*Bagnall* v. *State*).

real-estate law. On Lamb's retirement from active practice late in 1869, the firm became known as P. L. & J. C. Spooner, and their office was over the post office. Father and son took care of a variety of legal matters, many of them dealing with claims, settlement of estates, bankruptcies, land titles, and collection of debts. They had several cases, mostly injury suits, against the Milwaukee and St. Paul Railway, which, under the presidency of Alexander Mitchell, had become the most important road in the state. In one case young Spooner went over the head of the railroad's lawyer and appealed directly to the president of the company. He pointed out that the mechanic's lien law made the road responsible for claims for labor against a defaulting contractor employed by them. He suggested that if his client were paid for his work by the railroad company, he would not insist on payment of the other claims he had against the contractor. Failing to get a settlement out of court, the Spooners pressed and won the suit. The railroad then employed the firm to represent them in a case before the supreme court.[42]

The Spooners, although they had many clients, did not make much money; the fees they charged were low, ranging usually from $10 to $50. Once when they had set a rather large fee for a service, Spooner wrote the next day: "On reflection we prefer that you should change the figure in the bill we sent you yesterday from $500 to $300. This latter sum is the most we feel willing to accept and should not wish to subject ourselves to the imputation of having demanded an exhorbitant fee." [43] Though their fees were

[42] Spooner to A. Mitchell, January 1; to J. W. Carey, January 8; to H. Gilman, January 18, April 29, 1870, in Spooner Papers.
[43] Spooner to Frisby and Weil, November 6, 1869; to H. J. Smith, July 30, 1870, *ibid.*

very moderate, they frequently had difficulty collecting their money. Like many lawyers of the time, they often accepted produce in partial payment. They were reluctant to dun their clients but they needed money. To one, young Spooner wrote: "Please send me $50. Lawyers can't live in Madison without money." His letter to another was a little more specific: "It costs a great deal to live here and with office and other expenses, we must have our pay for services within a *reasonable* time or we can't keep out of debt." [44] It was always John Spooner who wrote the letters asking for payment of bills.

Young Spooner was ambitious; he wanted to make money. He was not content with his small salary as assistant attorney general and the meager income he and his father received from their law practice in Madison. He disliked not having a home of his own, for he and Annie had lived at the Main farm during most of their married life. With their son Charles Philip and the Main family, the small farmhouse was crowded. "There must be a swarming soon," Willett had noted in his diary. The elder Spooner was a man highly respected in the community, and John, much as he admired him, felt he was overshadowed by him. He complained: "I might sit far into the night to work out a point of law and when I delivered it at trial next day, court, bar and public would deny every particle of credit to me and would give it all to him." He also felt he ought to get away from Madison, where he was too dependent on the law library.[45]

[44] Spooner to A. D. Thompson, November 25, 1869; to C. Keogh, August 4; to Knute Nelson, August 4, 1870, *ibid.*

[45] Willett Main, Diary, September 26, 1869; *Milwaukee Sentinel,* June 11, 1919.

He began to look around for a more lucrative practice and a place where he could make a name for himself. Henry Chapman Baker, of Hudson, Wisconsin, twelve years his senior, became interested in the young man. He had represented Judge Spooner when he purchased some land in St. Croix and Pierce counties and he had met both father and son at the bar of the supreme court early in 1870. Baker had lived in Hudson since 1859, had built up a reputation as a lawyer in that section of the state, and was attorney for the St. Croix and Lake Superior Railroad.[46] He finally convinced young Spooner of the opportunities offered by that undeveloped section of the state. Arrangements for the dissolution of the Spooner partnership were made in August; Spooner senior was to continue his law practice and take ᴗver the work of the assistant attorney general. The young Spooners prepared to leave Madison. So meager were their financial resources that their departure had to be delayed until they received money from his mother's relatives in the East to help pay the moving expenses.[47] Finally the money arrived and the young couple with their year-old son started out to begin a new life in Hudson, Wisconsin.

[46] William H. C. Folsom, *Fifty Years in the Northwest,* p. 169; 25 Wis. 246 (*Schneider* v. *Evans*), 600 (*Hall* v. *Hall*).
[47] Willett Main, Diary, September 6, 1870.

2 : Life in Hudson
(1870-1884)

"GREAT FIGHTS, AND GREAT FUN"*

"COL. J. C. SPOONER and family have arrived here and taken up their permanent residence. They will be a valuable acquisition to the business and society of this city," noted the editor of the *Hudson Star and Times* on September 23, 1870. Hudson was then only a small "Arcadian village" but its residents were confident it would soon become a metropolis.[1] It was the county seat of St. Croix County and was located in the midst of one of the most valuable tracts of virgin timber at a time when, with settlers pouring into the treeless prairies west of the Mis-

---

* Spooner to J. E. Glover, February 27, 1898, in Spooner Papers: "I often live over again the years from 1870 to 1877 or 1878, when we traveled the circuit to-gether, and you and Gus, and Judge Weatherby, and Clinton, and some of the rest of us, had great fights, and great fun. They were happy years all things considered, and I, drifted as I have so far away from them, growing older, and burdened with a different sort of responsibility, look back upon them with a sort of longing."

[1] *Hudson Star and Times,* September 23, 1870, January, 1884 (special supplement).

sissippi, lumber was in tremendous demand. Down Wisconsin's many streams into that great river floated millions of board feet of lumber to build homes, barns, and stores for the settlers of the Great Plains. Hudson, on the St. Croix River near its junction with the Mississippi, commanded the mouth of a valley which that year alone had exported almost a million dollars' worth of lumber.[2]

Hudson, it was expected, would also become a railroad center. The settlers in the Northwest had long been clamoring for a railroad; lumbermen, although they floated logs down the streams, needed railroad transportation to bring in supplies. To facilitate the building of railroads in Wisconsin, Congress had passed on June 3, 1856, an act granting to the state millions of acres of the public domain. These lands were subject to disposition by the state legislature. For every mile of road built, the railroad company was to receive six sections (3,840 acres) of land—the odd-numbered sections on both sides of the road, for the federal government retained title to alternate sections. If the road were not completed within ten years, the unsold lands were to revert to the federal government. In 1864 the time limit had been extended to May, 1869, and the number of sections increased to ten per mile. The act of 1864 specified that there should be two roads in the western part of the state, one running from Madison or Columbus to some point on Lake St. Croix or the St. Croix River, and the other north from that point to the western end of Lake Superior and to Bayfield.[3] Hudson was almost certain to be the St. Croix terminus of the road from the south; it was the summer home of Daniel A. Baldwin, president of the

2 Agnes M. Larson, *History of the White Pine Industry in Minnesota*, pp. 132–34.
3 Frederick Merk, *Economic History of Wisconsin During the Civil War Decade*, p. 279.

West Wisconsin Railroad Company. This road had been designated to receive the land grant from Tomah to St. Croix and tracks had already been laid from Tomah to Black River Falls.[4] At Hudson the West Wisconsin could connect with the St. Croix and Lake Superior Railroad, on which had been conferred the land grant from the St. Croix River to Lake Superior. This small village would therefore be the center through which all traffic to the western end of Lake Superior must pass. Litigation between settlers and the railroad company over these millions of acres of valuable timber lands would provide ample practice for an ambitious lawyer such as John Spooner.[5]

Spooner's career in Hudson was to be closely linked with the railroad and lumber interests. Baker and Spooner opened offices in the First National Bank Building, a new brick structure occupied also by the *Star and Times*. Two of the firm's most important cases that first year were against Schulenberg and Company, of Stillwater, Minnesota, the most important lumber concern in that region. The first case was a dispute over the number of logs delivered by the plaintiff, Baker and Spooner's client, to the lumber company and whether he had been paid in full.[6]

[4] Willis H. Miller, "John Comstock: Banker," *Wisconsin Magazine of History*, 22 (December, 1948), 171–72. As early as 1864 Baldwin had written Comstock that he wanted his road to strike the St. Croix and Lake Superior road as near Hudson as possible. The Tomah and Lake St. Croix Railroad had been incorporated in 1863; one of the incorporators was Judge H. L. Humphrey, of Hudson, Republican congressman in the Forty-fifth and Forty-sixth Congresses. In 1866 the name of the road was changed to West Wisconsin.

[5] *Milwaukee Sentinel*, December 14, 1884.

[6] *Hudson Star and Times*, December 23, 1870, May 5, 1871; 34 Wis. 41 (*Smith* v. *Schulenberg*). Other cases concerning the lumber industry in which Spooner appeared before the Wisconsin supreme court: 34 Wis. 585 (*Durning* v. *Burkhardt*), 41 Wis. 584 (*Tewksbury* v. *Schulenberg*), 48 Wis.

The other case was of much greater significance. In this case Spooner's client was an agent of the state of Wisconsin, General Samuel Harriman. The General had been appointed to protect against trespassers the timber on the land granted to the St. Croix and Lake Superior Railroad, but which the company had not yet earned as it had laid no tracks in that region. The act passed by the state legislature on March 3, 1869, authorized the agent to take possession of any logs unlawfully cut on that property. Harriman had seized several million feet of logs he claimed had been cut by trespassers in 1870 and 1871. Schulenberg and Company sued for the return of these logs and claimed that the land from which they were cut no longer belonged to the state inasmuch as the railroad had not fulfilled the conditions stipulated in the Land-Grant Acts. Spooner and Cushman K. Davis, later governor of Minnesota and then United States Senator, argued the case before the Circuit Court for the District of Minnesota. Their client won. This was only one of many similar suits pending at that time but it was the one which finally went up to the Supreme Court and established the law on the reversion of railroad land grants.[7]

Just a year after Spooner's arrival in Hudson he sought the Republican nomination for the assembly. It was a

---

577 (*Tewksbury* v. *Schulenberg*), 48 Wis. 581 (*Tewksbury* v. *Bronson*), 52 Wis. 634 (*Collins* v. *Cowan*), 52 Wis. 647 (*Nelson* v. *St. Croix Boom Co.*), 60 Wis. 565 (*State* v. *St. Croix Boom Co.*).

[7] *Hudson Star and Times,* June 23, 1871; 21 Federal Cases, Circuit and District Court, 1789–1880, No. 12, 486 (*Schulenberg* v. *Harriman*). The trespass fund at that time credited to the St. Croix and Lake Superior Railroad amounted to $35,629.36; suits pending amounted to $75,000. See Lewis H. Haney, *Congressional History of Railways in the United States,* p. 23.

bitter fight, due not only to personal jealousy but also because of rivalry that existed between railroads and between communities favoring different lines. Spooner's nomination was opposed by the delegates from the southern section of the county; they were interested in the Prescott, River Falls and Northern Railroad, which, sponsored by Assemblyman Oliver S. Powell of Pierce County, had been incorporated in 1870. Residents of Hudson, however, favored the North Wisconsin, which had just been organized by Horace Thompson, Alpheus Beede Stickney, and Daniel A. Baldwin. Both companies proposed to build a railroad from the St. Croix River to Lake Superior and both wanted the land grant. Another grievance against Hudson (and its candidate) was that the town had, in March, 1871, been made the terminus of the West Wisconsin. Spooner was accused of being in the employ of that road and it was charged that he would do all he could to prevent the taxing of railroad lands by the county. The *Hudson Star and Times* called this a "falsehood" and pointed out that the West Wisconsin had already been granted tax exemption, but only for as long as it retained possession of the lands which, in view of the great demand for land, would not be long. Spooner's opponents declared that they would beat him or bust the Republican party, and when Spooner was nominated, a group bolted and nominated E. J. Dodge. After one of the most exciting campaigns in the history of St. Croix County Spooner won but by only a small plurality.[8]

Spooner, though not yet in the employ of either the West Wisconsin or North Wisconsin Railroad companies,

[8] *Hudson Star and Times*, March 3, October 13, 20, 27, November 3, 10, 17, 1871; *Wisconsin Assembly Journal*, 1870, p. 1009.

represented their interests in the legislature. These roads were important to St. Croix County. Spooner and Powell were rivals for appointment to the assembly committee on railroads; Spooner won.[9] Because of his efforts, several private bills repealing acts which it was feared might later cause legal difficulties for the West Wisconsin and North Wisconsin railroads were passed.[10] He also sponsored a general law perfecting the railroad incorporation act; it clarified the powers and liability of boards of directors and classified the rolling stock as fixtures so far as liens were concerned. His speech for a memorial to Congress urging renewal of the St. Croix and Lake Superior Railroad land grant had much to do with its passage by the assembly where, in spite of Governor Washburn's supporting message, it had encountered stiff opposition. Spooner also introduced a bill to confer this land grant on the North Wisconsin Railroad but the bill was pigeonholed.[11]

Spooner was chairman of the assembly committee on education. It was in this field that he made a most significant contribution. Up to this time the university had been supported by the University Fund, which had been created through the sale of land donated by the federal government for higher education. The sum realized from the sale of this land was smaller than it should have been, not only because much of the timber had been depleted by fire and cut by trespassers but because the land had been sold cheaply by the state in order to induce immigrants to settle in Wisconsin. It was argued that the state had failed in its

9 *Hudson Star and Times,* January 26, 1872.
10 *Wisconsin Private Laws,* 1872, pp. 311, 330, 339.
11 *Wisconsin General Laws,* 1872, pp. 137–65; *Wisconsin Assembly Journal,* 1872, pp. 24, 118–19, 278, Appendix; *Hudson Star and Times,* January 19, February 9, 1872.

trust, thus depriving children of their heritage; therefore the state should make annual appropriations for the support of the university. Spooner's bill, appropriating $100,-000 to supplement the income from the University Fund and authorizing the levying annually of a state tax for the support of the university, instituted regular state support of the university.[12]

While in Madison in the spring of 1872 Spooner combined the careers of legislator, politician, and attorney. He was elected by his assembly district as a delegate to the Republican state convention, which selected the delegates-at-large to the Republican National Convention. In spite of a protest by the same group that had opposed his nomination as assemblyman, Spooner and his associate Horace A. Taylor, owner of the *Hudson Star and Times,* were seated by unanimous vote.[13] This was the first state convention that Spooner attended as a delegate. He was to attend many more.

At the spring term of the supreme court Spooner appeared as attorney in four cases. They were all appeals from the circuit courts of St. Croix and Polk counties and were quite different in character. In one, the issue was the jurisdiction of the justice of the peace; another pertained to a claim for bounty money for a man who had enlisted as a substitute in the Civil War. Of particular significance in view of Spooner's later career as a railroad lawyer was the case of *Denniston* v. *Unknown Owners,* for it concerned

[12] Curti and Carstensen, *University of Wisconsin,* I, 116, 123, 148, 304–5, 309–10; *Wisconsin Assembly Journal,* 1872, pp. 31, 322; *Wisconsin General Laws,* 1872, chap. 100.

[13] *Hudson Star and Times,* March 15, 22, 1872.

the taxation of land granted by the federal government to the state for internal improvements. In this instance Spooner argued that the land granted to the state for the improvement of navigation of the Fox and Wisconsin rivers had been vested in the state in fee simple, and that when the land was given over by the state to the company, it was an absolute conveyance and therefore liable to taxation unless an act had been passed specifically exempting that land from taxation. The judgment of the circuit court in favor of Spooner's client was reversed. The court declared that although that land had not been specifically exempt from taxation, it was not liable to taxes at that time, for the state was still the owner of the land since all conditions for conveyance had not been fulfilled.[14]

The last case in which Spooner appeared at that term of the supreme court was a tiresome divorce case which the judge declared differed from other divorce cases only in the length of time that it had consumed in the circuit court, its expensiveness, and the eminence of counsel. This was the first of many cases in which Spooner appeared as a legal opponent of William F. Vilas. What a striking contrast they must have presented as they appeared before the bench of the highest court of the state! Spooner was twenty-nine, only five feet four, youthful looking, with a clean-shaven face and long, fiery-red hair. His opponent, three years his senior, was a handsome man, tall, spare, with lustrous dark eyes, swarthy complexion, and black, curly hair. Vilas was deliberate, careful in his choice of words, prone to the use of classical allusions. Spooner was excitable, vola-

14 30 Wis. 75 (*Howard* v. *Mansfield*); 29 Wis. 471 (*Wilkinson* v. *Martin*); 29 Wis. 351 (*Denniston* v. *Unknown Owners*). In every case the decision was against Spooner's client.

tile, dynamic. He used no written brief or notes as he pommeled the judge or jury with his arguments; he had his facts and authorities at his finger tips. When hard pressed, he was at his best; when particularly impassioned, he resembled a bantam rooster. Not only were the two men legal adversaries but they also became political opponents, each rising to positions of prominence in their respective parties at the same time. They were, however, good friends, were graduates of the same university and served together on the Board of Regents. They had fundamentally the same economic philosophy; both defended private property against legislative encroachment. Both were railroad attorneys and in several cases worked on behalf of the same railroad company.[15]

Spooner's triple job at the capital completed, he returned to Hudson and his law practice. It was at this time that he began to obtain a reputation as a trial lawyer in criminal cases. A story about one of his cases has become a legend in Hudson. After Spooner had succeeded in getting an acquittal for a man accused of burglary, the grateful client presented his lawyer with a traveling bag which,

[15] *Milwaukee Sentinel,* December 28, 1884 (description of Vilas); 29 Wis. 517 (*Williams* v. *Williams*). Other cases in which they were antagonists: 36 Wis. 362 (*Williams* v. *Williams*); 37 Wis. 75 (*Hersey and Others* v. *Board of Supervisors of Barron Co.*), concerning method of assessment of taxes—Spooner won; 44 Wis. 258 (*Geisinger* v. *Beyl*), concerning tax deeds—Spooner won; 42 Wis. 616 (*Fleming* v. *Hartford Fire Insurance Co.*), issue was responsibility of company for acts of agent; 47 Wis. 89 (*Redman* v. *Hartford Fire Insurance Co.*), 49 Wis. 431 (*Redman* v. *Aetna Fire Insurance Co.*), relation of application for insurance policy to the policy. Vilas won these insurance cases, although Spooner had written J. W. Lusk, April, 1879 (in Spooner Papers), that he thought Vilas' brief was "unfair, disingenuous to the Court, and *damned thin.* I examined while at Madison some of his authorities and they are shockingly remote and inconsequential."

when opened, was found to contain a complete set of burglar's tools. The bag was left in the hallway of the Spooner home, but the next morning it could not be found. Nothing else in the house had been touched. What became of the bag is still a mystery. Not only cases of burglary but also of murder and rape were undertaken by the firm. In the appeal of these cases Spooner was most successful. Here his intense study of Blackstone while on army duty in Dakota Territory was of value, for he based most of his appeals on the fact that some fundamental right guaranteed by English common law had been violated. Government of law, interpreted by impartial judges, was the foundation of Spooner's legal and political creed.[16] Nils P. Haugen, later a political enemy but at this time one of his great admirers, described Spooner as a "keen lawyer, forgetting himself in the interest of his client, diligent and fearless." He was always thoroughly familiar with his case and ready with his authorities. Haugen related how one judge was quite annoyed when, in a personal injury case, Spooner sprang some of his own decisions on him. At that time Haugen thought no one in the state excelled Spooner as a lawyer.[17]

By 1872 the Spooners had already become established in the life of the community. Mrs. Spooner was popular socially, was active in the Baptist church and sang in the choir. They had two sons: Charles, three years of age, and

16 *Hudson Star and Times,* May 30, 1873, March 13, November 21, 1874, November 22, 1945; 36 Wis. 424 (*Lamb v. State*), 41 Wis. 430 (*Anderson v. State*).

17 Nils P. Haugen, "Pioneer and Political Reminiscences," *Wisconsin Magazine of History,* 11 (March, 1928), p. 280. The case referred to was *Hoyt v. City of Hudson* (41 Wis. 105), which Spooner won. Similar case: 34 Wis. 590 (*McCabe v. Town of Hammond*).

a baby whom they named after Mrs. Spooner's brother Willett Main, though they spelled it with only one *t*. John Spooner entered enthusiastically into the activities of the town. He helped organize the volunteer fire department. As a member of Engine Co. No. 1, he attended fires dressed in a police-style blue cap, blue shirt trimmed in red, black belt, and dark pants. In the fall of 1872 he was appointed chairman of the Republican county committee, managed the campaign, and stumped the state for the re-election of President Grant.[18] This is the only time he ever officially managed a political campaign.

In December, 1872, Spooner made a trip to New York City and shortly thereafter it became known that he was to be the general solicitor of the West Wisconsin Railroad, of which Daniel A. Baldwin, of New York, was president, and Jacob Humbird the general manager. Spooner had insisted that his contract permit him to live where he wished and to continue his private law practice.[19] As solicitor for the West Wisconsin he was working for a going concern. The road had been completed from Elroy to St. Paul by way of Hudson. An agreement was made with the Chicago and Northwestern so that through service could be offered from Chicago to the Minnesota city. This brought the West Wisconsin into competition with the Milwaukee and St. Paul Railway, which since 1867 had controlled all rail transportation across Wisconsin from Lake Michigan to the Mississippi River.[20]

[18] *Hudson Star and Times,* June 14, October 18, 25, 1872.
[19] *Ibid.,* December 20, 1872; S. R. Stimson to Spooner, January 21, 1873, in Spooner Papers.
[20] William Francis Raney, *Wisconsin: A Story of Progress,* p. 189.

In January, 1873, Baldwin and Humbird assumed control of the North Wisconsin and Spooner became its general solicitor also. This road was to run from Hudson to the western end of Lake Superior and also to Bayfield. Only twenty miles of track had been laid. Spooner's first task was to obtain for the road the federal land grant which had been conferred by the legislature on the St. Croix and Lake Superior Railroad but which had been withdrawn in 1872 since the road had not fulfilled the conditions. It was a particularly valuable land grant—1,280,000 acres, most of which was covered by virgin timber.[21] The North Wisconsin's contestant for the grant was the Milwaukee and St. Paul road, sponsored by Spooner's old rival Assemblyman Powell. The St. Paul had a head start. Long before it was known that the North Wisconsin was going to make a fight for the grant, the St. Paul had lined up the newspapers of the section, had petitions circulated, and resolutions passed by the citizens of the towns through which the road might pass. Baker reported to Spooner in Madison that the time was too short to change public opinion and that the North Wisconsin could not compete with the St. Paul road in sending deputations to the capitol, for that road not only had passes to distribute but had promised to pay all expenses of the members of their delegations while they were in Madison. Both Baker and the officers of the road suggested that Spooner try to get the legislature to postpone

21 *Hudson Star and Times,* January 10, 17, 1873; John W. Carey, *Organization and History of the Chicago, Milwaukee and St. Paul Railway Company,* pp. 196–97; H. D. Barron to Spooner, December 31, 1872, in Spooner Papers. Barron was assemblyman from the northern tier of counties and introduced the bill to give the grant to the North Wisconsin. When opposition arose to the clause providing for exemption of the lands from taxation, it was deleted.

action until the following year. Spooner failed; the legislature conferred the land grant on the St. Paul road.[22] This was Spooner's first experience at lobbying.

The directors of the St. Paul road in New York, much to the chagrin of their officers in Wisconsin, turned down the land grant. The fight began anew in the legislature in 1874. There were three contestants for the grant this time: the North Wisconsin, the Chicago and Northern Pacific Air Line, and the Wisconsin Railroad Company. The latter did not have a chance; it had just been organized the year before and had so little financial backing that it was known as the "Dollar Company." Between the other two companies there was a bitter fight, with Spooner captaining the forces of the North Wisconsin. A bill was finally passed conferring the land from Lake St. Croix to Bayfield on the North Wisconsin and giving to the Air Line company the land between the intersection of the two roads to the west end of Lake Superior. The stockholders of the North Wisconsin accepted the land grant and the bonds were executed and presented to the governor by Spooner. The *Hudson Star and Times* hailed the completion of the transaction with headlines: "A Good Time Coming. The 'Great Northwest' Looking Up! Land Grant Accepted." [23]

As soon as that was accomplished, Spooner left for Washington as the legal title of the whole federal land grant was in doubt since the time limit had expired five years before. Wisconsin congressmen had not succeeded in getting the

[22] H. C. Baker to Spooner, January 6, 15, 16, 25, February 10, 13, 1873; A. H. Baldwin to Spooner, February 20, 1873, in Spooner Papers; *Hudson Star and Times,* January 17, March 21, 1873.

[23] *Wisconsin Assembly Journal,* 1874, p. 597; *Wisconsin Session Laws,* 1874, pp. 186–91; *Hudson Star and Times,* May 16, July 4, 1873, January 30, February 14, March 6, May 8, 1874.

time limit extended,[24] so Spooner decided to press the United States Supreme Court for a decision. Pending before the court was the case of *Schulenberg* v. *Harriman,* in which Spooner had appeared in the lower court in 1872. So that he might argue the case before the Supreme Court, Spooner, on motion of Senator Matt Carpenter, was admitted to the bar of that court on December 4, 1874.[25]

Almost immediately after his admission Spooner appeared before the court defending Harriman, the state agent for the protection of the railroad lands, against the Stillwater trespassers. Technically his client was the state of Wisconsin but in reality he was representing the railroad, for which he was the solicitor, for if the state's title was upheld, the North Wisconsin would receive not only the land but also the trespass fund. Spooner argued that the act of Congress had vested the lands *in praesenti,* and that according to English common law, the land did not revert back to the federal government unless some action were taken by that government. He claimed that since Congress had been the grantor, Congress alone could declare the intention to enforce the forfeiture. Congress had not done so; all bills declaring the grant forfeited had been defeated.

The Supreme Court handed down its decision in January, 1875. The justices agreed with Spooner that the land did not revert back to the federal government unless positive action were taken, but maintained that the judicial branch could have taken such action. Since no organ of the

---

24 *Hudson Star and Times,* October 14, 1870, June 5, 1874; *Congressional Record,* 41st Cong., 2d Sess. (1869–70), pp. 3134, 3940–41; 42d Cong., 2d Sess. (1871–72), p. 2521; 43d Cong., 1st Sess. (1873–74), p. 1527.
25 Spooner to G. W. Burnell, May 2, 1890, in Spooner Papers.

government had taken action, then the title to the land remained with the state.[26] This decision, according to Frederic L. Paxson, "helped establish the federal law as to railroad land grants, and pointed to the class of legal business for which he [Spooner] was fitted." [27] The muckraker David Graham Phillips declared that the "Supreme Court sustained this apparently fair but really dishonest Spooner proposition, so useful to land thieves throughout the West." [28] Before this decision was handed down, railroad companies had always been careful to get Congress to extend the time limit of their land grant if they could; now they needed only to prevent the passage of any law bringing about the forfeiture of their land. If the federal government were to regain the unearned land grants, reformers and antirailroad men had to take the initiative and obtain passage of a forfeiture act, a very difficult feat.[29]

Since the North Wisconsin had completed the first twenty miles of its road, Spooner, on behalf of the road, applied to the governor for the patents for the designated sections of land, totaling 128,000 acres. The patents were issued but the North Wisconsin was enjoined from disposing of any of the land or from receiving any of the St. Croix land-grant trespass fund pending settlement of a suit begun by the Madison and Portage Railroad Company. The latter road was joined in its suit by the West Wisconsin and Wisconsin Railroad Farm Mortgage Land Com-

[26] *Hudson Star and Times,* November 27, 1874, January 29, February 5, 1875; 21 Wallace 44 (*Schulenberg* v. *Harriman*).

[27] Frederic L. Paxson, "John Coit Spooner," *Dictionary of American Biography,* 17:465–66.

[28] Phillips, "Chief Spokesman of 'the Merger,'" *Cosmopolitan* 41 (June, 1906), 124.

[29] David Maldwyn Ellis, "The Forfeiture of Railroad Land Grants, 1867–1894," *Mississippi Valley Historical Review,* 33 (June, 1946), 27–35.

pany. They claimed some of this land under the indemnity clause of the act of 1856, which had provided that if any of the "odd" sections along the route of the railroad had already been disposed of by the federal government, the road would receive "indemnity lands" elsewhere, provided they were not more than fifteen miles from the line of the road. Since much of the federal land in the southern part of the state had been disposed of before the railroads put in their claims, these plaintiffs claimed part of the northern land grant. The suit dragged on for four years.[30]

The period from 1873 to 1875 was a difficult one for a railroad solicitor in Wisconsin. In the early days the farmers had eagerly sought railroads. They had welcomed the land grants given by the federal government to encourage the building of roads; they had supported their communities' subscriptions to railroad securities and many had mortgaged their farms to buy stock of a railroad which was supposed to be built in their locality. Many of the railroad companies had not lived up to their promises, had not built where they had said they would. Some had not built at all, had gone into bankruptcy, and the farmers had been left with worthless railroad stock and mortgages on their farms. With land becoming scarce, the farmers viewed with indignation the large land grants held by the railroads.

[30] *Hudson Star and Times*, July 2, 30, 1875; 16 Federal Cases 366, No. 8938 (*Madison and Portage et al.* v. *North Wisconsin*). Willett Main was appointed receiver of the North Wisconsin trespass fund. For a description of the Wisconsin Railroad Farm Mortgage Company see Merk, *Economic History*, p. 267. It was organized by the state legislature in 1868 and was granted lands claimed by the La Crosse and Milwaukee road for building from Portage to Tomah. The company was authorized to sell these lands for the relief of the farmers who had mortgaged their farms and had received railroad stock which turned out to be worthless.

The people in a community, heavily taxed for local improvements and educational facilities, resented the fact that large tracts owned by the railroads were exempt from local taxes. The farmers were at the mercy of the railroads; the roads charged all the traffic would bear, charged less where there was competition, and gave rebates to favored shippers. To maintain their favored position, railroad passes were widely distributed among public officials.

Resentment reached its height in 1873, when the farmers' already bad condition was made desperate by the panic. The Patrons of Husbandry, a farmers' organization that had grown up rapidly in the Middle West, provided a focal point for the expression of the grievances of the farmers. It was not a political organization, but in the election of 1873 in Wisconsin it had helped elect many antirailroad men to the legislature, and, as governor, the candidate of the reform wing of the Democratic party, William R. Taylor. Himself a farmer, Taylor had been president of the State Agricultural Society and was an active member of the Grange. He was determined to put through a reform program remedying many of the abuses of the railroads.[31]

The legislature of 1874 passed the famous Potter Law, one of the most radical of the so-called Granger laws. The act set up a railroad commission, classified the railroads as A, B, and C, and specified maximum freight rates to be charged on various commodities by the railroads in each class. It stated also that other rates were to be no higher than those charged in 1873, a low point.[32] The large rail-

[31] Solon Buck, *The Agrarian Crusade*, pp. 22–23, 36–38, 50.

[32] *Wisconsin Session Laws*, 1874, p. 599. For a discussion of the passage of the Potter Law see Robert T. Daland, "Enactment of the Potter Law," *Wisconsin Magazine of History*, 33 (September, 1949), 45–54.

road companies refused to accept the rate schedules and many of the smaller roads followed their lead. The West Wisconsin was brought up in a local court for violation of the law. Spooner contended that the Potter Law was unconstitutional. He maintained that a subsequent law, which provided that if any company should collect more than a fair and reasonable compensation it should be deemed guilty of extortion, abrogated the part of the Potter Law that fixed arbitrary rates of compensation. The justice agreed with Spooner and dismissed the case. Before this case reached the state supreme court the constitutionality of the Potter Law was upheld in a case concerning the St. Paul road. The court, having affirmed the validity of the law, reversed the decision in the West Wisconsin case.[33]

The Potter Law was the culminating blow to the already shaky West Wisconsin. That road had for some time been in financial difficulties, accentuated by the panic of 1873. Some directors of the Chicago and Northwestern Railway took advantage of the practically insolvent condition of the West Wisconsin to gain control of the road. On January 5, 1875, Henry H. Porter, David Dows, Roswell Pettibone Flower, James H. Howe, and Harvey Kennedy formed a pool to buy out Daniel A. Baldwin, to whom the stock of the company had been transferred in payment of claims held by him under a contract for building and equipping the road. They paid him $100,000, and in return received

[33] *Hudson Star and Times,* June 26, 1874; 37 Wis. 377 (*In re Langley*). For a discussion of the testing of the constitutionality of the law see Clara Lyon Hayes, "William Penn Lyon," *Wisconsin Magazine of History,* 9 (March, 1926), 263–64. Philip L. Spooner was one of the lawyers for the St. Paul in its suit; see 35 Wis. 425 (*Attorney General* v. *Railroad Companies*).

10,000 shares of preferred stock and 36,850 shares of common stock (Baldwin kept 3,150 shares for his family). In October, in order to raise funds the copartnership sold half of its common stock to the Chicago and Northwestern Railway for $100,000 and the rest was divided among the partners and the pool was dissolved. H. H. Porter, owner of almost half of the pool, became president of the road, and J. H. Howe, nephew of Senator Howe, became vice-president.[34]

The new owners found the West Wisconsin under attack from several directions. The legislature in 1864 had passed a special act exempting the lands of the West Wisconsin from all taxes for a period of ten years; this had been extended for another ten years on condition that the road should be completed by May 5, 1872. By large borrowings the road had been completed by November, 1871. That same year there had been passed a special act making subject to local taxes all railroad lands in Trempealeau County, except those used for roadbeds and stations. The lands were sold for nonpayment of taxes, the county becoming the holder of the tax certificates. Spooner filed a bill to set aside the sale and cancel the certificates, on the ground that the lands were exempt from taxation and the certificates were therefore void. The case was argued before the state supreme court by Spooner, with his father as counsel. They based their case for exemption on two points: First, that the lands had not been subject to taxation because they were given in trust by the federal government for the purpose of constructing a railroad, and until the lands were actually sold, this trust applied; sec-

[34] *Hudson Star and Times,* January 8, 1875; 109 New York 526 (*Harvey Kennedy* v. *Henry Porter et al.*); see brief of case of *Harvey Kennedy* v. *Henry Porter,* in Spooner Papers.

ond, that the act of the legislature exempting the lands from taxation was a contract which could not be impaired by a special act. The judges decided against them; they declared that as soon as the company acquired title to the land by the construction of the road, the trust was executed and the land liable to taxation. They also pointed out that the state constitution gave the legislature power to alter or repeal at any time special acts under which corporations were chartered or given privileges.[35]

The West Wisconsin appealed its case to the United States Supreme Court. There the railroad was represented by Philip L. Spooner and Senator Matt Carpenter. That court upheld the decision of the state supreme court. Justice Swayne, rendering the decision, declared "that the exemptions in question were gratuities offered by the State, without any element of a contract. There was no assurance or intimation that they were intended to be irrevocable." The court did insinuate that the legislature had been wrong in passing a special law for Trempealeau County, but declared the law had to be held good even if the legislature of Wisconsin was composed of "pretty dishonest men." The decision is "ill considered and against precedent," asserted Spooner, but he advised the railroad officials to pay the taxes assessed by Trempealeau County as soon as possible.[36]

The success of Trempealeau County led to attempts by other county governments to get repealed the law exempting from taxation the lands of the West Wisconsin. When

[35] *Hudson Star and Times,* January 9, June 19, 1874; 35 Wis. 257 (*West Wisconsin Railroad* v. *Board of Supervisors of Trempealeau County*); cf. Spooner's argument in *Denniston* v. *Unknown Owners.*

[36] Spooner to H. H. Porter, December 21, 1876; Judge Leonard to Spooner, January 11, 1877, in Spooner Papers; 93 U. S. 595 (*West Wisconsin Railroad* v. *Board of Supervisors of Trempealeau County*).

Spooner succeeded in getting such a bill defeated in the assembly,[37] efforts were made to have the Democratic party adopt a plank favoring repeal. Spooner appealed to Vilas, who was able to have substituted an innocuous plank urging the exercise of caution in granting exemptions from taxation.[38] Vilas was at that time representing the West Wisconsin in several cases pending before the courts.

One of the cases in which Vilas was defending the West Wisconsin was its fight with the town of Tomah over the removal of the tracks from Warren's Mills. The residents claimed that since the road had been chartered as the Tomah and St. Croix Railroad to build a road between those two terminal points, it had violated the charter when it had changed its name to West Wisconsin and had changed its route. The court had upheld the town and in the spring of 1875 Spooner had failed to get through the legislature a bill specifically legalizing the removal of the tracks.[39] Governor Taylor, the reform Democrat, was up for re-election and seemed inclined to support Tomah's case. Spooner appealed to Vilas; the two had a conference with the Governor and finally an agreement was reached. The attorney general consented to postpone the taking of judgment until the next term of the court. The West Wisconsin stipulated that it would accept judgment after the adjournment of the legislature the following year unless some law were passed which prevented such legal action.[40]

37 *Hudson Star and Times,* February 15, 1875.

38 Spooner to W. F. Vilas, August 27, 1875, in Vilas Papers at the State Historical Society of Wisconsin; *Milwaukee Sentinel,* September 9, 1875.

39 34 Wis. 197 (*State* v. *West Wisconsin Railroad*); 36 Wis. 466 (*Attorney General* v. *West Wisconsin Railroad*).

40 Spooner to W. F. Vilas, September 24, October 2, 4, November 5, 17; to J. H. Howe, December 16, 1875, in Spooner Papers; *Hudson Star and Times,* February 4, April 1, 1876.

By January, 1876, the situation had changed. Not only had Governor Taylor been defeated and a Republican governor, Harrison Ludington, been elected but the state legislature was safely Republican. As soon as the legislature convened, Spooner, accompanied by several other representatives of the road, descended on the capitol and prevailed upon the members to pass an act legalizing the removal of the tracks from Warren's Mills to Tomah. Spooner also succeeded in preventing passage of a bill repealing tax exemption for the lands of the West Wisconsin.[41] This legislature repealed the Potter Law, replacing it with the Vance Law, which provided for a supervisory railroad commission; it also amended Spooner's railroad law of 1872 so that fuel necessary for the operation of the road was subject to the same lien as fixtures and rolling stock.[42]

The reform movement had petered out. It had flared up too rapidly and went out as quickly. More than anything else, it had alarmed the corporate interests and aroused them to decisive action. The railroads for some years had had lobbyists at the capitol; they had asked for special favors and had granted passes to public officials. Now the corporations became more aggressive; their lobbies were better organized and the men who formerly had concentrated on building up big fortunes began to play a dominant part in politics. In Wisconsin one, if not the foremost, of these millionaire politicians was Philetus Sawyer, a lumberman from Oshkosh. He was to become both the financial benefactor and political sponsor of John Coit Spooner.

* *

[41] *Wisconsin Assembly Journal*, 1876, p. 710.
[42] Spooner to H. H. Porter, May 8, 1876, in Spooner Papers; *Wisconsin General Laws*, 1876, pp. 158, 758.

It was the lumber millionaire's interest in the West Wisconsin that brought Sawyer and Spooner together. By 1877 the road was again nearly bankrupt and more capital was needed. It was decided that a new company should be formed to buy out the West Wisconsin in foreclosure proceedings. The drawback was that by such action the lands of the railroad would no longer be tax exempt. Quietly, with no intimation of the plans afoot, Spooner prepared a bill to be presented to the legislature in January, 1877. The bill was general in scope; it merely stated that parties purchasing a road by foreclosure of mortgages would retain the special exemptions and privileges and immunities formerly granted the road. No specific railroad was mentioned, for then the act could be applied to the North Wisconsin also when the owners of the West Wisconsin decided to acquire that road. The act was passed with no difficulty; most of the members of the legislature had no idea of its significance.[43] The West Wisconsin was then sold at auction and was purchased by Porter, Dows, and Flower, the men who had bought out Baldwin's interest in 1875. They, with Philetus Sawyer and John Comstock, president of the First National Bank of Hudson, organized a new company —the Chicago, St. Paul, and Minneapolis Railway Company, with a capital of five million dollars. Spooner became not only the solicitor but also one of the directors of the new company.[44]

The purchase of the West Wisconsin through foreclo-

43 H. H. Porter to Spooner, January 8, 15, 29, February 16; to J. H. Howe, January 18, 1877, in Spooner Papers; *Wisconsin General Laws, 1877,* p. 321.

44 *Hudson Star and Times,* May 10, 1878; William H. Stennett, *Yesterday and To-day: A History of the Chicago and Northwestern Railway System,* pp. 82–83.

sure proceedings was a clever move on the part of the owners. It not only enabled them to get rid of the old mortgages which, according to Porter, had many objectionable features, but it also cut off any claims Baldwin might have against the West Wisconsin. The former president had caused Porter much anxiety and annoyance; the latter thought he was mentally deranged on the subject of the railroad. He probably was, for shortly after this transaction he hanged himself in a barn near Weehawken, New Jersey.[45] With Baldwin's death the only obstacle to complete control of the West Wisconsin was the ownership by the Chicago and Northwestern Railway of 18,425 shares. These were turned over to Porter in June, 1878, for the nominal sum of fifty dollars (they had no pecuniary value at that time) but really in return for Porter's resignation from the board of directors of the Northwestern.[46]

After taking over the West Wisconsin, Sawyer and Porter set about to gain control of the North Wisconsin. By July, 1879, Spooner was able to report that all the stock had been acquired. Communities that had earlier invested in the road had agreed to exchange their stock for bonds. Sawyer was elected president, Jacob Humbird, vice-president, William H. Phipps, Spooner's close friend and neighbor, secretary, and Spooner, general solicitor.[47] It was still not much of a railway, for only sixty miles of road had been constructed. It was not the road itself in which Saw-

45 H. H. Porter to Spooner, January 15, 18, 1877, in Spooner Papers; Miller, "John Comstock: Banker," *Wisconsin Magazine of History,* 22 (December, 1948), 172; *New York Herald,* December 3, 4, 1877.

46 Brief of case of *Harvey Kennedy* v. *Henry Porter,* in Spooner Papers. Flower, Dows, and Howe continued as directors until 1883–1884.

47 *Hudson Star and Times,* November 22, 1878, April 18, 1879; Spooner to P. Sawyer, July 13, 1879, in Spooner Papers.

yer was primarily interested but rather the land grant with its magnificent forests of pine.[48]

With the suit of the Madison and Portage, West Wisconsin, and the Wisconsin Railroad Farm Mortgage Land Company against the North Wisconsin still pending, the North Wisconsin could not obtain legal title or dispose of the lands. The hearing on this land-grant case was finally held in Boston on September 14, 1879, before Justices Harlan, Drummond, and Bunn. Philetus Sawyer, who accompanied Spooner, was full of admiration for the young lawyer as he presented the case of the North Wisconsin, arguing without written or printed brief or even memoranda. This was one of Spooner's best legal performances; the theme was a dry one, but he was cogent and eloquent as he expounded on the Land-Grant Acts of 1856 and 1864 on which the North Wisconsin based its claim.[49]

The decision was a great triumph for Spooner. The court rejected the claims of the two railroads, for they had been built under the act of 1864, which had provided for two roads. The claim of the Wisconsin Railroad Farm Mortgage Land Company was recognized, for the land grant it had been given came under the act of 1856, which had designated only one railroad. The company claimed approximately 160,000 acres, almost half of which were in the limits claimed by the North Wisconsin. The case was appealed to the Supreme Court.[50] Sawyer stepped in to break the deadlock. He privately arranged with the com-

48 *Hudson Star and Times,* June 7, 1879; Spooner to W. E. Smith, to S. U. Pinney, June 11, 1879, in Spooner Papers; *Madison Democrat,* January 7, 1885, describes Sawyer's and Spooner's activities in northwestern Wisconsin.

49 Spooner to W. F. Vilas, November 10, 17; to E. H. Abbott, November 29, 1879, in Spooner Papers.

50 *Hudson Star and Times,* October 21, 1879; 16 Federal Cases, 366, No. 8938 (*Madison and Portage Railway Company et al.* v. *North Wisconsin*).

missioner of the Farm Mortgage company to purchase the land claims of the company in the name of his son Edgar P. Sawyer. Spooner took care of the legal details. For this claim to 160,000 acres of pine lands, Sawyer paid $160,-000.[51] The land-grant issue, which had dragged on for almost a decade, was finally settled, and the North Wisconsin, when its line to Bayfield was completed, would receive 800,000 acres of rich timber lands.

In 1880 the Chicago, St. Paul, and Minneapolis (heir to the West Wisconsin) and the North Wisconsin were consolidated into the Chicago, St. Paul, Minneapolis and Omaha, usually called the Omaha. The management remained the same: H. H. Porter was president; Philetus Sawyer, vice-president; and Spooner, general solicitor. From two small roads in 1871 there had developed a powerful railroad system, with 1,147 miles of track stretching from the pinelands of northern Wisconsin through the cornfields of Iowa into Nebraska.[52]

In November, 1880, the law firm of Baker and Spooner was dissolved and Spooner took a suite of rooms in the Goss-Taylor Block, "the pleasantest and completest law

The Madison and Portage appealed the decision. To clear the title, the North Wisconsin purchased their claim and the case was dismissed by stipulation of counsel, April 8, 1884 (see Spooner to A. S. Sloan, December 6, 1883, in Spooner Papers).

[51] Richard Nelson Current, *Pine Logs and Politics: A Life of Philetus Sawyer, 1816–1900,* pp. 138–39; *Wisconsin Assembly Journal,* 1882, pp. 52, 231, 286; *ibid.,* 1883, Appendix, pp. 1–8; *Wisconsin General Laws,* 1882, p. 801; Spooner to W. H. Phipps, December 15, 1881, in Spooner Papers.

[52] *Hudson Star and Times,* March 26, 1880; Robert J. Casey and W. A. S. Douglas, *Pioneer Railroad,* pp. 151–52. The Omaha in 1881 took over the St. Paul and Sioux City Road, a line in Minnesota similar to the West Wisconsin. Later the Omaha had trouble over this line because of the liability clauses in the Minnesota constitution (see Spooner to M. Hughitt, February 11, 1885; to J. H. Howe, March 23, 1886, in Spooner Papers).

office in the city and hardly excelled elsewhere," declared the editor of the local paper. "Col. John C. Spooner has achieved a decided reputation as one of the finest lawyers in the country. He has been doing some fine work on the stump for the Republican ticket this fall." [53] He had devoted most of the summer to politics; he had declined most retainers but had agreed to try some cases in neighboring counties, as he wrote one of his cohorts, "just *to have business there,* under cover of which to do our work." Spooner was organizing the northwestern part of the state to bring about the election of Philetus Sawyer to the United States Senate in 1881.[54]

It was at this time that a revolution took place in the Republican party in Wisconsin—"Boss" Keyes was deposed. For almost twenty years he had been in control. For his aid in electing Timothy O. Howe as Senator in 1861 he had been rewarded with the Madison postmastership. This was a position with great potentialities; it was the most important federal office in the state capital, where the headquarters of the party organization were located and where the party conventions were held. Keyes had become chairman of the state central committee in 1869 and had built up in Wisconsin one of the most effective machines in the country at a time when the federal officeholders' control of the party was at its height in the United States. His agents were his fellow postmasters, the most numerous and most dispersed of the federal officeholders. They had managed the local caucuses and the county conventions and, through control of these local bodies, had exerted considerable influence in the Congressional, state, and national conventions. President Hayes had thoroughly dis-

53 *Hudson Star and Times,* October 22, November 12, 1880.
54 Spooner to W. T. Price, June 14, 1880, in Spooner Papers.

rupted the Republican party organization in Wisconsin when in June, 1877, he had issued a circular forbidding federal officeholders from taking part in the management of party conventions or campaigns. Keyes at first could not believe that this rule applied to him or to other postmasters. Protesting that it "relegates to the rear four of the five members of our Rep. State Exec. Com.," he had resigned as chairman of the committee rather than give up his postmastership. He had continued, however, to direct campaigns from behind the scenes. Much to his surprise, he had discovered that he did not have enough control of the party to bring about his own election in 1879 to succeed Senator Howe. When he found he could not obtain a majority of the votes, he had withdrawn in favor of Matthew Carpenter (who had been defeated for re-election in 1875), expecting that by so doing he would put himself in position to receive the coveted position in 1881.[55]

At the opening of the election year (1880) Keyes was confident he would be elected since Sawyer, his opponent, was sixty-five and had retired from Congress and public life five years before. The boss was sure he had an efficient machine of officeholders; but he did not realize that new influences were taking over control of the party. He soon, however, heard rumors that the lumberman millionaire was "rolling his bbl." with considerable effect. He received reports that Spooner and Hod Taylor were organizing the northwestern part of the state to elect members of the legislature pledged to vote for Sawyer and that they had the support of the leading capitalists among the lumbermen. "Sawyer's railroad connections tell heavily in his

[55] Richard W. Hantke, "Elisha W. Keyes, the Bismarck of Western Politics," *Wisconsin Magazine of History*, 31 (September, 1947), 29–42; Dorothy Ganfield Fowler, *The Cabinet Politician: The Postmasters General, 1829–1909*, pp. 169–70.

favor," wrote the postmaster of Eau Claire. "Business men seem to fear that by opposing him they will get no favors from the Board in the way of freights and that there will be a discrimination against them not that the Board has intimated any such thing but they seem to instinctively feel so." [56]

It was a severe blow to Keyes when Henry Clay Payne, postmaster at Milwaukee, threw his support to Sawyer. Payne had already acquired a reputation for party management. In 1872 he had organized the Young Men's Republican Club in Milwaukee, which had succeeded in carrying that city for the Republican party in 1875. Payne had become secretary of the county committee and a member of the state executive committee in 1876. In this capacity he had been closely associated with Keyes, but when the latter tried to bulldoze him into supporting him in his senatorial campaign, Payne came out openly for Sawyer.[57] This was the genesis of the triumvirate which for twenty years was to dominate the Republican party in Wisconsin—Sawyer the millionaire, Payne the political strategist, and Spooner the lawyer and stump speaker.

Spooner was not in Madison when the legislature convened in January, 1881, to elect a United States Senator; he was not on hand to help Sawyer during the last days of the campaign. He was not needed. He had done his work so well that all the votes of the members of the legislature from the northwestern part of the state were cast for the

[56] M. Herrick to E. Keyes, August 3; J. M. Brackett to E. Keyes, August 30; H. Cousins to E. Keyes, September 29, 1880, in Keyes Papers, at the State Historical Society of Wisconsin.

[57] H. C. Payne to E. Keyes, February 14; E. Keyes to H. C. Payne, February 20; F. A. Flower to E. Keyes, November 24, 1880, *ibid.;* William Ward Wight, *Henry Clay Payne,* pp. 24–25, 40–44; *Milwaukee Sentinel,* May 17, 1873, February 1, 1876. Only two Milwaukee men voted for Keyes.

lumber and railroad millionaire to help him defeat Boss
Keyes on the first ballot at the Republican caucus.[58]
Spooner probably would have been on hand but his youngest son and namesake was seriously ill with diphtheria.
The death of this child was the greatest agony of his life,
wrote Spooner twenty years later when he was trying to be-
friend the woman who had nursed young John during that
illness.[59]

Spooner was present at the state convention that met in
Madison in September. He had been elected a delegate by
his assembly district convention but by only 1 vote. The
convention had declared by a 3-to-1 vote in favor of Hans
B. Warner for the gubernatorial nomination. Spooner refused to be bound by this expression of opinion. He felt
Warner disliked him and was antagonistic to the Omaha
company.[60] He favored the nomination of Jeremiah Rusk,
whom Sawyer and Payne had picked as their candidate.
Rusk was a bluff, self-educated, and self-made man—stage-
coach driver, farmer, and banker from Viroqua. He had
long been in politics, had held the positions of sheriff and
coroner of Vernon County and had been a member of Congress from 1870 to 1876. Rusk was nominated on the fifth
formal ballot, defeating Warner by a vote of 135 to 97.[61] At
this convention Spooner's brother Philip was nominated
for the office of state insurance commissioner, which had

58 *Milwaukee Sentinel,* January 20, 1881; Current, *Pine Logs and Poli-*
tics, pp. 156, 178.

59 *Hudson Star and Times,* January 14, 21, 1881; Spooner to W. A. Scott,
January 9, 1898, in Spooner Papers.

60 *Hudson Star and Times,* September 23, 1881; Spooner to I. H. Wing,
September 13, 1881, in Spooner Papers. The other delegate from St. Croix
County voted for Warner.

61 *Milwaukee Sentinel,* September 22, 1881; Current, *Pine Logs and*
Politics, pp. 182–86.

just been made an elective position. He had held the office since its establishment in 1878. He, with Willett Main and Elisha Keyes, composed the "Madison Ring," which was said to control the Republican party in that Congressional district.[62]

The Republican party won an overwhelming victory in the election of 1881; it controlled all branches of the state government, and railroad and corporate interests were dominant in the party. When the legislature convened in January, 1882, Spooner was on hand (as he had been for the last ten years), "his hair awry, his long black pipe in constant puff, and his short, stubbed form in and out among the members, whenever railroad legislation was up for action." [63] Spooner's main task during that session was to obtain for the Omaha company the rest of the land grant, the part which in 1874 had been given to the Chicago and Northern Pacific Air Line Company, now called the Chicago, Portage and Superior Railroad. The grant would expire in May, 1882, if the road was not completed by that time. The company had been hard hit by the panic of 1873, had given a mortgage of its property to the Farmers' Loan and Trust Company, and had finally had to stop construction. In August, 1881, an arrangement had been made with H. G. Angle for him to build the necessary sixty-five miles of road from the intersection with the Omaha to the western end of Lake Superior. Though the Portage company was in bad financial straits, as long as it

[62] Ellis B. Usher, *Wisconsin, Its Story and Biography*, V, 1298–1301; Robert M. La Follette, *La Follette's Autobiography: A Personal Narrative of Political Experience*, pp. 45–46.
[63] *Milwaukee Sentinel*, December 18, 1884.

had the land grant it had a chance of obtaining enough credit to complete the line.[64]

The Omaha did not wait for the expiration of the time limit but prepared to fight for the grant as soon as the legislature convened in January, 1882. Spooner, in charge of the Omaha campaign, first arranged to secure the co-operation of the two major railroads of the state. The St. Paul was promised one-fourth of the land grant if it would take no part in the contest.[65] The Northwestern had always been friendly to the Omaha, but to be sure of its support, Spooner offered to represent its interests during that legislative session and to take over the distribution of their pass favors, although it would be a burdensome and distasteful job which he said he would not undertake for money. "The handling of the passes of such a Railway Company as the Northwestern brings one into relations with a great many members of the Legislature not so easily reached by one representing a road like ours," he explained in a confidential letter to the president of the Omaha. The chairman of the railroad and judiciary committees of the senate received passes not only for themselves but also for others for whom they requested them. The former "rendered service that was of the most friendly and zealous sort," Spooner wrote the general manager of the Chicago and

[64] Matilda Gresham, *The Life of Walter Quintin Gresham*, II, 530–50. She is very denunciatory of Spooner for the part he played in this land-grant fight.

[65] Spooner to M. Hughitt, February 8, 1884, in Spooner Papers; 75 Wis. 224 (*Chippewa Valley and Superior Railroad* v. *Chicago, St. Paul, Minneapolis and Omaha Railroad*). The Omaha did not give the St. Paul one-fourth of the land grant. The St. Paul brought suit but the court declared (August, 1889) that a contract whereby one railroad agrees with another not to make any effort to procure a land grant is void, being against public policy.

Northwestern, and the latter did "everything that we wanted done and took particular pains during the session to forward in every way our interest." [66]

A bill to annul the old land grant and to confer it on the Omaha road was introduced in the assembly on January 23, 1882. Spooner worked hard; he was on deck fully sixteen hours out of the twenty-four. On the whole, the outlook for the passage of the bill was good. The senate railroad committee unanimously favored its passage. The bill was all ready to be voted on when suddenly Spooner was told to delay it as a personal favor to Scofield, president of the Portage company. Spooner wired R. R. Cable, "What is the situation? Am I to have them to fight?" Spooner was aware that negotiations were being carried on between the officers of the Omaha and the Portage. A few days later he learned that the stock of the Portage company ($2,000,000 par value) had been sold for $200,000 to Cable, representing the Omaha. The Portage company ceased its opposition to the land-grant bill and it was passed on February 17, 1882.[67] This entire land-grant fight, with its many ramifications, had been a sordid mess, although all acts had been technically legal, for Spooner had seen to that. The participants were accused of opprobrious conduct. For years Spooner was on the defensive regarding this transaction. He seemed, however, more to resent the criticism rather than to be apologetic for the part he had played in it.[68]

[66] Spooner to H. H. Porter, December 13, 1881; to M. Hughitt, February 2, 1882, June 28, 1883, in Spooner Papers.

[67] *Hudson Star and Times,* January 13, 1882; Spooner to H. H. Porter, January 25, 31, February 1, 10; to R. R. Cable, February 6, 1882, in Spooner Papers; *Wisconsin Assembly Journal,* 1882, pp. 120–23. The act was confirmed by another act, March 7, 1883.

[68] Spooner to H. H. Porter, May 20, 1896, in Spooner Papers: "You will be glad to see that the court tears up the whole slander by the roots, sus-

The Omaha received the 400,000 acres of valuable timber lands, formerly granted to the Chicago and Northern Pacific Air Line, on condition that the line to Lake Superior be completed by December 1, 1882. The Omaha was required to give the governor $78,000 to be used to pay labor claims against the air line. That provision had been agreed on between Spooner and Governor Rusk before it had been incorporated into the bill.[69] These terms were met and the line to Lake Superior built. In honor of the general solicitor of the company, Chicago Junction, the point of intersection of the North Wisconsin and the Chippewa Falls and Superior branches of the road, was renamed Spooner [70] (see map of Wisconsin on p. 60).

Spooner was now realizing his ambition of making money. He had built up a lucrative law practice and his position as solicitor not only brought him a good salary,

tains Jackson's right to sell, and your right to buy, and says the action of the Omaha Co. was 'open and above board.' You and I know it but it is pleasant to have the Supreme Court of the U. S. unanimously say so." A good part of the decision was published in the newspapers of the state because Marvin Hughitt, president of the Northwestern, as well as Spooner, had been restive under the charges. Spooner wrote J. C. Gregory on May 23, 1896, *ibid.*: "I have been glad it was published because it is a complete explosion, by unanimous opinion of the Supreme Court of the United States, of the charges which were published so industriously against me in the Angle Case." Angle had been bankrupt when the Portage company lost the land grant. He had instituted suit against the Portage and Omaha companies, and after his death in August, 1882, his widow had continued the suit. The Farmers' Loan and Trust Company had also filed suit. The cases dragged on until 1896, when the Supreme Court ruled against them (see 39 Federal Reporter 912; 151 U.S. 1 (*Angle* v. *Chicago, St. Paul, Minneapolis and Omaha Railroad*); 39 Federal Reporter 143; 163 U.S. 31 (*Farmers' Loan and Trust Co.* v. *Chicago, Portage and Superior Railroad Co. et al.*). Spooner did not participate in the arguments in these cases but helped prepare some of the briefs (see Spooner to T. Wilson, May 21, 1896, in Spooner Papers).

69 *Wisconsin General Laws*, 1882, p. 11; Spooner to P. Sawyer, February 18, 1882, in Spooner Papers.

70 *Hudson Star and Times*, July 27, August 24, 1883.

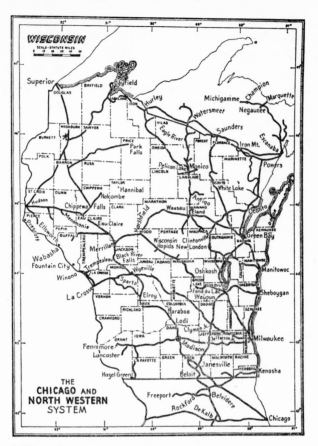

Map of Wisconsin, showing the Chicago and Northwestern and subsidiary lines. Spooner, formerly Chicago Junction, is marked with a star at a northwestern rail intersection in Washburn County. (Map from *Wisconsin*, by William Francis Raney, © 1940, Prentice-Hall, Inc., Englewood Cliffs, N. J. Used by permission.)

ten thousand dollars a year, it was said,[71] but also gave him opportunities for investment and excellent chances for speculation. Most of his ventures were done on borrowed

[71] *Milwaukee Sentinel*, December 18, 1884.

capital and there was hardly a time while he was in Hudson that he was not in debt to the First National Bank.[72] In 1882 he joined with Horace Taylor, John Comstock, and others to organize the Hudson Lumber Company, which built a modern mill calculated to cut between fifty and sixty thousand feet of lumber a day. It became one of the most important mills in St. Croix County.[73]

Spooner was a heavy investor in real estate. Even before he settled in that region, his father had bought land in St. Croix, Polk, and Pierce counties, and since 1872 John Spooner had purchased many acres of virgin timber lands which later were to be very valuable; one parcel alone was used as security for a fifty-thousand-dollar loan when he needed ready cash for his speculations.[74] Having inside information concerning the progress of the railroad, he bought land around what would become railroad termini; before the Omaha reached Lake Superior, Spooner had invested heavily in real estate in what was to become the city of Superior. He joined with Alpheus Beede Stickney, a St. Paul promoter formerly associated with the North Wisconsin, Humbird, superintendent of construction of the Omaha, and E. W. Winter, the general manager, to form the Bay Land and Improvement Company for the development of real estate around Bayfield. He helped form the Northern Nebraska and Improvement Company for the

72 A. Jefferson to Spooner, February 6, 1873. Spooner to D. C. Fulton, December 3, 1896, in Spooner Papers: "I think this will be the first time in twenty years that I have not owed that bank something. I am afraid it will make you feel lonesome."

73 Spooner to W. S. Main, July 17, 1883; to P. Sawyer, August 28, 1884, ibid.; *Hudson Star and Times,* July 6, 1883; Edward W. Durant, "Lumbering and Steamboating on the St. Croix River," *Collections of the Minnesota Historical Society,* 10 (February, 1905), 651.

74 Spooner to W. H. Rust, September 12, 1882; to R. J. Hoe, July 22, 1886, in Spooner Papers.

development of towns on the land received by the Omaha from the federal government. Besides these and many other financial enterprises, Spooner owned a good deal of stock in the Omaha railroad. This doubled in price when in the fall of 1882 there were rumors of competition between the Rock Island and the Chicago and Northwestern for control of the road.[75]

By November, 1882, the latter company had purchased a majority of the capital stock of the Omaha, and Marvin Hughitt, general manager of the Northwestern, replaced H. H. Porter as president. This was the era of consolidations, with smaller firms being crowded out by larger companies. Just as Porter had ejected Baldwin from the West Wisconsin, so William H. Vanderbilt, whose system controlled the Northwestern, was determined to ruin Porter, his rival in several railroad systems.[76] Porter was already involved in several suits, notably one with Harvey Kennedy, which grew out of the pool they had formed in 1875 to buy out Baldwin, and the stock deal with the Northwestern in 1878.[77] Vanderbilt, using these stock deals as a basis, filed a suit against Porter for $1,100,000. Spooner, as solicitor for the Northwestern, might be expected to pre-

[75] Spooner to D. G. Morrison, June 6; to C. Ives, September 21; to J. H. Peavey, June 28; to R. R. Cable, July 13; to Keep, Hughitt, and Sykes, July 25; to M. L. Sykes, September 21, 26; to E. W. Winter, June 30, 1883, May 28, 1886; to A. B. Stickney, November 24, 29, 1882, May 16, 1883; to E. G. Timme, June 5; to I. H. Wing, June 11; to H. P. Upham, October 31, 1883, *ibid.* See Frederic L. Paxson, "Alpheus Beede Stickney," *Dictionary of American Biography,* 6:479–80.

[76] Casey and Douglas, *Pioneer Railroad,* p. 145; *New York Daily Tribune,* April 11, 1884.

[77] Brief of case of *Harvey Kennedy* v. *Henry Porter,* in Spooner Papers; 109 N.Y. 526. The case dragged on for years. See Spooner to H. H. Porter, May 10, 1883, February 13, 1885, April 27, 1888; to D. McCurdy, May 14, June 1, 1883; to A. J. Vanderpool, September 23, 1882, in Spooner Papers. Finally in April, 1888, there was a compromise settlement.

pare the case against his former boss. It was a difficult choice—his old friends and business associates, or continued employment with the Chicago and Northwestern. His job was a good one, with a salary which was entirely satisfactory and duties easy of performance. Opportunities for advancement were immeasurable. The Northwestern was one of the two most important railroads in Wisconsin, and its association with the New York Central made Spooner "one of the right bowers in the Vanderbilt cabinet." [78]

Spooner, however, did not hesitate about taking sides. Although he refused the annual salary of ten thousand dollars, which Porter, Dows, and Flower offered to guarantee him for the next five years, he promised to give to the defense of their cases against Kennedy all the intelligent work of which he was capable. In May, 1884, he resigned as solicitor and as a director of the Omaha. [79] This marked the finale of his career as a railroad solicitor. Never again, although he had several offers, did he agree to accept such a position.

The opprobrium of having been a railway attorney shadowed him throughout his public career. Spooner was always indignant that this phase of his legal career was held against him and he never really understood why it should have been. [80] He was the victim of one of those shifts in

78 *Hudson Star and Times,* December 29, 1882, May 18, 1883, May 16, 30, 1884.

79 Spooner to P. L. Spooner, May 7; to H. H. Porter, May 6, 1884, in Spooner Papers.

80 Spooner to his son Willet, June 11, 1906, *ibid.:* "Of course if you have any idea of ever going into politics, . . . you will bear in mind that the fact that I was once a railroad lawyer, in connection with a general practice, has followed me through all my public life. It has annoyed me, but if my life were to be lived over again I should, as a matter of self respect, take such clients as I wished to take, and let the popularity or unpopularity of it take care of itself."

public morals which occur every once in a while. By the time he reached the zenith of his political career, the muckrakers had refashioned public opinion, but when he had been hired as a solicitor for the railroads, he had been considered very fortunate. Those were the Horatio Alger days, when the public admired the "robber barons," although they were not so denominated at that time. Money was the measure of success and the methods by which it was obtained were not closely examined. Control of governmental bodies to obtain special favors was taken for granted; the people were not concerned. There were unlimited public lands, plenty for both the railroads and individuals, and the timber was there, inexhaustible, it seemed, to be sold for the benefit of its owners. Conservation was not even contemplated. Little thought was given to the responsibility of a public carrier to the people or to its employees. That was the prevalent opinion of the 1870's and 1880's in spite of sporadic efforts of protest groups to change it. Spooner's job had been to see that the actions of the railroad owners were within the letter of the law. Deals had often been questionable and sometimes had resulted in more than financial casualties. Evidently none of these machinations, the ruining of a community or a man, the cheating of another railroad, or the winning over of legislators by means of passes seemed morally wrong to Spooner; he was a lawyer and the railroad was his client. He considered it his duty to represent the interests of his clients to the best of his ability and to carry out the instructions of his superiors "within the limit of honorable effort." [81]

[81] Spooner to J. Tillotson, September 5, 1892, *ibid.*

3 : *Apprenticeship in the Senate (1885-1887)*

"IF YOU EVER CALL ME A DAMNED FOOL I SHAN'T RESENT IT"*

TWO DAYS after Spooner presented his resignation as solicitor for the Omaha railroad he replied to an inquiry of one of his friends: "I have hardly given a thought to the matter of the Senatorship and the mention of my name in that connection has not been suggested or inspired by me in any way whatever. . . . That I am a candidate in the ordinary sense of the term I am not prepared to admit." [1]

Spooner might deny he was a candidate, but he had already succeeded in getting the top position in the state party machinery for the man who was to become his campaign manager. In April he had written Sawyer a long letter concerning the selection of a new chairman of the state central committee, since Edward Sanderson, who had held the office since 1881, did not want to be re-elected. Henry C. Payne would make an excellent chairman,

* Spooner to E. W. Winter, May 5, 1886, in Spooner Papers.
[1] Spooner to J. H. Waggoner, May 7, 1884, in Spooner Papers.

Spooner recognized, but as long as he was a postmaster he could not take the chairmanship, although he could continue to be secretary of the committee. Andrew J. Turner, former owner of the *Portage Register,* was being mentioned for the position, Spooner reported, but he warned Sawyer that Turner was treacherous, had been false to Sawyer in his senatorial campaign, and was working for the success of men who were not his friends. He recommended Horace A. Taylor, of Hudson, adding that in suggesting his neighbor he had no ax whatever to grind, that he was interested only in the good of the party.[2]

Spooner was a delegate, elected by acclamation by his senatorial district convention, to the state convention that selected Taylor for the chairmanship of the state central committee. This convention met in Madison on April 30, 1884, to elect delegates-at-large to the national convention. Spooner, a member of the resolutions committee, was able to substitute an ambiguous, complimentary resolution for one instructing the Wisconsin delegation to present the name of General Lucius Fairchild for the presidential nomination.[3] Friends of the General were under no illusion that he had a chance for the nomination, but they thought a boom at the national convention might put him in a favored position for the United States senatorship. Fairchild was sure the Wisconsin delegation would work for his nomination whenever there was a chance of winning.[4] In reality he was being gently eased out of the

[2] Spooner to P. Sawyer, April 16, 1884, *ibid.* Spooner also succeeded in getting Taylor elected a delegate to the Republican National Convention from the Eighth Congressional District (see Spooner to F. A. Myerey, April 21, 1884, *ibid.*).

[3] *Hudson Star and Times,* May 9, 1884; *Milwaukee Sentinel,* May 1, 1884.

[4] L. Fairchild to C. Fairchild, April 30, 1884, in Fairchild Papers.

political scene. The *Chicago Herald,* commenting on the proceedings of the convention, predicted the political annihilation of Fairchild and the rise into first place for the senatorship of John C. Spooner.[5]

Sawyer and Spooner both attended the Republican National Convention that met in Chicago the first week of June. They were only spectators. One evening during the convention Sawyer met Spooner on the sidewalk in front of the Grand Pacific Hotel and suggested that the young man be a candidate for the senatorship at the expiration of Senator Cameron's term. Spooner was aware that to be chosen by Sawyer for the toga made almost certain his receiving it. In flowery phrases he expressed his thanks: "I would rather be in the Senate *two* years with you there, than to be there *six* years, without you." He, however, did not commit himself to being a candidate.[6]

That same week there appeared in the *Hudson Star and Times,* under the heading "Our Washington Letter": "Rumor has it that Col. John C. Spooner will be urged by his friends as U. S. Senator from Wisconsin in place of Mr. Cameron, whose term soon expires. That he would fill such a position with honor and reflect credit upon the State, no one can doubt." The *Star and Times* was Horace Taylor's paper and Taylor was chairman of the state central committee.[7]

Spooner made no announcement of his candidacy and left Wisconsin to spend the summer on "the far-away Island" off the Atlantic coast. He explained to Payne that he had been working hard all year, was tired, and had

5 *Madison Democrat,* May 6, 1884.
6 Spooner to P. Sawyer, February 13, 1885, in Spooner Papers; Current, *Pine Logs and Politics,* p. 193.
7 *Hudson Star and Times,* June 6, 1884.

found that the seashore rejuvenated him. He picked for his retreat Siasconset, on Nantucket Island, thirty miles south of Massachusetts, with nothing beyond it but the shores of Spain. It was usually called S'conset, for Siasconset was too long a name for that Lilliputian village. It had been an old fishing settlement with no post office, no stores, and no churches when it had been discovered a few years before by some New York businessmen searching for a new resort. It was just beginning to become fashionable when the Spooners and their Hudson neighbors the Phipps began going there.[8]

True to his promise to Payne, Spooner returned to Wisconsin in time for the Republican state convention on September 3. While the convention renominated by acclamation all constitutional officers,[9] Spooner was performing his duty as a regent of the University of Wisconsin. He had been appointed by Governor Rusk to the Board of Regents in 1882 and had attended only one meeting, that of June 20, 1882. It was at that meeting that a report presented by William F. Vilas for the reorganization of the law department of the university had been adopted. Spooner had been appointed to the law committee, and at the September, 1884, meeting he presented for dean of the law faculty the name of Ithamar C. Sloan, the lawyer with whom he had pleaded his first case before the United States Supreme Court. At this meeting Spooner was also appointed chairman of a special committee to present to the legislature a request that additional compensation be given to the chairman of the new department of the Science and

8 *Ibid.*, July 25, August 29, 1884; *Nantucket Inquirer and Mirror*, August 20, 1887, August 4, September 8, 1888; Spooner to H. C. Payne, July 22, 1884, in Spooner Papers.
9 *Milwaukee Sentinel*, September 4, 1884.

Art of Teaching for his extra work in visiting schools throughout the state. Serving with him on this committee was his old lawyer-friend William F. Vilas.[10]

Spooner and Vilas left the meeting of the Board of Regents, where they had been working together on behalf of their alma mater, to fight each other on the political field, for it was generally understood that each was a candidate for the United States senatorship. That afternoon, September 3, Spooner attended the big rally held for General John A. Logan, the Republican vice-presidential candidate. Special trains had brought hundreds of Republican workers from all parts of the state. Spooner had a position of honor on the platform and held the crowd spellbound— so his friends said—with his stirring speech reviewing the records of Blaine and Logan and denouncing the Democrats. Many at the rally saluted him as the next United States Senator.[11] Throughout the campaign, despite his friends' entreaties, Spooner refused to admit—even to Payne and Sawyer—that he was a candidate.[12] Yet by the last of October he must have reached a decision, for when he wrote Winter, of the Omaha, asking him to make every effort to make available a special train to bring Democrats to a political rally in Hudson at which Vilas was to speak, he added: "Otherwise the railroad question will come into this contest I fear in a way that will not only hurt me but will hurt the railroad." [13]

The election was a critical one. The last one had re-

10 Wisconsin University, Board of Regents, Minutes, Vol. B, June 20, 21, 1882, September 3, 1884.

11 *Milwaukee Sentinel,* September 4, 1884; Spooner to M. M. Hill, August 26, 1884; N. L. James to Spooner, September 27, 1904, in Spooner Papers.

12 Spooner to H. C. Payne, January 27, 1885, in Spooner Papers.

13 Spooner to E. Winter, October 20, 1884, *ibid.*

sulted in a Democratic assembly and six Democratic congressmen. In this election not only were the state ticket and nine seats in the House of Representatives at stake but also the Presidency and a United States senatorship. Which party, not which Republican should win the senatorship, was the issue this time. In the contests for Republican nominations for assemblymen and senators the question of the United States senatorship was not raised as it had been in 1880.

From the time of the state convention until election night Spooner devoted every working day to campaigning for the Republican ticket. He was a brilliant orator who could hold the attention of a large audience for two and a half hours or electrify them by a two-minute speech.[14] His stump speaking was said to have been as big a factor as the organization work of Taylor and Payne in keeping Wisconsin in the Republican column in this election which put a Democrat in the White House for the first time in a quarter of a century. The Republicans made a clean sweep; their slate of state officers was elected by a plurality of 15,000, and they had a large majority in the state legislature, which ensured the election of a Republican to the United States Senate. Seven of the nine congressmen-elect were Republicans.[15] Among them, from Dane County, was Robert M. La Follette, the young aggressive district attorney (1881–1885) who had achieved his election to both offices in spite of the opposition of the local bosses, Elisha W. Keyes and Philip Spooner.[16]

14 *Hudson Star and Times,* September 12, 26, October 11, 18, November 21, 1884.

15 *Chicago Inter-Ocean,* November 11, 1884; Current, *Pine Logs and Politics,* p. 187.

16 La Follette, *Autobiography,* pp. 45–46.

By the time of the election it was definitely understood that the two major contestants for the Republican nomination for the United States senatorship would be General Fairchild and Colonel Spooner. The former had been an acknowledged candidate since the middle of July,[17] the latter after November 18.[18] A third candidate, William Thompson Price, congressman from Spooner's own district, entered the race in December but his candidacy was not taken seriously.[19] From all outward indications it would seem that Spooner would have little chance of winning against Fairchild. Willett Main, although he did not say so to his brother-in-law, thought Fairchild would be too strong for Spooner.[20] The former was his senior by eleven years and had had a notable public career, whereas Spooner had held only one elective position, that of assemblyman. Fairchild had been Wisconsin secretary of state for one term and governor for three terms. In 1872 he had gone into the foreign service, first as consul at Liverpool, then as consul general in France, and finally in 1880 as minister to Spain. He had also distinguished himself in the Civil War, having resigned from the army as a brigadier general after he had lost an arm at Gettysburg.[21] The veterans' organizations were his zealous supporters, ready

[17] C. Fairchild to L. Fairchild, July 21, September 22; H. B. Harshaw to L. Fairchild, November 15, 1884, in Fairchild Papers.

[18] Spooner Letterbooks 3G and 3EE contain almost a hundred letters from Spooner and Taylor, dated from November 18, 1884, to January 9, 1885. See *Hudson Star and Times*, November 28, December 5, 12, 19, 26, 1884, on Spooner's candidacy.

[19] *Milwaukee Sentinel*, December 7, 19, 23, 1884; H. Taylor to H. C. Payne, December 10; H. Taylor to Spooner, December 13; Spooner to N. Hicken, December 8, 1884, in Spooner Papers; W. H. Cash to J. C. Spencer, November 29, 1884, in Fairchild Papers.

[20] W. Main, Diary, November 18, December 3, 1884.

[21] *Milwaukee Sentinel*, April 26, 1884.

to bring all their influence to bear on members of the legislature.[22] He had the active support of two of the most important newspapers in the state, the *Milwaukee Sentinel* and the *Evening Wisconsin*. Some of the best-known politicians were working for him, notably Andrew J. Turner and Edward Sanderson. Fairchild was confident that he was the choice of a large majority of the people of Wisconsin.[23] But Fairchild had been away from the state too long; he was unaware of the transformation that had taken place in party politics during his absence. When he left, war glories and public service were significant factors in the selection of government officials. Now economic interests were a determining force in elections.[24]

Spooner was a product of this new political force. Some gave as their reason for supporting the younger man the fact that since a Democrat had been elected President, the Republican party needed a young, aggressive, hard-working man in the Senate—one who combined "the brains of statesmanship with the tongue of eloquence." It was not the time to use the senatorship just to reward a distinguished former soldier and public servant, and many felt that Fairchild had already had more than his share of political rewards anyway.[25] Spooner had the support of the *Chicago Tribune* and the *Chicago Inter-Ocean,* two influential dailies in that region.[26] He also had the party ma-

22 J. S. Bugh to L. Fairchild, November 15; A. M. Thomas to L. Fairchild, November 17; W. McBride to L. Fairchild, November 24, 1884, in Fairchild Papers.

23 A. J. Turner to L. Fairchild, November 21; W. E. Gardner to L. Fairchild, December 6, 1884; L. Fairchild to E. Sanderson, December 21, 1884, *ibid.; Milwaukee Sentinel,* December 9, 1884.

24 *Madison Democrat,* January 7, 1885.

25 *Chicago Inter-Ocean,* November 16, 30, 1884, January 3, 1885; H. O. Fairchild to Spooner, October 3, 1904, in Spooner Papers.

26 *Chicago Inter-Ocean,* January 18, 1885; Spooner to S. M. Booth, March 14, 1898, in Spooner Papers.

chinery on his side. Taylor, chairman of the state central committee, was his personal campaign manager; Payne, secretary-treasurer, was known to be friendly to Spooner, although he took no active part in the campaign. Governor Rusk used his influence with the representatives from his section of the state on behalf of Spooner.[27] But more than anything else, Spooner was the candidate picked by Philetus Sawyer. The Senator openly stated his preference but throughout the contest conspicuously remained in Washington.[28] His control of the party, however, was such that he did not have to be present to direct it. The *Madison Democrat* graphically presented the situation:

The senatorial plum which is to drop from the legislative tree this winter causes numerous republican mouths to water. . . . However, all of this shouldering and shoving and mouth opening is in vain. At the proper time Senator Sawyer will take the long pole with a little bag on the end, which he used in harvesting senatorial plums, and will quietly reach up, and that plum will detach itself from that tree and roll into that

[27] Spooner to J. Rusk, December 6; H. Taylor to O. B. Thomas, December 10, 1884, in Spooner Papers; C. E. Buell to L. Fairchild, November 20, 1884, in Fairchild Papers, saying that Vernon County members were for him; J. Rusk to H. Taylor, December 7, 1884, in Rusk Papers at the State Historical Society of Wisconsin: "I do not see why you should be annoyed that the members & Senator from Vernon are not committed. If nothing had been done they would have been committed to Fairchild. . . . While they are all friends of mine they do not wish it to be understood that I control them." They voted for Spooner.

[28] *Milwaukee Sentinel,* December 25, 1884, January 1, 1885; Spooner to A. Cameron, November 25, 1884, in Spooner Papers: "The situation was such, with Sanderson and other political friends committed to Fairchild, that he [Sawyer] was inevitably forced to declare his preference. And it was as certain as fate that in such case the keynote of the Fairchild campaign would be, and it has already been officially sounded—'Sawyer's money and friend'—some will say 'tool.' I regret very much on his account that I have allowed myself to be considered a candidate for the Senate. He is in every way one of my best friends, and I exceedingly dislike to appear to have dragged him into a fight."

bag. He will then hand it to the man of his choice and say: "Here, John, try some of this fruit, off from my tree." [29]

The campaign at first was distinguished by a complete lack of unpleasantness. Instead there was "an interminable lot of slush." Fairchild protested that the office was "too high and important to be run after" and that he could "not make an unseemly race for it." [30] Spooner also stated he thought the position was too exalted a one "to be *sought* in *customary* way." He professed to be reluctant to be a candidate against his former employer. Beyond writing letters to members-elect of the legislature and to other political leaders asking for their support, the young Hudson attorney made no personal campaign for the office. In fact, he was out of the state on legal business during most of December. He explained to his friends: "I am sorry to leave at this juncture. It may hurt me, and will unless my friends look after my interests, but . . . it is part of my religion that in the lawyer's duty and devotion to his client he must forget everything but his own self respect." [31]

Not until just before Christmas did the contest become a red-hot fight. Though the *Milwaukee Sentinel* preferred Fairchild, still up to that time it had printed no words derogatory to Spooner. The first attack, a rather subtle one, appeared in the *Sentinel* on December 24. It purported to

29 *Madison Democrat,* December 3, 1884.

30 *Chicago Inter-Ocean,* December 28, 1884; L. Fairchild to P. Norcross, December 5, 1884, in Fairchild Papers.

31 Spooner to F. Gilam, December 8, 1884; to E. G. Timme, November 20, 1884, asking him "at least preserve a neutrality?"; to H. B. Harshaw, January 2, 1885, in Spooner Papers: "You are a friend of Gov. Fairchild, who is a friend of yours; you are a friend of mine and I of yours. You support Gov. Fairchild. You ought to. I expected you would do so and would have thought less of you than I do had you done otherwise."

be a news item containing a report of a conversation with
a Fairchild man in Madison but was really an article written by Frederick Jackson Turner, young son of Andrew J.
Turner. It cited Spooner's activities as a railroad lobbyist
and also his relations with Senator Sabin of Minnesota,
who was at that time in disrepute for some fraudulent activities connected with the bankruptcy of the Northwest
Car Company and its adjunct, the Chicago Railway Equipment Company, which had been organized for him by
Spooner. The writer pointed out how shrewd Spooner was,
for although he had gotten more than a comfortable living
out of being a railroad solicitor, he could now disclaim any
railroad connection and also any relation with the Chicago
Railway Equipment Company.[32] It was true that Spooner
had had no dealings with that company since, as a lawyer,
he had been one of its incorporators; for that matter, he
was at that time retained by some of the stockholders to
protect their interests against Sabin and other managers
of the Northwest Car Company.[33] As members of the legislature began to gather in Madison, the *Sentinel* intensified
its attack on Spooner. He was pictured as "an unprincipled
railroad lobbyist," and a man who would be governed

[32] *Milwaukee Sentinel,* December 24, 1884. See also *Chicago Inter-Ocean,*
December 26, 1884, for a similar article, probably also written by Turner,
as he became special correspondent about that time; Fulmer Mood, "Frederick Jackson Turner and the Chicago *Inter-Ocean,* 1885," *Wisconsin
Magazine of History,* 35 (Spring, 1952), 189.

[33] *Milwaukee Sentinel,* December 19, 1884; Spooner to H. W. Cannon,
December 29; to S. U. Pinney, December 25, 1884, in Spooner Papers: "My
information is that you are right in your surmise as to the origin of the
attempt to connect me, to my prejudice, with the Chicago Railway Equipment Co., and I agree with you entirely as to the characteristics of the
gentleman you mention, only there must be added an element which has
long been very clear to my observation, and that is the element of *malice.*"
It is clear that Spooner meant A. J. Turner.

solely by corporations if he were elected to the Senate. Behind the movement to elect Spooner "is not the people, but an organization of special interests, and for this reason that movement should be defeated," concluded the editor.[34]

Both the major contestants had established headquarters in the Park Hotel in Madison. Fairchild had done so very reluctantly and only because his friends had insisted it was necessary.[35] Spooner was in New York City (January 9–18) as the case of Harvey Kennedy against H. H. Porter was to come up for argument on January 12. Porter had been defeated in the lower court, so Spooner felt obligated to be there to defend his former employer. However, Hod Taylor and Roger and Philip Spooner were on hand to take care of his campaign.[36] As members of the legislature arrived for the organization of the body, the candidates' headquarters became "lively." Taylor claimed Spooner had 45 votes and would also receive the votes of the Price men when he withdrew. Fairchild saw defeat in the air; he could count on no more than 25 to 30 votes. "Sawyer has evidently taken off his coat—he has the Rep. party by the throat," he noted in his diary.[37]

It was twenty-five degrees below zero in Madison on Monday, January 19, when the legislators convened to

34 *Milwaukee Sentinel,* January 14, 1885; *Chicago Inter-Ocean,* January 18, 1885.

35 L. Fairchild, Diary, January 10, 12, 1885.

36 Spooner to O. H. Fethers, January 9; to Roger, January 27, 1885, in Spooner Papers; W. Main, Diary, January 12, 1885.

37 *Chicago Inter-Ocean,* January 16, 17, 1885; W. Main, Diary, January 15, 1885; L. Fairchild, Diary, January 13, 14, 16, 1885. According to Fairchild's correspondence, Fairchild heard from or about thirty-seven of the Republican members of the legislature; twenty-one of these were reported to be for him but eight of them voted for Spooner.

make their momentous decision on the senatorship. Spooner had arrived the day before from New York and it was noted that he was in excellent spirits.[38] The caucus was set for Wednesday evening. The Fairchild men had wanted it postponed until after the opening of the G.A.R. encampment in Madison, for the veterans, who were to a man for the "one-armed General," would have furnished an enthusiastic claque. The issue was really settled Tuesday night when the Spooner men held their caucus. The Price men joined them, which gave Spooner 49 votes, a safe majority. The formal caucus was held the next evening in the senate chamber. Spooner on the first ballot received 54 votes to 25 for Fairchild. The latter's support came from the southern section of the state, much the same region which had favored Keyes in 1881.[39] The two candidates were summoned to speak before the caucus. "A tough place for me & a singular situation for me—but I bore it as best I could," Fairchild noted in his diary.[40] Spooner, addressing the members, said: "I pledge my word to have no interest but your interest, and will give the State of Wisconsin the highest effort of my life until I give back to your keeping this great trust." Vilas was already being mentioned for President Cleveland's cabinet, so he was not interested in the senatorial nomination. The Democratic caucus therefore selected Edward S. Bragg, who had made a name for himself at the Democratic National Convention when in nominating Cleveland he had declared, "They love him most for the enemies he has made." The formal

[38] *Chicago Inter-Ocean*, January 20, 1885; W. Main, Diary, January 18, 1885.

[39] *Chicago Inter-Ocean*, January 17, 22, 1885; W. Main, Diary, January 20, 21, 1885; *Madison Democrat*, January 16, 1885.

[40] L. Fairchild, Diary, January 21, 1885.

election, on January 27, merely ratified the caucus decisions; Spooner received 76 votes to 48 for Bragg.[41]

Spooner had won, but how and why he won was a question for discussion throughout his public career. David Graham Phillips, the muckraker, claimed that the election had been a fight between the two most important railroad systems in Wisconsin, that the Omaha crowd was the stronger, so Spooner was elected. Early in the campaign some of Spooner's opponents had claimed that his candidacy was "a bold attempt on the part of the Northwestern road to smuggle one of their own subservient tools" into the federal government.[42] The Spooner group charged that the Chicago, Milwaukee and St. Paul was working for the election of Fairchild. It had been reported that its president, Alexander Mitchell, in spite of his promise to Sawyer to take no part in the contest, had approached some of the Milwaukee delegates on the General's behalf. Fairchild's brother had written him that Mitchell knew he was not an antirailroad man and had no Granger tendencies and that his presence in the Senate would be better for the railways than Spooner's or any other professed railroad candidate. He had advised him to let Mitchell help him all he could if the Northwestern worked for Spooner, but suggested it might be better for all concerned if Mitchell got Vanderbilt and Hughitt to cease all interference in the contest.[43] Whether any agreement between the two railroad systems

41 *Milwaukee Sentinel,* January 22, 28, 1885.

42 Phillips, "Chief Spokesman of 'the Merger,'" *Cosmopolitan,* 41 (June, 1906), 126; A. W. Sanborn to L. Fairchild, December 17, 1884, in Fairchild Papers.

43 Spooner to A. Cameron, November 25; H. Taylor to G. C. Ginty, December 10, 1884, in Spooner Papers; W. A. Collins to L. Fairchild, November 19; C. Fairchild to L. Fairchild, November 21, December 2, 1884, in Fairchild Papers.

had been made, there is no evidence that either railroad company played a prominent part in the election, and by the middle of the campaign even charges of railroad interference had disappeared. There remained, of course, the accusation that Spooner had been a railroad lobbyist and that the lobby was "a poor school for statesmanship." [44]

Another explanation offered for Spooner's success is that the leading lumbermen in Wisconsin got together and bought the senatorship for the young railroad attorney. This story was first published by Lincoln Steffens in *McClure's Magazine* in 1904 in the middle of La Follette's campaign to destroy Spooner's control of the Republican party in the state. Steffens quoted a conversation which supposedly took place between the two millionaire lumbermen, Isaac Stephenson and Philetus Sawyer. It went as follows:

"Isaac," said Sawyer, "how much did you put in to get the legislature for Spooner that time?"

"It cost me about twenty-two thousand, Philetus. How much did you put in?"

"Why," said Sawyer, surprised, "it cost me thirty thousand. I thought it cost you thirty."

"No, it cost me thirty to get it for you when you ran."

It is undoubtedly true that the two millionaires contributed large sums of money in the campaign of 1884; they usually did. The money was spent to bring about a victory for the Republican party rather than to elect members of the legislature who would vote for Spooner rather than Fairchild. Actually, some on whose election Sawyer spent

[44] *Milwaukee Sentinel*, December 18, 1884, January 16, 1885.

the most money voted for Fairchild.[45] That Spooner was to be a candidate was not known until after the election. Stephenson later admitted this to be true.[46] Not even his most spiteful political enemies at the time the Steffens article appeared charged Spooner with any culpable conduct. He was considered to be "a victim—a willing one, it must be said," of the type of politics then in vogue.[47] He had been sponsored by Philetus Sawyer, who in the public mind was associated with large business interests—lumber and railroads. (Sawyer claimed he no longer owned railroad stock; Spooner made no such denial.) Some railroad scheme, although no one had been able to discover what, must be the reason for Spooner's election, the cynics said.[48] Whether Spooner, when in the Senate, represented the railroads and was Sawyer's tool, his record in the Forty-ninth Congress will demonstrate.

Railroads occupied a good deal of the attention of Spooner's first Congress. Their land grants had aroused so

[45] Lincoln Steffens, "Enemies of the Republic," *McClure's Magazine,* 23 (October, 1904), 568–69; Isaac Stephenson, *Recollections of a Long Life,* p. 197; H. O. Fairchild to Spooner, October 3, 1904, in Spooner Papers.

[46] *Milwaukee Sentinel,* December 2, 1904. See *Chicago Inter-Ocean,* January 25, 1885, for a purported statement of Hod Taylor's to the effect that they had elected a legislature to make Spooner Senator. The article asserts that even if that had been Taylor's object in the campaign, it had not been the object of the rest of the state central committee.

[47] W. L. Houser to W. Chandler, September 28, 1904, in Chandler Papers at The Library of Congress.

[48] *Chicago Inter-Ocean,* January 25, 1885; *Milwaukee Sentinel,* January 21, 1885; Spooner to P. Sawyer, February 13, 1885, in Spooner Papers: "I appreciate in every way the value and importance of your friendship and great influence." See Spooner to H. C. Payne, January 27, 1885 (*ibid.*): "The strictures upon my candidacy as you know and Ed. [Sanderson] knows are not fair, and I had on my own account, independent of the influences to which they impute my election, more strength than Gov. Fairchild developed, although not enough to elect me I grant."

much opposition that in 1884 all political parties had planks in their platforms demanding the return of all unearned land; minor parties had even demanded the forfeiture of all land where the terms of the grant had not been strictly complied with. Many bills were introduced in both houses of Congress providing for the forfeiture of certain specified grants.[49] It was in connection with a bill concerning a railroad land grant in Iowa that Spooner entered the debate. He presented an amendment that would exempt from forfeiture those lands which the Supreme Court should decide had been erroneously patented for the benefit of the Sioux City and St. Paul Railroad Company but had been earned by the Chicago, Milwaukee and St. Paul Company, which had completed its road on time. The Senate Committee on Public Lands had rejected the amendment. Spooner presented it on the floor of the Senate where, after a brief but heated debate with Senators Plumb and Ingalls of Kansas, it was adopted by a vote of 33 to 13.[50] Two of the negative votes were cast by the Iowa Senators, James F. Wilson and William Boyd Allison, in spite of the fact that many of their constituents had urged them to support this amendment. Allison's correspondents explained that the forfeiture of the land would not affect the railroad company but would injure

[49] Ellis, "Forfeiture of Railroad Land Grants," *Mississippi Valley Historical Review*, 33 (June, 1946), 44–52; Edward Stanwood, *A History of the Presidency*, pp. 422, 424, 431, 437. Not until 1890 was a General Forfeiture Act passed; this provided for the forfeiture of land grants not earned by 1890.

[50] *Congressional Record*, 49th Cong., 1st Sess. (1885–86), pp. 2287–91, 2322–25. The bill failed to pass the House because the Democrats wanted to strike out Spooner's amendment. A filibuster, led by Wisconsin Congressmen Guenther, Thomas, Price, and La Follette, blocked that plan (see *Milwaukee Sentinel*, June 18, August 5, 1886).

the settlers who had purchased the land from the railroad.[51]

Four days after the passage by the Senate of Spooner's amendment he appeared before the United States Supreme Court on behalf of the Sioux City and St. Paul Railroad in its suit against the Chicago, Milwaukee and St. Paul. Spooner was violently attacked by the *New York Herald* for combining the careers of lawyer and legislator. It was charged that he had tried as Senator to secure legislation in the interests of his client.[52] The charges were utterly false, for his amendment was designed to protect not the rights of his client but those of his adversary. In a personal letter to his brother he explained:

> It [St. Paul railroad] and its officers are constituents of mine, and I thought they had a right to call upon me to protect their interest, and that it would not be a very good reason for me to refuse, simply because I was retained *against* them in a lawsuit. I was so careful to be way above suspicion, that if I did anything wrong, I did an injustice to the Sioux City & St. Paul Company.

Though this accusation of the *New York Herald* was "a barefaced and malicious lie," it was later repeated by the muckrakers as proof that Spooner was a tool of the "interests." [53]

The Works Progress Administration's guide to Wisconsin says of Spooner: "While in the Senate Spooner acted as

51 Allison Papers; Box 251 contains several letters concerning this amendment; see, e.g., E. F. Drake to Allison, January 5, 1885, in Allison Papers at the Historical, Memorial, and Art Department of Iowa, Des Moines, Iowa.

52 *New York Herald,* April 9, 1886; 10 Federal Reporter 435; 117 U. S. 406 (*Sioux City and St. Paul Railroad* v. *Chicago, Milwaukee and St. Paul*). The court made an arbitrary division of the lands.

53 Spooner to Roger, April 16, 1886, in Spooner Papers; Phillips, "Chief Spokesman of 'the Merger,' " *Cosmopolitan,* 41 (June, 1906), 127–28.

chief counsel for the railroads on trial before the United States Supreme Court." [54] The Sioux City case was the only case in which Spooner appeared for a railroad during his senatorial career. He had expected to carry on some legal work while he was a member of the Senate. Several of his colleagues appeared frequently before the Supreme Court, notably George F. Edmunds, William M. Evarts, and George F. Hoar. Spooner soon found, however, that he could not serve faithfully in the Senate and at the same time practice law. [55] During his six years in the Senate he appeared in only one other case before the Supreme Court; it also concerned railroad land grants. The issue was the taxation of indemnity lands. Spooner represented Price County, while the Wisconsin Central Railroad was represented by Louis Brandeis, later an associate justice of the Supreme Court. It was quite a feather in the cap of this young lawyer, on his first appearance before that court, to win a case against Senator Spooner. The court ruled that title to federal lands remained in the United States government until all official acts transferring the land had been complied with and were therefore not subject to local taxes. [56] This was the only decision handed down by the

[54] Works Progress Administration, *Wisconsin: A Guide to the Badger State*, pp. 57–58.

[55] Spooner to I. Wiltrout, April 5, 1886; to H. Richardson, February 1, 1890, in Spooner Papers; *United States Reports*, Vols. 116–41. Spooner did present a brief on behalf of Frederick W. Cotzhauser in a debt case, 129 U. S. 330 (*White* v. *Cotzhauser*), and defended H. H. Porter in the Kennedy case before the New York Court of Appeals.

[56] 133 U. S. 496 (*Wisconsin Central Railroad* v. *Price County*). See also 57 Wis. 137 (*Wisconsin Central* v. *Lincoln County*). Alpheus Thomas Mason, *Brandeis: A Free Man's Life*, pp. 70–71, incorrectly states that Spooner was normally counsel of the Wisconsin Central but since he was not well versed in the facts of the case, Brandeis was asked to argue it before the Supreme Court. Because of his victory in this suit, Brandeis was retained as counsel for the Wisconsin Central.

Wisconsin Supreme Court in the 1880's to be overruled by the United States Supreme Court.[57]

Spooner was indirectly concerned with another railroad land-grant issue during his first session in Congress. This time it was not a bill in Congress or a case in the Supreme Court but a ruling of President Cleveland's new Commissioner of the General Land Office, William Jackson Sparks. Since his appointment, Sparks had with almost religious zeal approached the task of regaining from railroads the land grants they had not earned. When Governor Rusk, at the request of Sawyer, applied to the Secretary of the Interior for certification of certain indemnity lands selected by the state for benefit of the Wisconsin Railroad Farm Mortgage Land Company, Sparks denied the application. Spooner in disgust wrote E. W. Winter:

The old jackass who presided over the General Land Office yesterday rendered his decision, tearing the Farm Mortgage Co. up by the roots. He overruled Justices Harlan, Bunn and Drummond upon every point. Between you and me he has no sort of realization of what he does. An intelligent man, long experienced in that business in his office, wrote up carefully the decision in favor of certifying the lands to the Farm Mortgage Co. The old skunk sent it back, and told him to write it up the other way, and yet he could not tell, after it was written up adversely, upon what ground his decision was put.[58]

The issue was appealed to Secretary of the Interior Lamar, who reversed the decision. He declared that the decision

57 John D. Sanborn, "The Supreme Court of Wisconsin in the Eighties," *Wisconsin Magazine of History*, 15 (September, 1931), 19–20.

58 Spooner to P. Sawyer, February 13, 1885; to E. Winter, May 28, 1886, in Spooner Papers; J. Rusk to Spooner, November 25, 1885, in Rusk Papers; U. S. Department of the Interior, *Report of Commissioner of General Land Office*, 1887, pp. 288–92.

of the justices had been final since there had been no appeal and therefore the company had the right to the land. He directed his commissioner to submit for his approval the list of selections made by Wisconsin for the benefit of the Wisconsin Railroad Farm Mortgage Land Company. He pointed out that the right of the state of Wisconsin under Congressional grant had not been impaired by any Congressional declaration of forfeiture or judicial decree, as the Supreme Court had said was necessary in the *Schulenberg* v. *Harriman* case.[59]

Not only railroad land grants but also the abuses of the railroads, their excessive rates, and the need for federal regulation were taken up by the Forty-ninth Congress. Railroads had been so essential to the growth of the country and the rivalry between communities for a road had often been so great that they had been given many special favors. With consolidation, some systems had become so powerful that they thought themselves beyond the reach of the people. They charged all the traffic would bear, discriminated in favor of special shippers or certain localities, and gave passes to government officials. State legislatures had had, according to Spooner, "to teach them that in an

[59] Spooner to H. H. Porter, July 27, 1886, in Spooner Papers; *Decisions of the Department of the Interior Relating to Public Lands,* 5 (July, 1886–June, 1887), 81, 89–93. The following year Secretary Lamar restored to the Omaha railroad 200,000 acres of land which Sparks had denied it; thereupon Sparks resigned (see Allan Nevins, *Grover Cleveland: A Study in Courage,* pp. 226–27). When Lamar's appointment to the Supreme Court was brought up before the Senate, it was thought that the Wisconsin Senators would vote for confirmation of the appointment in spite of the adverse report of the Republican-dominated Judiciary Committee. Neither one did. See Willie D. Halsell, "The Appointment of L. Q. C. Lamar to the Supreme Court," *Mississippi Valley Historical Review,* 28 (December, 1941), 399–413, and *Senate Executive Journal,* 49th Cong., 2d Sess. (1886–87), pp. 139–40.

essential sense they were a public instrumentality and must consult and subserve the public interest." Twenty-six states had passed laws regulating railroads and for over ten years attempts had been made to pass a federal law. Bills had passed the House but had been blocked in the Senate. But in 1886 the effectiveness of state laws had been practically destroyed by the Supreme Court's decision, in the Wabash case, that a state could not regulate interstate commerce. Since most railroads, certainly all the important ones, crossed state lines, federal regulation was imperative.[60]

The fight on the railroad bill was not between Republicans and Democrats but between the rabid antirailroad men and those who represented business interests, between the House, with its extreme Reagan bill, and the Senate, with a moderate measure sponsored by Cullom of Illinois.[61] Few members in either House were impartial enough or had the requisite knowledge or experience to frame a bill that would effectively remedy the abuses of the railroads and yet would not destroy the systems which were still so essential to the prosperity of the country. Even Spooner, who had had more practical experience with railroads than most of his colleagues, still felt he was not well enough informed on that complex problem.[62]

Spooner, in a two-hour speech on May 5, 1886, urged passage by the Senate of the Cullom bill. This speech, like most others in Congress, was for public consumption and

[60] *Congressional Record,* 49th Cong., 1st Sess. (1885–86), pp. 4178–80; William Z. Ripley, *Railroads: Rates and Regulations,* pp. 440–55; Haney, *Congressional History of Railways,* pp. 290–92, 299–301.

[61] Shelby Cullom, *Fifty Years of Public Service,* pp. 321–22.

[62] Spooner to H. H. Porter, April 16, 1886, in Spooner Papers: "I wish I had, for use on the Interstate Commerce bill, some of your accurate and profound knowledge of the transportation question."

it was made from "the *popular* standpoint without any attempt to show its [the bill's] injustice to railroads," wrote Spooner to E. W. Winter, general manager of the Omaha. "The long haul short haul business would have gone entirely by default but for my starting the fight," he stated.[63] Spooner had championed all provisions of the railroad bill except a clause that would outlaw charging more for a short haul than a long haul under any circumstances. Such an absolute prohibition would benefit the railroads, he declared, for then they would raise their competitive rates. He admitted that there had been many abuses by the railroads in discrimination against localities, but pointed out that these abuses could be remedied by the enforcement of section three, which prohibited undue preference to individuals or localities. Common law also covered abuses of that nature but had not hitherto been very effective because of the expensiveness of litigation. Under the proposed bill a commission would investigate charges of discrimination and if railroads continued their unfair practices, then the commission could take the issue to court. The case would then be at the expense of the railroad or the government rather than the individual harmed, and the report of the commission would be prima-facie evidence. To forbid charging more for a short haul than a long haul under all conditions would destroy competition, Spooner argued, and to forbid competition "is a species of communism; it is an attempt to take from those who have competition that which they have and to give it to those who have it not and who, by the operation of natural laws, are not entitled to it." His whole argument was a plea for the West, which, he said, could never have been built up

63 Spooner to E. W. Winter, May 25, 1886, *ibid.*

if it had not been for the competition that had brought it near to the tidewater.[64]

The Senate adopted Spooner's amendment which gave the commission power to prohibit discrimination between long and short hauls provided the power were not used by the commission to deprive a community of its advantage of competition. The final bill, as reported by the conference committee, reversed the procedure and forbade the long and short haul "under substantially similar circumstances and conditions" but gave the commission power to grant exceptions. Spooner did not oppose this change. In his stand on this issue Spooner could not be said to be particularly prorailroad; instead, he was representing his section of the country.

Most of the conservative Senators, and those accused of having railroad interests, opposed section five, which forbade pooling. This had been one of the few provisions of the House bill that had been retained by the conference committee. Spooner clashed with Nelson W. Aldrich of Rhode Island and Orville H. Platt of Connecticut on this issue. Consolidation of competing lines "is a crime against the people," he declared, and pools have been bad not only for the public but also for the railroads. If pools were abolished, competing carriers would be placed under stronger incentive to attract business by merit, he argued.[65]

In public addresses and private correspondence Spooner tried to convince railroad men that some regulation would

64 *Congressional Record,* 49th Cong., 1st Sess., pp. 4181–85; *Milwaukee Sentinel,* May 6, 1886.

65 *Congressional Record,* 49th Cong., 1st Sess., p. 4178; 2d Sess., Appendix, pp. 36–43; Louis A. Coolidge, *An Old Fashioned Senator: Orville H. Platt of Connecticut,* pp. 455–56; Nathaniel Wright Stephenson, *Nelson W. Aldrich: A Leader in American Politics,* p. 62.

be beneficial to them. He recommended support of the Interstate Commerce Commission, especially with the increased powers given it by the conference committee. The provision for reasonable rates and for their publicity he thought excellent. Section three, "if plainly enacted and fairly enforced," would benefit both the railroad companies and the shippers, he declared. This section should be construed to prohibit altogether the issuances of passes on interstate travel. "The Companies will be damned fools," he wrote Winter, "if they do not unanimously give it that construction and stand by it throughout the country." Neither the railroads nor the commission, however, gave the section that interpretation. Spooner, from the time of the passage of the Interstate Commerce Act, returned all railroad passes sent him.[66]

Spooner had felt that the bill as presented by the conference committee was not only too inelastic but that it had many legal defects. The bitterness against the railroads had led to the inclusion of some unenforceable provisions. Spooner would have liked to have seen the bill recommitted if it could still have been passed during that Congress. Since that had not been possible, he had voted for the passage of the bill as it was, although he feared it would run into difficulties in the court.[67] (The effectiveness of

[66] Spooner to M. Hughitt, May 13; to E. W. Winter, May 25, 1886; to S. R. Ainslie, December 25, 1889, in Spooner Papers. It was in the Hepburn Act of 1906 that passes were forbidden.

[67] Spooner to E. W. Winter, March 7, 1888, *ibid.; Milwaukee Sentinel,* January 1, 15, 1887. During the Fiftieth and Fifty-first Congresses Spooner suggested two measures to strengthen government regulation of transportation and communication, both of which were included in the Mann-Elkins Act of 1910. One would prohibit changes in rates for thirty days while the I.C.C. investigated their reasonableness; the other would give the I.C.C. control of telegraph companies. See *Congressional Record,* 50th

the act was practically destroyed by the decisions of the Supreme Court during the following decade.)

Spooner, it seems, attempted to serve both the public and the railroads; he did not think their interests were diametrically opposed, as did so many of his colleagues. He believed regulation was absolutely essential to prevent abuses, to punish bad railroad men, and to promote competition. He was sure, though, that railroads were essential to the prosperity of the country and that if hamstrung, the public would suffer.

The Forty-ninth Congress was a notably barren one; with a Republican Senate and Democratic President and House of Representatives, the federal government was practically impotent. Only nonpartisan measures, such as the Interstate Commerce Act, could be passed. Two other acts of special interest to Spooner's constituents were the oleomargarine bill and the bill to establish agricultural experiment stations. Naturally, residents of the dairy state were in favor of the bill to define butter and oleomargarine and the Wisconsin Grange passed resolutions asking Spooner to support it. From the outset Spooner had favored the bill; not only was he always suspicious of substitutes but also he felt the farmer needed protection against what he called unfair and dishonest competition. This bill imposed not only annual taxes on manufacturers and wholesale and retail dealers but, in addition, levied a tax on each pound of colored oleomargarine sold. Spooner tried to prevent passage by the Senate of the Ingalls amendment, which reduced the tax per pound from five to two

Cong., 1st Sess. (1887–88), pp. 727, 6455, 7430–31; 51st Cong., 1st Sess. (1889–90), pp. 1059, 1931.

cents, but he did not succeed.[68] Many in the Senate thought the amount of the tax was not important, that even a small tax would bring the article under supervision and point out to the consumer that it was imitation butter.[69] Some questioned the constitutionality of the bill, for the taxes were obviously being levied for regulatory purposes rather than to raise revenue. Spooner assured his constituents, and the Attorney General convinced President Cleveland, that the bill was constitutional.[70] This act remained the basic law on this subject until repealed in 1951.

Spooner was severely criticized by some of his constituents for his amendment to the bill to establish agricultural experiment stations in connection with the colleges established in the several states under the Morrill Act of 1862.[71] Spooner, by his amendment, was trying to appease certain farmer organizations, notably the Grange and the Wisconsin Agricultural Society, which were opposed to the agricultural curriculum at the University of Wisconsin. In carrying out the provisions of the grant of 1862, Wisconsin had set up an agriculture department in the state university in 1868, and in 1883 had established an agri-

68 Spooner to H. Smith, July 12; to J. B. Quimby, July 22, 1886, in Spooner Papers; *Congressional Record,* 49th Cong., 1st Sess., pp. 5213, 7069, 7196, 7202, 7317.

69 B. Harrison to S. Spradling and to J. Mitchell, June 21, 1886, in Benjamin Harrison Papers at The Library of Congress.

70 Spooner to H. Smith, July 31, 1886, in Spooner Papers; *United States Statutes at Large,* 49th Cong., p. 209.

71 E. Keyes to R. M. La Follette, January 19, 1888, in Keyes Papers; Spooner to J. M. Smith, November 9, 1887, in Spooner Papers: "I am a graduate of the University, and a loyal one too, but I did not feel that I was representing the University in the Senate, and that I had any right, in dealing with a subject which related peculiarly to the farmers of the State, and with a fund intended primarily for their benefit, to consider any interest but their interest."

cultural experiment station. The farmer organizations had demanded a separate agricultural college, and in the fall of 1884 had appointed a committee to confer with the Board of Regents of the university on an equitable division of the funds derived from the sale of the Morrill Act lands.[72] The regents, at a special meeting on December 30, had adopted the motion presented by Spooner, which stated that although they had no hostility to the establishment of a separate agricultural college if the legislature thought it best, they could not assent to any proposition which would deprive the university of any of the Agricultural College Fund, since it had been given by Congress to the states for instruction in mechanical arts as well as all branches of agriculture. At the next meeting of the board, on January 20, 1885, it had been decided to set up a short, purely vocational, agriculture course at the university,[73] and the state legislature that session had passed a bill to appropriate five thousand dollars to the Board of Regents for holding farmers' institutes.[74] The Grange, however, had continued its agitation for a separate agricultural col-

[72] Wilbur H. Glover, "The Agricultural College Crisis of 1885," *Wisconsin Magazine of History*, 32 (September, 1948), 17–25.

[73] University of Wisconsin, Board of Regents, Minutes, Vol. C, December 30, 1884, January 20, 1885. This was the last meeting of the board that Spooner attended; he resigned in 1886. See Spooner to J. G. Thorpe, March 23, 1886, in Spooner Papers: "I cannot give the duties any attention, and, moreover, having been elected to the Senate, I think Republicans in the District have a right to feel that I should relinquish that position to some other man."

[74] Curti and Carstensen, *University of Wisconsin*, I, 470–73, 712–13; *Wisconsin General Laws*, 1885, p. 8. In the Fifty-first Congress Spooner introduced a bill to provide for establishment throughout the country of farmers' institutes similar to those in Wisconsin. The bill died in committee. See *New York Herald*, February 16, 1889; *Milwaukee Sentinel*, March 24, 1889; W. I. Chamberlain to W. B. Allison, March 4, 1889, in Allison Papers.

lege. It was for this reason that Spooner had presented his amendment, which declared that in case any state had established an agricultural department or experiment station in connection with the university, that if hereafter the state should establish a separate agricultural college, the legislature of the state might apply in whole or in part the appropriation made by this act to the separate agricultural college.[75] Spooner's amendment became a dead letter as far as Wisconsin was concerned, since agitation for a separate agricultural college practically disappeared when the College of Agriculture was established as part of the University of Wisconsin. This was done under the auspices of Thomas C. Chamberlin, whom Spooner helped persuade to leave his position as director of the United States Geological Survey for that of university president.[76]

Spooner's first Congress was a disillusioning experience. "I am not on a single committee the duties of which either give me an opportunity, or compel me, to become thoroughly familiar with any question of broad public policy, and if I knew everything that ever will come before the committees on which I am doing such hard work, it would be of little use to my constituents," grumbled Spooner.[77]

[75] *Congressional Record,* 49th Cong., 2d Sess., pp. 1042–43; *United States Statutes at Large,* 49th Cong., p. 442 (sec. 8).

[76] Spooner to J. G. Thorpe, March 23, 1886, in Spooner Papers; Curti and Carstensen, *University of Wisconsin,* I, 536. In the Fiftieth Congress, at the request of President Chamberlin, Spooner introduced a bill to make the appropriation for agricultural experiment stations a permanent one, but Allison, chairman of the Committee on Appropriations, stated that the only permanent appropriations were for the public debt. See *Congressional Record,* 50th Cong., 1st Sess., p. 22; Spooner to T. C. Chamberlin, December 12; to E. Keyes, December 15, 1887; to W. A. Henry, January 27, 1888, in Spooner Papers.

[77] Spooner to C. W. Porter, March 12, 1888, in Spooner Papers.

The *Milwaukee Sentinel* thought that for a new member Spooner had been pretty well treated in the make-up of committees. He had been appointed to the standing committees on Claims, on Public Buildings and Grounds, on Epidemic Diseases, and to the special committee on the Potomac River Front.[78] Spooner had hoped to be appointed to the Judiciary Committee but William Maxwell Evarts received the coveted position. Although he entered the Senate at the same time as the New York Senator, Spooner admitted the latter had already "won in a marvellous career a worldwide reputation as an orator, lawyer, statesman and diplomat." [79]

Spooner was made chairman of the Committee on Claims in December, 1886, when the death of Senator Pike of New Hampshire brought about the promotion of Senator Dolph of Oregon to that position. The latter preferred to retain the chairmanship of the Committee on Coast Defenses, which had been assigned to Spooner. The chairmanship of the Claims Committee was supposed to be the more important but entailed an enormous amount of work. Wisconsin Senators seemed to have a predilection for that position; Howe had held it for more than ten years and Cameron for six. One of the perquisites of the chairmanship was a clerkship; Spooner appointed to this position Horace C. Reed, who had been doing secretarial work for him since 1880. The chairmanship, although a minor one, brought Spooner to the attention of the Senate, for it necessitated the presentation of a great number of reports. It also brought him into close contact with some of

78 *Milwaukee Sentinel,* March 14, 1885; *Congressional Record,* 49th Cong., 1st Sess., pp. 37, 309.

79 *Milwaukee Sentinel,* December 13, 1887; Spooner to W. Evarts, November 23, 1890, in Spooner Papers. Evarts had been Attorney General, counsel in the Alabama Claims case, and Secretary of State.

the prominent Senators who were members of his committee, among them George Frisbie Hoar, the scholarly Senator from Massachusetts, chairman of the Committee on Privileges and Elections, Matt Quay, political boss of Pennsylvania, Edward O. Wolcott of Colorado, leader of the bimetallists, and John H. Mitchell, millionaire and dominant figure in the Republican party in Oregon.[80]

Spooner disapproved of the attempts of individuals to raid the United States treasury and worked very hard, harder than in any business in his life, so he said, to protect the interests of the government and yet to be just to claimants.[81] He refused to introduce any bills of this type himself unless for a constituent or in cases where he personally knew the merits of the claim.[82] Many claims were legitimate ones; they had to be presented as bills in Congress because of various legal technicalities that prevented payment through regular government channels.[83] Most of these relief bills were passed with little or no debate and were of no general interest. An exception was a bill to pay overtime to certain laborers. Congress in 1868 had passed an act establishing an eight-hour day for government employees, but some government officials had forced em-

[80] *Congressional Record,* 49th Cong., 2d Sess. (1886–87), pp. 273, 278. At the same time Spooner was excused from the Committee on Epidemic Diseases; *Milwaukee Sentinel,* December 21, 1886.

[81] *Congressional Record,* 56th Cong., 2d Sess. (1900–1901), p. 1329.

[82] *Ibid.,* 51st Cong., 2d Sess. (1890–91), p. 2538, describes one case he did sponsor. It was a bill giving compensation to the master of a whaling vessel who had broken his voyage to rescue passengers from a burning steamer. He learned about the incident while on vacation on Nantucket. See *Milwaukee Sentinel,* September 13, 1890; Spooner to W. W. Dudley, December 22, 1889, in Spooner Papers.

[83] *Congressional Record,* 49th Cong., 1st Sess., pp. 4395, 6816; 50th Cong., 2d Sess., p. 2371; 51st Cong., 2d Sess., pp. 3565–66; e.g., cases where taxes had been incorrectly assessed or illegally collected or where an individual performed some special service not provided for by Congressional appropriation.

ployees to agree to work ten hours. Spooner vehemently attacked this practice, pointing out that such agreements were not voluntary, that a man signed them because he wanted to feed his family. Eight hours a day, he declared, was long enough for any man to labor; a man needed time to think, to study, to invent, to get acquainted with his family. He was one of the few Senators to defend the bill; it did not pass.[84]

Holdups, Indian raids, and wars were the basis for most of the claims. There were still pending claims arising out of the War of 1812. Most numerous were those brought about by the War Between the States—claims for supplies furnished the Union Army and for property seized or damaged by it. In all such claims loyalty of the claimant was the chief issue involved. It was difficult for the committee to find out the truth about such claims, as they were frequently prepared by very skillful men. The Confederate Archives, Spooner found, were particularly valuable in protecting the government against millions and millions of unjust and fraudulent claims, seemingly fair on their face. An anonymous note, thrown into Spooner's home one night, led him to a search of these archives; there he found that a man who had put in a claim for $175,000 for some tobacco seized during the war had been a Confederate spy. Even when he presented this fact to the Senate, he had difficulty preventing the passage of the bill for his relief.[85]

84 *Ibid.*, 51st Cong., 1st Sess., p. 10564; 2d Sess., pp. 2239, 2242; *Milwaukee Sentinel*, September 28, 1890.

85 Spooner to F. Jones, March 8, 1891, in Spooner Papers. The Bowman Act, passed in 1883, stated that whenever claims for supplies furnished during the war involved investigation of facts, they could be referred to the Court of Claims. The report of the court, however, was only advisory. See *United States Statutes at Large*, 47th Cong., pp. 485–86; *Congressional Record*, 56th Cong., 2d Sess., pp. 1325–29; 50th Cong., 1st Sess., p. 9364; 51st Cong., 1st Sess., pp. 2901–2; 2d Sess., pp. 2482, 3431–33.

There were many illegitimate claims. Such a one was the Margaret Kennedy relief bill. She had put in a claim for timber taken from her farm in the District of Columbia when Fort Sedgwick was built. On recommendation of the Quartermaster General she had been awarded $1,500 but she was not satisfied and persuaded the millionaire Senator from California, Leland Stanford, to sponsor her claim for $10,000. He knew nothing about the claim but introduced the bill and when Spooner was absent from the floor called it up and got it passed. When Spooner heard of its passage, he got it referred back to the committee, where it was pigeon-holed.[86] Because of the vigilance of Spooner and other members of his committee, many bills for illegitimate claims failed to pass the Senate while he was chairman of the Committee on Claims.

Spooner tried to improve the method of disposing of these claims which overwhelmed the Congressional committees on claims. At one time there were eleven thousand such "relief" bills in the hopper of the Senate committee. He proposed that authority be given to the War or Treasury departments to pass on many of the claims. He encountered opposition in the Senate. Some Senators may have been thinking of the political advantage they gained when they succeeded in getting relief bills passed; others feared the growth of a government bureaucracy if too much authority were granted executive officials. Spooner, therefore, succeeded in getting through only a few measures that might aid the committees in their work.[87]

[86] *Congressional Record,* 50th Cong., 1st Sess., p. 2561; 51st Cong., 1st Sess., p. 5323; M. M. Bulkley to W. B. Allison, September 17, 1890, in Allison Papers.

[87] Spooner to W. C. Raymond, May 2, 1890, in Spooner Papers; *Congressional Record,* 51st Cong., 1st Sess., pp. 10464 (alphabetical list of all private claims before the Senate since 1881); 50th Cong., 1st Sess., pp.

Almost as much work was demanded by the Committee on the District of Columbia, to which Spooner was appointed on April 5, 1886.[88] That committee was really the city council for the District and Spooner was warned that no one was ever satisfied with its accomplishments. He soon discovered this to be true, that the committee was criticized not only by the citizens of Washington but also by members of the Senate. "It seems to be an impression here that the committee and each member of it is charged with the oversight of the streets of the city and with the administration of its affairs generally," Spooner complained one day when a Senator blamed the committee for the high fares charged by the local streetcar company. "I have not so understood the duty of that committee. I know of no committee connected with the Senate which gives more prompt attention, more laborious attention to every petition, every resolution, and every bill which is introduced in the Senate and referred to it than does the Committee on the District. It deals with tedious details and performs thankless tasks." [89] This committee, while Spooner was a member, passed on such diverse matters as legal holidays for the District, the appointment of police matrons, establishment of reform schools, regulation of the courts, the title to real estate, zoning rules, incorporation of companies, rights and liberties of married women, and regulation of the sale of intoxicating liquors.

7660, 7711–12 (Secretary of War to furnish list of Civil War claims on which War Department had taken adverse action); 51st Cong., 2d Sess., pp. 3431–33 (claims covered by Bowman Act were not to be paid until the Attorney General certified as to the loyalty of the claimant and the justice of the amount).

[88] *Congressional Record,* 49th Cong., 1st Sess., p. 3106; Spooner to E. Keyes, February 10, 1887, in Spooner Papers.

[89] *Congressional Record,* 50th Cong., 1st Sess., p. 7659.

Spooner was concerned mainly with the public utilities of the District. During his first Congress he was chairman of a subcommittee to pass on a bill to regulate the manufacture and sale of gas in Washington. Although the bill failed to pass the House after having been passed by the Senate, the Washington Gas Company, under threat of regulation, reduced its rates. (A bill regulating it was finally passed in the Fifty-fourth Congress.) [90] Spooner was also chairman of a subcommittee, created on his motion, to investigate street railway corporations to see if they were paying a fair proportion of taxes. Spooner favored a tax on gross earnings rather than an assessment on tracks.[91] "Senator Spooner is possessed of a strong judicial mind. . . . He was tenacious in maintaining the rights of the corporations, but he insisted that the public had rights which is the duty of Congress to protect," said the *Washington Star* in an article devoted to Spooner's work on that committee. The paper declared that he was recognized as one of the best workers the committee had ever had.[92]

Senator Sawyer had advised Spooner not to accept appointment to the District of Columbia Committee, had warned him it would not increase his popularity in Wisconsin, and that his constituents would not be interested in the measures for the District which would consume so

[90] *Ibid.*, 49th Cong., 1st Sess., pp. 6613, 7961; 2d Sess., p. 1605; Spooner to J. C. Blackburn, September 25, 1886, in Spooner Papers; *Milwaukee Sentinel*, November 20, 1896.

[91] Spooner to Commissioners of the District of Columbia, March 30, 1888, in Spooner Papers; *Congressional Record*, 50th Cong., 1st Sess., pp. 370, 1331, 1338, 1363–65, 1409–14.

[92] *Milwaukee Sentinel*, December 18, 1887. Citizens' associations passed resolutions expressing gratitude to Ingalls, the chairman, and to Spooner for their interest in the District; see Spooner to E. B. Stocking, March 23, 1889, in Spooner Papers.

much of his time.[93] He urged him to concentrate on the passage of legislation that would more directly affect Wisconsin individuals and communities. In that field the senior Senator excelled.[94] He was more successful in obtaining public buildings for Wisconsin towns than was Spooner, who was on the Committee on Public Buildings and Grounds. The junior Senator did succeed in getting passed a bill appropriating almost two million dollars for a new federal building in Milwaukee. It entailed a tremendous amount of work and Spooner was distressed when his efforts were not fully appreciated.[95]

Spooner did not agree with many Republicans who felt a surplus in the treasury was a valid reason for free spending.[96] He even broke with his party during the Forty-ninth Congress and voted for the River and Harbor bill, which had been scaled down 25 per cent by the Democratic

[93] Current, *Pine Logs and Politics*, p. 197. About one bill concerning the District, Spooner did hear from his constituents; that was about a measure to establish prohibition in the District. Spooner wrote G. Gilkey, May 11, 1888, in Spooner Papers: "I am a temperance man myself and there has never been a drop of wine upon my table. The subject is beset with difficulties, from the political and the reform standpoint. I have always believed that the true interests of temperance lay in the direction of Republican success."

[94] For a description of Sawyer's private pension bureau see Dorothy Ganfield, "Influence of Wisconsin on Federal Politics" (unpublished doctoral dissertation, University of Wisconsin, 1928), pp. 62–63.

[95] Spooner to G. Paul, December 5, 1887, March 7, 1888; to W. P. McLaren, December 30, 1887, February 24, March 7, 1888; to W. E. Gardner, January 10; to H. M. Mendel, January 10, February 21; to C. E. Andrews, February 17; to E. Elliott, July 27; to J. B. Weaver, August 3, 1888; to F. Holton, April 4, 1889; to C. D. Booth, May 5, 1890; to J. H. Windrim, March 6, 1891, in Spooner Papers; *Congressional Record*, 50th Cong., 2d Sess., p. 833; 51st Cong., 1st Sess., pp. 22, 125, 302, 1587, 7231, 7250; *Milwaukee Sentinel*, December 13, 1887, January 10, 1888, January 21, February 27, 1891.

[96] Spooner to J. Spalding, January 23, 1888, in Spooner Papers.

House of Representatives.[97] He did appear before Senate committees on behalf of Wisconsin projects and defended them on the floor of the Senate because it was expected of him.[98] He also did not approve of many of the private pension bills which, in spite of President Cleveland's vetoes, were being passed by the hundreds by the Senate. Many of them he thought were frauds.[99] When convinced of the justice of a claim, he spared no effort to put it through. Before bringing a claim before Congress, he tried the Pension Bureau.[100] When it was impossible to get action through the bureau, he would introduce private pension bills, but he introduced few compared to other Republican senators.[101]

Not only were Senators expected to get through Congress bills of special interest to their constituents but they were expected to intercede with various departments to obtain special favors. Many thought a congressman was in Washington to be an errand boy for his constituents. It was this part of his senatorial job that Spooner disliked. He complained:

With haunting the corridors of the Departments . . . and attending to the errands of constituents, and committee meet-

[97] Spooner to N. Smith, July 22, 1886, *ibid.*
[98] *Madison Democrat,* July 9, 1886, February 13, 1887; *Milwaukee Sentinel,* May 11, 1888, June 6, September 30, 1890.
[99] Spooner to P. L. Spooner, September 11, 1883, in Spooner Papers. See William Henry Glasson, *History of Military Pension Legislation,* p. 121, and Nevins, *Grover Cleveland,* p. 326.
[100] Spooner to J. C. Black, September 1, 1886, December 31, 1887; to Mrs. S. Lewis, January 27; to R. C. Lee, March 3, 1888, in Spooner Papers.
[101] Spooner to R. Joyce, May 29, July 31, 1886; to Mrs. F. Hauser, January 5; to J. A. Watrous, February 7, 1888; to Mrs. G. F. Street, April 14, 1890, *ibid.* Three of the five pension bills Spooner succeeded in getting passed were on behalf of widows.

ings and the Senate and so on *ad infinitum,* I am terribly pressed with work. . . . I am so engrossed with the routine work, and errands and pensions and the like, that I find little time to read, or to study great questions. It is almost impossible for a man under such circumstances to grow, however ambitious and anxious he may be, up to the creditable discharge of the higher duties of so great a position.[102]

[102] Spooner to J. H. Howe, December 18, 1889, *ibid.*

4 : *Reluctant Excursion Into Politics (1888-1890)*

"I AM HERE TO ATTEND TO *LEGISLATIVE* DUTIES"*

SPOONER was forced to assume a very active role in practical party politics in 1888. That was another feature of public life he disliked and in that also he differed from Sawyer. The leaders of the Republican party were preparing for a particularly intensive campaign that year for they were determined to regain control of the federal government. Although Wisconsin had remained Republican in the previous election, it was thought that special efforts should be made to ensure another Republican victory. It had been decided to organize a permanent Wisconsin League of Republican Clubs to supplement the work of the state central committee. When consulted about it, Spooner advised that the headquarters be located in Milwaukee so as not to interfere with the party machinery in Madison. He suggested that the officials of the league be

* Spooner to W. E. Gardner, September 29, 1888, in Spooner Papers.

men who could spend all their time in the state and devote most of their attention to the work of the clubs. He thought by this advice he would forestall any attempt to make him president of the league.[1] He deliberately remained in Washington when the launching convention was held in Madison the middle of March. When at the end of the convention he was informed that he had been elected president, he tried to decline but the convention had adjourned before his reply was received. After consulting Sawyer, he decided he had no recourse but to accept the office. As he had warned the leaders, Spooner was able to give little time to the work of the league but did contribute money and campaign material.[2]

Spooner was also elected a delegate-at-large to the Republican National Convention. This too was done despite his protest that he had already received one honor from the party and that his selection as delegate would prevent the election of Sawyer, who really enjoyed participating in the activities of national conventions, for he cared more for personal party power than Spooner did. A contributing factor to Spooner's reluctance to be a delegate was his desire to avoid the task of putting in nomination for President the name of Governor Rusk, whom Sawyer had

[1] Spooner to W. E. Gardner and to M. Herrick, March 7, 1888, in Spooner Papers.

[2] *Milwaukee Sentinel*, March 17, 1888; Spooner to B. F. Bryant, March 25; to O. H. Fethers, March 26; to W. J. McElroy, July 27, 1890, in Spooner Papers. See especially the letter to F. Gilson, March 7, 1888 (*ibid.*), in which he says that La Follette, who had charge of the meeting, had spoken to him about it but had never sent him a written invitation, which would have given him a chance to address the convention by letter. He explained that his main reason for not attending was the recent death of his father. "You know, that he was my idol, as a lawyer and as a man. Somehow I cannot bring myself to stand now within sight of his snow covered grave to make a political speech."

picked to be Wisconsin's favorite son that year.[3] Some Republicans thought Wisconsin should present the name of former Governor Fairchild. The one-armed General had gained national prominence when, as grand commander of the G.A.R., he had denounced President Cleveland for his order offering to return to the South the rebel flags. The General had protested that those running him again for President were "dampfools," but he still had a faint hope that the party might support him.[4] The state convention, however, adopted a resolution to the effect that Wisconsin would present Governor Rusk to the Republican National Convention "as a candidate in every respect worthy to receive its nomination for the presidency." Even before the convention met it had been decided that Governor Rusk should have the privilege of selecting the delegates-at-large. He named only two of them, Henry C. Payne and John C. Spooner, the latter to be chairman of the delegation and the one to make the speech presenting his name to the national convention.[5]

The convention opened in Chicago on Wednesday, June 20. Spooner, busy in Washington, arrived in Wisconsin the Friday before. That evening he addressed the Merchants and Manufacturers Association of Milwaukee on "The Age in which We live, the Era of Commerce." [6] The following Monday the Wisconsin delegation gathered in Chi-

[3] Spooner to W. Main, April 3; to O. H. Fethers, April 26; to H. C. Payne, May 3, 15; to W. E. Gardner, May 15, 1888, in Spooner Papers.
[4] L. Fairchild to C. Fairchild, June 4, 1886; C. Fairchild to L. Fairchild, September 12, 1887; J. H. Blair to L. Fairchild, February 28, 1888, in Fairchild Papers; see Robert McNutt McElroy, *Grover Cleveland*, I, 208–9.
[5] J. Rusk to Spooner, May 11, 1888, in Rusk Papers at the State Historical Society of Wisconsin; *Milwaukee Sentinel*, May 10, 1888.
[6] Spooner to C. E. Andrews, May 26, 1888, in Spooner Papers; *Milwaukee Sentinel*, June 16, 1888.

cago prepared to put on a show, at least, for their favorite son. Up and down the streets of the convention city they paraded with two brass bands and shouts of "What's the matter with Jerry Rusk? *He's all right.*" The headquarters at the Grand Pacific Hotel displayed a large banner-portrait of Rusk with the slogan "Three years a soldier, six years Congressman, seven years Governor, not a weak spot in his record." Spooner spent little time at headquarters; he was too busy hobnobbing with the big guns, some said.[7] It was after seven in the evening on June 21 when the Wisconsin Senator, the last of twenty-four orators, rose to nominate Governor Rusk for the Presidency. Many of the delegates were on their feet ready to leave the auditorium as they wanted a recess. Spooner began: "It is hard to attempt to wrestle with a cyclone, but it is my duty to do it." Throughout his fifteen-minute speech there was noise and confusion and, much to his chagrin, his voice gave out. He was crestfallen, for he felt that the speeches on the whole had not been very good and that he had missed such a chance to make himself a favorite with the convention.[8]

[7] Henry Casson, *"Uncle Jerry": Life of General Jeremiah M. Rusk*, pp. 213–14; C. D. Smith to J. Rusk, March 9, 1889, in Rusk Papers; *Madison Democrat,* June 20, 1888.

[8] *Official Proceedings of the Ninth Republican National Convention, 1888,* p. 148; *Milwaukee Sentinel,* June 22, 1888; Spooner to W. Main, July 11, 1888, in Spooner Papers. It had been suggested that Spooner might soft-pedal Governor Rusk's actions in the labor riots in Milwaukee in 1886 because of the labor vote. Spooner replied to F. A. Flower, June 4, 1888, in Spooner Papers: "I do not see how his name can be presented without a reference to the firmness and promptitude with which he met the emergency to which you refer. I have not been at all backward on the stump in justifying this course. I do not intend to say anything about the use of the military, in terms, but I do feel like drawing attention to the executive capacity which he manifested on that occasion." In his speech Spooner said that Governor Rusk had met the emergency "with hand of iron" and had insisted that this was a "nation of law."

The next day the balloting began; Governor Rusk made a poor showing even on the first ballot, receiving only 3 votes besides Wisconsin's 22. On the second, three Wisconsin men broke away from him and voted for Judge Walter Quintin Gresham, the federal judge whose circuit included Wisconsin. Three more deserted Rusk on the third ballot, and on the fourth, taken Saturday morning, 20 of Wisconsin's votes were cast for Benjamin Harrison of Indiana.[9] After the withdrawal of Chauncey Depew, who really had no chance of being nominated, for he was anathema to the farmers of the West because of his connection with the New York Central Railroad, New York delegates cast 58 of their votes for the former Senator from Indiana, bringing his total to 216. The convention recessed so party leaders could find some way to break the deadlock between Harrison and John Sherman, of Ohio. The latter had had a notable political career but the Ohio delegation was divided and he had few warm partisans.[10] At the Grand Pacific Hotel key men from Massachusetts, New York, Pennsylvania, Illinois, and Iowa met to decide who should be the Republican presidential candidate; Spooner was one of the participants at that conference. According to George Frisbie Hoar, they decided to support Senator William Boyd Allison, who had represented Iowa in Congress since 1863. Just before the convention reconvened, the group met again; the New York delegation reported that Depew was opposed to Allison and that they would continue to vote for Harrison. Wisconsin followed New

9 *Official Proceedings*, pp. 160, 163–64, 178; *Milwaukee Sentinel*, June 23, 1888; Spooner to J. Rusk, August 7, 1888, in Rusk Papers.

10 Spooner to J. Spalding, June 22, 1886; to J. M. Bundy, February 17, 1888, in Spooner Papers.

York's lead; others made haste to climb on the bandwagon and Harrison was nominated on the eighth ballot.[11] Levi P. Morton, of New York, was selected as his running mate.[12]

Judge Gresham blamed Sawyer, Payne, and Spooner for the poor showing he had made in the race for the Republican presidential nomination. He was sure that he had been the choice of the people of Wisconsin and that Governor Rusk had been put up as a candidate merely to hold delegates away from him. Sawyer and Spooner, he declared, were opposed to him because he had been judge of the court which the year before had awarded Mrs. H. G. Angle $351,965.50 damages for breach of contract by the Portage company. Since the Omaha company had taken over its property, it would be responsible for the money.[13] Sawyer was opposed to Gresham's nomination but Spooner was inclined to favor it if it were politically feasible. Shortly before the convention had convened, Spooner had written Payne that Gresham was perfectly agreeable to him in every way, but that the judge was unpopular in Washington with those who had known him when he was Postmaster General in President Arthur's cabinet. Gresham's associate on the bench, Charles E. Dyer, had assured Gresham that Spooner was unqualifiedly for him and that Payne was also all right but that he did not trust Sawyer.[14]

[11] George Frisbie Hoar, *Autobiography of Seventy Years*, I, 411–13. See also Leland L. Sage, *William Boyd Allison*, chap. 14, and Oscar Doane Lambert, *Stephen Benton Elkins*, pp. 118–19, for different accounts.

[12] Spooner to J. Spalding, June 22, 1886, in Spooner Papers: "Morton is undoubtedly an able man, in his way, and a fair politician, but he would be denominated all over the country as a boodle candidate."

[13] Gresham, *Life of Gresham*, II, 583.

[14] Spooner to C. W. Porter, March 12; to H. C. Payne, May 3, 1888, in Spooner Papers; H. C. Payne to C. E. Dyer, May 8; C. E. Dyer to W. Gresham, May 9, 22, June 13, 15, 1888, in Gresham Papers at The Library of Congress.

There are several divergent accounts of what took place during the various conferences of the Wisconsin delegation at the convention. One member claimed that Spooner had tried a dozen times to get his delegation away from Harrison to vote them for Gresham. He related how once when he and Henry C. Adams were absent, Spooner had persuaded the delegation to agree to cast a unanimous vote for Gresham on the next ballot. He, however, had frustrated this plan of Spooner's. The fact that the author of the story was trying to persuade Harrison to give him a position somewhat destroys its validity.[15] Harrison's campaign manager, L. T. Michener, reminiscing years later, claimed that the Gresham supporters had constantly hammered Spooner and that he had rather favored him; that it had been Payne who had held the Harrison men in line so that not one of them had escaped. Rusk also claimed that he had selected Payne as one of the delegates-at-large because he could be relied on to oppose Gresham, who was anathema to railroads and other corporations, and Payne was a lobbyist for such organizations. After weighing all the different accounts, one is compelled to believe that Spooner told the truth when he wrote that he had been faithful to the sentiment of the state for Judge Gresham but that it was impossible to nominate him as long as the Indiana delegation was opposed to him and supported Harrison. It would have been political suicide for Wisconsin to have tried "to force another Indianian down the throats of the people of that doubtful State," he explained.[16]

15 H. G. Kress to B. Harrison, March 5, 1891, in Harrison Papers; see H. C. Payne to B. Harrison, June 20, 1889, *ibid.*, about Kress.

16 J. Rusk to L. T. Michener, December 13, 1888, in Michener Papers at The Library of Congress; Spooner to J. F. Fuller, July 3; to W. E. Gardner, July 11, 1888, in Spooner Papers; Dorothy Ganfield, "Influence of Wisconsin on Federal Politics," p. 81.

* *

Despite the election, Congress remained in session throughout Washington's sweltering summer, for President Cleveland had forced it to consider the tariff issue. For two decades both parties had been straddling that issue, both paying lip service to reform but doing nothing. When the Republican party had come into power in 1861, it had supported a moderate protective tariff, but the duties had been increased at a great rate during the war to compensate for the internal revenue taxes levied on American manufactures. These excise taxes had been repealed shortly after the war but there had been no real revision in tariff rates. The industries built up by this "accidental protection" blocked all attempts to lower the duties. Neither party had come out specifically for a high protective tariff or for a tariff for revenue only, and the "sugar" Senators in the Democratic party were as zealous for protection as "Pigiron" Kelley in the Republican. Some in the Democratic party had, however, become advocates of free trade, or at least for drastic revision downward.[17] Among that group were the Wisconsin Democrats, led by William F. Vilas, and it was the rumor that they favored the election of Spooner for Senator, rather than Fairchild, that had forced Spooner to make his first public statement on that issue. He had declared that he was "in favor of encouraging by means of a tariff American industries and of protecting by means of a tariff American labor against the cheaper labor of other countries." [18] The statement was in line with the Republican party platform of that year.

[17] Arthur T. Volwiler, "Tariff Strategy and Propaganda in the United States, 1887–1888," *American Historical Review*, 36 (October, 1930), 76–96.
[18] Spooner to P. L. Spooner and to S. H. Reese, December 24, 1884; to W. B. Parker, January 9, 1885, in Spooner Papers.

President Cleveland, in his message of December 6, 1887, had stated his position unequivocally. He demanded that the tariff be revised downward. He ridiculed the argument that a protective tariff protected American laborers; he declared it enriched only the manufacturer and at the expense of the consumer. More than anything else, he stressed the fact that revision downward would reduce the embarrassing surplus in the United States treasury. To some Democrats the message brought consternation, but Vilas was delighted for he thought it would give the party a rallying point and make it a "great, united cohering body aligned on well defined principles," while previously it had been a mere opposition, not a party.[19] Spooner crowed "that the Democratic party has come out from ambush, and its attitude of duplicity, to a point in the open field, where we can get a 'whack' at them." He thought the chances of the Republican party carrying the election had improved immeasurably since the message. The Republicans might win back some of the Irish who had deserted the party when the Reverend Samuel Dickinson Burchard in 1884 had insulted them by declaring the Democratic party to be one of "rum, Romanism, and rebellion." The Republicans could use this tariff message to show that Cleveland was pro-British in his advocacy of free trade. "The transports of delight manifested by almost every leading English paper over the President's message, ought to be almost conclusive evidence that it is not in the line of American policy and American interests," wrote Spooner.[20]

[19] James D. Richardson (ed.), *A Compilation of the Messages and Papers of the Presidents*, VII, 5165–76; W. F. Vilas to Judge Endicott, May 10, 1891, in Cleveland Papers at The Library of Congress.
[20] Spooner to S. L. Lord, December 8, 1887; to J. W. Hoyt, January 17, 1888, in Spooner Papers. This point was a favorite one with Republicans.

As soon as the message was delivered, the Democratic members of the House Committee on Ways and Means, under the chairmanship of Roger Q. Mills of Texas, had begun holding hearings and meetings to try to frame a tariff bill in accordance with the President's message. The Democratic party was so divided on the issue that it was possible that the House would adjourn without passing any tariff bill. Spooner thought the House would pass a bill of some sort which the Senate could then amend by attaching to the enacting clause a good Republican tariff bill. There was no chance of a tariff law being enacted by the Fiftieth Congress since the House was Democratic and the Senate Republican. Until the House passed a bill, however, the Senate could only mark time, for it had no primary jurisdiction over financial measures.[21]

While waiting for the Mills bill, the Senate considered United States–Canadian relations, closely related to the tariff issue. The Treaty of Washington, of 1871, which had given certain inshore fishing privileges to American fishermen, had been abrogated as of July 1, 1885. The Senate had passed resolutions authorizing the President to exclude Canadian vessels from American waters and expressed its opposition to any treaty being negotiated which would give to Canadians tariff reductions. Secretary of State Bayard, on February 15, 1888, had negotiated a treaty which, although it gave Americans some fishing privileges, recognized the Canadian claim of jurisdiction beyond the three-mile limit along the sinuosities of the coast. Since the Republicans controlled the Senate, it was obvious that

21 Nevins, *Grover Cleveland,* pp. 389–93; Spooner to J. Spalding, January 23; to S. W. Hunt, February 27; to H. Fink, March 12, 1888, in Spooner Papers.

the treaty would not be approved in that form.[22] Spooner thought it would be more expedient, from the political standpoint, to amend the treaty and thus delay its ratification rather than to defeat it with a negative vote at that time. He wrote Harrison, the Republican presidential nominee:

I have feared that, if rejected, Cleveland would at the opportune time before election, show his teeth to England under the retaliatory legislation—not in a *general way*, or as to interfere with large interests or commerce, but by refusing admission of some Canadian ships, etc. etc. which he could do with England's consent and cheerful connivance and thus try to make for campaign purposes an American administration of this one, demoralize possibly our Irish & take the "tuck" somewhat out of our strong position that this is an English administration.

Spooner presented these arguments at a conference of Republican Senators held at Chandler's home on July 14, and at the Republican caucus, but the New England Senators demanded prompt rejection.[23] Two days after the treaty was rejected by the Senate, President Cleveland, in a special message to Congress, suggested applying the retaliatory act of 1887. "The President has done just what I expected him to do," Spooner wrote Payne. "He has run up the American flag. The Democrats think it will knock out the tariff issue, and it is their trump card." [24]

The Democratic tariff bill finally passed the House on

22 Spooner to J. Humbird, July 16, 1888, in Spooner Papers; James Morton Callahan, *American Foreign Policy in Canadian Relations,* pp. 371–80.
23 Spooner to B. Harrison, July 15, 1888, in Harrison Papers; Spooner to E. Keyes, September 17, 1888, in Spooner Papers.
24 Richardson, *Messages of Presidents,* VII, 5205–12; Spooner to H. C. Payne, August 24, 1888, in Spooner Papers.

July 21. Republican Senators were in a quandary. Some Senators whose political fences at home needed attention did not want to spend months in stifling Washington in futile debate. Others felt they would be doing more service to the party by remaining at the capital endeavoring to frame a Republican tariff bill, which could be presented to the country in answer to the Mills bill, than by making speeches on the stump explaining why they had not done so. The question was threshed out at a caucus meeting on July 25, and the second course of action was decided on. The Senate Finance Committee set to work. Justin Morrill, chairman of the committee, was old and ill, so responsibility for framing the bill fell to Nelson W. Aldrich of Rhode Island and Allison of Iowa.[25]

Throughout the summer and into the fall congressmen remained in Washington while political managers clamored for their participation in the campaign. Henry C. Payne, chairman of the Wisconsin state central committee and member of the national committee, accused Spooner of merely using the Senate session as an excuse to stay out of the campaign. As usual, Spooner's feelings were hurt. He promised that he would take the stump in October if he could possibly get away. He pointed out that he had already helped the campaign by sending into the state at his own expense almost one hundred thousand documents, protective tariff speeches, printed in German, English, and the Scandinavian languages, folded and franked, all ready to be addressed. He also arranged for speakers to campaign in Wisconsin, some of whose expenses he paid out of his

[25] Spooner to E. Keyes, July 24; to H. C. Payne, July 24, 31; to H. Rublee, July 27, 1888, in Spooner Papers; Stephenson, *Aldrich*, pp. 70–77; Sage, *Allison*, pp. 232–33.

own pocket. He sent Payne drafts for five thousand dollars and wrote he wished he had a million so he could send him all he needed to carry the state.[26] Payne still did not think Spooner had done enough and insisted that if he wanted to, he could get away to participate in the campaign. Spooner maintained that it was his duty to remain in Washington as long as the Senate was in session. He wrote:

I not only represent the Republicans, but I represent the people, in the Senate. I am here to attend to *legislative* duties. Politics *"is" incidental,* and it has seemed to me that my course would be justly animadverted upon if I should leave the Senate, with our small Republican majority here, when a matter of so great consequence was pending, in order to make political speeches, in what is regarded as a safe Republican State.[27]

Finally, on October 8 the Finance Committee reported out the Mills bill with a substitute, a protective tariff measure. On the sixteenth Spooner spoke briefly on the question of free trade—his first tariff speech in the Senate. Concerning it he said:

I made a unique sort of tariff speech to-day in the Senate, intended simply to show the depressed condition of industry, trade and agriculture in the United Kingdom, its long continuance and its causes, consisting mostly of quotations from reports of Boards of Trade to the Royal Commission in 1885, and extracts from the report of that Commission. It may not be fair in all its inferences, but I think it is on a line which has not been much pursued, and which will be of some utility.[28]

26 Spooner to A. W. Young, May 12; to D. C. Lamb, July 16; to H. C. Payne, July 31, August 18, 20, 24, September 7, 17, 1888, in Spooner Papers.

27 Spooner to W. E. Gardner, September 29, 1888, *ibid.*

28 Spooner to R. P. Porter, October 16, 1888, *ibid. Congressional Record,* 50th Cong., 1st Sess., pp. 9502–8; *Madison Democrat,* October 17, 1888.

The Senate was rapidly falling to pieces and it was difficult to obtain a quorum. It was decided that the Senate should take a recess on October 20, but during it the Committee on Finance was empowered to continue its study of the tariff.

Shortly before adjournment Spooner left for Indiana in obedience to a command which he could not disregard. At the personal request of Harrison, the Republican presidential nominee, he made eight speeches in the state in six days [29] and on October 25 he left for Wisconsin to wind up the campaign there. He brought it to a grand finale with a big rally at West Side Turner Hall and Schlitz Park in Milwaukee the night before the election. There was an immense crowd to hear him and he received a great demonstration as he denounced the Cleveland administration, stressing the President's pension vetoes. The election resulted in a Republican landslide in Wisconsin, with 176,-553 votes being cast for Harrison; only eight other states made a better showing. Her vote in the election and the shrewdness of her delegation at the national convention in dropping the favorite son on the fourth ballot and casting their votes for Harrison put Wisconsin Republicans in an excellent position to demand some recognition—even a cabinet position.[30]

Wisconsin had several candidates for positions in President Harrison's cabinet. Spooner was mentioned for the Attorney Generalship, but he declined to have his name even considered since Wisconsin already had two anxious

[29] Spooner to H. C. Payne, October 11, 1888, in Spooner Papers; Spooner to J. Rusk, October 10, 1888, in Rusk Papers.

[30] *Milwaukee Sentinel,* October 26, 30, November 2, 30, 1888; *Madison Democrat,* June 26, 1888.

aspirants for cabinet positions—Governor Rusk and Chairman Payne. There was also some mention of former Governor Fairchild as Secretary of War.[31] Late in November, Spooner, at Harrison's request, visited him in Indianapolis. On the train he met Allison, who was interested in obtaining a cabinet appointment for James S. Clarkson, vice-chairman of the Republican National Committee and manager of Allison's preconvention campaign for the presidential nomination. Returning from Indianapolis, Spooner reported to Sawyer, Payne, and Rusk that if Wisconsin was represented in the cabinet, the selection of the man would depend upon the office to be given that state. If it were the Postmaster Generalship, then Payne would be the one selected; if it were the War Department, Rusk would be appointed. Rusk's ambition clouded his judgment and he tried to get the Senators to drop Payne. This they would not do, and Spooner also refused to pester Harrison for the appointment of a Wisconsin man to the cabinet.[32]

President-elect Harrison was having considerable difficulty making up his cabinet. Again and again he called on Spooner for advice. In response to his urgent call, Spooner left for Indianapolis on Christmas afternoon. "How he does bemoan his having to go," noted Mrs. Spooner in her diary, "no man ever loved his home & family better." The whole family were together for the holiday, as Charles, the

[31] Spooner to J. Rusk, November 20, 1888, in Spooner Papers; *Milwaukee Sentinel*, November 9, 17, 29, 1888.

[32] Spooner to A. W. Sanborn, November 24; to L. Fisher, December 3; to H. C. Payne, December 6; to W. Main, December 17; to H. Rublee, December 20, 1888, in Spooner Papers; W. B. Allison to B. Harrison, December 11, 1888, in Harrison Papers; H. C. Payne to E. Keyes, November 27, 1888, in Keyes Papers.

eldest son, was home from Princeton. When in February Spooner was asked to make a third trip he demurred, pointing out that each visit aroused too much speculation and created such a racket in the newspapers. In a long letter he gave his views on the composition of the cabinet.[33] It began to look as if Wisconsin were to receive no cabinet post. Redfield Proctor of Vermont was given the War Department and, at the insistence of Matt Quay, chairman of the National Committee, the Postmaster Generalship went to John Wanamaker. James S. Clarkson was made his first assistant.[34] When the Department of Agriculture was raised to cabinet status on February 9, Harrison had another high office to fill. The day before the inauguration Spooner called on the President-elect and was able "to land Governor Rusk in the Cabinet" for that position.[35]

The Republican party came back into power on March 4, 1889, and Senator Spooner became one of the leaders in the new administration. He was probably as intimate with President Harrison as any member of the Senate and closer than many of the cabinet members. They were born only a few miles apart, Spooner in Indiana, Harrison in Ohio. While in Indiana, their fathers had become acquainted and later, when the Spooners moved to Wisconsin, the senior Spooner had carried on some real-estate transactions for J. S. Harrsion. John Spooner and Benja-

[33] Annie Spooner, Diary, December 25, 1888; Spooner to B. Harrison, December 20, 1888, January 30, February 16, 1889, in Harrison Papers.

[34] Spooner to J. Rusk, February 5, 1888, in Rusk Papers; Spooner to H. C. Payne, December 24, 1888, in Spooner Papers. Concerning the Wanamaker appointment see Fowler, *Cabinet Politician*, pp. 207–12.

[35] Spooner to W. R. Finch, March 21, 1889, in Spooner Papers; Elijah W. Halford, Diary, March 3, 1889. I wish to record my indebtedness to Professor Arthur T. Volwiler, who furnished me items about Spooner in this diary.

min Harrison had been associated in some legal work and had been colleagues in the Forty-ninth Congress. Spooner was one of three Senators to whom the President-elect had read his Inaugural Address. The Wisconsin Senator was invited to the White House frequently, not only to give the President the benefit of his advice but also because Harrison enjoyed his company.[36]

President Harrison had considered calling Congress in special session to take up the tariff issue but instead he merely convened the Senate on March 4 to confirm cabinet appointments; it remained in session less than a month. Spooner wrote:

The Senate has adjourned, but the officeseekers have not. The rush and pressure is unprecedented in the history of the Government, I believe. I have between 700 and 800 applications from Wisconsin. It is all right, of course, for people to seek positions, and I do not mention it to find fault with it at all, but it brings to one in my position great embarrassment and anxiety; the applicants, worthy in every way, are so numerous, and the places are so few.[37]

Spooner spent April writing letters, "letters begging, letters threatening, and letters of every imaginable description," in an effort to secure places for Wisconsin Republicans. They were followed "by trip after trip, wearisome and humiliating" to federal departments.[38] One of the first positions he obtained was that of railroad commissioner, a five-thousand-dollar job, for his old neighbor and cam-

36 E. Halford, Diary, March 2, 1889; P. L. Spooner to J. S. Harrison, June 19, 1866, July 24, 1867; J. S. Harrison to B. Harrison, June 20, 1866; Spooner to E. Halford, April 18, July 2, 1890, in Harrison Papers; *Milwaukee Sentinel*, May 7, 1890.
37 Spooner to J. R. Bennett, April 4, 1889, in Spooner Papers.
38 Spooner to F. A. Flower, January 3, 1895, *ibid*.

paign manager Horace A. Taylor. The latter had been a
candidate for the gubernatorial nomination the year before but had been defeated by W. D. Hoard. Spooner had
publicly stated that Taylor was his choice and had done
all on his behalf that he had felt proper for a Senator to
do, but Taylor's nomination had been opposed by both
Sawyer and Rusk. Taylor had been very bitter at his defeat
and had "served notice" on Spooner that if Rusk got some
government position and he did not, he would fight him in
Wisconsin and that he had the force with which to do it.[39]

An appointment Spooner was to regret was that of his
youngest brother Roger to be consul at Prague. The Senator knew he was a drunkard and a profligate spender, for
he had had to get him out of many scrapes. Roger, however, pestered his brother with letters and telegrams until
he finally yielded and arranged his appointment. Less than
a year later the Senator had to bring him home at considerable expense to himself, for Roger had incurred many
debts in Prague.[40]

Spooner's opponent in the senatorial race in 1885,
Lucius Fairchild, was appointed chairman of the Cherokee
Indian Commission. It had been established to purchase
the so-called "Cherokee outlet," so it could be added to
the Oklahoma Territory that Congress intended to create.
The job was a vexatious one, for the cattlemen in that area

[39] Spooner to W. R. Finch, November 20, 1888; to H. Taylor, April 25,
1889, *ibid*. Concerning Spooner's actions in regard to Taylor's candidacy for
the gubernatorial nomination, see Spooner to W. Finch, February 18,
October 1; to W. E. Gardner, March 7; to H. C. Payne, August 16, 24; to
W. Phipps and H. L. Humphrey, September 6, 1888, *ibid*.

[40] Roger Spooner to J. Rusk, November 22, 1888, in Rusk Papers;
Spooner to Uncle Elisha, April 5, 1889; to Willet, February 11, 1890, in
Spooner Papers; A. J. Daugherty to Lije, June 1, 1889, April 22; J. G.
Blaine to B. Harrison, June 6, 1890, in Harrison Papers. Roger Spooner
was replaced by William A. Rublee, son of the editor of the *Milwaukee
Sentinel* (see *New York Herald*, June 7, 1890).

put all kinds of obstacles in the way of the negotiations. When they finally succeeded in convincing the Indians that they should not sell for the $1.25 an acre which the government offered them, Fairchild, "mad as a March hare," resigned.[41]

To escape for a while from the office seekers, Spooner went to Europe. The night before his departure he had a long discussion of the patronage problem with Senator Sawyer, who did not mind coping singlehandedly with the ambitious office seekers of Wisconsin.[42] Spooner returned two months later to find the scramble for offices as great as before. He had hardly gotten his family settled in their new Cape Cod style house on the north bluff of Nantucket Island when he received a note from Secretary Rusk urging him to return to Washington, for he thought the President was inclined to do something more for Wisconsin. The result of Spooner's visit with the President was the appointment of William E. Gardner, editor of the *Evening Wisconsin,* as consul at Rotterdam. The appointment was a surprise to Wisconsin Republicans, for that paper had been one of the foremost supporters of Fairchild in the senatorial race. After the election Gardner and Spooner had become good friends and the latter had tried to interest Sawyer and Taylor in buying two Milwaukee papers for Gardner. The proposition had fallen through since Sawyer did not like newspaper ventures and Spooner did not have enough money to undertake the enterprise

41 President Harrison's secretary to L. Fairchild, June 14; J. M. Rusk to L. Fairchild, June 14; L. Fairchild to his wife, November 10, December 12, 1889; Spooner to L. Fairchild, March 17, 1890, in Fairchild Papers. See *Congressional Record,* 51st Cong., 1st Sess., p. 1274, for Spooner's speech defending Fairchild and the Cherokee Commission. Angus Cameron, a former Senator, replaced Fairchild in March, 1890.

42 *Milwaukee Sentinel,* April 26, 1889.

by himself. The editor had suffered a nervous breakdown and needed a rest so Spooner thought a government job would be just the thing for him.[43]

Wisconsin was generously treated by President Harrison in the matter of diplomatic and consular appointments. Only New York and Indiana fared better. The Badger State received one ministership, to Peru, a ten-thousand-dollar position,[44] two consul generalships, and five consular appointments.[45] Concerning them Spooner wrote: "After the advent of President Harrison, I did an immense deal of fairly successful work in hunting up positions and obtaining appointments for Wisconsin Republicans. The President recently said that for its population this State had received more from the administration than any other State in the Union."[46]

Aside from the diplomatic posts and a few executive positions in the departments, there was little patronage. Most of the minor government jobs had been incorporated into the classified civil service. This system had been established by the Pendleton Act, of January, 1883, after at least a decade of hard campaigning by the reformers. At that

[43] J. Rusk to Spooner, August 3, 1889, in Rusk Papers; Spooner to W. E. Gardner, January 10, February 20, 1888; to F. A. Flower, December 14, 1889, in Spooner Papers; *New York Herald*, November 30, 1889.

[44] *New York Herald*, March 28, April 3, 1889. John Hicks, editor of the *Oshkosh Northwestern*, was appointed minister to Peru at the insistence of Sawyer. Spooner was afraid it might lessen Wisconsin's chances for consulships (see Spooner to J. L. Linderman, March 17, 1889, in Spooner Papers). *The Times* (London), June 12, 1919, said that Spooner was offered the post of minister to the Court of St. James but refused it.

[45] The two consuls general appointed were Julius Goldschmidt to Vienna (*New York Herald*, March 20, 1889) and Richard Guenther, defeated for re-election to Congress, to Mexico City (*ibid.*, January 29, 1890). Consular appointments were to Canton, Prague, Dublin, Rotterdam, and Brookville, Ontario.

[46] Spooner to G. G. Cox, January 15, 1892, in Spooner Papers.

time it had included the departments in Washington and customhouses and post offices having more than fifty employees. The President had been given the power to classify other offices. Civil service reform had been one of the issues in the election of 1884 and it had been the support of these reformers, the Mugwumps, that had helped elect President Cleveland. Under the heavy pressure put upon him by the politicians of his party and by the famished Democrats who had been out of office for a quarter of a century, he had made concessions to the spoilsmen of his party. Postmaster General Vilas' "confidential circular," which had asked congressmen to pick out for removal the most obnoxious and pernicious partisan postmasters in their districts, had caused a tremendous outcry by the reformers.[47]

During the Fiftieth Congress Spooner had been appointed a member of a special committee (four Republicans and three Democrats) to investigate Cleveland's civil service policy. He had been in charge of the investigation of the customhouse in New York City, the prize of the spoils system. His 310-page report was purely a political document; it showed that the practice of levying assessments had been continued in that office, that systematic efforts had been made by various officials to turn their departments into political machines, and that the civil service law had been violated both in removals and appointments.[48] During the campaign of 1888 the Mug-

47 Carl Russell Fish, *The Civil Service and Patronage*, pp. 221–23; Fowler, *Cabinet Politician*, pp. 191–93. H. C. Payne was dismissed at this time from the postmastership at Milwaukee.

48 *Congressional Record*, 50th Cong., 1st Sess., pp. 34, 370, 1994, 2069, 3498, 3555; *Senate Report*, 50th Cong., 1st Sess., No. 2373 (serial number 2528), pp. 3–15; *Madison Democrat*, May 25, 1888.

wumps of the Middle West had deserted Cleveland and had supported the Republican nominee. On this important issue Spooner sided with the reformers. He even suggested to President Harrison that he return to their positions in the New York customhouse two Democrats who had been removed by the preceding administration for political reasons. It would not only be a "conspicuous act of justice, of adherence to the principles of civil service reform," he wrote, but also "good politics." [49] (The appointments were not made.) Spooner thoroughly approved of the Civil Service Law and declared that the longer he remained in public life the more enthusiastic about it he became. If it were repealed and there were "super-added to the work members of Congress are obliged now to do in the matter of patronage the pressure to fill clerkships in the Departments, upon my word I doubt if we would have any time to attend to the principal legislative duties for which we are sent here to perform." [50]

The method of nominating people to fill the federal offices in the state had been pretty well established by 1850. The customs, land, and judicial officials were named by the Senators of the party in power. If there were two administration Senators, they divided the state; therefore Sawyer recommended men for the offices in the eastern judicial district and Spooner in the western. Spooner refused to sponsor the removal of Democrats before the expiration of their terms. "Of course, they [Democratic incumbents] could hardly expect to be reappointed, . . . for there are many applicants for the places, and some of them are un-

---

[49] Spooner to B. Harrison, April 11, 1889, in Spooner Papers.
[50] Spooner to H. Sanford, December 17, 1889; to H. Beach, May 2, 1890, *ibid.*

questionably in every way competent and worthy, and they are Republicans," he explained.[51]

The postmasterships were the perquisite of the congressmen, except that Senators could nominate the postmasters of their home towns and in districts represented by members of the party not in power. At this time there were two districts represented by Democrats, so Sawyer made the recommendations for postmaster appointments in the fifth district, and Spooner for the second. As far as the distribution of patronage was concerned, there was perfect harmony between the two Senators. Spooner disliked that function, and if his colleague wanted to make a postmaster appointment in his district, he did not "hesitate to accede to his wishes." Spooner despised this scramble for these small jobs, the local factional quarrels, the balancing of nationalities, the care to see that an appointee had never engaged in some work of which someone in the community might disapprove, such as being a saloonkeeper, and the political necessity of appointing the one he felt the least fit for the position.[52] He resented the complaints of disappointed applicants, those who, when he had said he would see what he could do, claimed he had made promises he had not fulfilled. The few for whom he had been able to obtain places never seemed to appreciate his service, he grumbled. Patronage is "a curse to a party or to a public man," Spooner declared.[53]

51 Spooner to J. L. Linderman, February 14, 1890; to L. Luchsinger, December 14, 1889, *ibid.*; P. Sawyer to E. Keyes, January 30, 1892, in Keyes Papers. See Dorothy Ganfield Fowler, "Congressional Dictation of Local Appointments," *Journal of Politics,* 7 (February, 1945), 39.

52 Spooner to Uncle Elisha, April 5; to L. S. Caswell, April 22; to H. C. Payne, April 6, 24, 1889, June 1, 1890; to W. Main, April 14, June 12, August 8, 1890, in Spooner Papers.

53 Spooner to H. Kress, February 8, 1890, *ibid.*

5 : *The Fifty-First Congress (1889-1891)*

"CREDITABLE DISCHARGE OF THE HIGHER DUTIES"*

"THE TIME HAS COME, as you are aware, in my Senatorial career when I have some influence in shaping the party policy," Spooner wrote Payne during the Fifty-first Congress.[1] After the barren Forty-ninth and Fiftieth Congresses, this one seems notable indeed. Many of the measures discussed during this Congress—for example, trust control, reciprocity, federal aid to education,[2] elections in

* Spooner to J. H. Howe, December 18, 1889, in Spooner Papers.
[1] Spooner to H. C. Payne, July 23, 1890, in Spooner Papers.
[2] Senator Blair of New Hampshire was sponsor of a bill to distribute to the states $77 million on condition that the states raise an equal sum. The money was to be apportioned on the basis of illiteracy as shown by the census of 1880 and could be used both for the establishment and support of common schools. In the use of the money there should be no discrimination based on color. Spooner had voted for the bill in the Forty-ninth Congress but spoke against it in the Fiftieth and Fifty-first Congresses. It was claimed that his speech against the bill had much to do with its defeat. See *Congressional Record*, 49th Cong., 1st Sess. (1885–86), pp. 2086, 2105; 51st Cong., 1st Sess. (1889–90), pp. 1865–76; *The Nation*, February 23, 1888, March 13, 1890; Spooner to J. B. Thayer, January 27, 1888; to G. Esterley, December 25, 1889, in Spooner Papers.

the South, and cloture in the Senate—are significant today. It is interesting, therefore, to note Spooner's views on these issues and the part he played in framing measures connected with them.

The major measure passed by that Congress—practically the only one still on the statute books—was the Sherman Antitrust Act. To this bill Spooner contributed an amendment which made it possible for the government to bring into court the larger trusts. It *would* take a corporation lawyer to frame a measure from which other corporation lawyers would not be able to extricate their clients!

Throughout the 1880's businessmen had tried many devices to eliminate competition, and state governments had tried to outlaw them. Rockefeller's oil trusteeship, from which was derived the term "trust" to designate a monopoly, had been declared illegal in the Ohio courts on the basis that it violated English common law as a combination in unreasonable restraint of trade. In spite of that decision monopolies had flourished. State legislatures passed laws but they proved ineffective. Not only did the minor parties include in their platforms antimonopoly planks but also, in 1888, both the major parties declared their opposition to combinations of capital organized as trusts and called for federal legislation to prevent abuses.[3] The Constitution, with its delegation of powers to Congress, made it difficult to fashion a federal law regulating trusts, for, as Spooner pointed out, "nearly all exist under State laws, and our jurisdiction, at the utmost, seems to be limited to their interstate commercial operation." [4]

[3] Carl Brent Swisher, *American Constitutional Development*, pp. 420–25; Stanwood, *History of the Presidency*, pp. 462, 470, 474.
[4] Spooner to A. A. Arnold, December 22, 1889, in Spooner Papers.

Senator Sherman of Ohio had, on the opening day of the regular session, presented his bill to regulate trusts. It merely provided that manufacturing combinations producing goods for interstate commerce were illegal and injured parties might sue for damages. The bill had been referred to the Senate Committee on Finance, which had added a section providing penalties of fine and imprisonment for participation in illegal combinations. Spooner thought Sherman's bill absurd in many of its features and that it would be better to pass no bill than one which would turn out to be a humbug.[5] He thought the efficacious remedy against trusts would not be criminal prosecution but the vigorous and drastic use of the writ of injunction. But according to the law at that time, a writ could be served only within the district over which the court had jurisdiction. Spooner pointed out that most of the big combinations, especially the notorious beef and sugar trusts, were made up of several different corporations in different states. To deal effectively with such a trust, it must be possible to bring all the corporations into one court in one action. To this end he introduced his amendment whereby a writ of injunction could be served in any court district within the United States, and if it were disobeyed, the attachment for contempt could be served anywhere. He explained:

Now, the object of one branch of the amendment is to enable the United States court, when the suit is brought in the name of the United States to suppress one of these combinations or trusts made up of citizens or corporations of different States, to bring them all into that suit, wherever they may hap-

[5] Spooner to G. Edmunds, March 19; to H. H. Porter, April 14, 1890, *ibid.*

pen to reside. I have no doubt it is within the constitutional power of Congress to do this, because I think the entire power to regulate the procedure is under the Constitution in Congress.[6]

Spooner suggested that since the subject of trust regulation involved complicated questions of law, therefore the antitrust bill should have been referred to the Judiciary Committee instead of the Committee on Finance. In spite of Sherman's protest, the bill was sent to the Judiciary Committee. A few days later it was reported out and was passed with little debate and with only one dissenting vote. It had been carelessly drawn; some charged that it had been thrown together in a hurry just so the Republicans could use it for propaganda purposes in the campaign of 1890. The new bill merely re-enacted as to federal jurisdiction the common law against agreements in restraint of trade; it omitted, however, the word "unreasonable," which was part of common law. It retained the provision for criminal penalties and it did contain Spooner's amendment, although reworded and simplified. Spooner thought the law would be "efficacious, if properly enforced, . . . against the beef combine, and some other like conspiracies." [7]

Several Senators besides Sherman in later years claimed credit for the Sherman Antitrust Act—notably Hoar, Ed-

6 *Congressional Record,* 51st Cong., 1st Sess., p. 2642. It is interesting to note that one of the reasons for Justice Holmes's dissent in the Northern Securities case was his opposition to the provision in the Sherman Act providing for criminal penalties (193 U. S. 197).

7 When the bill was finally referred to the Judiciary Committee, Spooner voted against it since he felt the original bill had been perfected by amendments; see Spooner to G. Martin, March 31, to E. G. Moore, April 20, 1890; to H. W. Morley, June 25, 1890, in Spooner Papers; *United States Statutes at Large,* 51st Cong., pp. 209–10 (sec. 5).

munds, and Evarts. They were all members of the Judiciary Committee and two of them represented the Senate on the conference committee.[8] Yet it was Spooner's amendment that made possible the bringing into court of some of the largest and most notorious trusts. Years later the *Chicago Record Herald* related how some governmental officials, when studying the history of the Sherman Act, discovered

that the little amendment on a point which the author of the measure (Senator Sherman) had overlooked, has sixteen years later afforded the means of getting a grip on the great Standard Oil company, by which it is likely to be dissolved. Senator Spooner of Wisconsin, who has been charged by his political enemies with being the advocate of the "interests" in the upper branch of congress, was the man who proposed and finally put through the amendment to the Sherman Act which now enables the government to get action on the whole seventy-three of the constituent corporations of the Standard Oil company in a single judicial district, regardless of the location, or in what state of the union their officers may have their headquarters.

The article pointed out how valuable a constitutional lawyer can be in Congress.[9]

The new Republican administration claimed it had received a mandate from the people to pass a high protective tariff measure. The leaders might so interpret the election but they had great difficulty passing such a measure. Not only did several other bills block its passage but the party's

[8] Hoar, *Autobiography*, I, 362–63; Selig Adler, *Senatorial Career of George Franklin Edmunds*, pp. 10–11; Chester L. Barrows, *William M. Evarts*, p. 462; John Sherman, *Recollections of Forty Years in House, Senate, and Cabinet*, II, 1071–74.

[9] *Milwaukee Sentinel*, January 8, 1907.

control of Congress was so slight as to be uncertain. In the House there were only three or four more Republicans than the majority required for a quorum and at that time a quorum was determined by the roll call. When a few Republicans were absent, the Democrats, by refusing to answer when there was a call for a quorum, could obstruct all legislation. The new Republican Speaker, Thomas B. Reed of Maine, finally took extreme measures. When the Democrats refused to answer the roll call, he counted enough of them present to make a quorum. There was an uproar but he continued the practice until finally he got adopted a rule incorporating the idea that a quorum should be determined on the basis of those present. Spooner, although admitting that Reed was probably technically wrong, admired his splended leadership which had opened the door for the revision of the tariff.[10] The protective tariff measure, named after William McKinley, chairman of the Committee on Ways and Means, was passed on May 21 after a little over a month of debate.[11]

In the Senate the Republican majority was slightly larger. It had been increased on April 16 by the seating of two Republican Senators from Montana. Because of election frauds there had been a dispute over which party had control of the Montana legislature and two sets of Senators had been elected. Spooner, a member of the Committee on Privileges and Elections, had made a four-hour speech, dry, technical, legal, and exhaustive, in support of the majority report seating the Republican Senators. By a purely

10 William A. Robinson, *Thomas B. Reed: Parliamentarian*, pp. 207–17, 224; Spooner to W. E. Carter and to H. G. Kress, February 8, 1890, in Spooner Papers.
11 See Charles S. Olcott, *Life of William McKinley*, I, 158–93.

party vote this report had been adopted.[12] That gave the Republicans a majority of ten, but eight of these Senators were from the newly admitted western states,[13] which, though nominally Republican, were not in sympathy with the commercial interests in the East, especially as regards a protective tariff.

Before these western Senators would support a protective tariff bill they wanted some protection for silver. This could be obtained only by enlarging the demand for silver by the United States Mint. They were insistent on a liberalization of the Bland-Allison Act, which required the purchase of two million dollars' worth of silver bullion each month to be coined into silver dollars. The administration was willing to make some concessions to this group but the Democrats in the Senate wanted free and unlimited coinage of silver, and with the support of Republicans from the silver mining states they could pass such a bill. Spooner was not only afraid of the effect such an expansion of currency would have on business but feared

[12] *Congressional Record,* 51st Cong., 1st Sess., pp. 3107, 3136–44; *Milwaukee Sentinel,* April 9, 1890. Spooner had been appointed to the Committee on Privileges and Elections on January 21, 1887.

[13] The omnibus bill providing for the admission of North and South Dakota, Montana, and Washington by proclamation of the President, when constitutions acceptable to him had been drawn up, had been passed at the end of the Fiftieth Congress. The Dakotas had been ready for statehood for some time but their admission had been blocked by the Democratic House of Representatives. Spooner had delivered a major speech in favor of their admission during the Fiftieth Congress. When the election of 1888 brought about a Republican victory, the Democrats decided to make political capital out of the statehood issue and added to the Dakota bill amendments providing for the admission as states of Montana, Washington, and New Mexico. The latter, however, was eliminated. See *Congressional Record,* 50th Cong., 1st Sess. (1887–88), pp. 2996–3003; *Milwaukee Sentinel,* May 6, 1888; and Spooner to H. C. Payne, April 26, 1888, in Spooner Papers, about having four thousand copies of his Dakota speech printed and franked for distribution in the campaign.

that such a measure would wreck the party whichever way the President acted on it. He and Senator Hiscock of New York called on President Harrison to see if he could exert some pressure on the Republican Senators to keep them from voting for bimetallism.[14] Because of the "demagogism or treachery of 5 or 6 Republicans"—according to Spooner —a free-silver coinage bill was passed by the Senate, but the House refused to concur in the Senate action and the result was a compromise. The Sherman Silver Purchase Act, as the bill came to be called, provided for the purchase of four and one-half million ounces of silver per month, to be paid for by legal tender treasury notes redeemable in gold or silver. This proposition was the one favored by Spooner and was acceptable to the administration; in fact, it had been proposed by Secretary of the Treasury Windom.[15] It did not, however, satisfy the advocates of cheap money.

Some Republican leaders felt that important as a protective tariff measure was, it was even more vital to enact a federal election law. Spooner took this point of view and in the Fifty-first Congress became the champion of the Negro's right to vote. In this fight he was allied with Senator Hoar, chairman of the Committee on Privileges and Elections, and with William E. Chandler, the radical antirailroad Senator from New Hampshire.[16] Spooner had become in-

[14] Spooner to G. F. Edmunds, March 19; to H. H. Camp, May 8, 1890, in Spooner Papers; E. Halford, Diary, June 16, 1890, in Harrison Papers. See Sherman, *Recollections*, II, 1061–73.

[15] *Congressional Record*, 51st Cong., 1st Sess., pp. 6169–72; Spooner to J. Johnston, June 18; to C. K. Wells, June 25, 1890, in Spooner Papers; W. Windom to B. Harrison, January 14, 1890, in Harrison Papers.

[16] Leon Burr Richardson, *William E. Chandler: Republican*, pp. 390, 395–97.

terested in the issue of suppression of the Republican vote in the South when, as a member of a subcommittee with Evarts of New York and Henry Moore Teller, free-silver Republican from Colorado, he had investigated frauds in the Washington County, Texas, elections. Throughout the Fiftieth Congress he had brought in resolutions and made speeches on the subject. He had accused the Southerners of frauds in elections, of swiping ballot boxes, of terrorizing Negroes to prevent them from voting, and of even countenancing lynching. Debates had been very heated and insults had been exchanged on both sides; southern Senators dragged in Spooner's career as a railroad attorney and declared he had been responsible for robbing women and children of their land.[17] Spooner had wanted the issue of a "free ballot and a fair count" to be stressed in the presidential campaign of 1888. The Republican platform had demanded "effective legislation to secure the integrity and purity of elections." Yet the national committee, headed by Quay of Pennsylvania, had sidetracked that issue for fear it might deter some Democrats, who favored a protective tariff, from voting Republican.

"I think they are mistaken," Spooner had written Quarles. "No party ever made anything yet by being cowardly, especially where the right of citizenship (even the right to live) are involved." [18]

After President Hayes's withdrawal of the federal troops from the southern states there had been practically no fed-

[17] Spooner to A. L. Sanborn, December 5, 1887; to J. Farwell, May 11, 1888, in Spooner Papers; *Congressional Record*, 50th Cong., 1st Sess., pp. 7825–26, 8523–24, 8564, 9004–10; *Milwaukee Sentinel*, February 16, 1887, September 13, 1888.

[18] *Official Proceedings*, 1888, p. 109; Spooner to J. V. Quarles, October 10; to H. C. Payne, October 11, 1888, in Spooner Papers.

eral supervision of elections; consequently, in many sections of the South fraud and terrorism had led to the virtual disfranchisement of the Negro. In order to remedy this, Spooner, during the second session of the Fiftieth Congress, had introduced two bills to enforce the laws then on the statute books relative to Congressional elections and to punish offenses thereat. He had introduced them again at the beginning of the first session of the Fifty-first Congress.[19] Senator Hoar introduced a bill providing for a separate registration list and a special election of members of Congress. This was objected to by many because of the expense of double registrations and elections. "So I drew another Bill," the Massachusetts senator wrote in his *Autobiography*. "I say I drew it. But I had the great advantage of consultation with Senator Spooner of Wisconsin, a very able lawyer who had lately come to the Senate, and I can hardly say that the Bill, as it was finally drafted, was more mine than his." [20]

The Hoar-Spooner proposals were attached to the preamble of the House bill sponsored by Representative Lodge of Massachusetts, chairman of the House Committee

[19] *Milwaukee Sentinel*, April 1, December 5, 1889; Spooner to A. J. Turner, December 11, 1889; to J. M. Smith, February 4, 1890, in Spooner Papers: "We will attempt to enact at this session of Congress a law which shall in some degree, if enforced, remedy the evils, in their relation to elections, but, as you know, it is difficult to enforce a law in a community the entire sentiment of which is opposed to it. The principal hope I have is, that the north will solidify, as these fellows solidify the south, and, if that shall be done, when the southern leaders find they can no longer win politically on that score, and on those lines, they may quit and divide on industrial and other issues."

[20] Hoar, *Autobiography*, II, 152. The new bill provided that there should be national officers present at the registration and election of members of Congress and a federal board to canvass the vote. See Spooner to G. Farnam, May 8; to C. H. Williams, July 27, 1890, in Spooner Papers, for Spooner's objections to Hoar's original bill.

on Elections.[21] The new bill provided that, upon petition of five hundred voters in any election district, federal officials would be appointed to election boards to inspect and verify returns and pass on the qualifications of voters. In case of a dispute concerning an election certificate of a member of Congress, the judges of the circuit court would determine which name should be put on the clerk's roll of the House of Representatives. The Massachusetts Senator said that the bill "only extended the law which, with the approbation of both parties, had been in force in cities of more than twenty thousand inhabitants, to Congressional districts when there should be an application to the Court, setting forth the necessity for its protection." Arthur P. Gorman, chairman of the Democratic caucus, admitted that it was an innocent-looking measure but thought it was a threat to States' rights. Since the bill was framed by northerners, southern Democrats became alarmed. They envisioned a return of the Reconstruction era, a revival of the hated carpetbag governments. They dubbed it the "force bill" and resorted to all sorts of obstructive tactics, blocking not only the federal election bill but also the tariff measure.[22]

Senate leaders considered adoption of cloture measures. A committee consisting of Aldrich, Sherman, Ingalls, Hoar, Spooner, Frye, and Moody was appointed by the caucus on July 10 to draw up a rule to limit debate. When the report

21 Karl Schriftgiesser, *The Gentleman from Massachusetts: Henry Cabot Lodge*, pp. 104–7; John A. Garraty, *Henry Cabot Lodge: A Biography*, pp. 117–20. Spooner wrote J. Johnson, July 13, 1890 (in Spooner Papers), that he thought Lodge's bill was "too cumbersome and rasping."

22 Hoar, *Autobiography*, II, 152–53; Richardson, *Chandler*, pp. 410–14; Barrows, *Evarts*, pp. 458–61; John R. Lambert, Jr., *Arthur Pue Gorman*, pp. 149–50.

was presented, the caucus, by an overwhelming vote, decided against adoption of any drastic measures. Many, knowing Spooner's zeal for the federal election bill, were surprised when Spooner spoke in favor of keeping the Senate a deliberative body. Yet shortly afterward Spooner wrote Payne that he thought the day was coming, and very soon, when the Senate would have to adopt a

rule which, while providing for the right of every Senator to be heard after the previous question is ordered, shall at the same time put it in the power of the majority to do business, and to prevent the defeat of important public measures simply by the obstructive tactics of a factious minority. The time never has been when the principle of majority rule everywhere, at the polls and in the legislative and deliberative bodies of the country, was dearer to or more popular with our people than now.[23]

The summer dragged on. Spooner complained it was the second one he had had to spend alone in Washington and that he was "awful homesick" for his wife and children. Frequently in the evenings after Senate sessions he went with other Senators to the home of Senator James McMillan of Michigan, chairman of the Committee on Manufactures. These stag gatherings gradually developed into an informal club. Among the members were Nelson Aldrich of Rhode Island, William Allison of Iowa, Joseph Hawley of Connecticut, Eugene Hale of Maine, Charles F. Manderson of Nebraska, William D. Washburn of Minnesota, and Frank Hiscock of New York. Most of them had served in the Senate for several terms—longer than Spooner—and were among the most influential members of that body.

[23] G. Edmunds to N. Aldrich, July 11, 1890, in Aldrich Papers at The Library of Congress; *New York Herald*, July 15, 1890; Spooner to H. C. Payne, August 23, 1890, in Spooner Papers.

Three of them (Aldrich, Allison, and Hiscock) were members of the Finance Committee and the Rhode Island Senator was in charge of the tariff bill. With full freedom, frankness, and friendliness, said Spooner, they discussed problems confronting them in the Senate. He felt that on more than one occasion they were a potent force for good.[24]

They were able to defeat the Quay-Democratic trade, under which, if the Senate would drop the federal elections bill, the Democrats would agree to an early date for a vote on the tariff bill. Quay, on August 12, presented a resolution incorporating these ideas. Spooner was furious. It was a cowardly surrender, he declared. "The almighty dollar obscures their vision. I mean by that, that the commercial spirit which held back the anti-slavery men, is holding them back against anything that might sacrifice commerce to the rights of citizenship." At the Republican caucus Hoar and Spooner read the riot act to the Senators; they insisted the election bill must be passed at that session. Finally after an informal conference at McMillan's home, an arrangement was made among the Republicans whereby they agreed that the federal election bill would go over but would be brought to a vote during the second session of the Fifty-first Congress.[25]

On August 25 it was decided that, except for appropriation bills and conference reports, the tariff bill was to be the exclusive order of the day. As did other Senators,

24 Spooner to F. Hiscock, April 1; to W. D. Washburn, April 9, 1892, in Spooner Papers; Stephenson, *Aldrich,* pp. 91–92, says this group was called the "School of Philosophy Club" and was really a select card club.

25 Spooner to H. Fink, July 27; to W. W. Lockwood, August 18; to H. C. Payne, August 23, 1890, in Spooner Papers; *Congressional Record,* 51st Cong., 1st Sess., p. 8842; *Madison Democrat,* August 15, 22, 23, 1890.

Spooner insisted on protection for certain products in which the people of Wisconsin were interested: tobacco, lumber, barley, iron ore, vinegar, and fresh-water fish. He defended the duty on vinegar mainly because of the interest in it of Paul Bechtner, owner of an important German newspaper in Wisconsin, which at that time Spooner was helping finance.[26] He spoke against a low duty on iron ore to prevent competition from Cuba, which would be detrimental to the Bessemer iron mines around Lake Superior. He himself had invested considerable money in the Pioneer Vermillion Iron Company in conjunction with his old friends John Humbird and William H. Phipps. At that time, however, the owners of Pioneer stock were not much worried about competition from foreign iron for they had not been able to strike "pay dirt." [27]

There was considerable interest among Spooner's correspondents in the tobacco duty. Wisconsin farmers, in order to develop diversified agriculture, had begun experimenting with the raising of tobacco. Representative La Follette, a member of the Ways and Means Committee, had gotten into the House bill a provision raising the duty on tobacco from Sumatra from 35 cents and 75 cents to $2.00 and $2.75 a pound. It encountered heavy opposition in the Senate. Manufacturers who used the tobacco from Sumatra for wrappers fought to have the provision cut from the bill. Harrison's campaign manager wrote that if this duty were increased, it would mean the loss of thousands of votes.

[26] *Congressional Record,* 51st Cong., 1st Sess., pp. 9227, 9778, 9781–83, 9109; Spooner to P. Bechtner, April 28; to H. C. Payne, July 23, 1890, in Spooner Papers.
[27] *Congressional Record,* 51st Cong., 1st Sess., pp. 8194, 8198–99; Spooner to J. Humbird, June 12, July 16, 1888; to W. D. Parker, December 18, 1889, in Spooner Papers.

The Tobacco Growers Association of Wisconsin appealed to Spooner. He, with the aid of Platt of Connecticut, succeeded in persuading the Finance Committee to retain that provision of the House bill in spite of the opposition of Allison of Iowa. On the floor of the Senate Spooner argued for that increased duty, pointing out that Sumatra tobacco was produced entirely by coolies who received about 15.8 cents a day. Farmers of Wisconsin, Ohio, Pennsylvania, and Connecticut should be protected against cheap labor, he maintained.[28] (The high tobacco duty was kept and today Wisconsin ranks seventh in the production of tobacco.)

Spooner spoke very briefly—the five-minute rule was in effect—in opposition to Senator Vest's proposition to put white pine on the free list. Spooner declared that amendment discriminatory, for there were duties on other kinds of lumber, and if the duty on white pine were removed, competition from Canada would bring disaster to a great industry in Wisconsin. He made his appeal for retention of the duty on behalf of the laborers in the lumber camps rather than the owners; the workers would want to know, he declared, why American miners were protected but they were not. Spooner himself still owned considerable timberland although most of the white pine on his lands had been cut. Sawyer did not oppose the reduction in the lumber duty; he had hedged by investing in lumber mills in Canada.[29]

28 *Congressional Record*, 51st Cong., 1st Sess., pp. 9214–15; *Milwaukee Sentinel*, June 4, September 1, 1890; Spooner to L. Kittelsen, June 12; to H. C. Payne, August 25, 1890, in Spooner Papers; L. T. Michener to E. Halford, March 24, 1890, in Harrison Papers.

29 *Congressional Record*, 51st Cong., 1st Sess., pp. 9715, 9719; Spooner to C. H. Cooke, September 28, 1890, in Spooner Papers; Current, *Pine Logs and Politics*, pp. 218–19; see Robert F. Freis, *Empire in Pine*, pp. 116–18.

Aside from these duties, which were mainly on raw materials, Spooner worked for a lower tariff. He was not a high protectionist and felt high duties should not be levied just to protect a few manufacturers. That is why he presented his amendment to the tin schedule. Several attempts had been made in the United States to develop the tin industry but the Welsh had a monopoly and had always been able to ruin the infant industry by cutting prices. Some businessmen in the United States, interested in starting the industry, had persuaded McKinley to include in his bill a duty on tin plate. Spooner was skeptical and thought the men who said they had the capital ready to engage in the manufacture of the thinner grades of tin plate should either "put up or shut up." He was willing to give them an opportunity to experiment but wanted a time limit put on the duty so that the people would not continue to be taxed until a new tariff bill was passed if there were no increase in the amount of tin plate manufactured in this country. After a conference with these men, he introduced and got adopted an amendment to the effect that unless within six years the amount of tin produced in the United States annually equaled one-third of that imported, the duty would be repealed and thereafter tin plate would be admitted free of duty. That precaution, however, was not necessary, for the tin industry flourished in the United States.[30]

The sugar duty was one favored by Democrats and opposed by Republicans. Spooner felt sugar should be on the

[30] Olcott, *William McKinley*, I, 172; *Congressional Record*, 51st Cong., 1st Sess., p. 8780; *Milwaukee Sentinel*, July 27, August 20, September 7, 1890; Spooner to B. Stone, September 16; to J. W. Hinton, August 25, 1890, in Spooner Papers.

free list; he did not see why Americans should be taxed sixty or seventy million dollars a year by a duty on sugar when there was almost no home production of sugar to be protected. Although on general principles he was opposed to bounties, he defended the proposal to give one to domestic producers of sugar. The bounty would serve two purposes: it would reduce the surplus and at the same time protect the domestic producer and might so stimulate beet sugar production that importation of sugar would no longer be necessary.[31] Opposed to putting sugar on the free list was Secretary of State Blaine. He wanted to bring the United States and the Latin American countries into closer economic relations, and at the Inter-American Conference, held in November, 1889, he had proposed a customs union. Latin American countries, suspicious of the United States, had rejected it but had agreed to try to negotiate reciprocal trade treaties. Blaine therefore wanted a provision for reciprocity included in the tariff bill and a duty on sugar. If sugar were on the free list, the United States would lose one of its chief assets in bargaining with those countries for tariff concessions on United States products.[32] Leading Senators, Spooner among them, had conference after conference with the President on this issue and several Republican caucus meetings were held. A compromise was finally reached on August 28—sugar was to be kept on the free list, with a bounty given to sugar producers in the United States. The President was to be given the power to put into effect, by proclamation, duties on sugar, molasses, tea,

31 *Congressional Record,* 51st Cong., 1st Sess., pp. 9856–57; Spooner to H. Sanford, December 19, 1889; to J. Johnson, July 13, 1890, in Spooner Papers.
32 David Saville Muzzey, *James G. Blaine,* pp. 443–49; J. G. Blaine to B. Harrison, July 21, 22, 24, 1890, in Harrison Papers.

coffee, and hides from countries that refused to agree to reciprocity commercial agreements.[33]

At the special request of Aldrich, Spooner spoke extemporaneously on the reciprocity clause shortly before midnight on September 8. He explained that the amendment had been prepared with great care by the Committee on Finance, and he pointed out that there was considerable precedent for giving such discretionary power to the President. He concluded:

I am in favor of protecting, as we are doing by this bill, our home industries, and caring for the well being of our labor, and developing the home market for our products; and with the surplus products of farm and factory and mine for which we have no market, I would trade with any government under the shining sun for those things which they produce that we want, and which *we do not produce*. It need not be confined to Latin America, either, this reciprocity for which I am willing to vote.

The one country with which he did not favor a reciprocity agreement was Canada; instead, he expressed the hope that the day would come when the American flag would float over Canada and the British flag be eliminated from that domain. Eastern newspapers declared that Spooner's argument really influenced votes, "a thing rarely true of speeches made in Congress." Two days after his speech the tariff bill was passed by the Senate.[34]

So many congressmen had left Washington that it was difficult to keep a quorum. "I have heard it said that we

[33] Spooner to H. C. Payne, August 25, 1890, in Spooner Papers; E. Halford, Diary, August 7, 14, 17, 1890, in Harrison Papers; Stephenson, *Aldrich*, pp. 87–88.

[34] *Congressional Record*, 51st Cong., 1st Sess., p. 9879; *Milwaukee Sentinel*, September 17, 1890.

have as many as fifteen members sick in the Senate—not seriously, I presume," Platt wrote the President.[35] Spooner thought it was his duty to remain on the job until Congress adjourned. More than anything else, he thought it important that the McKinley tariff bill become a law very soon. He considered it on the whole a fair bill—not perfect by any means, for it was impossible to frame a tariff bill to please every Senator since duties were frequently determined on a give-and-take basis. The agricultural schedules, the sugar bounty, and the provision for reciprocal trade agreements were new features in a tariff act.[36] The latter, although in a Republican tariff measure, formed a precedent for the Hull reciprocity agreements of 1934.

Throughout the summer Payne, chairman of the state central committee, had kept urging Spooner to come home to help in the Congressional campaign. Spooner's own political future was at stake. Lack of enthusiasm for the Harrison administration, dissatisfaction among party workers who had not received the jobs they coveted, hard times among farmers, and the fact that it was an off year politically made the outlook for the Republican party throughout the nation seem a "little blue." In Wisconsin the situation was complicated by the Bennett Law and the state treasury question.[37]

It was not, however, the discovery that the Republican state treasurers had for years received large sums of money

35 O. H. Platt to B. Harrison, September 19, 1890, in Harrison Papers.

36 Spooner to F. Avery, August 17, 1890; to E. Coe, April 14, 1890, in Spooner Papers: "The contest over a revision of the tariff brings to light a selfish strife which is not far from disgusting."

37 Spooner to J. G. Clark, February 2; to A. Cameron, February 27, 1890, in Spooner Papers.

from their investment of state funds that was to cause the Republicans the most apprehension;[38] it was the Bennett Law, an innocuous compulsory education law, signed by the governor on April 18, 1889. This law required children between the ages of seven and fourteen to be sent to school in the district in which they resided for not less than twelve weeks a year. It defined a school as one in which reading, writing, arithmetic, and United States history were taught in the English language. The English language requirement had been included at the request of Governor Hoard, who, in his annual message that year, had declared that a child as a future citizen had a right to demand a reasonable amount of instruction in English. William Dempster Hoard had long been interested in public education; he was of American stock and of evangelical Protestant background. He had been active in the Wisconsin State Dairyman's Association and in Fort Atkinson had established a paper called *Hoard's Dairyman*. As the "Jersey cow candidate," his nomination for governor had been brought about by the farmers and the *Milwaukee Sentinel*, to the astonishment of the party leaders. Although the Governor had been interested in the education bill, it had not been a party measure; in fact, it had passed the assembly without even a dissenting vote. At the time of its passage it received almost no attention.

Two months later, however, two Lutheran synods passed

[38] Spooner to E. Timme, March 24, 1890, *ibid.*: "I think the party must commit itself in unmistakable terms to a proper disposition of the State funds, so that if loaned or invested the increment will inure to the benefit of the owners of the principal—the people. Save from rumor, and a report of ex-State Treasurer Kuehn, made at one time to the legislature, I of course have never known anything of the loaning of State funds." See Clara L. Hayes, "William Penn Lyon," *Wisconsin Magazine of History*, 9 (March, 1926), 279.

resolutions denouncing it; they felt the law was directed against their parochial schools where most of the instruction was given in German. The *Milwaukee Sentinel* took up the challenge and sent reporters to visit the private schools. In analyzing the series of articles describing conditions, the editor pointed out that 16 per cent of the children in Wisconsin attended parochial schools. The official Lutheran paper, the *Germania,* denounced the *Sentinel* as a Know-Nothing sheet, reviving the antiforeign, anti-Catholic attacks of the 1850's. The Roman Catholic Church, fearful that its parochial school system might be affected by the residency requirement in the law, joined with the Lutherans, and in March, 1890, the three Roman Catholic bishops in Wisconsin issued a formal manifesto denouncing the law as unnecessary, offensive, and unjust, and an encroachment by the state on religious schools.[39]

The Democrats, quick to take advantage of the chance to capture the combined German Lutheran and Catholic vote, made the Bennett Law an issue in the Milwaukee city election that spring. Their candidate for mayor, George W. Peck, with his entire ticket, was overwhelmingly elected in what had been for years a Republican city.[40]

The leaders of the Republican party became thoroughly alarmed. Payne and Spooner feared the Bennett Law might cause the loss of the state, for there were over 42,000 German Lutheran voters in Wisconsin, over half of whom had

[39] William A. Sumner, "William Dempster Hoard," *Dictionary of American Biography,* 9:90; Louise P. Kellogg, "The Bennett Law in Wisconsin," *Wisconsin Magazine of History,* 2 (September, 1918), 3–25; William F. Whyte, "The Bennett Law Campaign," *Wisconsin Magazine of History,* 10 (June, 1927), 364–90.

[40] *Milwaukee Sentinel,* March 2, 6, 23, 1890; *New York Herald,* April 28, 1890; Spooner to H. C. Payne, March 24; to R. Guenther, March 31, 1890, in Spooner Papers.

usually voted the Republican ticket. They were for upholding what they considered the essential principles of the law, "reasonable instruction in the English language, prohibition of child labor, and the care of the incorrigible truant," but they were not willing to rally to the defense of that particular statute. Spooner felt that private and parochial schools were entitled to be exempt from legislative regulation as far as term and curriculum were concerned; he thought the requirement concerning instruction in English might be limited to a knowledge of reading and writing English. Governor Hoard, however, wanted to make "the little schoolhouse" the slogan of the campaign. He insisted that one of the features of Americanism was state-supported schools with instruction in the English language. The right of the state to regulate education had been challenged by ecclesiastical authorities in a most offensive manner, he declared. Spooner thought Hoard's defense of the law a "barefaced and asinine" blunder.

The differences between Spooner and Hoard were not only ones of point of view; there was considerable personal animosity between the two. They had disagreed over the distribution of patronage, and Spooner believed that Hoard was considering supporting Congressman La Follette, instead of him, for the United States senatorship. Hoard was aware that he had not been the choice of either Payne or Spooner for the gubernatorial nomination in 1888 and knew they would be glad to drop him at this time if it were not the tradition of the party to renominate a governor for a second term.[41]

41 J. Rusk to H. Casson, May 8, 1890, in Rusk Papers; Spooner to W. Main, May 16, June 12; to H. C. Payne, September 11, 1890; W. D. Hoard to Spooner, June 16, 1890, in Spooner Papers. See Belle Case La Follette

Spooner met Governor Hoard, Horace Rublee, editor of the *Milwaukee Sentinel,* and Payne at the Auditorium Hotel in Chicago on May 18 to see if they could not come to some agreement that would eliminate the objectionable features of the Bennett Law. It was decided that Spooner should draw up a draft of a plank to be incorporated in the Republican platform. The one he framed was not acceptable to Governor Hoard. The latter was still unwilling to give up his defense of the Bennett Law, for he was confident that "the little schoolhouse" slogan was arousing "the old time American feeling" and that the Republicans were not in favor of compromising on this issue. He was sure that since he was in Wisconsin, he could better evaluate public opinion than could Spooner in Washington. Several times during the summer Spooner "played hooky" from the Senate to confer with Hoard, Rublee, and Payne in Chicago, Milwaukee, and Boston. Finally, early in August the Governor, after making a few changes, accepted a plank written by Spooner.[42]

This plank was included in the platform adopted by the Republican state convention, which met on August 20, about two weeks earlier than usual, and in Milwaukee rather than at the state capital. It read as follows:

The Republican party, in convention assembled, declares its devotion to the common school as the chief factor in the education of the people and pledges itself to support, strengthen and defend it. . . .

and Fola La Follette, *Robert M. La Follette,* I, 87, about a conference at Sawyer's home when Payne tried to persuade the Wisconsin Congressional delegation to bring pressure on Hoard to get him to refuse to run for re-election; La Follette and Caswell refused.

42 Spooner to W. Main, May 16, June 12, August 8; to H. C. Payne, July 23, 25, 1890; W. D. Hoard to Spooner, June 16, 1890, in Spooner Papers.

We believe that the compulsory education law passed by the late legislature is wise and human in all its essential purposes and we are opposed to its repeal [put in at Hoard's insistence] but at the same time we assert that the parent or guardian has the right to select the time of the year and the place, whether public or private and wherever located, in which his child or ward shall receive instruction and we pledge ourselves to modify the existing law so that it shall conform to the foregoing declarations. . . .

We are unalterably opposed to any union of church and state, and will resist any attempt upon the part of either to invade the domain of the other.

Another plank in the platform recognized Spooner's splendid services and recommended that earnest efforts be made to secure his return to the United States Senate. When it was read, "the yells were like the sounds from an Apache scalp dance," commented the *Milwaukee Sentinel*. Governor Hoard was renominated by acclamation and was greeted with enthusiasm when in his acceptance speech he hailed "the little schoolhouse." Payne agreed to remain chairman of the state central committee for another term. There was apparent harmony in the Republican party and Spooner was confident that the party would march forward to a magnificent Republican victory.[43]

Efforts were made to win over the German press. Before the presentation of the platform to the convention, Spooner had shown the plank on the Bennett Law to George Koeppen, editor of the *Germania*. He had cautioned him not to make any statement of public approval until after its adoption, for he feared that if Hoard thought it was satisfactory to any Lutheran, he would not stand by it. Spooner had

[43] Spooner to H. C. Payne, August 23, 25, 1890, *ibid.; Milwaukee Sentinel*, August 20, 21, 1890.

pointed out that every limitation the Germans wanted was in the platform:

The right of the parent and guardian to select the school, and the time and the place, with plain and unequivocal declaration upon the part of the party that they will not interfere with the curriculum, government, etc. of the private and parochial schools, and the amount of English itself the minimum. It is confined to reading and writing. The duty is laid upon the parent and the guardian, and not upon the school.[44]

When he was unable to secure the complete support of the *Germania,* he and Payne decided to underwrite Paul Bechtner, who in January of that year had combined the *Volksreitung* and the *Freie Presse* into the *Abend Post.* They thought it was important that the Republican party should have one German paper that would stand by the party through thick and thin. They did not have enough ready cash, so they endorsed notes of Bechtner's on which Sawyer advanced the money. Spooner assumed responsibility for ten thousand dollars. It turned out to be a losing financial venture for both Spooner and Payne, for they had finally to reimburse Sawyer.[45]

A week after the Republican convention the Democrats held their convention and nominated for the governorship the successful standard-bearer in the Milwaukee election, George W. Peck, the humorist, founder of the weekly

[44] Spooner to H. C. Payne, August 6; to Paul Bechtner, September 16, 1890, in Spooner Papers.

[45] Payne to Spooner, July 12, 1893, *ibid.;* Spooner to Payne, July 23, 1890; to P. Bechtner, September 16, 1890, October 23, 1893; to P. Sawyer, November 6, 1893, *ibid.* In 1897 the property was sold to George Brumder for $13,250. The following year Spooner sold some of his stock in the First National Bank of Milwaukee to pay off the note (see Payne to Spooner, April 21, May 13, 1897, *ibid.;* Spooner to Payne, April 17, 22, May 4, 1897; to F. Bigelow, September 30, 1898, *ibid.*).

Peck's Sun and creator of "Hennery" in *Peck's Bad Boy*. The platform, presented by Vilas, demanded outright repeal of the Bennett Law, assailed the national Republican administration for extravagance, and denounced the tariff and force bills. They began an intensive campaign, one of the chief objects of which was to elect a Democratic state legislature that would select William F. Vilas as Senator to succeed Spooner.[46]

Throughout September Spooner remained in Washington, for the Republicans were having great difficulty keeping a quorum in the Senate. Payne begged him to come home to attend the convention of the League of Republican Clubs on September 4. It was a large rally, attended by five hundred members representing ninety-nine clubs from all parts of the state. Spooner, chagrined as he had been "barren of service" to the organization since his election as president in 1888, resigned that position and, since he could not be present at the convention, sent a check for a thousand dollars for their campaign chest.[47] In addition, he authorized Payne to draw on him for five thousand dollars and arranged for some Republicans of national prominence to make speeches in the Wisconsin campaign, but he refused to come until after Congress adjourned. He promised Payne that then, after a few days of absolute rest, he would "carry the flag, without complaint, wherever I am ordered to go, and I realize how much that means, for you are a pretty tough taskmaster when you get the whip in your hands." He added: "You must remember that we

46 *New York Herald,* August 28, 1890; see Spooner to B. M. Malone, June 4; to H. Tarrant, September 16, 1890, in Spooner Papers, about Vilas as a candidate for the Senate.
47 *Milwaukee Sentinel,* September 4, 1890; Spooner to H. C. Payne, August 25, 28; to W. J. McElroy, July 27, 1890, in Spooner Papers.

have been here since December—that I have had no vacation—that for thirty days we had met at ten o'clock, and held until six—that we have had a considerable number of evening sessions, and that I have from the beginning of the session to the end of it done an immense deal of hard work." Then in a postscript, he said: "No from Sturgeon Bay to Racine very often as in 'the days that are gone.' " [48] It was at Racine that he delivered his first campaign speech on October 7. From then until election night he toured the state, delivering long addresses, usually lasting two and a half hours, covering the tariff and the silver issue, as well as the Bennett Law. Everywhere, the *Sentinel* noted, he received a rousing welcome by immense audiences.[49]

The Republicans received an "infernal licking"; the Democrats carried not only their state ticket and won control of the state legislature but also elected eight congressmen. The approaching hard times, the growing unrest among farmers in the Middle West, their discontent at the moderation of the Sherman Silver Purchase Act, and the fear of higher prices because of the McKinley tariff were factors in the defeat. Dr. Joseph Schafer, editor of the *Wisconsin Magazine of History*, writing in 1927, stated that these factors, especially the tariff, were more responsible for the defeat of the Republican party in Wisconsin than the Bennett Law, and pointed out that the party had also been defeated in neighboring states. He admitted, however, that most of the German Protestants voted against Hoard; yet, according to Payne, the German Republican vote was essential if the party were to carry Wisconsin

[48] Spooner to H. C. Payne, April 23, September 11, 22, 1890, in Spooner Papers.
[49] *Milwaukee Sentinel*, October 7, 8, 16, 17, 1890.

elections.[50] Contemporaries, however, believed the Bennett Law was responsible for the overwhelming defeat in Wisconsin. George Hazelton, former congressman from Wisconsin, wrote: "All the Wis. Republican Delegation are beaten except Haugen and he got in by a small majority. Hoard with his school question drove all the Lutherans away from our party, the German Lutherans especially, and the Norwegians stayed away from the polls." [51] Spooner was very bitter against Hoard and declared the party had "gone to hell through his stupidity." To another he wrote: "The school law did it—a silly, sentimental and damned useless abstraction, foisted upon us by a self-righteous demagogue." The one satisfaction he got from the election was that Governor Hoard had been defeated. Jokingly he suggested to Payne that the letterhead on the official stationery which read "For Governor William D. Hoard, of Fort Atkinson" should be changed to read "For Fort Atkinson, William D. Hoard, Governor." [52]

The overwhelming defeat of the Republican party in Wisconsin in 1890 meant, of course, the retirement of Spooner from the Senate. Although he had rather expected the victory of the Democratic party, "he had unconsciously counted on being returned to the Senate, which he has so much adorned," admitted his wife.[53] Immediately there

[50] Joseph Schafer, *Wisconsin Magazine of History*, 10 (June, 1927), 455–61.

[51] G. Hazelton to son John, December 4, 1890, in Hazelton Papers; E. Keyes to H. C. Payne, November 6, 1890, in Keyes Papers.

[52] Spooner to H. M. Kutchin, November 18; to H. C. Payne, November 19, 1890, in Spooner Papers.

[53] Annie Spooner, Diary, November 5, 17, 1890. In the Wisconsin legislature Spooner received the unanimous Republican vote and Vilas the unanimous Democratic vote. Vilas was elected Senator over Spooner by a vote of 82 to 45 (see *Milwaukee Sentinel*, January 28, 1891).

were rumors that Spooner would receive some federal government position. The one mentioned most often was a seat on the Supreme Court bench, as there was a vacancy. A meeting of the Wisconsin Bar Association was called to prepare a petition to President Harrison for Spooner's appointment. As soon as Spooner heard about it he wired Payne that he wished no such action to be taken. Not only did he not want such an appointment to come after solicitation but also he did not want the position at that time, for it would be *"too fosselizing."* He felt he was too young —not yet fifty—to enjoy the "isolation and seclusion of an appellate bench." He wanted to be able to go where he chose, to make a political speech if he chose, and to live generally in the world.[54] He had a conference with President Harrison on November 13, but whether an appointment for Spooner or legislative business was discussed is not known. Spooner was also mentioned for the Attorney Generalship and for the positions of Secretary of the Treasury and Secretary of State. The President, however, could hardly invite Spooner to become a member of his cabinet as long as Wisconsin was represented by Secretary of Agriculture Rusk.[55]

Spooner devoted most of his last session in Congress to trying to obtain passage of the federal election bill. He

[54] Spooner to H. C. Payne, November 11; to H. S. Sacket, December 28, 1890, in Spooner Papers.

[55] E. Halford, Diary, November 13, 1890; W. B. Allison to B. Harrison, January 30; G. Edmunds to B. Harrison, January 30; J. S. Morrill to B. Harrison, February 17, 1891, in Harrison Papers. See Annie Spooner, Diary, November 27, 1890, concerning Secretary Rusk. "He . . . is a crafty old fellow, & false as can be—& so vain—I do not like him & wish he were what he appears—a bluff genuine man—for he *is* bluff & illiterate & is large, but far from genuine. His eyes are very near together for his big face & the peculiar drawing of the upper lid gives a sly look to his face—& he is sly."

wrote: "If this Congress fails to take action on the subject I cannot answer your question as to what can decently be said in the next national platform, unless it be a condemnation of the Senate, which in my opinion would be justified." [56] On his way to the Capitol for the opening of the second session of the Fifty-first Congress, Spooner stopped for a last-minute conference with President Harrison. The President had agreed to stress, in his state of the union message, the necessity of passing an effective federal election law. He pointed out that there had been such a law on the statute books for twenty years but that law had been unenforceable in certain sections of the country, since local authorities had full control of the certification of congressmen.[57]

At the Republican caucus meeting that day Spooner succeeded in getting the federal election bill made the main order of business and it occupied almost the exclusive attention of the Senate from December 2 until January 5.[58] On December 20 Spooner delivered his major address on the subject, a five-hour speech. He carefully explained every provision of the bill. He cited Supreme Court decisions to prove that the bill was constitutional and quoted statistics to show that there was discrimination against the Negro in the South. He read the requirements for voting contained in the new Mississippi constitution—the payment of a poll tax and an understanding of the constitution. He pointed out that, according to Senators from the South, few Republican Senators interpreted the United

[56] Spooner to I. W. Morley, January 23, 1891, in Spooner Papers.
[57] Annie Spooner, Diary, December 1, 1890; Richardson, *Messages of Presidents,* VIII, 5564.
[58] *Milwaukee Sentinel,* December 2, 1890.

States Constitution correctly; that being so, how could a Negro be expected to interpret the Mississippi constitution to the satisfaction of a white southern board of elections? He concluded: "The guarantees of the Constitution and the majesty of the law are not for any race or class. They are for all, strong or weak, proud or lowly, white or black, rich or poor, learned or ignorant. The power of Government for the protection of its citizens is a trust from the people for all the people." [59]

This time it was not Quay but the defection of the silver Republicans that blocked the passage of the federal election bill. The number of silver Senators had been increased by the admission of Wyoming and Idaho during the first session. [60] On January 5, while Vice-President Morton was at lunch and a Democrat was presiding officer, a motion, made by Stewart of Nevada, to take up his free-silver coinage bill, was carried by a vote of 34 to 29, with 8 Republican Senators voting with the Democrats. After the passage of the bill on January 14, Spooner proposed the election bill be again discussed. It was only with the casting vote of the Vice-President that the Senate agreed to do so. [61] Discussion continued for a week. The southern Democrats were defiant; it was obvious they would filibuster. Aldrich, chairman of the Rules Committee, reported out the resolution for stopping debate, which he had introduced on De-

[59] *Ibid.*, December 21, 1890; *Congressional Record*, 51st Cong., 2d Sess. (1890–91), p. 730; see also pp. 168, 171–72, 713–30.

[60] *Congressional Record*, 51st Cong., 1st Sess., p. 6518 (Wyoming's admission and discussion on provision in its constitution prohibiting alien land ownership); 51st Cong., 2d Sess., pp. 844, 846–47, on seating of Idaho Senators.

[61] Fred Wellborn, "The Influence of the Silver Republican Senators," *Mississippi Valley Historical Review*, 14 (March, 1928), 476–80; Elmer Ellis, *Henry Moore Teller*, pp. 193–201.

cember 23. This resolution declared that if a bill had
been under consideration a reasonable length of time, any
Senator could demand that debate be closed. If this demand were seconded by a majority of Senators present,
then the vote would be taken. There was not to be any debate on the demand for a vote.[62]

Spooner had persuaded Vice-President Morton to agree
to enforce any rule the Senate adopted to bring the federal
election bill to a vote. The problem was how to get the
cloture rule voted on, for the Democrats were united in
obstructing this as well as the "force bill." The Vice-President insisted on impartially enforcing existing rules of the
Senate. The sponsors of the bill tried to get him out of the
chair but he resisted all such attempts. Finally on January
22, Wolcott of Colorado moved that the Senate proceed to
other legislative matters. His motion was adopted by a vote
of 35 to 34, the Democrats being joined by the Republican
Senators from the silver states of Colorado and Nevada and
by Cameron of Pennsylvania and Washburn of Minnesota.[63] That meant the defeat of the federal election bill.
Spooner wrote:

I am too angry to write. . . . We are fallen upon bad times
for the party. The Confederacy and the Western Mining
Camps are in legislative supremacy. Think of it—Nevada, . . .
barely a respectable county—furnishes two senators to betray
the Republican party and the rights of citizenship for silver.

[62] *Congressional Record*, 51st Cong., 2d Sess., pp. 819, 1468, 1667–82,
1706.

[63] Thomas F. Dawson, *Life and Character of Edward Oliver Wolcott*, II,
36–59; Robert McNutt McElroy, *Levi Parsons Morton*, pp. 187–90, 194;
Lambert, *Gorman*, 152–65; Spooner to F. Hiscock, April 1, 1892, in Spooner
Papers: "Washburn acted a little 'bad' to be sure, but then he is an awfully
good fellow, and I like him."

. . . We are punished for making too easy the pathway of rotten boroughs into the Union.[64]

The advocacy of a federal election bill in 1890 has been treated by historians as a part of the "waving-the-bloody-shirt" phase of Republican party politics. Yet many of the sponsors of the bill were sincerely interested in the issue of Negro disfranchisement. Politics also motivated them, for they hoped that by the passage of such a bill to break the hold the Democratic party had on the Solid South. Over half a century elapsed before the issue of disfranchisement of the Negro was again seriously discussed in Congress, and again southern Senators, by filibustering, were able to block not only the anti-poll tax and antilynching bills but also all attempts to bring about a cloture rule in the Senate. Debates during the Eighty-first Congress were reminiscent of those of the Fifty-first, just as the Civil Rights Act of 1960 is similar to the federal election bill of 1890 in that both emphasize civil remedies rather than criminal penalties.

Spooner spent most of his last month in Congress presenting reports from the Committee on Claims.[65] This was an appropriate finale for a term devoted so much to the "demnition grind" of committee work. In token of his service as chairman of the Committee on Claims, the committee members gave a dinner in his honor the day after adjournment and presented him with a heavily embossed silver pitcher and tray. The menu card was enclosed in a silk cover containing Spooner's picture and a picture of

64 Spooner to J. Rusk, January 27, 1891, in Spooner Papers.

65 *Congressional Record*, 51st Cong., 2d Sess., pp. 2481–82, 2538, 2862, 2905–6, 2911–15, 3431–33, 3565–66.

the committee room where they had spent so many hours. The dinner was held at Chamberlin's and the menu was typical of the banquets of that time, with seven courses, each with its appropriate wine. Short toasts to Spooner were offered by President Harrison, Vice-President Morton, Secretary Rusk, and several members of the committee. Spooner was overwhelmed and for once found himself at a loss for words.[66]

Spooner's keenest regret on leaving the Senate was that he had allowed himself to be burdened too long by unimportant committee work and had not cut loose earlier from such details to devote himself to the higher duties of the Senate which he found delightful. He wrote an old friend: "I feel that with the experience gained in one term I could strike out in such a way in another term as to leave some creditable impress upon the legislative history of the country." [67]

[66] *Milwaukee Sentinel,* March 7, 1891; Spooner to John Mitchell, March 7, 1891, in Spooner Papers.
[67] Spooner to W. E. Gardner, April 14, 1890; to W. Evarts, November 23, 1890, in Spooner Papers.

6 : *Counsel of Northern Pacific Receivers (1891-1896)*

IMMEDIATELY after the adjournment of Congress the Spooners packed their goods, shipped them to Hudson to be put into storage, and then left for Europe. This was their third trip; they had gone after the two previous short sessions. The Senator, Mrs. Spooner, Willet, and Phil sailed on May 5 on the *Teutonic*. They had a roomy upper-deck stateroom, light and airy but "awfully expensive," Mrs. Spooner thought. Every time they went abroad they visited the same places; they spent a short while in England, mainly in London, crossed over to Paris, then traveled to Nice, to Milan, to Switzerland and then back to Paris, England, and home. Mrs. Spooner wrote: "I don't know whether I am odd in the respect of wanting to go over a pleasant time again—the same route or not."

The Spooners were typical American tourists. The Sena-

* Spooner to S. H. Clough, February 14, 1897, in Spooner Papers.

tor could not speak French but they were seldom in places where that was necessary. Confronted one time with a railroad guard who understood no English, Mrs. Spooner described how her husband, in order to keep their compartment for themselves, exclaimed "amidst a comprehensive flourish in a circle with his hand—aloney-aloney? with a rising inflection." She added: "Evidently Mr. Frenchy had met with 'aloney's' before—& nodded assent." The Spooners made no effort to meet Europeans and were delighted when they encountered prominent Americans. They ate only food familiar to them—beefsteak or chops, fried potatoes, bread, coffee or cocoa every morning and evening. Each time they did some sightseeing, went driving in the parks, attended the theater and opera, and shopped. Mrs. Spooner was impressed by the cost of things and invariably listed the prices on the clothes she bought. On this trip her husband succumbed to Paris fashions and had a suit made for himself ($43) and bought a mink-lined overcoat at Bon Marché ($100).

The Spooners were restless, seemed always ready to move on to the next place. They were glad to escape from the disagreeable climate of England to find warmth and sunlight in France. Yet Mrs. Spooner thought Paris the most Godforsaken place—"church in the A.M. & theatre & all sorts of fun & drinking afterwards—way into the early morning hrs." Nevertheless, when they returned to England she wrote:

When we come to London from wicked Paris—we *love* England. After a few meals at the Metropole—we are cursing the tea in this land of Eng. Breakfast tea is abominable—nothing like that in Paris & the Continent generally—nor can the rolls compare nor anything but prices. . . . The contrast is almost

calculated to make one lonesome—that between London &
Paris. In the former the homes look so shut up & so few really
gay people on the streets. While in Paris the sidewalks are
lined with people, eating, drinking & chatting. Yet, in another
way—England—or London seems far more American & decent.
Who ever saw such vile pictures on the streets in L——— as
they allow in Paris—& people seem to have some sober idea of
life & its better possibilities in London—where, of course, vice
flourishes also in hideous forms.

After a few weeks in Europe they impatiently awaited the
day their steamer would sail for America. In a letter written the year before this trip, Spooner well expressed their
feelings toward Europe:

How I envy you your quiet and restful situation over the
sea. While I am over there I am homesick, get out of sorts with
the country and with the people, damn the swindling trades-
men and tradeswomen, cuss the lying dressmakers in Paris, and
so on and so on, swearing that if I ever get home again I will
stay home, and before long I catch myself, as I do now, looking
forward with the utmost impatience and delight to another
trip across the ocean, and to the infinite number of short and
delightful journeys open to one over there. We are never satisfied, are we? [1]

The Spooners landed in New York on July 4; the customs officials hardly looked at their baggage, for some of
the officers knew the former Senator. A day later they went
by boat to 'Sconset, where they remained for the rest of
the summer. In the fall they returned to Wisconsin, all
except Charles, who was a senior at Princeton. Willet had
transferred to the University of Wisconsin. The Spooners
settled down in their old home in Hudson which, when

[1] Annie Spooner, Diary, May 5–July 3, 1891; Spooner to C. H. Haskins,
January 26, 1890, in Spooner Papers.

they built it in 1877, had been considered one of the handsomest houses in the town. It was at Third and Myrtle streets, overlooking Lake St. Croix to the steep bluffs of Minnesota. It was a large and roomy two-story frame building, with a wing on one side for a library. Spooner had built up one of the finest private law libraries in the state, insured for fifteen thousand dollars.[2]

Wisconsin Republicans had been impatient for Spooner to return and settle down in Wisconsin, for he had promised to help with the apportionment case. There had been no reapportionment of the state into senate and assembly districts since 1877, so one of the first acts of the new Democratic legislature had been to pass an apportionment act. The Republicans denounced it as a gerrymander designed to perpetuate the Democrats in power. Spooner had one hundred thousand copies of a pamphlet, prepared by Andrew J. Turner, printed and distributed throughout the state so the people could be well informed on the issues.[3] Spooner suggested that the case testing the constitutionality of the law be brought before the Wisconsin Supreme Court on the first day of the January term, for by that time his old legal associate Silas U. Pinney would be one of the judges. The action could be brought by means of petitions from county boards, and the more counties that expressed themselves the better, he thought. They could all condemn the act and then point out their local injustices, how they

2 *Hudson Star and Times,* December 7, 1877, September 5, 1884; *Milwaukee Sentinel,* August 28, 1892.

3 Raney, *Wisconsin,* p. 275; H. C. Payne to A. J. Turner, April 23, May 4, October 19, 1891; C. E. Estabrook to A. J. Turner, May 4, September 11, October 2, 1891, in Turner Papers at the State Historical Society of Wisconsin; Spooner to P. Sawyer, January 15, 1892, in Spooner Papers.

had been dismembered or combined with other counties, and how county lines had been ignored.

From October to February Spooner devoted his days and many of his nights to the apportionment case. In spite of attempts by the attorney general to delay the hearing,[4] the case was finally argued before the Supreme Court on February 10. Spooner represented the county governments, while E. S. Bragg presented the case of the Democratic administration.[5] The court, composed of three Democrats and two Republicans, handed down a unanimous decision on March 22. After declaring it had jurisdiction, the court said that an apportionment act, like other acts, had to be in accordance with constitutional restrictions, and that this apportionment act violated the constitution, since many districts were not bound by county lines nor were they as compact as possible. The justices also agreed that the secretary of state could, under this apportionment act, be enjoined by injunction from sending out election notices. The *Milwaukee Sentinel* issued a supplement devoted to the case. The editor noted that although Spooner was showered with congratulations he took the decision so modestly that one might have thought that he had won an ordinary lawsuit.[6] Concerning the significance of the case

[4] C. E. Estabrook to A. J. Turner, October 2, November 14, 25, December 3, 1891, January 7, 23, February 2, 4, 1892, in Turner Papers; Spooner to A. J. Turner, November 16, 1891; to P. Sawyer, January 15; to J. A. Watrous, January 16, 1892, in Spooner Papers.

[5] Spooner to W. E. Carter, February 16; to L. J. Perry, February 16; to F. Hiscock, April 1, 1892, in Spooner Papers.

[6] 81 Wis. 440 (*State ex rel. Attorney General* v. *Cunningham*); *Milwaukee Sentinel,* March 23, 1892. The Democratic legislature passed another apportionment act on July 2, 1892. This also was declared unconstitutional; see 83 Wis. 90 (*State ex rel. Lamb* v. *Cunningham*). Spooner filed a brief and closed the presentation. Vilas represented the Democrats. See C. E. Estabrook to A. J. Turner, May 11, July 5, October 1, 1892, in Turner Papers.

Spooner wrote: "It is not only a notable professional triumph, but the court has struck a sturdy blow for good government, which will bear rich fruit long after we are all dead and gone." This was a pioneer case—the first time an apportionment act had been declared unconstitutional by the courts. Several of his former colleagues in the Senate asked Spooner for his brief, as they might be able to institute similar suits in their own states. It did result in the general curbing of the practice of gerrymandering.[7]

The year 1892 Spooner devoted to politics. The Republican state convention met in Milwaukee on May 6. Although its purpose was to elect delegates-at-large to the national convention, the leaders, at Spooner's suggestion, had decided it should also adopt a platform to let the Wisconsin Germans know as early as possible that the Bennett Law was buried beyond resurrection. Spooner, chairman of the committee on resolutions, presented the platform, which declared in unmistakable terms that the "educational issue" of 1890 was permanently settled and would never be revived by the Republican party. The convention strongly endorsed the Harrison administration but did not pledge its delegation for his renomination. Spooner, Payne, and Fairchild were elected delegates-at-large by acclamation, but much to Spooner's dismay, Isaac Stephenson, former congressman and millionaire lumberman, defeated Ogden H. Fethers for the fourth position.[8]

Spooner and Payne arrived early in Minneapolis, where

[7] Spooner to J. A. Watrous, March 25; to F. Hiscock, April 1, 1892, in Spooner Papers; S. Cullom to Spooner, May 28, 1893, *ibid.;* B. Harrison to Spooner, April 27, 1893, in Harrison Papers; Hayes, "William Penn Lyon," *Wisconsin Magazine of History,* 9 (March, 1926), 273–80.

[8] *Milwaukee Sentinel,* May 6, 1892; Spooner to H. C. Payne, February 25; to O. H. Fethers, May 14, 1892, in Spooner Papers.

the national convention was to meet. Louis T. Michener, Harrison's personal campaign manager, reported on June 2, in code: "Seventy-two [Spooner] is all right. Will speak and help. Fifty-eight [Payne] is here and wrong, his people are pounding him; sixty-seven [Rusk] must reach him. Telegrams from the State ought to be sent to fifty-eight." [9] Payne could not, however, be persuaded to support President Harrison. He, like many other members of the national committee, was sure the President, even if nominated, could not be elected.[10] This was one of the few times that Spooner and Payne disagreed on a party candidate.

On June 4, the very day the Harrison men held their first meeting in Minneapolis, Blaine submitted his resignation as Secretary of State. This, his supporters interpreted as an indication that he had reconsidered his February letter in which he had declared he was not a candidate for the presidential nomination. A Blaine boom was launched.[11] The Harrison forces, however, had things well in hand. Their choice for permanent chairman, William McKinley, was elected; Spooner and Samuel Fessenden of Connecticut escorted him to the chair. Satisfactory rules were adopted. Spooner contested the idea that a man should vote on his own seating and the chair finally ruled that delegates-at-large could vote in cases where a district delegate's seat was contested, and vice versa. Delaying tac-

[9] L. T. Michener to E. Halford, June 2, 1892, in Harrison Papers. See *New York Herald,* May 31, June 3, 1892, for interviews with Spooner in which he came out unqualifiedly for Harrison. See also Donald Marquand Dozer, "Benjamin Harrison and the Presidential Campaign of 1892," *American Historical Review,* 54 (October, 1948), 49–78.

[10] H. C. Payne to J. Rusk, May 2, 1892, in Rusk Papers.

[11] *New York Herald,* June 5, 1892; J. G. Blaine to B. Harrison, June 4, 1892, in Harrison Papers.

tics in making up the permanent roll were not successful and by June 10 the nominating speeches were begun. Spooner seconded the nomination of President Harrison.[12] Many called it one of the "handsomest speeches" of the convention but the *Chicago Tribune* described it as follows:

Now came up the champion of the light weights, Spooner, in a brown head of hair and a concave mouth. He came from Indiana, has delicate, female features, and his gift of oratory is packed in a confectionary box. His plumage of reddish hair made him look like a sparrow-hawk. He was hoarse and the people were tired, so he could not keep the excitement up. Spooner and Vilas are the two juvenile public rivals of Wisconsin. Before Spooner ended everybody yawned and wanted a vote to be taken.[13]

The *Milwaukee Sentinel* claimed Spooner was virtually head of the Harrison forces on the convention floor. Spooner had worked very hard and felt that "his work was efficient in contributing" to the nomination of Harrison on the first ballot. He lost eight pounds during the fight and never got to bed until three or four in the morning. It was a "hell of a whirl," Spooner wrote. "The National Committee used all of the machinery of the party against us, and took a position at once unprecedented, dictatorial and offensive." [14] Because of the opposition of so many members to the renomination of President Harrison, the selection of a new national committee was a problem.

12 *Official Proceedings of the Tenth Republican National Convention, 1892*, pp. 26, 71, 128, 140; *New York Herald,* June 9, 11, 1892.

13 N. McKay to E. Halford, June 14, 1892; B. Harrison to Spooner, June 14, 1892, in Harrison Papers; Spooner to W. H. Taft, June 25, 1892, in Spooner Papers; *Chicago Tribune,* June 11, 1892.

14 *Milwaukee Sentinel,* June 11, 1892; Spooner to W. E. Gardner, June 26; to I. H. Wing, July 13, 1892, in Spooner Papers.

Spooner thought Payne should be retained, for he was a "good Republican and a good worker" although he "got wrong this time." Spooner was urged by President Harrison and by Secretary Rusk and Senator Sawyer to take the chairmanship of the committee but he refused. He explained: "Our situation in this State is very peculiar. We are engaged in a fight for life, against great odds. If I were in charge of the national campaign it is absolutely certain that I could not give in any degree whatever the attention to the campaign in this State which I would otherwise give." [15]

Spooner was selected as standard-bearer in the Wisconsin campaign; the Republican state convention on August 18 nominated him for governor, unanimously, and, according to the press, spontaneously and enthusiastically.[16] Former Congressman La Follette, however, claimed Spooner had been selected by the machine at the insistence of Sawyer and Payne, and that the rank and file of the party had had nothing to do with his nomination. La Follette was resentful that the chairmanship of the Dane County committee had been given to Spooner's brother Roger.[17] Although La Follette campaigned under

[15] Spooner to J. A. Watrous, June 25; to O. E. Britt, June 25; to E. Halford, July 14; to P. Sawyer, July 14, 1892, in Spooner Papers; E. Halford to Spooner, July 13, 1892; H. C. Payne to E. Halford, July 22, 1892, in Harrison Papers. Payne was also offered the chairmanship of the committee but declined. See George H. Knoles, *The Presidential Campaign and Election of 1892*, pp. 122–24.

[16] *Milwaukee Sentinel*, August 18, 1892. Spooner accepted the nomination reluctantly and only because he felt he was so indebted to the party for past honors that he had to obey the party's command; see Spooner to K. Nelson, September 5, 1892, in Spooner Papers.

[17] La Follette, *Autobiography*, p. 170; Albert O. Barton, *La Follette's Winning of Wisconsin*, p. 51; Spooner to J. Conley, November 26, 1892, in Spooner Papers.

the auspices of the Republican party, he never mentioned John C. Spooner's name. Former Governor Hoard, thinking he should have had the gubernatorial nomination, was also lukewarm, and H. C. Thom, a Hoard man who had been made chairman of the state central committee, was not the political manager and organizer that Payne was. For that matter, throughout the nation, listlessness, indifference, and inactivity characterized the Republican party campaign.[18]

The odds were against Spooner's election. The Democrats had carried the state by a tremendous plurality two years before and his opponent was the successful vote getter of 1890, Governor George Peck. Spooner's successor in the Senate, William F. Vilas, stumped the state on behalf of the Democratic nominee. The Democratic party speakers dealt in personalities, accusing Spooner of sacrificing settlers to the interests of the railroads when he was in the Senate, and of being opposed to organized labor not only when he was a railroad solicitor but in 1892, when the Typographical Union failed in its attempts to unionize the office of the *Milwaukee Sentinel*. Most of these accusations were lies or misrepresentations.[19] The *New York Herald* described the situation:

[18] E. Keyes to G. Weeks, September 3, 1892; P. Sawyer to E. Keyes, October 24, 1892, in Keyes Papers.

[19] *Milwaukee Sentinel*, September 3, 1892, contains a cartoon showing the records of the two candidates; Nils P. Haugen, "Pioneer and Political Reminiscences," *Wisconsin Magazine of History*, 11 (June, 1928), 429–30; Spooner to J. McClure, September 6; to J. Tillotson, September 5; to C. D. Booth, November 26, 1892; H. M. Teller to Spooner, September 14; H. Reed to Spooner, October 26, 28, 1892, in Spooner Papers; G. Hazelton to son, November 4, 1892, in Hazelton Papers at the State Historical Society of Wisconsin.

The campaign in Wisconsin is and has been throughout a peculiar one, neither party seeming at any time to attack the position taken by the other. . . . The Republican party is conducting its campaign largely, indeed almost entirely, upon a basis of national issues, and ignoring State issues, while on the other hand the Democrats practically ignore national issues and are conducting a vigorous campaign on State issues.[20]

Spooner personally carried on a very intensive campaign and to some effect. The Republicans succeeded in cutting down the Democratic plurality from 32,000 to about 7,000, and elected three congressmen. Spooner wrote: "I think we have left the party by this fight, which to me was a sacrificial one, in good shape to win the State two years from now, with proper effort and *good organization*." [21]

In one of his speeches during the campaign Spooner had stated that Sawyer wished to retire from the Senate on March 4, 1893. Newspapers had taken up the statement, had exaggerated it, and intimated that it was a trick to get Sawyer out of the way so Spooner would have no competition for the Republican nomination. Sawyer's feelings had been hurt; he was approaching seventy-seven and sometimes realized he should retire, but at other times he felt he was too young to be put on the shelf. Shortly after the election the two, the old Senator and his ambitious protégé, had a conference in Milwaukee. It was agreed that Sawyer would not be a candidate for the senatorial nomination.[22]

Spooner was nominated by acclamation by the Republi-

20 *New York Herald,* November 4, 1892.

21 Spooner to E. S. Minor, November 25, 1892; to T. H. Mosher, November 29, 1896, in Spooner Papers; *Milwaukee Sentinel,* October 26, 27, November 1, 5, 6, 1892.

22 Spooner to P. Sawyer, June 12, 1893, in Spooner Papers; Current, *Pine Logs and Politics,* pp. 275–76.

can caucus on January 19, 1893. The Democratic caucus
came to no agreement before the legislature was convened.
The contest was chiefly between veteran politician Edward
S. Bragg, former congressman and minister to Mexico, and
John Mitchell, millionaire congressman, son of Alexander
Mitchell, of the Chicago, Milwaukee and St. Paul Railway
Company. There was a third candidate, John H. Knight,
business partner of Vilas. Early that spring Spooner had
prophesied that if the Democrats carried the legislature,
Bragg would not have a chance at the senatorship, that
Vilas and Edward C. Wall, chairman of the state central
committee, would try to elect Mitchell. He was right, for
finally after several days of balloting, Knight withdrew and
Mitchell was nominated by the Democrats and then was
elected, defeating Spooner by a vote of 77 to 46.[23]

Twice defeated for the senatorship, Spooner decided to
take up again his private law practice. For two years he
had devoted his time and his talents to the Republican
party. He had refused retainers from several railroad companies and estimated that he had turned away $100,000
worth of law business from would-be clients from many
parts of the country who had sought him out in his
"country home." [24] By 1893 he needed to make money.
The financial tornado had struck him, as it had so many
others. He declared he had never been harder up financially than he was that year. He had too much capital tied

[23] Spooner to J. J. Jenkins, May 14, 1892; to M. McCord, January 28,
1893, in Spooner Papers; *Milwaukee Sentinel,* January 20, 27, 28, 1893;
Horace S. Merrill, *William Freeman Vilas,* p. 196.

[24] Spooner to S. H. Clough, February 14, 1897; to F. H. Finney, November 19, 1890; to J. H. Swan, November 4, 1891; to W. E. Gardner, June 26,
1892; to E. S. Smith, January 9, 1893, in Spooner Papers.

up in real estate, land companies, a gold mine in North Carolina yielding no more gold, and especially in the Pioneer Iron Company, into which he had sunk thousands of dollars but from which he had not received a cent.[25]

Spooner had considered opening an office in Milwaukee but finally decided to settle in Madison, the site of the university, so the whole family could be together. Charles had entered Wisconsin University Law School and Willet was a junior at the University of Wisconsin. The youngest, Philip, Mrs. Spooner's favorite, would soon be ready for college and Mrs. Spooner refused to be separated from him. Their home in Madison was a comparatively modest one; it was on Langdon Street at the corner of Henry, not far from the university campus. They had a cook—not fancy—and a second girl. Mrs. Spooner was happy with her family around her, with her home to oversee, with time for singing, church work, and an occasional trip with her husband. She was particularly delighted to have no official social demands.[26]

Spooner entered into a partnership with Arthur L. Sanborn, who had been a law partner of S. U. Pinney, the new justice of the Wisconsin Supreme Court. Their office, near the state capitol, was at 2–4 South Carroll Street. H. C. Reed continued as Spooner's private secretary. There were seven law students working in the office, and when Charles finished his law course, he entered the firm as a partner.[27]

The firm of Spooner and Sanborn appeared in a wide

[25] Spooner to B. F. Callahan, February 18, 1892; to W. H. Phipps, June 9, October 13, December 6, 1893; to I. B. Bradford, September 24, 1893; to D. M. Shannon, July 3, 1893, *ibid.*

[26] Spooner to T. M. Blackstock, February 2, 1893; to L. H. Catchpole, January 9, March 8, 1892; to H. Sanford, April 21, 1893, *ibid.*

[27] Spooner to A. Sanborn, May 18, 1893, July 2, 1894; to S. W. Hunt, September 24, 1892; to S. D. Howe, April 9, 1895, *ibid.*

variety of cases. Their first case before the state supreme court, early in 1893, was similar to one in which Spooner had appeared almost twenty years before; again he successfully defended a married woman's right to hold property free from attachment by her husband's creditors. He lauded the Wisconsin Married Woman's Property Law of 1850, based on the New York statute of 1848, which had removed the disabilities of common law.[28] Most of the cases handled by the firm were in the field of civil and equity law, but they did take on some criminal cases with such dissimilar clients as an Indian charged with murder and a bank president indicted for embezzlement of funds. Spooner was gratified that the *Chicago Tribune* had a long article on the latter case, with special attention given to his oral presentation. He had argued, successfully, that the indictment had been incorrectly drawn because it charged the defendant with ten different offenses, while under common law only one offense could be charged in each indictment.[29] Injury suits,[30] disputes over inheritances, settlement of estates,[31] land transactions, fulfillment of contracts,[32]

[28] 85 Wis. 214 (*Le Saulnier, Appellant* v. *Krueger and Wife, Respondents*); 47 Wis. 113 (*Dayton* v. *Walsh*). See similar case, 95 Wis. 456 (*Davenport* v. *Stephens*).

[29] Spooner to A. Sanborn, May 18, 1893; to L. S. Butler, June 24, 1894; to J. V. Quarles, January 25, 1896, in Spooner Papers; 59 Federal Reporter 677 (*U. S.* v. *Cadwallader*).

[30] 86 Wis. 64 (*Johnson* v. *Lake Superior Terminal and Transfer Company*); 91 Wis. 214 (*McVoy* v. *Oakes*); 89 Wis. 119 (*Craven* v. *Smith*); 92 Wis. 629 (*Sharp* v. *City of Mauston*).

[31] 90 Wis. 427 (*Cooper* v. *Reilly*); 95 Wis. 405 (*Markwell* v. *Pereles*); 68 Federal Reporter 61 (*Hodge* v. *Palms*); 68 Federal Reporter 64 (*Morancy* v. *Palms*).

[32] 86 Wis. 661 (*Gilbert* v. *Loberg*); 88 Wis. 672 (*Edwards and McCulloch Lumber Co.* v. *Mosher*); 91 Wis. 221 (*Lehigh Coal and Iron Co.* v. *West Superior Iron and Steel Co.*); 94 Wis. 251 (*Westurn* v. *Page*); 62 Federal Reporter 173 (*Wetherby* v. *Stinson*); 157 U. S. 327 (*Bardon* v. *Land and River Improvement Co.*).

and receivership and bankruptcy[33] cases kept the firm busy.

Several lawsuits concerned a city's authority under its charter: Whether a city could levy taxes for general improvements or only for a specific object and only on the property improved; whether a city could borrow money to build waterworks and electric lighting plants; whether a city could demand five hundred dollars for a liquor license when the state had specified two hundred.[34] The most important of these city cases was that between Milwaukee and the Milwaukee Street Railway Company, with which Henry C. Payne was connected. The issue was whether the franchise of the company was taxable as property. When the case was appealed to the supreme court, Spooner appeared on behalf of Payne's company. The decision, handed down by Justice Pinney, accepted Spooner's argument that franchises could not be assessed, as was the other property of a railway, because they were not transferable and the company could not disable itself from performing the duties owed the public. Franchises were to be regarded as personal property, not as real estate. Payne sent Spooner one thousand dollars for his services.[35]

Although busy with his new law practice, Spooner could not stay entirely aloof from politics. The Republican party

[33] 86 Wis. 661 (*Gilbert* v. *Loberg*); 90 Wis. 581 (*In re Rosenberg*); 91 Wis. 76 (*Johnston* v. *Humphrey*); 91 Wis. 90 (*Thayer* v. *Goss*); 91 Wis. 98 (*Dowie* v. *Humphrey*); 91 Wis. 111 (*Gibbs* v. *Humphrey*); 91 Wis. 276 (*Thayer* v. *Humphrey*); 94 Wis. 523 (*Warner* v. *Rosenberg*).

[34] 92 Wis. 429 (*Hayes* v. *Douglass Co.*); 91 Wis. 131 (*Ellinwood* v. *City of Reedsburg*); 95 Wis. 530 (*State ex rel. Farrell* v. *Howe*).

[35] 90 Wis. 550 (*State ex rel. Milwaukee Street Railway Co.* v. *Anderson*); H. C. Payne to Spooner, June 18, July 28, 1894, February 3, May 11, 1895, in Spooner Papers.

in Wisconsin in 1894 was in a demoralized state. Not only was it out of power but it was split into two camps by a quarrel between Sawyer and La Follette. The new Democratic administration, in accordance with its campaign pledge, had brought action against Republican former treasurers and their bondsmen to recover the interest they had received on state funds. The first case, against former Treasurer Harshaw and Sawyer, his bondsman, had been scheduled to be heard in September, 1891, in the circuit court of Dane County, with Robert G. Siebecker, brother-in-law of Robert M. La Follette, as presiding judge.[36] Suddenly Judge Siebecker had announced that he would not hear the case. There had been all kinds of rumors to explain his withdrawal, until finally both Sawyer and La Follette had given statements to the *Milwaukee Sentinel.* Their accounts disagreed. La Follette claimed that Sawyer had tried to bribe him and that the judge therefore felt he could not preside over the case. Sawyer, denying that he had tried to bribe La Follette, declared that he had merely offered the former congressman a retainer and that he had not known of his relationship to the judge.[37] Sawyer was rabid against La Follette and accused him of attempting his political assassination. Spooner had not taken the quarrel very seriously; he thought it deplorable but felt that it would not have any lasting effect on the Republican

[36] Raney, *Wisconsin,* pp. 274, 285; 84 Wis. 532 (*State* v. *Harshaw, State* v. *Sawyer*). The court held Harshaw and his sureties liable for the interest on the state funds deposited in banks.

[37] *Milwaukee Sentinel,* October 27, 1891; La Follette, *Autobiography,* pp. 139–46; La Follette, *La Follette,* I, 95–99; Current, *Pine Logs and Politics,* pp. 259–64. See the following letters for two interesting and somewhat conflicting stories about the incident: Horace Rublee to J. Rusk, November 3, 1891, in Rusk Papers, and N. L. James to Spooner, September 27, 1904, in Spooner Papers.

party and would be political suicide for La Follette.[38] He was badly mistaken.

This incident completed the break between Sawyer and La Follette. The young congressman had long been resentful because the Sawyer-Payne-Spooner machine had never supported his political ambitions and he had been restive under the attempts of the senior Senator to control his actions in Congress. Since the old Republican leaders were then discredited by the party's defeat at the polls, La Follette decided it was a propitious time for him to take the lead in opposing Sawyer. He then came out as a reformer. He traced this interest in the underdog to his early life, when he had to work so hard on the farm and had had to earn money at the same time he was studying at the university. He blamed the adversities of the working class on the political bosses. He set out to wrest control of the Republican party in Wisconsin from the "corrupt machine." He selected, as his gubernatorial candidate for 1894, Nils P. Haugen, a Norwegian, the only Republican congressman who had survived the Democratic landslide of 1890. Former Governor Hoard joined him [39] and they tried to win over Horace Rublee, editor of the *Milwaukee Sentinel,* but Spooner persuaded him to remain aloof from that cabal.[40]

Spooner was opposed to Haugen, considered him per-

38 P. Sawyer to E. Keyes, November 1, 1891, in Keyes Papers; Spooner to J. Treat, November 4; to P. Sawyer, November 16; to H. H. Rand, December 6, 1891, in Spooner Papers.

39 La Follette, *La Follette,* I, 103–9; Blair Bolles, *Tyrant from Illinois,* pp. 26–27; Haugen, "Pioneer and Political Reminiscences," *Wisconsin Magazine of History,* 12 (September, 1928), 43–45.

40 C. W. Mott to Spooner, May 24, 1894; Spooner to H. Rublee, May 29, 1894; to J. T. Murphy, June 24, 1894, in Spooner Papers.

sonally hostile, and felt that his candidacy would bring up again the Bennett Law issue, for he had at that time publicly favored the law.[41] Even more, he disliked Hoard, whom he still blamed for the defeat of the party in 1890. He was also provoked that Hoard for the past year or so had been spreading rumors throughout Wisconsin that Spooner, when senator, had sacrificed the dairy interests by not getting the Senate to concur in the House amendment to the Wilson Original Package bill, which made intoxicating liquors subject to state law. This amendment would have made oleomargarine imported into a state subject to its laws. Spooner claimed that he had tried his best but that the amendment had been badly drawn and that it would have been impossible to have made a successful fight for concurrence with the members of the Senate Judiciary Committee opposed. To have insisted on it would have jeopardized the bill itself.[42]

Spooner's candidate for the gubernatorial nomination was his old friend Horace A. Taylor, who early in 1890 had bought the *Wisconsin State Journal,* Madison's leading paper.[43] There were many other candidates, among them Edward Scofield and William H. Upham. They had both been in the Civil War and had been captured and imprisoned by the Confederates. They were now prosperous

[41] Spooner to G. Koeppen, July 7, 1894, *ibid.;* see G. Koeppen to Keyes, May 31, 1890, in Keyes Papers.

[42] Spooner to W. D. Hoard, September 22, 1890; to F. Hiscock, July 11; to J. F. Wilson, July 7, 1894; F. Hiscock to Spooner, July 7; G. Edmunds to Spooner, July 9, 1894, in Spooner Papers.

[43] Spooner to Willet, January 9, 1889, February 11, 1890; to H. C. Payne, February 23, 1890, *ibid.* Spooner had considered going in with Taylor on this project and had also tried to interest Sawyer in it. The *Madison Democrat,* April 13, 1890, claimed there had been a struggle between the supporters of La Follette and Spooner for the paper.

businessmen, interested in lumber.[44] John C. Koch, who
had been candidate for lieutenant governor on the ticket
with Spooner in 1892, withdrew from the race early in
July. Spooner was mortified when he learned that one of
the factors in his withdrawal had been an insulting letter
from his brother Roger.[45]

Critical for the success of the Republican party in 1894
was the platform. The formulating of it was left in
Spooner's hands. The main issues were the silver question,
major plank of the new Populist party, the labor situation,
the Bennett Law, and the American Protective Association
(A.P.A.). Although the Bennett Law had been repealed by
the Democratic legislature in 1891, and the Republican
party in 1892 had declared the educational question permanently settled, there were still some in the party who
wanted the law revived. Spooner thought the issue should
be permitted to drop into oblivion. The A.P.A. had been
organized in Iowa in the 1880's. Its avowed purpose was to
prevent the appropriation of public money for sectarian
schools but it soon began an antiforeign and anti-Catholic
campaign. The bitter controversy over the school question
in Wisconsin and other states aided the growth of the
movement, which by 1894 claimed a membership of over
one million. It had come to be very influential in the Republican party in the Middle West and in many sections it
controlled nominations. In Wisconsin the chairman of the
state central committee reported: "The A.P.A.'s are becoming very earnest and doing their utmost to concentrate

44 George W. Hotchkiss, *History of the Lumber and Forest Industry of
the Northwest,* p. 443; *National Cyclopedia of American Biography,* 12:80.
See P. Sawyer to E. Keyes, May 28; W. H. Upham to Keyes, June 9, 1894,
in Keyes Papers.
45 Spooner to J. C. Koch, July 11, 1894, in Spooner Papers.

their forces. The rank and file of the party is becoming more determined that the new element shall not control, and I am quite apprehensive that the outcome is bound to prove disastrous to the party." Spooner thought it best for the party to ignore the organization both in the platform and in speeches. "It will inevitably be like the Know-nothing movement. It will have its time, and, as all other things based on so narrow a view of liberty, will pass away."

By the time the Republican state convention met in Milwaukee on July 25, Spooner had gone east to Nantucket. Chairman H. C. Thom had urged him to be present. "We will need you here convention day, with your counsel and influence, and we will need you badly; and so far as your personal interest is concerned I think you owe it to yourself to be here," he had written.[46] Spooner refused; he had decided several years ago that neither business nor politics should interfere with his summer vacation. As it turned out, his presence was not necessary. The platform he had drawn up was adopted. It was a very brief one—it reaffirmed the national platform, declared in favor of honest money, stated that the Republican party was the friend of organized labor, and the party of religious liberty, nonsectarianism, and free common schools. After a deadlock between Upham, Scofield, and Haugen, with Taylor trailing, Upham was finally nominated.[47]

Spooner returned to Wisconsin in October and devoted

[46] H. C. Thom to Spooner, July 17, 1894; Spooner to G. F. Hoar, April 19, 1895, in Spooner Papers. See Frederick H. Gillett, *George Frisbie Hoar,* pp. 187–93, and Carl F. Wittke, *We Who Built America,* p. 498, on the A.P.A. movement.

[47] Spooner to G. Koeppen, July 7, 1894; P. L. Spooner to J. C. Spooner, July 21, 27; C. W. Mott to Spooner, July 27; H. Reed to Spooner, August 9, 1894, in Spooner Papers; *Milwaukee Sentinel,* July 25, 26, 27, 1894.

that month to his party. He made his first political speech
in Milwaukee on the fifth and then stumped the state,
speaking every day except Sundays and twice on many
days. He stressed the tariff and silver questions and ignored
state issues. "The State Is Swept as by a Cyclone," the headlines of the *Milwaukee Sentinel* on November 7 described
the victory of the Republican party. Upham was elected
governor by a plurality of over 50,000 and the Republicans
had complete control of the state legislature and the Congressional delegation.[48] Party leaders celebrated with a tremendous jollification banquet in Milwaukee on November
10. Spooner declared the wonderful victory meant the return to prosperity. His political obligations fulfilled, he
returned to his professional duties; leaving early, he took
the train to Helena, Montana, on legal business for the
Northern Pacific Railroad.[49]

Spooner was one of the counsels for the Northern Pacific
receivership. Remembering the opprobrium attached to
his former employment by a railroad, Spooner was insistent that he was not the attorney for the railroad but
only for the receivers who were really moral officers of the
court. He was offered the general counselship of the receivers but refused it since that would have meant moving
away from Wisconsin and giving up his general practice.
William Nelson Cromwell, a well-known New York lawyer, became chief counsel and Spooner was one of seven
or eight other counsels.[50] It was a lucrative position; he

48 Memorandum: Route of J. C. S., 1894, in Spooner Papers; *Milwaukee
Sentinel*, October 3, 5, 13, 17, 23, November 3, 4, 6, 7, 1894.

49 *Milwaukee Sentinel*, November 9, 10, 1894; H. C. Payne to Spooner,
November 7; Spooner to F. A. Flower, December 5, 1894, in Spooner
Papers.

50 Spooner to J. C. Clark, March 2, 1896; to J. N. Scott, May 5, 1895, in
Spooner Papers. Spooner wrote W. J. Curtis, December 5, 1894 (*ibid.*),

was paid a retainer of $5,000 and a salary of $15,000 a year, plus other allowances for special services.[51] He earned his salary, for the pressure of the work was heavy and he often sat up most of the night preparing cases or going over with other counsels the arguments to be presented before court the next day. Since the Northern Pacific extended from the Great Lakes to the Pacific Ocean and the headquarters were in New York City, Spooner lived a strenuous life. One week he would be in New York City, the next in Wisconsin, the next in Montana, then Walla Walla, Washington, then back in New York.[52]

The Northern Pacific had been chartered by Congress in 1864 and, although it had received an immense land grant, it had not completed its line to the Pacific until 1883. Many well-known railroad builders had been connected with it but it was Henry Villard who had finally brought the project to fruition. For a while the line had prospered, but the passing of the preferred stock dividend in 1892 indicated that the road was in financial difficulties. An investigating committee, headed by Brayton Ives, reported

---

about Cromwell: "You told me long ago that he was a remarkable man, and I long ago came to agree with you on the subject, but he cannot keep up the same rate of pressure that he has since I have known him, and I presume since you have known him, without wearing out. He is wonderful in his energy, in his quickness of comprehension, his mastery of details, his power of rapid generalization, his fertility of resources, etc. etc., and with it all he is generous, full of good impulses, and altogether a lovable man, and, in addition to his other accomplishments, he can bulldoze like damnation when he wants to, and I have seen him when he wanted to; and he can take care of himself. As this is a confidential letter, and as I am writing to *you*, I have taken the liberty to '*put upon the record* if not for present purposes, at least for the benefit of future generations,' a partial estimate of Cromwell." Cromwell lived to be ninety-four (see *The New York Times,* July 20, 1948).

[51] Spooner to F. Stetson, July 13, 1896, in Spooner Papers.

[52] Spooner to W. G. Collins, September 24, 1893; to James McNaught, February 1, 1895; to H. B. Sloan, April 19, 1895, *ibid.*

that the management had been extravagant, had acquired entirely too large a floating debt, that the company was overloaded with branch lines, and particularly that it had subordinated the interests of the Northern Pacific to that of the Wisconsin Central, with which a 999-year lease had been made so that the eastern terminal could be transferred from St. Paul to Chicago. This committee finally, in June, 1893, forced the resignation of Villard as chairman of the board.[53] Two months later, on August 15, the company, admittedly insolvent, went into receivership. Judge James G. Jenkins, whose appointment in 1888 as United States judge of the Eastern District of Wisconsin had been sponsored by Senator Spooner, appointed as receivers Henry C. Payne, Henry C. Rouse, and Thomas F. Oakes, manager of the Northern Pacific. Because of Payne's influence, Spooner was called in as counsel for the receivership on September 1.[54]

One of the first legal problems that Spooner took up was the Wisconsin Central lease. When Judge Jenkins ordered the surrender of the lease by the Northern Pacific receivers, the Wisconsin Central sued for rent for the forty days it had been under the receivership. The railroad was represented by Louis D. Brandeis and for the second time he defeated Spooner in a legal engagement.[55]

53 Robert E. Riegel, *Story of the Western Railroads*, pp. 203–4; Stuart Daggett, *Railroad Reorganization*, pp. 263–89; William Z. Ripley, *Railroads: Finance and Organization*, pp. 379–83.

54 Daggett, *Railroad Reorganization*, pp. 289–90; Spooner to J. G. Jenkins, July 11, 1888; to S. S. Rockwood, September 3, 1893, in Spooner Papers.

55 *Railway Age*, 18 (September 8, 1893), 678; (September 29, 1893), 735; 58 Federal Reporter 257 (*Farmers' Loan and Trust Co.* v. *Northern Pacific*); Spooner to G. P. Miller, September 24, 1893, in Spooner Papers. See Spooner to E. D. Moe, February 15, 1899 (*ibid.*), for his estimate of Brandeis: "I know a lawyer in Boston, whom I often met in opposition in the

There were a great number of other claims brought against the Northern Pacific and referred to Spooner as counsel for the receivers. These ranged from such minor ones as a claim for $40 for a cow injured by a train, one for $50 for some fish spoiled because of delay in transit, to one by Westinghouse Air Brake Company for some $40,000. There were also many claims for injuries to employees. Most of these claims Spooner turned over to other lawyers to be handled, although he went over with them the docket of cases; one docket in Milwaukee included sixty cases.[56] There were also a great number of cases concerning the Northern Pacific land grant. Spooner helped prepare the briefs in many of these suits but did not personally argue the cases.[57]

The Northern Pacific was also involved in serious labor troubles. Because of decreased earnings, due to the depression, notice that wages would be cut had been issued. Fear-

---

Northern Pacific and Wisconsin Central litigations, of whose legal ability and power I have a high opinion—Louis D. Brandeis. If I had a case in Boston, of any sort, I should not hesitate to entrust it to Mr. Brandeis. I have heard him argue cases in the Supreme Court of the United States and in Circuit Courts of the United States, and he is persuasive, and strong, and accurate, and learned."

[56] Spooner to J. McNaught, November 26; to Finch and Barbe, December 7; to T. Jewell, December 16, 1893; to T. H. Gill, January 16, March 6, April 17, 1894; Paul Cravath to Spooner, November 8, 1893, January 10, May 18, 1894, in Spooner Papers; 63 Federal Reporter 43, 102, 114, 527, 530; 64 Federal Reporter 84, 211.

[57] Spooner to W. N. Cromwell, March 23, April 4, 13, May 2, 23, June 29, 1895; to C. Bunn, October 5, 1896, in Spooner Papers; 46 Federal Reporter 239; 47 Federal Reporter 604 (*Northern Pacific* v. *Sanders*); 46 Federal Reporter 224, 237; 54 Federal Reporter 252 (*Northern Pacific* v. *Cannon*); 54 Federal Reporter 67 (*Northern Pacific* v. *Wright*); 166 U.S. 620 (*Northern Pacific* v. *Sanders*); 158 U.S. 1 (*Roberts* v. *Northern Pacific*); 172 U.S. 589 (Montana tax case). Spooner refused to have anything to do with injunction suits against settlers (see Spooner to W. N. Cromwell, April 4, 1895, in Spooner Papers).

ing a strike, Spooner, as a precautionary measure, asked Judge Jenkins to grant a writ of injunction against the executive heads of the various railway unions forbidding any interference with the operation of the lines. Thus was presented to the court the direct issue whether an injunction could be used to restrain employees from striking. Judge Jenkins took up the challenge. He ordered the new wage schedule to go into effect January 1, 1894, and at the same time he issued a writ of injunction precisely as Spooner had requested. In a very impressive manner the judge delivered his momentous decision. First he discussed the right of the court to assume a part in the contest between capital and labor; he declared: "It is the duty of the courts to restrain those warring factions, so far as their action may infringe the declared law of the land, that society may not be disrupted, or its peace invaded, and that individual and corporate rights may not be infringed." He pointed out that the strike would disable the receivers from operating the road and would also prevent the road from carrying the mails. Since pecuniary compensation would be wholly inadequate in case of such a strike, the injunction was the appropriate weapon.[58] An amicable settlement of the troubles between the receivers and the employees was finally reached.[59]

[58] Spooner to W. N. Cromwell, December 19, 1893; G. P. Miller to Spooner, April 6, 1894, in Spooner Papers; 60 Federal Reporter 803 (*Farmers' Loan and Trust Co.* v. *Northern Pacific Railroad Co.*); *Railway Age*, 19 (April 13, 1894), 209.

[59] *Railway Age*, 19 (February 16, 1894), 93. The Northern Pacific also became involved in the eastward march of Coxey's Army. Again injunctions were issued and finally President Cleveland called out the troops. See Donald L. McMurry, *Coxey's Army*, pp. 199–205; *Senate Executive Document*, 52d Cong., 2d Sess., No. 120. See also J. W. Kendrick to Spooner, April 23; H. C. Payne to Spooner, April 25; W. Curtis to Spooner, April 25; Spooner to J. McNaught, July 11, 1894, in Spooner Papers.

When in July of that year President Cleveland and Attorney General Olney used similar methods to put down the Pullman strike, W. E. Gardner wrote Spooner:

> Has it struck you . . . that the position of Senator Spooner and Judge Jenkins with reference to the Northern Pacific strike injunction merely anticipated by about three months, the position now occupied by the courts and substantially by all the people, in consequence of the recent Chicago strike.
>
> Everybody then said that your identity with that Northern Pacific injunction was surely fatal to Spooner. I predict that what was then deemed to be an element of greatest weakness, is soon to prove a source of your greatest strength before the public.[60]

Spooner's major job as counsel was to defend the receivers of the Northern Pacific against the attacks of Brayton Ives and his committee. Ives, backed by August Belmont, had gained control of the board of directors of the Northern Pacific Railroad Company and Ives had been elected president. The receivers, having control of the funds of the company, refused to grant the new officers any salaries. This action was upheld by Judge Jenkins. The new board of directors passed a resolution asking for Oakes's resignation and the appointment of Ives in his place. When Oakes

[60] W. E. Gardner to Spooner, August 7, 1894, in Spooner Papers. In answer to warnings of the effect his use of the injunction in a labor dispute would have on his reputation, Spooner wrote W. H. Phipps, March 11, 1894 (*ibid.*): "If to be popular with the public and eligible to public office I must be a coward at the Bar, and think as a lawyer of my interest instead of my clients, the price of popularity is altogether too high. I enjoy popular approval as well as any man living, but as a lawyer I must do my duty, or deserve the contempt of decent men, and lose my respect for myself. This I will not do. The argument did not add a penny to my income. . . . It was my duty to do what I did, and with me that is the only question."

refused to resign, they filed a petition for the removal of the receivers. They claimed the receivers had been illegally appointed, that they were friends of Villard and had really been nominated by the management of the road.[61] Judge Jenkins dismissed outright the petition for the removal of Payne and Rouse and referred the charges against Oakes to a master for investigation.[62]

Before taking on the defense of Oakes, Spooner received assurance from him that he had no interest, direct or indirect, in any of the branch lines. Oakes said he had kept in mind from the beginning "the importance to him personally, to his reputation, and to his family, that he should so conduct himself as to be exempt from such impeachment of his integrity." Spooner, in his defense, decided to treat the inquiry as to illegal profits as merely incidental to the paramount question of Oakes's fitness. In preparation for this he requested some officers of competing railroads in the West to furnish affidavits stating "that they always found him not only able and industrious and painstaking, but *alert, zealous* and *faithful* in *advocacy* and *protection* of the N.P. interest." They were also asked to declare that it was important to the receivership and the trust estate "that one of the receivers should have the full and complete knowledge, to be acquired only by long experience, of the physical characteristics of the property." [63] Spooner

61 W. Curtis to Spooner, October 23, December 6; W. N. Cromwell to Spooner, November 29, December 8, 1893; Spooner to J. McNaught, November 26, 1893, in Spooner Papers; *Railway Age,* 19 (January 5, 1894), 11; (February 2, 1894), 73.

62 *Railway Age,* 19 (April 29, 1894), 231; 61 Federal Reporter 546 (*Farmers' Loan and Trust Co.* v. *Northern Pacific*); G. P. Miller to Spooner, January 30, 1894, in Spooner Papers.

63 Spooner to J. McNaught, December 5, 1893; to W. N. Cromwell, January 16, 1894; H. C. Payne to Spooner, January 13, 1894, in Spooner Papers.

was able to get Oakes completely exonerated and the petition for his removal was dismissed.[64]

The Ives group continued its efforts to obtain a change of receivers. Since the Northern Pacific stretched across the continent, it came under the jurisdiction of several United States courts. It was customary, however, for each court to recognize the proceedings of the court which possessed "primary jurisdiction"—in this case the Eastern District of Wisconsin. Judge Caldwell, of the Eighth Circuit, at Spooner's request, had officially done so in November, 1893.[65] Judge Hanford, of the District Court of Washington, and Judge Gilbert, of the Ninth Circuit, declared on September 2, 1895, that the principle of comity did not of necessity apply in this case because no part of the road of the Northern Pacific was in Wisconsin. They then directed the receivers to answer charges of malfeasance one month later. The receivers immediately resigned, not because they were afraid to answer charges but to solve the problem of the divided receivership. They prepared, with the aid of Spooner, a report for Judge Jenkins, which Spooner thought was "the best chance the receivership will ever have to vindicate itself." [66]

Judge Jenkins appointed as the new receivers, Frank Bigelow, president of the First Wisconsin National Bank of Milwaukee, and Edwin H. McHenry, chief engineer of the Northern Pacific; Judge Sanborn of the Eighth Cir-

[64] Spooner to T. F. Oakes, July 11; to W. N. Cromwell, July 11; to J. T. Hanson, October 16, 1894, *ibid.; Railway Age,* 19 (October 19, 1894), 599.

[65] Spooner to W. N. Cromwell, November 15, 1893, in Spooner Papers.

[66] Spooner to W. N. Cromwell, July 5, 1895, *ibid.;* 69 Federal Reporter 871 (*Farmers' Loan and Trust Co. v. Northern Pacific*); *Railway Age,* 20 (August 9, 1895), 394; (September 6, 1895), 442; (September 27, 1895), 467; (October 4, 1895), 490.

cuit confirmed their appointments. However, the District
Judges of Montana, Idaho, Oregon, and Washington refused to recognize them as the receivers and appointed
instead Andrew Burleigh.[67]

Spooner did not take a position with any of these new
receivers although he agreed to advise Bigelow when he
wanted him to, as a matter of friendship. He was still employed by the trust estate and was retained by the old receivers to present the defense of their receivership.[68]

The Northern Pacific receivership was in a chaotic condition. Spooner spent the next two months trying to bring
about some sort of coherence. Failing to get the various
Circuit Judges to agree on a four-man receivership, he decided to submit the controversy over jurisdiction to the
Supreme Court. *Railway Age* pointed out that it was "entirely unprecedented, in the history of receiverships for the
supreme court to take charge of such matters, but the conflict of authority which has led to the appointment of rival
receivers is also unprecedented." Spooner had considerable
difficulty persuading Justice Field to sit on the case but
finally it was arranged that he, with Justices Brewer,
Brown, and Harlan, the Supreme Court justices responsible for the four circuits having jurisdiction over the Northern Pacific receivership, would take up the matter in their
conference room on January 14, 1896. Spooner, assisted

67 *Railway Age*, 20 (October 11, 1895), 503; Spooner to C. C. Beaman,
October 7, 1895, in Spooner Papers.
68 Spooner to J. Scott, November 4; to W. N. Cromwell, December 19; to
H. C. Payne, December 25, 1895, January 24, 28, 1896; to H. C. Rouse,
February 3, 1896; Payne to Spooner, December 2, 1895, in Spooner Papers.
The old receivers were finally relieved of all indebtedness by order of
Judge Lacombe in July, 1896. For his defense of the receivers Spooner got
a special allowance of ten thousand dollars. See 70 Federal Reporter 423
(*Farmers' Loan and Trust Co.* v. *Northern Pacific*).

by Joseph H. Choate and H. B. Turner, presented the case on behalf of the Farmers' Loan and Trust Company, and Silas W. Pettit, general counsel, for the Northern Pacific Company. The latter asked that primary jurisdiction be established in the state of Washington but Spooner insisted it should remain in the Eastern District of Wisconsin. In his argument before the justices he pointed out that if the situation were allowed to continue, the road would soon be split in two, which would be injurious to all interests. The justices sustained Judge Jenkins' jurisdiction and declared that the court for the Eastern District of Wisconsin must be regarded as the court of primary jurisdiction.[69]

Judge Jenkins immediately reappointed Bigelow and McHenry as receivers; the judges of the Second and Eighth Circuits followed his lead.[70] Spooner took a trip west to try to persuade Judge Gilbert, of the Ninth Circuit, to carry out the order of the Supreme Court justices. He took Mrs. Spooner, Willet, and Phil with him. They traveled in a private car furnished by the Northern Pacific.[71] The trip was unsuccessful, for Judge Gilbert, while acquiescing in the Supreme Court decree, left in force the order appointing Burleigh receiver.[72] Judge Jenkins, disgusted with the whole receivership mess, decided he could not consent to

69 Spooner to Justice Field, January 7; to E. D. Adams, January 8; to H. C. Payne, January 28; to J. M. Harlan, January 20, 1896; G. R. Peck to Spooner, January 28, 1896, in Spooner Papers; 72 *Federal Reporter* 26; *Railway Age* 21 (January 10, 1896), 15; (January 17, 1896), 39.

70 W. N. Cromwell to Spooner, February 21; Spooner to W. N. Cromwell, March 1, 1896; memorandum, February 21, 1896, in Spooner Papers.

71 Annie Spooner, Diary, February 5–March 26, 1896, describes the trip. She was particularly thrilled when her husband, learning that she had admired a screen on her visit to Chinatown in San Francisco, surprised her by purchasing it for her; it cost eighty dollars.

72 Spooner to W. N. Cromwell, March 2, 6, 10, 1896, in Spooner Papers.

its continuance any longer and on April 28, 1896, signed a decree authorizing the sale of the Northern Pacific Railroad under foreclosure proceedings.[73]

Spooner was charged with the duty of arranging the purchase of the old company by a new company. Edward D. Adams, heading a committee of consolidated bondholders, had succeeded in reorganizing the Northern Pacific Company and had arranged that it be financed by Morgan and Company and the Deutsche Bank.[74] The company, however, needed a new charter. Since the original company had had a federal charter, Spooner tried to get through Congress a joint resolution recognizing the reorganization of the railroad and giving it the right to acquire and hold any property and branches of the old Northern Pacific Railroad Company. The resolution passed the House but was blocked in the Senate. It was reported to Spooner that the opposition there came from Cullom of Illinois, "inspired through the Armour influence," and from Platt, "because some of his constituents were heavily interested in the securities of the Seattle, Lake Shore and Eastern road." [75] When action by Congress that session seemed im-

[73] Spooner to C. W. Bunn, March 31; to D. J. Crowley, April 30, 1896, *ibid.*

[74] Spooner to W. N. Cromwell, May 12, July 5, 23, 1895; R. Benson to Spooner, February 16, 1895, *ibid. Railway Age*, 21 (April 4, 1896), 186; Daggett, *Railroad Reorganization*, pp. 293–95, 302–10. Earlier, Adams had planned that the securities of the new company should be guaranteed by the Great Northern, in return for which James J. Hill would receive one-half of the capital stock. Spooner was opposed to that scheme and had warned Adams that it would be declared illegal, for such a merger of competing lines was contrary to the laws of Minnesota; see 161 U. S. 647 (*Thomas Pearsall v. Great Northern*).

[75] Spooner to F. L. Stetson, March 30; to E. D. Adams, June 10, 1896; F. L. Stetson to Spooner, March 26; E. V. Smalley to Spooner, April 25; Britton and Gray to Spooner, May 7, June 15, 1896, in Spooner Papers. The bill contained a provision forbidding consolidation with a competing

probable, Spooner suggested they use the charter of the Superior and St. Croix Railroad Company, which he had gotten amended by the Wisconsin legislature the previous year. The amendment authorized the railroad company to survey, locate, acquire, maintain, and so forth, a road from Superior to such point in Minnesota as it wished and thence westward to the Pacific Coast (the words Pacific Coast had been used instead of Puget Sound because the latter would have warned the public of the particular road for which they were working).[76] To be sure that the question of the constitutionality of the amended charter would not later be raised, Spooner arranged for a test case to be brought before the Wisconsin Supreme Court. Quo warranto proceedings were instituted by the attorney general. He claimed that the Superior and St. Croix Railroad Company, since it had stopped building in 1872 and had never completed a road, had been dissolved. Spooner represented the railroad company. The decision, handed down by S. U. Pinney, declared that suspension by a corporation of its business did not *ipso facto* dissolve the company.[77]

Everything was then in readiness for the sale of the

line. Spooner wrote E. W. Winter, May 15, 1897 (*ibid.*), when J. J. Hill was attempting to take over the Northern Pacific: "If Senator Mitchell and some others had not defeated the proposition in Congress to give the purchasers of the Northern Pacific a Federal charter, I think Mr. Hill would have had a long and rocky road to gain control of the Northern Pacific. It is a damned outrage that he should be permitted to take into his clutches that great property, and obliterate it as a competitive factor in the great transcontinental commerce of this country."

76 W. N. Cromwell to Spooner, March 21, 1895; Spooner to W. Curtis, April 11, 1895, in Spooner Papers; *Wisconsin Assembly Journal*, 1895, pp. 885–86, 933, 959, 965; *Wisconsin Session Laws*, 1895, p. 475.

77 Spooner to F. L. Stetson, March 30; to E. D. Adams, April 14, May 23, 1896; F. L. Stetson to Spooner, March 26, 1896, in Spooner Papers; 93 Wis. 604 (*Attorney General* v. *Superior and St. Croix Railroad*).

Northern Pacific Railroad. The first sale took place at the passenger station in West Superior on July 25, 1896. It was purchased by E. W. Winter, the new president of the Northern Pacific Railway Company, chartered in Wisconsin and Minnesota. The receivership was at an end.[78]

Spooner's professional connection with the Northern Pacific was terminated on September 1, 1896. He had faith in the company, for shortly before the sale he purchased 5,000 shares at $12.50 a share. This was later exchanged for 2,500 shares of preferred stock and the same number of common stock of the new company. (A year later the common was selling for $15 and the preferred for $24 a share.) Spooner's three years with the Northern Pacific receivership had been profitable ones for him; he had received over $100,000 for his work.[79] He also considered it a thrilling experience. He wrote Curtis, a member of Cromwell's firm: "What an epoch in a professional way it has been, and what a flood of memories, splendid and fraternal and delightful, as well as of treachery and conspiracy, and dishonesty, it will always bring to a few of us who from the beginning to the end have been in the fight. It has been a wonderful litigation." [80]

[78] *Railway Age*, 22 (July 31, 1896), 92. The sale had to be conducted in the several states along the line of the road.

[79] Flower and Company (brokers) to Spooner, April 23, December 8, 1896, December 21, 1897; Spooner to Flower and Company, July 13; to F. L. Stetson, July 13; to H. Hayes, November 16, 1896; to A. C. Prescott, February 4, 1897, in Spooner Papers.

[80] Spooner to W. Curtis, September 1, 1896, *ibid.*

7 : *Return to the Senate (1896-1898)*

FOR TWO YEARS Spooner had remained aloof from politics. Many of his friends had urged him to take an active part and not to allow matters just to drift along; they warned him that if he continued to do nothing, he might find that someone else would be the Republican party's choice for United States Senator in 1897. Spooner was of two minds about a return to public life. He could lead a much happier, healthier, and more satisfactory life in the practice of law. "There is not much but ashes in a public career," he wrote a friend. "The people glorify you one day, and stone you to death the next, and one is a target for every malicious and envious liar who lives." Yet he was reluctant to leave, as his political record for all time, two defeats for the senatorship and one for the governorship. It was probable, therefore, that he would be a candidate,

* Spooner to S. H. Clough, February 14, 1897, in Spooner Papers.

especially if there were no opposition in his own party.[1]

Former Senator Sawyer kept Spooner guessing whether he would be a candidate. It had been understood at the time of the 1893 election that he had no desire to return to the Senate. Since then, however, Sawyer had become very active in politics; he had attended meetings of the state central committee and state conventions and had been a delegate-at-large to the Republican National Convention in 1896. It was not so much personal ambition that spurred him on to political exertions but rather his desire to prevent control of the party from falling into the hands of La Follette, his bitter enemy since the treasury cases.[2]

Spooner, on the other hand, had never liked the details of party management and, although he distrusted the former congressman from Dane County, he had no personal grievance against him. In reality, they had much more in common than had Sawyer and Spooner. They were somewhat similar in appearance, both very short and with long reddish hair, but while Spooner wore his parted on the side, La Follette's stood straight up, so he was nicknamed "La Pompadour." They had both attended the University of Wisconsin, where debating and oratory rather than studies had been their main interests. Both had been admitted to the bar in Madison and both had, because of their need of money, obtained their first legal experience as a public official. Spooner, however, had soon struck out into a private law practice and had made a fortune while La Follette

1 Spooner to G. F. Hoar, April 19, 1895; to W. H. Burkhardt, December 14, 1894; to L. S. Fisher, May 16, 1896, in Spooner Papers.

2 H. Reed to Spooner, January 3, January 7, 1895; W. H. Upham to Spooner, March 6; H. M. Kutchin to Spooner, March 28, 1896; Spooner to J. D. King, March 2; to J. W. Stillman, December 4, 1895; to P. Sawyer, March 12, 1896, *ibid.*

had remained in politics, keeping his position as district attorney of Dane County while he built up a private civil-law practice. Both had been elected to Congress in the same year and both had been retired to private life by the Democratic avalanche of 1890.[3]

Mutual friends tried to bring the two together, to persuade them to join forces, since La Follette was a candidate for the gubernatorial nomination and Spooner for the United States senatorship.[4] Governor Upham had been an unpopular governor and had been persuaded to withdraw from the race. Sawyer and Payne picked Edward Scofield, of Oconto, to be their candidate. Spooner took no part in the preconvention contest; in fact, he deliberately remained out of the state.[5] He was kept informed of the prog-

3 Spooner to C. S. Crosse, September 1, 1896, *ibid.:* "I have not been able to understand why a man might not be a good friend of Mr. La Follette's and a good friend of mine. I came to Dane county in 1859, went through college here, went from here into the army, and remained here until 1870. The first political speeches of my life were made for the republican ticket in Dane county." See La Follette, *La Follette,* I, 28–34, 51, 65, 90.

4 H. C. Adams to Spooner, March 2, 1896, in Spooner Papers. He was working to get La Follette elected delegate to the national convention from Dane County. "Before I left Madison Phil [Spooner] came to me and wanted to know if I had obtained any promise from Mr. La Follette and his friends, with reference to their attitude towards you and the Administration. I told him that I had not—that I knew Mr. La Follette too well to suggest anything of the kind. I did not tell him that I had enough confidence in La Follette's appreciation of an act of this kind, to feel that he would not be unmindful of it when other questions came up. . . . I can conceive of nothing which would be more prejudicial to you in your candidacy for the United States Senate, than to permit your friends to make a fight on La Follette at this time. I understand that your relations with Bob have become reasonably friendly of late, and I want to see that feeling grow."

5 C. W. Mott to Spooner, June 22; H. C. Payne to Spooner, July 11, 1896, *ibid.* He asked Spooner to get Frank Flower to cease his opposition to Scofield: "I think a line from you telling him about the combine which means the overthrow of you, Mr. Sawyer, and all of us, and that Scofield is the crucial point."

ress of the race by his secretary. Events in the convention were as Reed had predicted. La Follette led on the first ballot but on the third Scofield took the lead and was nominated by acclamation on the sixth. One of Spooner's admirers wrote that two-thirds of La Follette's supporters were also friends of Spooner's and that if La Follette had publicly announced that he favored Spooner for Senator, he would not have been defeated for the governorship.[6] It was generally understood by Spooner's supporters that La Follette was sponsoring Hoard for the senatorship.[7]

The Republican leaders were furious because Spooner had not attended the state convention. Charles F. Pfister, wealthy Milwaukee businessman who had become the unofficial boss of the party and whose hotel since 1894 had been the party headquarters, was "ugly as a groundhog" on the subject. Sawyer was much put out and complained to many at the state convention that Spooner was a coward, that he had left him to carry on the fight alone at the convention for the purpose of sustaining his own position at the expense of those who had befriended him. Even Payne, who had gotten Spooner the receivership job which took him away from the state so frequently, was feverish over his absence and called Reed to tell him to urge Spooner to return immediately. "John will be mighty lucky if he don't find himself shipwrecked when he returns," he warned.[8]

A few days later Spooner returned to Wisconsin from the West where he and his family had been camping in the

6 H. Reed to Spooner, August 4; C. W. Mott to Spooner, September 14, 1896, *ibid.*; *Milwaukee Sentinel*, August 5, 6, 7, 1896. See La Follette, *La Follette*, I, 116–17.

7 Spooner to H. M. Kutchin, April 26, 1896; H. Reed to Spooner, July 22, August 8, 17, 1896, in Spooner Papers.

8 C. F. Pfister to Spooner, April 16, 1894; C. W. Mott to Spooner, July 30, September 14; H. Reed to Spooner, August 17; M. Herrick to Spooner, August 24, 1896, *ibid.*

Teton Mountains in Wyoming. He met former Senator Sawyer in Milwaukee and there, in the presence of Payne and Pfister, they thrashed out the question of the senatorship. Sawyer retracted the charges he had made at the state convention and declared he was heart and soul in favor of Spooner's election.[9] When Spooner made his first campaign speech, in Schlitz Park in Milwaukee on September 20, Sawyer was with him on the platform.[10]

Therefore when the election turned out to be a landslide for the Republican party, it was a foregone conclusion that Spooner would be elected to the Senate. The *Milwaukee Sentinel* on November 8 prominently displayed Spooner's picture with the heading "Spooner for the Senate." In order to stress the unanimity in the party, the editor canvassed the members of the legislature as to their senatorial preferences, and by the end of the month announced that over one hundred had declared in favor of Spooner's election. The editor, in describing the Republican caucus of January 14, 1897, declared:

Never before in the history of the state was a United States senator chosen except to succeed himself without a contest in his own party. . . . Probably none of those who applauded the proceedings tonight will live to see another joint legislative caucus with 119 votes for any one party out of a possible 133 and they will be a long time dead before the chairman of another such joint caucus will announce after a roll call 118 votes for any one candidate.[11]

9 Spooner to M. Herrick, August 31; to S. H. Clough, September 8, 1896, *ibid.*

10 *Milwaukee Sentinel*, September 20, 1896. Two days later Sawyer celebrated his eightieth birthday (see Spooner to J. Hicks, September 18, 1896, in Spooner Papers).

11 *Milwaukee Sentinel*, November 8, 1896, January 14, 1897. See Spooner to A. S. Burt, November 16; to O. E. Britt, November 29, 1896; and to T. H. Carter, January 17, 1897, in Spooner Papers: "It is worth having been turned out in 1891 to be sent back in such a manner in 1897."

The formal election was held on January 27 and Spooner was declared elected, receiving 118 votes, while the Democratic caucus candidate, W. C. Silverthorn, received 8 votes and E. S. Bragg 2 votes. The legislature remained in session while a committee of five was sent to inform Spooner of his election. "If my heart beats too fast for comfort, it is your fault not mine," he began his short speech to the joint convocation. He then paid tribute to former Senator Sawyer and to Senator Vilas, whom he was succeeding. Spooner could afford to be generous to his rivals. To a friend who commented on his forgiving spirit, he wrote: "But life is short. There is 'lots' to do and little time to do it in." [12]

Mrs. Spooner did not rejoice over her husband's election. She wrote in her diary: "I had had enough 'agony' over going & it all did no good—so I have to be philosophical & accept & leave my boys." [13] In Washington the Spooners leased from Admiral Upshur a furnished twenty-room house at 1721 Rhode Island Avenue. It was a big house for only the two of them, especially since they did very little formal entertaining. Mrs. Spooner could be a charming hostess when she wished; there was much wit and sparkle in her conversation. Sometimes she would sit down at the piano and sing to entertain her guests, for she had a beautiful coloratura soprano voice. She held her at homes on Thursdays, as did the wives of other congressmen, but

12 *Wisconsin Assembly Journal,* 1897, pp. 117–22; C. W. Mott to Spooner, February 3, 1897; Spooner to C. W. Mott, February 9, 1897, in Spooner Papers. See *Madison Democrat,* January 27, 1897: "It is the nicest illustration in recent history of the office seeking the man—and would there were more of it."
13 Annie Spooner, Diary, November 30, 1896.

if too many came to call, she complained of the crowds and declared she was exhausted. She avoided as many social occasions as possible, but when she did attend, she often stayed for just a short while and then quietly left. She was scornful of those who preferred fashionable receptions to great music. She even refused the invitation of Vice-President Hobart's wife to meet President and Mrs. McKinley since the date conflicted with an opera performance. The grand opera season in Washington was about the only thing that reconciled her to being away from her boys.[14]

Spooner hoped that this time he would be able to continue his law practice. Charles had, in June, 1896, married his cousin Susie Main and had moved to Milwaukee, where he had become a partner in the law firm of Spooner, Rosecrantz, and George. The Senator had written a friend when Charlie was packing, getting ready to move away from their home forever: "It is the course of nature, and therefore all right, but it nearly broke my heart to part with him." Willet had taken Charles's place in the firm but the Senator felt that was not the place for him and that after a while he would either "have to go with him to a larger place or send him away also." In November, 1898, Willet married Katherine Noyes, a recent graduate of the University of Wisconsin. They established themselves in the family home in Madison; Philip, attending the university, lived with them. Even with Willet as a partner, Spooner was finding it unsatisfactory to be so far away from his law firm. He was frequently irritated because Sanborn did not keep him informed on pending cases. Since he was still

14 La Follette, *La Follette*, I, 85; Annie Spooner, Diary, January 3–February 6, 1899. For a description of the social life of Washington during this period see Julia B. Foraker, *I Would Live It Again,* pp. 256–59.

head of the firm, he felt himself responsible for its reputation. By the end of his first Congress he had decided to dissolve his law partnership,[15] for he found himself busily engaged in public duties and in a position of influence in the Senate.

Spooner was received by the Republican leaders in the Senate as one of the old-timers; he had already served his apprenticeship. In spite of the Democratic victories of 1890 and 1892, which had weeded out so many Republicans from the Senate, there were still some who had greeted Spooner in 1885: Hoar of Massachusetts, Hale and Frye of Maine, Aldrich of Rhode Island, and Platt of Connecticut. These New England states, reliably Republican, had continued to keep the same men in office term after term. Even a few of the Middle Western states, where Populism had made such inroads, had continued to re-elect and re-elect some of the same Senators; Allison, for example, had represented Iowa in the upper house since 1873 and Cullom of Illinois was serving his third term. With seniority the guiding rule of the Senate, these men were in control when the Republican party returned to power. Within this group of elder statesmen there was gradually developing a small steering committee. Aldrich, with his flair for organization, was welding it. As chairman of the Committee on Rules and dominant member of the Finance Committee, he was in a position of influence. Working with him was Allison, chairman of the Appropriations Committee and

15 Spooner to A. L. Sanborn, February 15, March 23; to Willet, April 9; to W. B. Allison, July 27; to S. H. Clough, September 8, 1896, November 29, 1898; to D. B. Cheney, December 3, 1898; to C. Folger, March 20, 1899; H. Reed to Spooner, August 5, 11, 1898; to W. H. Bennett, March 20, 1899, in Spooner Papers.

head of the Republican caucus, and Orville H. Platt, rugged, resolute, straightforward, devoted to principle, chairman of the Committee on Patents and member of the Finance and Judiciary Committees. Spooner was to become the fourth member. For such a comparatively young member that was a tribute. They, however, needed a lawyer, one who could spot the legal flaws in objectionable or foolish measures, one to perfect and to make constitutional the laws they desired. They needed a spokesman to present the constitutional arguments that might win votes for their measures. Spooner had made a name for himself as an orator and, what was even more important, as a masterly debater. They wanted another senator from the Middle West, that region so unstable politically. Yet he must be a sound conservative, one whose economic philosophy agreed with theirs, one who would help bring about business prosperity. The Fifty-fifth Congress saw the beginning of that unique senatorial cabal known as "The Four." [16]

Little time elapsed before Spooner was initiated into the inner circle of the Senate. During the first month after his return he was elected by the Republican caucus to be a member of the committee to reorganize the Senate committees; he was the only new member named to that committee, headed by James McMillan, his old friend and host of the "club" of which he had been a member in the Fifty-first Congress. [17] Spooner was given excellent committee appointments. He received a position on the Judiciary

[16] Stephenson, *Aldrich*, pp. 134–37; Richardson, *Chandler*, p. 542; Orlando O. Stealey, *Twenty Years in the Press Gallery*, pp. 175–83, 390; Arthur Wallace Dunn, *From Harrison to Harding: A Personal Narrative, Covering a Third of a Century*, I, 218.

[17] W. B. Allison to Spooner, March 31, 1897, in Spooner Papers; *Milwaukee Sentinel*, April 2, 1897.

Committee, one he had coveted throughout his first term. Even before he had been formally elected, friends of his had enlisted the support of Senator Hoar, chairman of that committee, for his appointment. He was also made a member of the Committee on Privileges and Elections, on which he had served during the last Congress of his first term, and of the Committee on Rules.[18] He was given the chairmanship of the Committee on Relations with Canada. It was a minor committee but the best that could be given him at that time. In those days when there was no Senate Office Building, any chairmanship was important because it carried with it an office (his was in the Maltby Building). It also gave him one position to fill. To this he naturally appointed H. C. Reed, his secretary, for he was invaluable in keeping Spooner's affairs in order.[19]

The Fifty-fifth Congress had been called in special session by President McKinley on March 15, 1897, to carry out Republican party pledges. As was to be expected, the platform had praised the Republican policy of protection and reciprocity and denounced the Democratic Wilson-Gorman Tariff Act. The Republicans had also declared their opposition to the free coinage of silver except by international agreement, and stated that until such an agreement could be obtained, "the existing gold standard must be maintained." This plank had split the party, for when it was adopted a group of silver Republicans, led by Teller

18 H. H. Rand to Spooner, January 19, 1897, in Spooner Papers. Rand also arranged to get a good seat for Spooner in the Senate. *Congressional Record*, 55th Cong., 1st Sess. (1897–98), p. 942; *Milwaukee Sentinel*, May 6, 1897.

19 Spooner to W. E. Gardner, to H. L. Austin, May 15, 1897, in Spooner Papers.

of Colorado, had walked out of the convention and had supported William Jennings Bryan, who, with his cross-of-gold speech, had captured the Democratic party nomination. The conservative Republicans were aware that they did not have enough strength to put through a gold standard act during this Congress. Even to get passed a protective tariff measure, it would be necessary to have the votes of the moderate silver Republicans. Aldrich therefore allied himself with the other Senator from Colorado, Edward O. Wolcott, who was willing to follow the Republican party platform and work for an "international bimetallic agreement with the leading commercial nations of the earth." In accordance with this pledge the Republicans, with the endorsement of President-elect McKinley, during the closing days of the Fifty-fourth Congress, had put through a bill providing for United States participation in any monetary conference that might be called. The rabid free-silver Senators called it merely a dodge to obtain silver votes for a protective tariff bill—which it probably was.[20]

Spooner agreed that a Republican tariff measure was a must to replace the Wilson-Gorman Act, but he was less convinced than his associates of the benefits of a high protective tariff. He had repeatedly rebuffed the American Protective Tariff League, founded in 1885 to lobby for a high tariff. In 1897 the league was headed by Cornelius N. Bliss, who had become Secretary of the Interior in President McKinley's cabinet.[21] Spooner had turned down the

[20] Richardson, *Chandler*, pp. 526–31; Ellis, *Teller*, pp. 290–91; W. McKinley to Hoar, Chandler, and Carter, December 28, 1896, in McKinley Papers at The Library of Congress.
[21] When Bliss resigned in December, 1898, President McKinley asked Spooner to take his place as Secretary of the Interior. Spooner finally de-

League's invitation to be vice-president and ignored their appeals for money. He felt he did enough for the cause by his work as Senator and by making campaign speeches, and he thought the manufacturers ought to finance all propaganda.[22]

Spooner did present to the Senate Finance Committee the appeals of his constituents. They were numerous and asked for duties on all sorts of products—on lumber, zinc, tobacco, mineral waters, china clay, poppy seeds, sage, cranberries, agricultural implements, and so forth.[23] Other constituents expressed opposition to duties on such things as scientific books and apparatus, gypsum in the rock, naphthazarine black, bleaching powder, and brimstone.[24] He also presented to the committee the opposition of some of his constituents to the proposed nonprotective taxes, ones on tea and beer. The committee felt they were necessary to offset the loss of revenue from the higher protective duties. It was Payne, at the request of the brewers of Milwaukee, who urged Spooner to use his influence to prevent these taxes; he declared that the reaction to a tax on tea would be no less serious than that which followed the attempt of the British government to collect such a tax from

clined the honor as he felt the senatorship was the more important position; see Spooner to McKinley, December 10, 1898; to W. S. Grubb, February 14, 1899, in Spooner Papers; *Washington Post,* December 22, 1898.

22 Spooner to W. F. Wakeman, July 15, 1893, December 2, 1895, February 12, 1897, February 10, 1902, in Spooner Papers.

23 Spooner to M. J. Peck, to J. H. Pierce, to E. R. Richards, March 25; to F. P. Brown, to W. R. Goodrich, March 28; to J. A. Johnson, to W. M. Tanner, April 4; to E. P. Arpin, April 7; to D. Buchanan, May 15, 1897; L. Schneider to Spooner, July 2, 1897, *ibid.* For a history of this tariff bill see Ida M. Tarbell, *The Tariff in Our Times,* pp. 242–58.

24 Spooner to C. K. Adams, March 15, April 4; to G. B. Congdon, to E. Brunchen, March 28; to W. H. Rosenstengel, to E. Reynolds, April 4; to J. A. Kimberley, July 4, 1897, in Spooner Papers.

the colonists. The Republicans would be committing suicide if they levied such taxes, he added. These proposed
taxes were dropped.[25]

The Senate Finance Committee, finally on May 24, reported to the Senate the Dingley tariff bill with many
amendments. With a narrow Republican majority in the
Senate (only 46 out of 90 members) strict party discipline
was necessary. The caucus practically took the bill away
from the Finance Committee. It elected a committee of
three to map the strategy for the passage of the bill.
Spooner was a member of this committee and throughout
June worked late into the night on the tariff bill.[26] Dis-
puted schedules were thrashed out in caucus and compromises reached. Once a majority of the members of the
caucus decided on a schedule, party members agreed to
abide by it. "It is the first time we have ever had anything
like a republican organization and caucus action since I
have been in the Senate," Spooner wrote Governor Scofield. "In order to get a bill through at all we have to vote
together, and in doing that I am voting for some duties I
don't like, and may have to take some bitter medicine before we get through." [27]

The two caucus-adopted schedules to which Spooner was
most opposed were the duties on sugar and hides. The
Finance Committee had proposed a high ad valorem duty
on sugar, which was said to favor the sugar trust. Spooner
insisted he would not vote for a rate higher than the one

[25] H. C. Payne to Spooner, April 6, June 1; J. G. Gregory to Spooner,
May 19; F. A. Flower to Spooner, May 27, 1897, *ibid. Congressional Record,*
55th Cong., 1st Sess., p. 2245.
[26] G. C. Tichenor to Spooner, May 27, 1897; Spooner to J. T. Murphy,
July 4, 1897, in Spooner Papers; *Washington Post,* May 28, 1897.
[27] Spooner to E. Scofield, May 28, 1897, in Spooner Papers.

in the existing law or for a differential a breadth of a hair higher than absolutely necessary to protect the small independent refiners in the country. In the caucus one fraction after another was proposed, and finally the compromise rate suggested by Spooner was adopted. He was still uneasy about it for he felt it meant an additional tax on consumers and additional profit to sugar refiners on all sugar consumed in the United States.[28] He also wanted incorporated in the bill some provision that would make the sugar trust pay duties on their "devilish anticipatory importations" of sugar. He prepared such an amendment but it was turned down by the caucus, for it was felt such action could not be taken on one schedule only.[29]

Spooner fought in the caucus for free hides. The constituent who was most interested in this was Charles F. Pfister, Republican boss. Spooner declared a duty on hides would not benefit the farmers of Wisconsin but rather the beef combine of Chicago. Over the opposition of Wisconsin, Ohio, Pennsylvania, Indiana, and Massachusetts, the caucus voted a 20 per cent ad valorem duty on hides. Spooner accepted the caucus decision and did not speak against the duty on the Senate floor.[30]

On only one duty did Spooner speak in the Senate; that was on the lumber duty, and his arguments were the same as those he had presented in 1890. When accused of being

[28] Spooner to H. C. Payne, to W. Smith, June 9; to A. A. Paulson, June 14; to H. A. Taylor, June 15, 1897, *ibid.*; W. Chandler to E. Wolcott, June 14, 1897, in Chandler Papers at The Library of Congress; *Washington Post*, June 9, 13, 1897.

[29] G. C. Tichenor to Spooner, June 10, 11, 13, 1897, in Spooner Papers; *Washington Post*, June 13, 15, 16, 1897.

[30] Spooner to C. F. Pfister, April 4, June 15; to P. Norcross, June 14; to A. Trestel, July 4, 1897, in Spooner Papers; W. Chandler to E. Wolcott, June 27, 1897, in Chandler Papers.

personally concerned in the matter, he denied he had any interest in any lumber company.[31] Most of the Republicans had agreed not to make any long speeches on the general question of protection but to confine themselves to short debate on items in which their constituents were interested. They hoped they could thereby induce the Democrats to follow this self-denying ordinance, for they knew they did not have the votes to pass a rule limiting debate, even if they wanted to. They were intent on getting the bill through as soon as possible, not only because the uncertainty as to tariff rates hindered business but also because Washington in July was unbearably hot.[32]

More than anything else, Spooner opposed the method by which tariff bills were framed. He did not think Senators really knew enough to frame a good tariff measure. Each Senator was interested in particular duties and voted for the duties desired by other Senators so they in turn would vote for the ones he wanted. The result of this logrolling was a hodgepodge tariff bill that had nothing to do with the general economy of the United States. With the aid, if not the prodding, of George C. Tichenor, a native of Wisconsin who was at that time president of the Board of United States General Appraisers, Spooner framed an amendment which he introduced on July 1.[33] This amendment authorized the Secretary of the Treasury to

31 Spooner to L. S. Tainter, April 28; to H. C. Putnam, May 14, 1897; to E. C. Young, October 12, 1898; National Lumber Company to Spooner, April 14; H. C. Putnam to Spooner, May 27, 1897, in Spooner Papers; *Congressional Record,* 55th Cong., 1st Sess., pp. 1554–60, 2184–86; *Milwaukee Sentinel,* June 8, 1897.

32 Spooner to C. F. Freeman, May 14; to H. C. Payne, June 22, 1897, in Spooner Papers.

33 G. C. Tichenor to Spooner, May 27, 1897; Spooner to G. C. Tichenor, May 28, 1897, *ibid.*

designate three of the general appraisers, only two of one party, to investigate the industries in the United States which received protection and also competing industries in foreign countries. They were to figure out what the duty should be from the point of view of bringing in revenue and also to equalize the cost of production. They were also to see what products of other countries could be admitted free into the United States. They would report to the Secretary of the Treasury, who would then recommend to Congress certain changes in tariff duties. Spooner made a gallant fight for his amendment. It would do away with logrolling; it would eliminate frequent tariff revisions which gave business no rest; it would give the Senators accurate information on a subject on which they were little informed, he pointed out. "The report of a tariff commission would be simply advisory," Spooner explained, "as Congress cannot delegate to any commission the power to make revenue laws, or, in other words, to control the tariff." This amendment was opposed not only by the Democrats but also by members of his own party. "We are becoming a nation of commissions," complained that "damned blatherskite" from Nebraska, as Spooner designated Senator Allen.[34] Since the passage of the bill was being delayed by this discussion, Spooner, a member of the steering committee which was trying to obtain prompt passage of the bill, asked for its withdrawal. "It is difficult to induce Congress to adopt anything that is new," Spooner wrote Joseph V. Quarles. "There are selfish reasons why any scheme for better tariff bills is antagonized."

34 Spooner to E. Colman, June 15, 1897; to H. S. Town, March 14, 1898, *ibid.; Congressional Record*, 55th Cong., 1st Sess., pp. 2166–67, 2292–99; *Milwaukee Sentinel*, July 1, 2, 6, 1897.

He declared that before he left the Senate he proposed to get through something that would lead to a better future for the system of tariff making.[35]

Spooner also aided in drawing up an amendment which would give the President general authority for a period of two years to negotiate reciprocity treaties.[36] It was an innocuous provision, for the President already had that power, and was included not necessarily to promote freer trade but to salvage, if possible, the international bimetallic conference for which preparations were being made in Europe by the commission appointed by McKinley on April 12, 1897. England was only lukewarm to the proposal and France had made her co-operation in such a project conditional on lower tariff duties for her products. The House bill had been unsatisfactory to France. Edward O. Wolcott, chairman of the commission and also a member of the Senate Finance Committee, had, before he left for Europe, secured a promise from the Republican members that the duties on French goods would be lowered. Aldrich, although a high protectionist, had incorporated into the Senate bill lower duties on French products but the bill, as recast by the Republican caucus, had raised them again. In an attempt to save the situation, the reciprocity amendment was included in the tariff bill just before it was passed by the Senate on July 7.[37]

While the tariff bill was in conference, President Mc-

[35] J. V. Quarles to Spooner, July 10, 1897; Spooner to E. W. Arndt, July 11; to J. V. Quarles, July 23, 1897, in Spooner Papers.

[36] Spooner to W. D. Anderson, May 29, 1897; G. F. Edmunds to Spooner, June 23, 1897, *ibid.*; G. F. Edmunds to W. B. Allison, June 22; E. B. Elkins to W. B. Allison, July 9, 1897, in Allison Papers.

[37] Richardson, *Chandler*, pp. 551–56; Stephenson, *Aldrich*, pp. 147–50; J. Hay to President McKinley, May 6, 1897, in McKinley Papers.

Kinley considered sending to Congress a message recommending currency legislation. Mark Hanna, chairman of the Republican National Committee, wired him not to do so. Allison, chairman of the Republican caucus, asserted that nothing could be done concerning financial legislation during that session of Congress, for it would be impossible to keep a quorum in the Senate twenty minutes after the tariff was cleared away.[38] The conference bill was completely unsatisfactory to France, so negotiations for an international bimetallic conference were suspended and finally dropped entirely when the British government in October refused outright to consider bimetallism. The monetary issue was left for the next Congress.[39]

Another measure of interest to the businessmen of the country was the bankruptcy bill. Although the Constitution specifically gives Congress the power to pass a uniform bankruptcy law, there had been only three (1800, 1841, and 1867) and they had been of short duration; the last had been repealed in 1878. During Spooner's first term he had supported the Torry bill, which had been passed by the House but had failed in the Senate. Creditors, Populists, Democrats, and those who feared the encroachment of the federal government into the realm of state jurisdiction opposed such a law.[40] Merchant organizations, such as the Merchants and Manufacturers Association of Milwaukee, urged enactment of some bankruptcy law by that Congress.

38 M. Hanna to McKinley, July 6, 1897, in McKinley Papers; W. B. Allison to W. W. Baldwin, July 15, 1897, in Allison Papers.

39 E. Wolcott to McKinley, August 6; J. Hay to McKinley, August 7, October 11, 19, 1897, in McKinley Papers; W. Chandler to McKinley (copy), September 21, 1897, in Allison Papers.

40 Spooner to H. M. Mendel, April 1; to H. W. Morley, September 22, 1890; to A. J. Frame, January 23, 1891, in Spooner Papers; Gillet, *Hoar*, p. 159.

Businessmen felt that because the financial depression had been so long continued and so widespread only a federal law would aid them to recovery, and the Republicans of this Congress had been pledged to restore prosperity, for the slogan of the campaign of 1896 had been the return of the "full dinner pail." Spooner supported the bill with a brief speech, entirely legal in character. The bill was passed by the Senate on April 22, 1897, with only 8 negative votes, but because of opposition in the House it did not become a law until July, 1898.[41]

Another important act passed by this Congress was the Erdman Act, providing for the settlement of railroad labor disputes. The secretary of the Interstate Commerce Commission had interested Spooner in the measure and the Wisconsin Senator suggested amendments to perfect the bill, got it made a special order of business, which facilitated its passage, and spoke in favor of it during the debate. The bill provided that the Commissioner of Labor and the chairman of the Interstate Commerce Commission could mediate in labor disputes at the request of either party; in case mediation failed, they were to try to arrange for settlement by a board of arbitration. The latter, Spooner admitted, was an experiment but he thought it worth trying if it would prevent the great strikes which brought not only loss to the country but also to the men who were engaged in the strikes. Another provision of the bill prohibited yellow-dog contracts and black-listing of employees by employers. To this section Spooner added an amendment which extended the prohibition of black-listing to

41 J. C. Spence to Spooner, March 29, 1897, February 8, 1898; Spooner to J. B. Cassoday, April 8; to C. D. Booth, April 10, May 16, 1897, in Spooner Papers; *Congressional Record*, 55th Cong., 1st Sess., pp. 601, 626–28.

men who quit as well as to those who were discharged. He pointed out that many men might quit for good reasons and should also be protected.[42]

In light of Spooner's conservative legalistic approach to legislation, it is surprising that he should support a bill which extended the interstate commerce clause of the Constitution to railroad labor disputes, especially where the issue was union membership. It is even more surprising that he did not think that the prohibition of yellow-dog contracts was a violation of the Fifth Amendment, depriving railroad owners of property without due process of law and laborers of their freedom of contract. (The Supreme Court later declared that part of the law unconstitutional.) [43]

The bill had been opposed by Samuel Gompers, president of the American Federation of Labor, for he feared the encroachment of the government into problems concerning labor.[44] It had received the support of the Railroad Labor Brotherhoods and they formally, by convention resolutions, expressed their gratitude to Spooner for his aid in passing the bill. E. E. Clark, of the Order of Railway Conductors, promised to take great pains to see that railroad men in Wisconsin learned of his work.[45]

During the Fifty-fifth Congress, although much of its attention was focused on Cuba and the problems of war, the conservative Republicans had succeeded in getting

[42] John Lombardi, *Labor Voice in the Cabinet*, p. 97; E. A. Moseley to Spooner, March 29, 1897, May 3, 11, 1898, in Spooner Papers. *Congressional Record*, 55th Cong., 2d Sess. (1898–99), pp. 4772, 4848; *United States Statutes at Large*, 55th Cong., pp. 424–28.

[43] 208 U. S. 172 (*Adair* v. *United States*).

[44] Samuel Gompers, *Seventy Years of Life and Labor*, II, 136.

[45] P. H. Morrisey to Spooner, May 5; P. M. Arthurn to Spooner, May 13; E. E. Clark to Spooner, May 4, 14, 1898, in Spooner Papers.

through a major portion of their program to bring about prosperity. They had put into effect the highest tariff rates in United States history, enacted a national bankruptcy law, and an act to prevent disruption of transportation by strikes. They had defeated all silver bills (these had been blocked in the House rather than the Senate).[46] This meant that the United States remained on the gold standard, since the Sherman Silver Purchase Act had been repealed in 1893 [47] and the Resumption of Specie Payment Act was still in force. The election of 1898 gave the Republicans a workable majority in the Senate, making possible the passage of the Gold Standard Act in the next Congress.[48]

By the end of the Fifty-fifth Congress the influence of "The Four" was generally recognized. Albert Beveridge, the newly-elected Senator from Indiana, noted that "the Senate was dominated by a 'marvelous combination,' composed of Aldrich as manager, Allison as 'conciliator and adjuster,' Spooner as floor leader and debater, and Platt as 'designer and builder.'" "Spooner of Wisconsin was the spokesman who sallied forth in the shining armor of his

46 *Congressional Record,* 55th Cong., 2d Sess., pp. 311, 790, 854, 968, 982, 1171, 1309.

47 See Spooner to F. G. Bigelow, March 4, 1893, in Spooner Papers, criticizing the narrow partisanship of the Republicans who refused to vote for repeal.

48 The Gold Standard Act, passed on March 14, 1900, merely put on a legislative basis what had been executive policy for several administrations. It defined the standard unit of value as the gold dollar and declared all moneys would be maintained at a parity with it. Spooner had considerable to do with the framing of the act, for he was appointed to the Senate Finance Committee in December, 1899. That meant that all "The Four" were members of that committee. See W. B. Allison to Spooner, May 13, 20, 1899, in Spooner Papers; N. W. Aldrich to W. B. Allison, May 19, 26, November 2, 29, 1899, in Allison Papers; *Congressional Record,* 56th Cong., 1st Sess. (1899–1900), pp. 650, 1825–26.

genius when the occasion called for a defense of the machine," he wrote. "These men and their disciples ruled the
Senate through the packing of the important committees
with their creatures." [49] Allison, as head of the Republican caucus, designated the members of the caucus committee, which decided what committee appointments
Republican Senators would have; that committee was composed of Aldrich, Spooner, Cullom, McMillan, Lodge,
Elkins, Hansbrough of North Dakota, Perkins of California, and Platt of New York. Allison considered it of utmost importance that no mistakes be made in reorganizing
the committees of the Senate. It was a complicated and
troublesome job to try to satisfy the desires and claims of
various members as to committee positions and Spooner
complained that it took up many of his evenings. Spooner
and Aldrich were also members of the committee on order
of business, which was headed by Allison; since this committee determined the place of a bill on the calendar, it
really decided what bills could be brought up for discussion and to a vote. [50]

With Aldrich's promotion to the chairmanship of the
Finance Committee, Spooner became chairman of the
Committee on Rules. This gave him one of the coziest
committee rooms in the Senate wing of the Capitol, a large,
sunny room on the ground floor, with a huge fireplace. [51]
As chairman, a position he held throughout the rest of his
Senate career, he was really the parliamentarian of the
Senate. The committee was composed of such influential

[49] Claude G. Bowers, *Beveridge and the Progressive Era*, pp. 138, 313.
[50] W. B. Allison to Spooner, November 7, December 6, 1899, February 23,
1900; Spooner to P. A. Orton, December 16, 1899, in Spooner Papers.
[51] Annie Spooner, Diary, February 10, 1899.

senators as Aldrich, Hoar, Elkins, Teller, Cockrell of Missouri, and Bacon of Georgia. Besides being responsible for formulating the rules of the Senate, it also had the disagreeable task of assigning committee rooms. This job Spooner thoroughly disliked; he complained, "I am utterly weary of being the room clerk of the Senate." The office situation was bad. There were only a few decent rooms in the Capitol and most of them were in the crypt, which was cold and damp. Other offices were in the Maltby Building, which was some distance away from the Senate chamber and had been condemned as a fire hazard. Old-timers cautioned new senators not to carry too many books into the building for fear it might collapse. When the Congressional Library was moved into its own building and an appropriation was finally made for the reconversion of the space vacated into committee rooms, Spooner had to supervise this remodeling. Again and again he tried to get an appropriation through Congress for the erection of a new Senate office building, even presenting to the Senate a model of the proposed building, but nothing was accomplished until after his retirement.[52] As chairman of the Rules Committee, Spooner also had charge of allotting space in the Senate gallery for use of the President and cabinet members.[53] In addition, he supervised the Senate restaurant, audited its accounts, gave permission for the purchase of new equipment, and was even expected to see that the rule against serving liquor was enforced. This chairmanship was a very important one while the Senate

[52] R. J. Bright to Spooner, April 29, 1899; Spooner to J. H. Gear, March 8, 1899, in Spooner Papers; *Congressional Record*, 58th Cong., 2d Sess. (1904–5), pp. 3921–23.

[53] J. A. Porter to Spooner, December 11, 1899, in McKinley Papers.

was in session and a vexatious one when Congress was in recess.[54]

During the Fifty-fifth Congress there had been close co-operation between the conservative leaders of the Senate and Speaker Reed of the House, for they were in agreement on the fundamental issues of tariff and currency. When at the end of that Congress Reed announced his intention to retire, they decided to put into that position David B. Henderson of Iowa, a friend of Allison's. Spooner agreed to do all he could to bring about his election, as he wanted the speakership to go to a man from the Middle West and thought Henderson the best of those mentioned; his chief rivals were Joseph G. Cannon and Albert J. Hopkins of Illinois. Spooner was sure he could deliver the votes of the Wisconsin delegation, as Allison, Aldrich, and Platt would see that the Representatives from their states voted for Henderson.[55] Thus "The Four" made certain of their influence in both houses of Congress. Also their dominant position in the federal government was assured as long as William McKinley was in the White House, for he had neither the ability nor inclination to make the Executive the leader nor the initiative to upset the custom of Congressional control.

Spooner had been a little apprehensive about his status with President McKinley. He had not been well ac-

[54] T. L. Page to Spooner, December 7, 1899; see also W. F. Adams to Spooner, April 21, 1906; Spooner to H. Colman, June 27, 1902, in Spooner Papers.
[55] D. B. Henderson to Spooner, May 6, 9, 12; W. B. Allison to Spooner, May 13, 1899; Spooner to W. B. Allison, to D. B. Henderson, May 27, 1899, *ibid.;* D. B. Henderson to W. B. Allison, April 29, 1899, in Allison Papers; *Congressional Record,* 56th Cong., 1st Sess. (1899–1900), pp. 4–5. See Sage, *Allison,* pp. 274–75.

quainted with him before his election, as he had been with the preceding Republican President. In fact, in 1888 he had expressed the opinion that McKinley was of no account except as a tariff specialist. "He is much overrated," he had written his brother-in-law, "and except on that subject does not amount to much." [56]

During the first year Spooner found he did not have the influence with McKinley that he had had with President Harrison when it came to obtaining political plums for Wisconsin Republicans. The pressure for offices had been heavy; during the first month in Washington Spooner had received nineteen hundred letters, most of them asking for jobs.[57] During that year only three bureau positions at the capital were obtained for Wisconsin men.[58] President McKinley did give Spooner the opportunity of offering as an olive branch to Robert M. La Follette the position of Comptroller of the Department of the Treasury, a six-thousand-dollar job. La Follette promptly turned it down and even refused to recognize it as an overture from Spooner; he claimed it had been offered him by McKinley out of friendship, since they had served together on the Committee on Ways and Means in the House. Sawyer, Payne, and others blasted Spooner for making the tender to the former congressman; La Follette is "one who must

[56] Spooner to W. Main, July 11, 1888, in Spooner Papers.

[57] Spooner to A. L. Sanborn, to I. H. Wing, March 24, 1897, *ibid.*

[58] Spooner to L. A. Pradt, April 3; to S. W. Reese, April 8, 1897; to Representative Jenkins, June 6, 1899, *ibid.; Washington Post,* March 23, April 21, 1897. Spooner also got his brother Roger appointed an inspector in the Indian Service. He held the office until 1906, when his resignation was requested by President Roosevelt (see *Milwaukee Sentinel,* June 4, 1897); Elting E. Morison (ed.), *Letters of Theodore Roosevelt,* V, 379.

either whip or be whipped—he cannot be placated," one correspondent declared.[59]

Spooner gave the best of the federal jobs in Wisconsin, that of pension agent in Milwaukee, to his old friend and classmate Edwin D. Coe, who had been elected chairman of the state central committee in 1896, defeating Samuel Harper, La Follette's candidate. He had conducted a splendid campaign, Spooner thought, and as chairman was titular head of the party in Wisconsin. Spooner begged him not to encourage too many to think they could get government jobs.[60] As postmaster of his home town, Spooner got Elisha W. Keyes appointed. That displeased many but Spooner explained to Coe that Keyes had served the party "with a great deal of zeal through many years," that he was getting old and was poor, and it seemed to be "a gracious and decent thing to give him this little lift." [61]

Spooner wanted to satisfy the political ambitions of his old friend Henry C. Payne more than anyone else. Before the inauguration Spooner had visited McKinley at Canton, Ohio, on Payne's behalf to try to get him appointed Postmaster General. In spite of Payne's services as vice-chairman of the Republican National Committee and the backing of Mark Hanna, who had been largely responsible for McKinley's nomination, McKinley refused to

[59] Spooner to R. M. La Follette, July 2; to P. Sawyer, August 5, 1897; R. M. La Follette to Spooner, July 4; C. Ingersoll to Spooner, July 7; M. Herrick to Spooner, July 17, 1897, in Spooner Papers; R. M. La Follette to W. T. Lewis, July 9, 1897, in La Follette Papers at State Historical Society of Wisconsin; La Follette, *La Follette*, I, 120–21.

[60] Spooner to H. L. Humphrey, March 12, 1896, asking him to support Coe for the chairmanship; to C. Carlin, November 16, 1896; to E. D. Coe, April 4, 1897, in Spooner Papers; Secretary of the President to Spooner, August 9, 1897, in McKinley Papers.

[61] Spooner to McKinley, February 7, 1898; to E. D. Coe, February 14, 1898, in Spooner Papers.

appoint Payne. He felt he was unacceptable because of his connection with the Northern Pacific Railroad and his attitude toward labor during the strike on that road.[62] Later Payne was proffered a choice of diplomatic posts but he refused them all.[63]

In 1899 Payne rather hoped he might become Spooner's colleague in the Senate, although he publicly denied that he was a candidate. There were many acknowledged aspirants for the position: Representatives Michael Griffin and Joseph W. Babcock, former Congressman S. A. Cook, Joseph V. Quarles, Isaac Stephenson, and Charles M. Webb, judge of the seventh judicial circuit. Quarles had been prominent in local politics, as district attorney of Kenosha County, mayor of the city, and member of the state legislature. Since 1881 he had devoted his attention to his flourishing law practice in Milwaukee.[64] Isaac Stephenson was in many ways a counterpart of Sawyer, a self-made man who had begun as a timberman getting logs out of the woods and had become one of the wealthiest lumbermen in the state. He had been active in politics since the birth of the Republican party; he had been a delegate to the national conventions in 1880 and 1892, had been a member

[62] Spooner to McKinley, January 16, 18, 23, February 5, 1897; to H. M. Kutchin, February 4, 1897, *ibid.* See Fowler, *Cabinet Politician*, pp. 247–48; La Follette, *La Follette*, I, 118–19.

[63] Spooner protested to President McKinley that notwithstanding the offer of diplomatic posts to Payne, Wisconsin was still entitled to at least one or two of the smaller missions. Finally W. R. Finch was appointed minister to Paraguay, Julius Goldschmidt was made consul general at Berlin, Richard Guenther at Frankfort, and William Rublee at Hong Kong. See Spooner to L. Lienloklen, February 3; to L. T. Pullen, March 25; to President McKinley, April 16; to W. R. Finch, July 18; to W. R. Day, September 30, 1897, in Spooner Papers.

[64] *Milwaukee Sentinel,* September 5, November 18, 1898; J. V. Quarles to E. Keyes, November 25; E. Keyes to J. V. Quarles, December 5, 1896, in Keyes Papers.

of the state assembly, and for three terms a member of Congress. He had contributed hundreds of thousands of dollars to the party's campaign chest and he wanted his reward. He claimed he entered the race for the senatorship at this time because of the solicitation of Sawyer, Payne, and Spooner, and he expected the latter's support, if not his active participation, in the contest.[65]

Many in the party thought that it had been decreed by the powers that be that Payne was to be the one elected.[66] When after five days of balloting the Republicans had not agreed on a candidate, it looked as if Payne's chance had come. Payne wired Spooner: "I think you are in a position to decide contest in Madison in manner that will be to your satisfaction. Your friends and I think you should be here or in Chicago next Saturday and Sunday to advise and confer." Pfister added his plea: "The time has come to do something for Henry." Spooner hesitated and wired Keyes, Taylor, Willet, and others for information. They all replied that Quarles still had a chance of winning. Keyes wrote: "There is no earthly show for Payne under any circumstances. This Legislature would not touch him any more than it would touch contagion, still I think he has got it in his head, and it manifests itself in very many mys-

[65] *Milwaukee Sentinel,* September 21, 1898; *Superior Telegram,* March 15, 1918; Stephenson, *Recollections,* p. 200; I. Stephenson to Keyes, September 24, December 7, 1898, in Keyes Papers. Willet to Spooner, January 10, 1899, in Spooner Papers: "Stephenson says he knows of and appreciates your lack of desire to participate too much if any extent in this fight, but that he knows where you stand (for him, at any rate *prefer* him to any others) and wanted you to take a little more active part. I told him you had a high regard for him—that you had told me that you & Stephenson had been life long friends, etc. etc. but nothing further nor *more* than you told me to say to him if he came here."

[66] La Follette, *Autobiography,* p. 228; G. H. Ryland to E. Keyes, January 26; E. Keyes to P. Sawyer, July 29, 1898, in Keyes Papers.

terious directions." Payne was insistent, so Spooner finally agreed he would try to meet him in Chicago on Sunday but added: "Unable to see what can honorably do without knowing exact situation." On Friday, January 27, Payne wired: "Situation too uncertain to justify attempt which will embarrass my friends and myself. Do not come on." [67]

The legislature adjourned on the twenty-eighth, to meet again Monday night. It was a weekend of intrigue. What took place was "interesting," Payne wrote Spooner, and said he would explain the "true inwardness of the whole situation" when he saw him. Several attempts had been made to combine against Quarles, who was leading in the balloting, and secret conferences of representatives of the four other candidates were held on January 27–28. It was proposed that their supporters hold a separate caucus and that a series of ballots be taken with the lowest one dropping out each time until there was only one candidate left and then all the votes be cast for him. Payne and Pfister refused to enter into the combine against Quarles and the scheme fell through. Evidently the leader in these maneuvers was Babcock, for Payne wrote Spooner that he had had a narrow escape from having the congressman as his colleague. Spooner had supported Babcock for re-election to Congress in 1898 but did not want him in the Senate. Babcock blamed Payne and Pfister for the failure of the scheme and was very bitter against Spooner. Just before the caucus meeting Monday night he withdrew from the contest, the other candidates followed suit, and Quarles was

[67] Willet to Spooner, January 20, 24; H. C. Payne to Spooner, January 24, 25, 27; H. Taylor to Spooner, January 24, 25, 27; E. Keyes to Spooner, January 26, 28; C. Pfister to Spooner, January 24, 1899; Spooner to C. Pfister, January 24; to H. C. Payne, January 26; to H. Taylor, January 26, 1899; to F. Bigelow, February 20, 1899, in Spooner Papers.

nominated by acclamation. The next day he was formally elected by the legislature, receiving 110 votes to 18 cast for Timothy E. Ryan, the Democratic nominee.[68]

Spooner was satisfied with the outcome. Although he had never come out publicly for any of the candidates, Quarles believed he favored his election. He thanked him for his cordial aid during the campaign. "The support of your personal friends in Madison [Philip Spooner and Willett Main] was something to be proud of," he wrote.[69] Spooner was assured of a colleague who would follow his leadership in the Senate. This senatorial election, however, further split the Republican party in Wisconsin, for two of the defeated candidates, Babcock and Stephenson, blaming Spooner for their defeat, joined the La Follette group.

[68] E. Keyes to Spooner, January 28, 30; H. C. Payne to Spooner, January 31; J. V. Quarles to Spooner, February 25, 1899; Spooner to J. G. Clark, May 9, 1898, *ibid.*

[69] J. V. Quarles to Spooner, February 3, 1899; Spooner to J. V. Quarles, January 31, February 10; to E. Keyes, February 17, 1899, *ibid.* In September, 1899, Willet Spooner moved to Milwaukee to become a member of the firm of Lines, Spooner, and Quarles [Louis].

8 : *Spokesman for the President in the Senate (1898-1901)*

"THE BITTER FRUITS OF THE WAR"*

I T   W A S   D U R I N G   the anxious days when President Mc-
Kinley was exerting every effort to prevent a crisis ensuing
from the Cuban situation that Spooner earned the sobriquet "defender of the President." A revolution had
broken out in Cuba in 1895. It was caused not so much by
the economic depression or the colonial policy of the Spanish government, for that was the most liberal period of her
rule, but by the desire of some Cubans for complete independence. A revolutionary junta, organized in New York
City, had, on July 15, 1895, formally declared Cuba independent and had styled itself the "Republic of Cuba." The
revolutionists and the Spanish armies embarked on a campaign that threatened to devastate the whole island.[1] The

* *Congressional Record,* 55th Cong., 3d Sess., p. 1376.
[1] Charles E. Chapman, *A History of the Cuban Republic,* pp. 73-82.

reconcentrado policy and atrocities of the Spanish army under General Valeriano Weyler made headlines for the yellow press, Pulitzer's *World* and Hearst's *Journal*. The American public became very emotional over the plight of the unhappy Cubans.[2] Congressmen excitedly took up the issue. The war party, urging American intervention in the island, was led by Morgan, Democrat from Alabama, and he was supported not only by such independent Republicans as Chandler and Teller but by many so-called administration Senators, Lodge, Cullom, Foraker, and Frye. Opposed to them were the "Big Six"—Aldrich, Allison, Hanna, Hoar, Platt, and Spooner; they rallied around the President as he endeavored to avert a war.[3]

During the special session of the Fifty-fifth Congress, called to revise the tariff, Morgan had succeeded in getting before the Senate for debate a joint resolution recognizing the belligerency of Cuba. It was a political trick; by threatening to delay the tariff bill, the Democrats thought to force Congress to act upon a Cuban resolution. From April 6 to May 20, during the morning hours, the Senators debated this resolution. Spooner had been gathering material— Supreme Court decisions, precedents, and utterances of distinguished statesmen—for an exhaustive argument to demonstrate that recognition of belligerency and independence was primarily an Executive function. The debate ended sooner than he had expected and the call for the vote caught him without his notes. He insisted, however, on making a short, impromptu speech. He appealed to the

2 Walter Millis, *The Martial Spirit*, p. 77.
3 Everett Walters, *Joseph Benson Foraker*, pp. 144–45, 148; Olcott, *McKinley*, II, 28; Richardson, *Chandler*, p. 570; Stephenson, *Aldrich*, p. 152; Oscar Doane Lambert, *Stephen Benton Elkins*, pp. 228–34.

Senators not to treat a President of their own party more shabbily than they had treated one they had so disliked. He pointed out that President Cleveland had been in office fourteen months before the Senators had raised the issue of Cuban belligerency and then they had passed only a concurrent resolution, but now, after President McKinley had been in office only two months, a Republican Congress was trying to force his hand by passing a joint resolution which he would have either to veto or sign. Spooner spoke before hostile galleries and a contrary Senate, which immediately after his speech passed the Morgan resolution with only 14 negative votes.[4] Those Senators who opposed the resolution had, Foraker claimed, "constituted themselves the special guardians of the peace and the deputized protectors of the business of the country." [5] Spooner was accused of being merely the President's understudy in the Senate. This he hotly denied; he declared he thought the President was right in this case and he did not want to see his hand forced and negotiations hampered. He admitted that a recognition of belligerency was not a *casus belli*, but he feared that with the hotheaded Spanish people such a resolution might lead to war. Congress adjourned without the House acting on the resolution, so the President was left

[4] Spooner to I. M. Bean, May 30; to W. Smith, June 9, 1897, in Spooner Papers; *Congressional Record*, 55th Cong., 1st Sess. (1897-98), pp. 1182-84; *Washington Post*, May 21, 1897. Several years later Teller asked what was the difference between a concurrent and a joint resolution and why the former did not have to go to the President. The Chair referred the question to Spooner. He explained that a joint resolution was a rule of action, binding on the Executive Department, and therefore had to be presented to the President, while a concurrent resolution merely expressed the opinion of the two Houses (see *Congressional Record*, 58th Cong., 1st Sess. [1903-4], pp. 438-39).

[5] Joseph Benson Foraker, *Notes of a Busy Life*, II, 18.

free to continue his negotiations with the Spanish government.[6]

The President appointed, as minister to Spain, General Stewart L. Woodford; he was instructed to explain to the Spanish government that the United States was very anxious about the situation, that she had been extremely forbearing but she thought Spain should have, before this, made peace. Within a month after his reception at Madrid, a new government, headed by Práxedes Mateo Sagasta, a Liberal, came into power. General Weyler was immediately recalled from Cuba and a program leading toward political autonomy by January, 1898, was instituted.[7] The crisis seemed to be past when suddenly the American public was electrified by the news that a United States battleship had blown up in Havana harbor. Whether the Spanish authorities were responsible was unimportant to the warmongers; they now had a rousing slogan—"Remember the *Maine*."[8] It was a time of burdensome suspense. One day it looked like war and the next there were hopes of peace. In order that the United States should be prepared for war, Congress put at the disposal of the President fifty million dollars. This appropriation had been passed by the Senate, with every Senator present or accounted for, without debate and by unanimous vote.[9]

[6] Spooner to W. S. Main, May 26; to C. W. Mott, May 29; to G. W. Hazelton, May 30, 1897, in Spooner Papers; Robinson, *Reed*, p. 359.

[7] S. Woodford to President McKinley, June 16, September 14, 1897; A. A. Adee to the President, August 21, 1897, in McKinley Papers; U. S. Department of State, *Papers Relating to the Foreign Relations of the United States, 1898*, pp. 558–61. See Olcott, *McKinley*, II, 1–30.

[8] Spooner to J. H. Palmer, April 9, 1898, in Spooner Papers: "Since the explosion of the Maine it has seemed to me inevitable, unless independence were granted to Cuba, that there must be war, on account of Cuba, and later a settlement on account of the Maine."

[9] Spooner to F. Bigelow, March 9; to J. V. Quarles, to H. S. Town, March 14, 1898, *ibid*.

While the yellow press and the jingoists in and out of Congress shouted for war, President McKinley and a small group of Senators bent every effort to bring about a peaceful settlement of the Cuban situation and the *Maine* incident. The friends of peace—Aldrich, Allison, Hale, Hanna, Platt, and Spooner—met with Assistant Secretary of State William R. Day at the home of Senator Fairbanks; there they worked out the terms of an armistice to be presented to the Spanish government. Their hopes for success were somewhat shaken when they heard that the Naval Commission, which had been studying the *Maine* explosion, would report the next day, March 26, that the cause of the explosion of the *Maine* came from outside the ship, although not necessarily brought about by Spanish agents. Woodford was instructed to try to get the Spanish government to agree to an immediate cessation of hostilities and to accept certain terms of peace outlined in the cable. When three days elapsed and there was no answer, Day, after a conference with Spooner and the President at the White House, cabled that they must receive a reply by the next day, that the conservative Senators feared a resolution for intervention would be passed by Congress unless the President assured them that if he failed in the negotiations, he would submit the facts to Congress.[10] Senators Spooner, Hanna, and Aldrich, with the President and most of his cabinet, waited anxiously the next evening for the reply of the Spanish government. It was very late when the message, in cipher, began to arrive. It was a disheartening one; the Spanish government, while accepting most of McKinley's demands, did not agree to the paramount one,

[10] Memorandum, April 11, 1898, in Chandler Papers; O. L. Pruden to Spooner, March 29, 1898, in Spooner Papers; *Papers Relating to Foreign Relations, 1898,* p. 721.

an immediate armistice. Woodford was still hopeful; he thought he could persuade the government to agree to an armistice if he had a little more time.[11]

While Woodford continued negotiations, the President, as he had promised, prepared a message presenting the problem to Congress. That there might be the closest cooperation between the Senate and the President, Hanna wrote the President:

> I have been talking with some of our friends this morning, particularly Senators Platt of Conn and Spooner. They think . . . it is very *important* that some *one man* (Senator) should be so far taken into confidence and consulted before your message went to Congress that your friends in the Senate for *that* body should be *prepared* to meet the situation and intelligently support your policy. In that connection I have no hesitancy in saying that Senator Spooner should be that man. And I *know* it will cause no jealousies among them.[12]

This letter indicates how much respect and trust his colleagues accorded Spooner.

The President did not follow Hanna's advice and the administration leaders had a difficult time staving off action in Congress as time and time again the delivery of the President's promised message was postponed.[13] When

[11] *Milwaukee Sentinel,* April 1, 1898; French Ensor Chadwick, *The Relations of the United States and Spain: Diplomacy,* pp. 566–74.
[12] M. Hanna to President McKinley, April 3, 1898, in McKinley Papers.
[13] *Congressional Record,* 55th Cong., 2d Sess. (1898–99), p. 3453. On April 1 Senator Quay had introduced a resolution that the Committee on Foreign Relations be instructed to report before April 5 a bill to recognize the independence of Cuba. Spooner to H. B. Turner, April 2, 1898, in Spooner Papers: "Apparently Congress cannot keep its head. It looks at this writing as if a majority had their watches out, waiting for the arrival of a particular hour on Monday, to force the hand of the President, and let loose the dogs of war."

finally the message was sent to Congress on April 11, Spooner was surprised at its tone.[14] After dwelling at length on the terrible situation in Cuba and the interest of the United States in the island, McKinley asked Congress to empower the President to take measures to bring about an end to hostilities and to secure the establishment of a stable government on the island.[15] Historians have described this as a war message and have declared that McKinley surrendered to the interventionists.[16] In spite of the emphasis on the atrocities, Spooner thought that war could still be averted if the President were given the powers for which he asked. This the House resolution did. That resolution would leave to "Spain a *locus penitentiae,* and to McKinley a chance to work it out," Spooner said. Chandler, the leader of the Republican warmongers, declared the House resolution did little more than give McKinley authority to continue negotiations.[17] The President's message and the House resolution, in fact, followed exactly the lines suggested by Minister Woodford in his cable of April 10.[18]

In a long, although extemporaneous, speech Spooner implored the Senate to accept the simple House resolution

14 Spooner to E. Keyes, April 23, 1898, in Keyes Papers; F. Bigelow to Spooner, April 12, 1898, in Spooner Papers: "The President's message is all right but dull."

15 Richardson, *Messages and Papers of Presidents,* IX, 6281–92. Only at the very end did he mention Woodford's wire of April 10, in which he stated that Spain had issued orders for the suspension of hostilities and that an autonomic constitution would soon be put into effect in Cuba (see *Papers Relating to Foreign Relations, 1898,* p. 747; Garraty, *Lodge,* p. 189).

16 Thomas A. Bailey, *A Diplomatic History of the American People* (4th ed.), p. 508; Samuel Flagg Bemis, *A Diplomatic History of the United States* (3d ed.), p. 450; Walters, *Foraker,* p. 150.

17 Spooner to C. F. Freeman and to J. H. Knight, April 23; to F. Bigelow, April 27, 1898, in Spooner Papers; Richardson, *Chandler,* p. 582.

18 *Papers Relating to Foreign Relations, 1898,* p. 747.

rather than the amendments the warmongers wished to tack on its enacting clause. One amendment declared the people of Cuba free and independent and recognized the Republic of Cuba, a second demanded that Spain relinquish authority over Cuba, and a third directed the President to use military forces to carry out these resolutions. A fourth, added later, declared the United States had no intention of exercising sovereignty over Cuba.

Spooner, in his address to the Senate, declared he favored the independence of Cuba, had for some time believed that it was inevitable, but thought it could be brought about without war. He was, however, vehemently opposed to recognition of what he termed "the paper government now called the Republic of Cuba." He declared that it was not a government, it controlled a very small part of the island, and it had not been sanctioned by the people of Cuba. He beseeched the Senators to let the President handle the situation in his own way and maybe war could be averted. He pictured the horrors of war, illustrating with his own experiences in the Civil War; then he added: "Moreover, the war of which we knew was, I fear, little like war of to-day, with the death-dealing instrumentalities of this inventive civilization." Spooner admitted that armed intervention in Cuba was necessary to put an end to the shocking situation there. In a burst of oratory he concluded:

We intervene . . . not for conquest, not for aggrandizement, not because of the Monroe doctrine; we intervene for humanity's sake; we intervene to gain security for the future; we intervene to aid a people who have suffered every form of tyranny and who have made a desperate struggle to be free. We intervene for our own permanent peace and safety. We intervene upon the highest possible ground . . . ; and upon this case we may, although with the utmost reluctance—for we are a people devoted to the arts of peace—go into the war, if it must come, confidently "invoking the considerate judgment of mankind and the blessing of Almighty God." [19]

The President was pleased with Spooner's speech, the press declared that he had magnificently supported the President's policy and that his argument was "exhaustive, profound and brilliant," and some of his colleagues thought it a great pleading.[20] Most Senators, however, were unconvinced by it and passed the Senate resolutions on April 16 by an overwhelming vote of 67 to 21. The House, under the influence of Speaker Reed, a noninterventionist, eliminated the resolution recognizing the Republic of Cuba; the Senate accepted this change. After it was all over, Spooner wrote: "I am very glad we succeeded in beating the recognition of independence, although the resolutions as they were passed are very absurd, and so insulting, being legislative notice to Spain to quit her own property, that it precluded all possibility of arrangement, except by war." [21]

Spain immediately declared these resolutions equivalent to an evident declaration of war, and Congress on April 25 formally declared a state of war existed between the United States and Spain. "It will be no picnic although of course we will win," Spooner wrote Keyes. "But when our people

19 *Congressional Record,* 55th Cong., 2d Sess., Appendix, pp. 286–301; see also pp. 3699, 3702, 3847, 3988, 3993. See Ellis, *Teller,* pp. 310–12, for the framing of the fourth resolution, the so-called Teller Resolution.

20 Spooner to E. Keyes, April 23, 1898; W. B. Allison to Spooner, May 9, 1898, in Spooner Papers; *Washington Post,* April 16, 1898.

21 Spooner to E. E. Bryant, April 23, 1898; *Congressional Record,* 55th Cong., 2d Sess., pp. 3993, 4017, 4032, 4040, 4081.

begin to pay war taxes, and a battleship or so is sunk, and the yellow fever begins to send our boys home in boxes, a lot of the shouters who have been in too big a hurry will get the benefit of the sober sentiment of the people." [22]

The Spanish-American War, although of short duration, revolutionized the attitude of Americans toward the acquisition of territories. It was probably inevitable that the United States should become part of the world-wide scramble for colonies at the time she did. She had expanded to the Pacific and there was no longer a frontier. Her natural resources were being developed too rapidly, her industries were being increased so that they would soon need foreign markets, her capitalists would before long need new financial outlets for investment. Yet it was not the businessman who first realized the time had come for the United States to expand beyond continental limits; this was discovered, according to Julius Pratt, by "historians and other intellectuals, by journalists and politicians." Missionaries, such as Josiah Strong, preached that "on this continent God is training the Anglo-Saxon race for its mission"—the domination of the world; and intellectuals, such as Columbia University Professor John W. Burgess, influenced by the Darwinian theory of the survival of the fittest, taught that Americans were destined to conquer the weaker races and they should be prepared to shoulder the "white man's burden." Politicians scorned a "little America" and insisted that the United States must develop a big navy, acquire naval bases and colonies, or retrogress. Admiral Alfred T. Mahan propagated this idea and Theodore Roosevelt and

[22] Spooner to E. Keyes, April 23, 1898, in Spooner Papers; Chadwick, *Relations of United States and Spain*, p. 585.

Senators Lodge, Foraker, Morgan, and Chandler tried to make it a reality.[23]

Spooner very slowly and exceedingly reluctantly accepted the concept that the United States should acquire colonies. Up to the bitter end he fought the annexation of the Hawaiian Islands. On this issue he broke not only with such expansionists as Lodge and Foraker, who had favored United States intervention in Cuba, but also with President McKinley and with his close associates Aldrich, Allison, and Platt. This was one of the most independent actions of his public career.

It was Dewey's victory at Manila Bay that finally made it possible for the expansionists to get passed a joint resolution annexing the Hawaiian Islands. Throughout the nineteenth century Americans, especially missionaries, whalers, and sugar producers, had been interested in the Sandwich Islands, as the Hawaiians were then called. A treaty of annexation had been negotiated and submitted to the Senate early in 1893 but had been withdrawn by President Cleveland.[24] Senator Lodge convinced President McKinley that the United States needed these islands, that it was manifest destiny that the United States should acquire them. During the special session of the Fifty-fifth Congress (June 16, 1897), a treaty of annexation had been submitted to the Senate but Congress adjourned without taking any action on it. The treaty had been debated off and on during the regular session but had never been brought to a formal vote, as it was clear it could not re-

23 Julius W. Pratt, *Expansionists of 1898*, p. 22; Ralph Henry Gabriel, *The Course of American Democratic Thought*, pp. 339–56.

24 John W. Foster, *American Diplomacy in the Orient*, pp. 98–132, 365–85; Nevins, *Grover Cleveland*, pp. 549–62.

ceive the necessary two-thirds affirmative vote. On March 16, 1898, the Senate Committee on Foreign Relations presented a joint resolution for the annexation of Hawaii, but no action was taken on it until the victory of Admiral Dewey made the islands strategically important. Three days after Dewey's exploit, a joint resolution for the annexation of the Hawaiian Republic was introduced in the House of Representatives and was passed on June 15 by an overwhelming vote.[25]

Spooner was sure there would be extended debate in the Senate on the resolution. He was not aware of the change in attitude toward colonial possessions that had taken place with the outbreak of war. During the debate Spooner spoke several times against annexation. His chief antagonist was Foraker, also a constitutional lawyer. Spooner denied that Congress had the power to acquire territory by joint resolution, and he pointed out that Alaska had been annexed by a treaty and Texas had been admitted by joint resolution but as a state, not as a territory. Spooner also felt it would be undesirable to annex the islands. He feared that in the long run the annexation of Hawaii to the United States would be a detriment rather than a benefit to the people of the islands and not in the best interests of the United States.[26] Less than three weeks after the bill entered the Senate it was passed on July 6 by a vote of 42 to 21. The biographer of Aldrich said that "The Four" had come to an agreement whereby Spooner

[25] Schriftgiesser, *The Gentleman from Massachusetts,* p. 172; Olcott, *McKinley,* I, 376–79; *Senate Report,* 55th Cong., 2d Sess., No. 681.

[26] Spooner to C. Schurz, January 15, asking for his articles on the annexation of Hawaii; to F. Winter, February 14; to W. F. Vilas, June 3, 1898, in Spooner Papers; Walters, *Foraker,* pp. 152–53; *Congressional Record,* 55th Cong., 2d Sess., pp. 6366, 6584–87.

would go on record as opposing the annexation but would not vote against the resolution. On the vote he was paired but announced that he would have voted "nay." [27]

Congress had hardly adjourned on July 8 when rumors of peace led Senate leaders to fear they might all be together again "in that hot box before very long." The President did not call the Senate in special session but did summon Spooner from S'conset to the White House on August 16. It was reported that he was to be asked to be a member of the commission which was to draw up a final peace treaty with Spain.[28] At the conference the President probably asked Spooner to be a member of the commission; if not, he undoubtedly consulted him as to the personnel of the commission. McKinley had already arranged for John Hay to return from England to become Secretary of State, so that Secretary Day could head the commission. Among those the President asked to serve with Day were Senators Allison and Frye and Chief Justice Melville Fuller.[29] Chandler, when he heard that Spooner and other antiexpansionist Senators were to be members of the peace commission, protested to President McKinley. He declared it would be unconstitutional for him to include members of the Senate on the commission since that body would have to act on the finished treaty. The New Hampshire Senator had fought so hard to get the United States into the war that he was unwilling to have antiexpansionists de-

[27] Stephenson, *Aldrich,* p. 161.

[28] Spooner to W. B. Allison, July 27, 1898, in Spooner Papers; *Milwaukee Sentinel,* August 17, 1898.

[29] J. Hay, August 15; W. Frye, August 18; M. Fuller, August 18, 1898, to President McKinley, in McKinley Papers. W. R. Day to Spooner, August 6, 1898, in Spooner Papers, indicates the President knew Spooner's views on the annexation of the Philippines.

cide the terms of peace.[30] After the declination of Allison and Fuller, the President seemed to tend toward the selection of men more favorable to the annexation of the Philippines, which was the major issue. Senators William P. Frye and Cushman K. Davis favored the annexation of the islands and Whitelaw Reid, of the *New York Tribune,* was an outspoken imperialist. The last man selected was Senator George Gray of Delaware, a Democrat and anti-expansionist.[31]

After two months of negotiations with the Spanish commissioners in Paris, the United States peace commission returned with the completed treaty. It was sent to the Senate by the President on January 4, 1899. The treaty adhered to the protocol, which, through the good offices of the French ambassador, had been signed by the United States and Spanish representatives on August 12, 1898. It had provided that Spain should relinquish all sovereignty over Cuba and cede to the United States Puerto Rico and Guam. The protocol had left the status of the Philippines to be decided by the peace commission, and the treaty provided for the cession to the United States of all of the Philippine Islands. This had been President McKinley's own decision, arrived at, he said, after days and nights of meditation and prayer.[32]

By the time the Spanish treaty reached the Senate, Spooner and most of the small group who had opposed

30 W. Chandler to W. Frye, August 31, 1898, in Chandler Papers.

31 W. Reid to President McKinley, August 25, 1898, in McKinley Papers; Royal Cortissoz, *The Life of Whitelaw Reid,* II, 225–27.

32 J. Cambon to President McKinley, July 22; McKinley to J. Cambon, July 26; to Duke Almodovar del Rio, July 30; W. R. Day to J. Hay, October 29, November 2, 3, 11, 15, 25, December 10, 1898, in McKinley Papers; Olcott, *McKinley,* II, 93–112; *Senate Document,* 55th Cong., 3d Sess., No. 62, pp. 108, 119, 129–31.

entrance into the war had been won over to the idea that the United States must acquire colonies. It was a very distressing situation for Spooner. Finally, after painful doubt and hesitation, he had come to the conclusion that the only way to get out of a bad situation was to ratify the treaty. He explained to his old friend Bigelow:

> I tried to put myself in the President's place, to see what I would have done under the same circumstances. I took up each of the alternatives in my own mind, analyzed them and worked them out, and was obliged to reject everything except the treaty. All lines of thought converged to an acceptance of the cession and the acquisition of the title and sovereignty of Spain.[33]

From January 4 until February 6 the treaty was debated in executive session, but the Senators also publicly debated the issues involved in the treaty. The same Democrats who had voted for entrance into the war now attacked the treaty under the guise of debating resolutions declaring the federal government had no power to acquire territory which was to be governed permanently as colonies. Since this was a constitutional issue, and Spooner was one of the leading, if not the foremost, constitutional lawyers in the Senate, he had to reply. Feverish, sick with a cold, and against doctor's orders, he left his bed to deliver his speech, for he had given notice and "either had to speak or flunk." Before a large audience in the galleries and an unusually large number of Senators he defended the administration's

[33] Spooner to F. Bigelow, February 20; to C. K. Adams, February 24, 1899, in Spooner Papers; Stephenson, *Aldrich*, p. 161; O. Platt to President McKinley, August 15, 1899, in Platt Papers at Connecticut State Library, Hartford, Connecticut. He wrote that he would be compelled to vote against any treaty which allowed Spain to keep the Philippines.

expansion policy. He declared the Philippine question was one of the fruits of the war—to him "one of the bitter fruits of the war"—and he wished they were honorably quit of it. He maintained, however, that there was no question about the constitutionality of the treaty. He cited as his authority Chief Justice Marshall, who had declared that the United States, not Congress, had the absolute right to acquire territory either by the treaty-making power or as an inherent element of sovereignty. From that power to acquire came also the power to govern, the Chief Justice had said, and the territories thus acquired were considered property of the United States and the people could be governed forever in accordance with the mandates of Congress. He disparaged Chief Justice Taney's decision in the Dred Scott case, on which the resolution under debate was predicated, and asserted that it was a political, not a constitutional, decision and had long since ceased to be regarded as the law of the land.

After a lengthy and highly technical legal discussion, Spooner explained his own attitude toward the acquisition of the Philippine Islands. He described himself as a commercial expansionist, in favor of extending United States trade and her merchant marine, of building an interoceanic canal, and of acquiring naval bases. "But," he added, "I shrink from the notion that the interests of this country will be subserved by making permanently a part of our land territory thousands of miles away, inhabited by peoples alien to us, not of our blood, not of our way of thinking, foreign to all our associations, living in a tropical climate, where the white man cannot work, under labor conditions of necessity which we would not permit to exist in the United States." With a fervent appeal for the ratification of the treaty to bring peace to this country, he concluded his speech: "Let us take this sovereignty and title, and then do with it what is right, leaving to the people to determine hereafter what the permanent policy of this Government with reference to it is to be." [34]

Spooner was surrounded by his colleagues, all anxious to congratulate him; among them was "Pitchfork" Ben Tillman of South Carolina, with whom he had had a sharp personal wrangle during the debate. His speech was hailed by the press as a notable one, the most logical, comprehensive, and able speech made on the question, one in which he had displayed brilliant oratory, splendid qualities as an advocate, and cleverness at repartee. Some reporters were aggrieved that he had not furnished them advance copies of his speech. He explained that he never wrote out his speeches. He always thought a good deal about the subject, looked up authorities, and arranged in his mind the order of presentation, but he finally formulated his sentences while on his feet. Besides, he was always being interrupted and frequently had to discuss collateral questions. He admitted that he envied those who could sit down and write a speech and then read it or memorize it, but he had become, as a lawyer, accustomed to the other practice and was now too old to change.[35]

Spooner's speech was said to have convinced several wavering Senators that it was not necessary to be an imperialist in order to vote for the treaty. He was not able to win over two of his close friends, Hoar and Hale; the former delivered what Mrs. Spooner thought was an eloquent speech

[34] *Congressional Record,* 55th Cong., 3d Sess. (1898–99), pp. 20, 1376–89; Spooner to J. W. Stillman, February 14, 1899, in Spooner Papers.

[35] Spooner to L. W. Nieman, February 10; to F. W. Kelsey, February 27, 1899, in Spooner Papers; *Washington Post,* February 3, 1899.

against expansion, "Mostly the constitutional aspect.—Partic'ly against the con'ty of annexing a people against their will." Several Democrats and Populists, however, voted with the Republicans, and the resolution of consent to the ratification of the treaty was passed with one vote to spare.[36]

The main problem confronting the Fifty-sixth Congress was the government of the recently acquired territories. Drawing up an organic act for a noncontiguous territory was an entirely new proposition.[37] Although Alaska had been a possession for over thirty years, only piecemeal legislation had been passed for it: laws providing for an appointed governor, judicial officials, and for the extension of the laws of Oregon and some of the laws of the United States, notably the homestead laws, to that region.[38] "We have made a bull in attempting to legislate . . . for Alaska without careful preliminary investigation, and we now have some bad spots upon the statute books, leading to great trouble and some scandal because of it," wrote Spooner.[39]

Congressmen were surprisingly indifferent to the need for establishing civil governments in these new territories. Those who had been most anxious for the United States to enter the war—the Democrats and independent Repub-

36 *Milwaukee Sentinel,* February 6, 1899; Annie Spooner, Diary, January 9, February 6, 1899; *The Nation,* February 9, 1899.

37 Spooner to F. Bigelow, May 17, 1898, in Spooner Papers: "It is quite evident now that the best statesmanship of this country will be taxed in solving some of the questions which the war will leave upon us, problems new to us."

38 *Congressional Record,* 55th Cong., 2d Sess., pp. 456, 2368, 2463–64; 56th Cong., 1st Sess. (1899–1900), pp. 3119–20. See *United States Statutes at Large,* 56th Cong., p. 321.

39 Spooner to J. G. Gregory, January 29, 1901, in Spooner Papers.

licans—now washed their hands of the fruits of the war. The bills were repeatedly postponed as Senators declared there was no need wasting time discussing them while there was more important legislation pending. When the bills were finally brought up for debate, so many Senators absented themselves that calls for a quorum were frequent. Spooner, one of those most opposed to the expansion of the United States and her entrance into the war, took a leading part in the framing of the government bills. For that he has been branded as an imperialist. He had not approved of the annexation of the new territories but, since they had been annexed, he bowed to the decision of the majority and helped to construct their governmental framework. The impress of his political ideas is seen on every one of what might be called the constitutions of these new territories—the Hawaiian Government Act, the Foraker Act for Puerto Rico, the Spooner Amendment for the Philippines, and the Platt Amendment for Cuba.

Spooner, on the whole, approved of the Hawaiian government bill presented by Senator Cullom, who had been a member of a commission sent by President McKinley to the islands. He praised especially the provision which declared that the laws of Hawaii not inconsistent with the Constitution of the United States and the organic act should remain in force. It is wise, he said, to "leave in force the laws which are peculiar to their conditions over there, . . . the perpetuation of customs peculiar to that people, to that climate, and to their former organization, property rights, and all that." [40]

He was opposed to the amendment providing for a com-

[40] Cullom, *Fifty Years,* pp. 287–89; *Congressional Record,* 56th Cong., 1st Sess., pp. 89, 1559, 1918–33, 2190–91, 2391–98.

plete civil government for Puerto Rico, which Foraker, chairman of the new Committee for Pacific Islands and Puerto Rico, added to the House bill. The latter had merely made provision for the collection of import duties. Spooner declared that he thought no organic act should be framed for a territory until after a Congressional committee had visited the region and made a careful study of local conditions.[41]

To both government bills Spooner suggested several improvements that were adopted. The major changes dealt with the judicial systems. In the Hawaiian bill he helped Platt of Connecticut frame an amendment which provided that the judges of the Hawaiian courts should be appointed by the President with the consent of the United States Senate, instead of by the governor and senate of the island. He insisted that there should be a federal district court in both territories. The original Foraker bill had attached Puerto Rico to the Second Circuit without an intermediary federal court. The final act provided for a district court with appeals directly to the Supreme Court.[42]

Spooner particularly objected to the suffrage provision in the Hawaiian bill, for it required ownership of property for those voting for members of the senate. He declared that he would not vote "for any proposition which gives intelligent men no right to vote unless, in addition to intelligence, they own property." It was finally decided that there should be no property requirement, but that to be eligible to vote, a man should be able to speak, read, and write English or Hawaiian. He vehemently protested the pro-

---

41 *Congressional Record*, 56th Cong., 1st Sess., p. 2469; Walters, *Foraker*, pp. 161–73.

42 *Congressional Record*, 56th Cong., 1st Sess., pp. 1981–89, 2190–99, 3082.

visions conferring United States citizenship on the citizens of the Hawaiian Republic and on Puerto Ricans. He was able to get the latter provision eliminated. He was willing that Hawaii be given a territorial government based on our traditional policy, but he did not want Hawaii ever to be admitted as a state and he hoped it might eventually become independent again. He was even more opposed to the idea that Puerto Rico might become a state, and he fought against permitting it to send a delegate to Congress, as territories heretofore had done, for that might be considered a sort of pledge of future statehood. Instead, Puerto Rico was allowed to send a resident commissioner.[43]

It was the tariff issue that presented the difference in the constitutional status of the two new possessions. The argument came up only in connection with Puerto Rico, for the Hawaiian Islands were immediately incorporated into the United States customs system. President McKinley in his message to Congress in December, 1899, had declared it was "the plain duty" to inaugurate free trade between Puerto Rico and the United States. There was considerable opposition to this in the House so a compromise was reached. Instead of taxing goods coming into the United States from Puerto Rico the full tariff rates as prescribed by the Dingley Act of 1897, duties amounting to only 15 per cent of those rates were to be assessed. The money collected was to be put into a separate fund in the United States Treasury to be spent to maintain the government of the island. The President privily gave his support to this provision.[44] Advocates of free trade claimed that Republi-

[43] *Ibid.,* pp. 2243–45, 3632; *Washington Post,* February 21, 27, 1900.
[44] Olcott, *McKinley,* II, 215–19; Spooner to M. B. Rosenberry, May 4, 1900, in Spooner Papers.

cans who supported the compromise were defying the President. Spooner and Foraker urged McKinley to send a message to Congress to clarify the issue but he was unwilling to do so. To obtain passage of the Puerto Rican bill, it was necessary to employ the party caucus and to include in the bill a provision that free trade would be established as soon as the Puerto Rico legislature made provision for local taxes.[45]

Spooner was selected to expound the constitutional issues involved in the Republican colonial policy, to make clear whether the Constitution *in toto* applied to the territories. The specific clause in the Constitution which was under dispute was that (Art. I, sec. 8, clause 1) which declares that all duties "shall be uniform throughout the United States." Spooner began: "The Constitution does not follow the flag, . . . the flag follows the Constitution." That issue had been raised at the time of the Louisiana Purchase in 1803 and Congress then had decided that the Constitution did not by its own force go into the territories. Spooner pointed out that there had been many laws and many Supreme Court decisions that had not been applied to the territories; whenever the Constitution was extended by statute to the territories, it had gone there as

---

[45] *Washington Post*, March 13, 21, 1900; *Madison Democrat*, March 14, 1900; Spooner to G. W. Hazelton, May 5, 1900; to H. Fink, March 19, 1900, in Spooner Papers: "I think the attitude of the newspapers is not very strange. When the President came out for 'the plain duty of free trade' most all the republican papers, of course, lined up to it. Most all of the free trade democratic papers did, because they are for free trade anyhow everywhere. The newspapers cannot change with the same facility that Presidents and Members of Congress can, and it came about that while the President was under cover helping to pass the House bill the newspapers of the country were damning the men who were voting for it and supporting it, as being in opposition to the President. All together it is a mess."

a statute, not as the Constitution. "Puerto Rico belongs to the United States," he declared. "We obtain our right from the Constitution to legislate for Puerto Rico. I do not think the Constitution *ex proprio vigore* extends over Puerto Rico." As he finished his speech applause broke out in the galleries but the presiding officer quickly squelched it.[46]

A year later, on May 27, 1901, the Supreme Court, in the *Downes* v. *Bidwell* case, confirmed the views on the relationship of Puerto Rico and the United States expressed by Spooner; in fact, many claimed that the opinion was largely a restatement of his argument in the Senate. The Court recognized two sorts of territories, incorporated and non-incorporated. In the first, the Constitution, *ex proprio vigore,* extends over it; in the second, the fundamental parts of the Constitution (which were not defined) automatically apply to the territory but other parts could be applied by Congress whenever it wished to do so. The uniformity tax clause was considered a formal part of the Constitution. Spooner, although he could not see any sense in the notion of different kinds of territories, approved the decision. He was afraid that if the territories became integral parts of the United States and their citizens became United States citizens, there would be no way in which the territories could ever be given their independence.[47]

Although many acts reflect Spooner's legal and political

[46] *Congressional Record,* 56th Cong., 1st Sess., p. 3220; see also pp. 3217–23, 3623–35; *Washington Post,* April 3, 1900.

[47] 182 U. S. 244; *Milwaukee Sentinel,* September 9, 1901; Spooner to C. K. Adams, June 13, 1901, in Spooner Papers. See Walters, *Foraker,* p. 173, who says that Justice Brown's remarks revealed the influence of Spooner, Root, and Foraker.

ideas, only two measures bear his name. One of these was passed at the very end of the Fifty-sixth Congress and provided for the establishment of civil government in the Philippines. Spooner was not even a member of the Senate Committee on the Philippines. It had been reported that he had been urged by the caucus committee on committees to accept the chairmanship of that Senate committee but he preferred the Committee on Rules. Beveridge of Indiana had had fond hopes that he would receive the chairmanship; he considered himself an authority on the Philippines, for he had made a fleeting visit to the islands between his election and his first session. The chairmanship, however, had been given to Henry Cabot Lodge of Massachusetts.[48]

The Philippine archipelago was the most difficult possession for which to provide a government. Not only was it the most distant and least known, but the situation was further complicated by a revolt led by Emilio Aguinaldo, who had expected the United States to recognize him as head of an independent Philippine government. President McKinley had sent a civil commission, headed by Jacob Gould Schurman, of Cornell University, to study conditions in the islands. It had arrived after hostilities had broken out so it had not been recognized by the military authorities. Major General Elwell S. Otis had insisted that the war must be prosecuted until the insurgents submitted and only then could civil government be established. The commission, in its report to the President, stated that the people of the islands did not desire immediate independence but considerable self-government and it recommended

48 *Milwaukee Sentinel,* December 15, 1899; Bowers, *Beveridge,* pp. 112–16.

that, pending action by Congress, the President inaugurate a form of civil government.[49]

Spooner, early in the first session of the Fifty-sixth Congress, introduced a bill providing that, after the insurrection was suppressed and until Congress acted, all military, civil, and judicial power necessary to govern the islands should be vested in the President. (It was practically a copy of the bill passed for Louisiana in 1803.) The bill, without amendment, was reported out by Lodge on March 5, 1900. Morgan called it a "dangerous measure. . . . It takes from the President his present ample power under the Constitution and law of nations to introduce civil government in these islands, and changes it to power granted by act of Congress," he maintained.[50]

Spooner in a three-day speech defended his proposal. He explained:

It [the bill] recognizes that we acquired the archipelago by the treaty. It assumes the fact that we will enforce obedience to our authority over there, and then provides, after the war shall have ended, for a government by the President, through his appointees (not to be permanent, not to make the President a proconsul) until *Congress shall otherwise provide*. . . .

The President has the power now and it will continue until Congress acts, under the war power, to establish a government and maintain it.

My purpose in this bill was first to show to the people that the Congress is behind the Administration in the Philippines. . . . Moreover, I thought that Congress ought to put this measure of authority behind the President, when insurrection

[49] Olcott, *McKinley*, II, 173–79, 181–84; W. Cameron Forbes, *The Philippine Islands*, I, 74–76, 93–94, 119–23.

[50] J. T. Morgan to President McKinley, April 4, 1900, in McKinley Papers; *Milwaukee Sentinel*, January 12, 1900.

shall have been suppressed, in governing a people seven thousand miles away, ten million comparative strangers.[51]

Congress took no action before it adjourned for the summer recess. The situation in the Philippines had changed considerably by the time Congress convened in December for the short session. American troops had captured most of the towns, General Arthur MacArthur had been made military governor of the islands, and a second civil commission, headed by Judge William Howard Taft, had arrived in Manila. The military governor was the chief executive, but the commission had control over appropriations and many appointments and, after September 1, all legislative power. Relations between the military and civil authorities were anything but harmonious.[52] Taft, on January 2, 1901, cabled Secretary of War Root: "Passage of Spooner bill . . . greatly needed to secure best results from improving conditions. Until its passage no purely central, civil government can be established; no public franchises of any kind granted, and no substantial investment of private capital in internal improvements possible." [53]

On January 18 Spooner called the Senate's attention to the fact that it still had done nothing about a government for the Philippines although it had legislated for the other territories. He admitted that Congress was not ready to frame detailed laws for the Philippines and would not be until a joint Congressional committee had been sent to

51 *Congressional Record,* 56th Cong., 1st Sess., p. 5961, see also pp. 2767–71, 5895–5903, 5950–61; *The Nation,* May 31, 1900.
52 Forbes, *Philippine Islands,* I, 102–4, 124–29; Philip C. Jessup, *Elihu Root,* I, 354–58.
53 W. H. Taft to E. Root, January 2, 4, 1901, in McKinley Papers; see Chamber of Commerce of Manila to McKinley, January 30, 1901, *ibid.*

investigate conditions on the spot.[54] Instead of calling up his original bill, Spooner redrafted it in the form of an amendment to be added to the Army Appropriation bill.[55] He made no long speeches in support of his amendment for fear passage might be delayed and an extra session have to be called.[56] Although there was considerable opposition to the passage of such a measure as an amendment to an appropriation bill, it was adopted by the Senate on February 27 by a strictly party vote, and by the House on March 1. The next day President McKinley directed that the power to govern the Philippines be vested in the same persons who had been exercising it. The Spooner Amendment had merely changed the basis for the authority of the commission from that of the military power of the President as Commander-in-Chief, to his civil authority as President of the United States.[57]

Attached to the same Army Appropriation bill was an amendment defining relations between the United States and Cuba. This amendment bears the name of Orville H. Platt but Spooner was coframer. Cuba was not a possession, but in the Treaty of Paris the United States had agreed to "assume and discharge the obligations that may under in-

[54] *Congressional Record*, 56th Cong., 2d Sess. (1900–1901), pp. 1170–71.

[55] *Ibid.*, pp. 2117, 2955–56, 3025, 3141, 3145; *Washington Post*, February 9, 1901. To the original amendment Senator Hoar added a provision limiting the granting of franchises. See Jessup, *Root*, I, 358, who claims that the Spooner Amendment was drafted by Root and cites a letter from Adjutant General Corbin to Spooner, February 8, 1901. Yet the amendment was based on a bill introduced by Spooner a year earlier.

[56] Spooner to T. F. Barr, March 9, 1901, in Spooner Papers.

[57] *Washington Post*, February 28, March 2, 1901; memorandum, March 2, 1901; E. Root to W. H. Taft, June 20, 1901, in McKinley Papers. Aguinaldo was captured in April and on July 4, 1901, civil government was inaugurated in the Philippines.

ternational law result from the fact of its occupation, for the protection of life and property." [58] With the evacuation of the Spanish troops on January 1, 1899, the United States had established a military regime, first under General John R. Brooke and then under General Leonard Wood. The only basis of authority in Cuba was the law of belligerent right over conquered territory, and the only lawful authority until Congress acted was the President of the United States as Commander-in-Chief.[59]

A new standing committee had been set up in the Senate to deal with legislation concerning Cuba. Platt was chairman and associated with him were Aldrich, Spooner, Cullom, McMillan, and Chandler. It is interesting to note that most of these men had tried to prevent United States interference in the Cuban insurrection. During the summer Platt, Aldrich, and Spooner had worked on the Cuban problem; the New Englanders had visited Cuba and had sent Spooner reams of reports and documents to study. Immediately after the election Platt called a meeting of the Republican members of the committee to map their program for the short session of Congress.[60] They hoped that the convention meeting in Cuba to draw up a constitution would also formulate a statement of relations between

[58] *Senate Document,* 57th Cong., 1st Sess., No. 182; Coolidge, *Platt,* p. 326. Concerning the necessity for framing some measure for Cuba, Platt wrote: "It is right that I should do it, and when I look the Senate over there seems to be no one to do it, or I might say, that can do it, except Spooner and myself."

[59] McKinley to J. R. Brooke, December 22, 1898; R. Alger to W. McKinley, July 31, 1899, in McKinley Papers.

[60] O. H. Platt to Spooner, July 26, August 14, 16, 18, 30, October 6, November 8, 1900, in Spooner Papers; O. H. Platt to N. Aldrich, September 28, October 6, 18, 29, 1900, in Aldrich Papers; Stephenson, *Aldrich,* p. 166; *Washington Post,* December 14, 1899.

Cuba and the United States, but in case it did nothing they would have to do so.[61]

Time was short, for Congress had to adjourn on March 4. The Republican members of the Committee on Relations with Cuba met at Chandler's home two Sunday afternoons (February 3, 10). Resolutions defining the relationship between Cuba and the United States were outlined; the final drafting was left to Platt and Spooner, the latter because he was the "master of parliamentary phraseology." During the discussion, Chandler, the Senator who had been so sympathetic to the plight of the Cubans in 1898, suggested Cuba should be required to issue bonds amounting to $100 million to pay for the war. He thought Spooner rather naïve when he objected and said the United States should not ask money for freeing Cuba.[62]

In order to avert an extra session it was decided to incorporate the resolutions into an amendment to the Army Appropriation bill. Thus it was the Platt Amendment

[61] Chapman, *Cuban Republic,* pp. 131–34; Jessup, *Root,* I, 306–12; E. Root to J. Hay, January 11; to L. Wood, February 9, 21, 1901, in McKinley Papers.

[62] O. H. Platt to Spooner, February 1, 1901, in Spooner Papers; Richardson, *Chandler,* pp. 604–5; Coolidge, *Platt,* pp. 339–40. See Lambert, *Elkins,* pp. 238–42, for Elkins' plan to admit Cuba as a state. Later when Root was given credit for the Platt Amendment, Platt wrote to C. H. Clark, editor of the *Hartford Courant* (see O. H. Platt to C. H. Clark [copy] January 1, 1904, in Spooner Papers): "It is not a matter that I care enough about to make an issue of but Mr. Wellman is a little off. The letter of instructions to Gen. Wood was written by Secretary Root after the 'Platt' amendment had been considered by the republican members of the Cuban Committee. The original draft was my own, and contained substantially the terms on which the withdrawal of American forces was to take place as shown in the instructions to Wood. It was changed from time to time, somewhat in language but not in spirit, in consultations both with the republicans of the committee, President McKinley, and Secretary Root. A final consultation between myself and Senator Spooner put the document in its complete form."

rather than the Platt Act which governed relations with Cuba from 1901 to 1934. It limited the sovereignty of Cuba by preventing her from entering into treaties with foreign powers, which might impair her independence, and by limiting her public debt. It also gave to the United States the right to intervene in the island and the right to lease naval bases.[63] These resolutions were finally, although reluctantly, accepted by the Cuban constitutional convention and were later incorporated into a treaty.[64] Not only Cubans but many Europeans and some Americans looked on the Platt Amendment as another evidence of United States imperialism. Spooner, however, felt it was the first step in paving the way toward Cuban independence, which he thought should be granted as soon as possible.[65]

Imperialism had been the major issue in the election of 1900. There had been no question about the stand the Republican party would take. The platform, about which Spooner had been consulted before it had been taken to the national convention at Philadelphia, was unanimously adopted. There was also no doubt as to the presidential nominee—McKinley was the only candidate. It was the vice-presidency that threw Mark Hanna, chairman of the national committee, into a panic and caused him to sum-

[63] M. Hanna to W. McKinley, February 14; E. Root to W. McKinley, February 27, 1901, in McKinley Papers; *Congressional Record,* 56th Cong., 2d Sess., pp. 2954, 3145–52.

[64] O. H. Platt to Spooner, April 21; G. B. Cortelyou to Spooner, April 23; E. Root to Spooner, May 21, 1901, in Spooner Papers; *Milwaukee Sentinel,* May 31, 1901. Spooner had to make several trips to Washington during April and May to meet with representatives of the Cuban constitutional convention. Elections held in December, 1901, resulted in the choice of Tomás Estrada Palma as president, and the United States Army withdrew on May 20, 1902.

[65] Spooner to F. O. Holt, May 6, 1902, in Spooner Papers.

mon friends of the President to the Quaker City.[66] The rank and file of the delegates wanted Theodore Roosevelt, the "Rough Rider" Governor of New York. Payne, vice-chairman of the national committee, and the political bosses of New York and Pennsylvania, T. C. Platt and Matt Quay, were in accord with this enthusiasm. Not that the latter two liked Roosevelt, but they wanted to embarrass the administration and Platt wanted to get "Teddy" out of the governor's chair. Roosevelt, however, refused to commit himself on the subject of that national office.[67]

Spooner was summoned from Wisconsin so the friends of the President could decide if they should yield on this issue. Besides Hanna and Spooner there were at these conferences Senators Allison, Burrows, Fairbanks, and Lodge, Postmaster General Charles E. Smith, and Henry C. Payne. At the request of President McKinley they decided to let the convention delegates select the candidate for the second place on the ticket. Spooner believed, however, that if Roosevelt had not appeared at the convention or had been firm in his insistence that he did not want the office, John B. Long, Secretary of the Navy, would have been nominated.[68]

In Wisconsin imperialism was not the issue in 1900; in fact, the real contest was not between the Republican and Democratic parties but within the Republican party itself, and there the question was the position of Robert M. La

66 M. Hanna to Spooner, May [no day], 1900; H. Reed to C. E. Tobey, June 17, 1900, *ibid*.

67 H. C. Payne to T. Roosevelt, February 2, 8, 1900, in Roosevelt Papers at The Library of Congress; Henry F. Pringle, *Theodore Roosevelt*, pp. 222-23.

68 Charles G. Dawes, *A Journal of the McKinley Years*, pp. 232-33; *Washington Post*, June 20, 1900; Spooner to J. B. Long, June 29, 1900, in Spooner Papers.

Follette. He had, by the beginning of the century, won a large following for his progressive program, the central plank of which was the direct primary. He maintained that the old caucus-convention system was too easily controlled by the bosses, and suggested instead that candidates for all offices be nominated in a preliminary election to be held by both parties on the same day. It was a new idea and had never been tried on a large scale. Since 1897 he had flooded the state with material on the subject and had made the circuit of county fairs explaining his program.[69] Several of the reforms he advocated had been incorporated into the Republican party platform in 1898 and two of his followers had been nominated: James O. Davidson as treasurer and Emmett Hicks as attorney general. La Follette, however, had been defeated by Governor Scofield for the gubernatorial nomination.[70]

La Follette and his supporters, since their former technique had not succeeded, decided this time to try the policy of conciliation. When La Follette announced his candidacy for the governorship on May 16, he did so with a declaration of harmony. Although Spooner and his friends had no faith in these "peace proposals," no one of them was anxious to lead the fight against La Follette. Philetus Sawyer, his bitterest enemy, had died in March. Payne, tired and not very well, had won what he most de-

[69] Allen Fraser Lovejoy, *La Follette and the Establishment of the Direct Primary in Wisconsin, 1890–1904*, pp. 17, 37–41; La Follette, *La Follette*, I, 121–23.

[70] *Milwaukee Sentinel*, August 18, 1898. Spooner played some part in Scofield's renomination. Many leaders considered dropping Scofield since he was very unpopular but Spooner, in a public statement, came out for his re-election. Spooner also had recommended that no concessions be made to the La Follette group either in platform or offices (see E. Coe to Spooner, April 19; H. C. Payne to Spooner, August 8; Spooner to E. Coe, May 3; to J. Stone, August 12, 1898, in Spooner Papers).

sired, reappointment on the national committee. Spooner, hating party fights, was not a political strategist and whenever possible had shunned such party councils and party conventions. Spooner's absences so annoyed Pfister that the latter wrote Payne: "I see no reason why I, who has no political ambition at all should do the fighting for others. John Spooner has the most at stake and ought to be the leader." Neither Payne, Pfister, nor Spooner endorsed any of the men who had announced their candidacy for the gubernatorial nomination, so one by one the aspirants withdrew from the race.[71]

In this campaign La Follette had two new supporters— two of the defeated senatorial candidates of 1899 who had sworn they would get even with the Payne-Pfister-Spooner combination. Congressman Babcock also hoped to replace Payne on the national committee and later to take Spooner's place in the Senate. Stephenson, whom the La Follettes regarded as a genuine convert to the progressive cause, claimed he was responsible for La Follette's agreeing to run for a third time. He had promised to finance him and had put up a dummy candidate, Senator De Wayne Stebbins, to aid him in his preliminary campaign, with the understanding that after he had canvassed the northern part of the state, he would withdraw in La Follette's favor.[72]

71 E. Keyes to Spooner, May 6, 21; Spooner to F. A. Dennett, May 19; H. C. Payne to H. Fink, June 4; C. Pfister to H. Fink, June 8, 1900, in Spooner Papers; Barton, *La Follette*, pp. 152–53.
    72 E. D. Coe to Spooner, December 4, 1899; Spooner to H. C. Payne, February 19; to F. Bigelow, February 20, 1900, in Spooner Papers; H. A. Taylor to E. Keyes, December 5, 1899; E. Keyes to Spooner, March 28; to H. A. Taylor, April 9, 1900, in Keyes Papers; H. B. Tanner to La Follette, July 10; J. W. Babcock to La Follette, July 12, 1900, in La Follette Papers at the State Historical Society of Wisconsin; Stephenson, *Recollections*, pp. 215–16.

The last obstacle to La Follette's nomination was removed by the announcement on July 5 that Spooner would not be a candidate for re-election. In preceding campaigns party leaders had argued that if La Follette were elected governor, he would then try to replace Spooner in the Senate.[73] Spooner gave as his reason for his intention to retire from public life, his wife's health and her preference for a quiet, peaceful home life in Madison. He hotly denied that the political "ruction" in his party had anything to do with his decision and declared that he had never been backward about fights either in the Senate, in his profession, or in politics. He did feel that he had brought prestige to Wisconsin and to his party by his work in the Senate and should not have to "get down on his marrow bones, and beg for support in the matter of a re-election." [74]

The state convention met in Milwaukee on August 8; La Follette was nominated by acclamation for governor; the platform endorsed the direct primary, the establishment of a tax commission, legislation to prevent abuses by corporations, and regulation of lobbies. La Follette, however, did not have everything his own way. A former chairman of the state central committee described the proceedings in a letter to Spooner:

> The great day has come and gone, and we on whom the brick house fell salutamus te. We still live. It was in all truth very much of a Spooner day. . . .
> Quarles' tribute to yourself was most handsomely rendered, and its sincerity and earnestness were manifest to every one.

[73] La Follette, *La Follette,* I, 131–32.

[74] *Milwaukee Sentinel,* July 6, 1900; Spooner to I. H. Wing, July 2; to W. R. Durfee, July 9; to S. H. Clough, December 15, 1900, in Spooner Papers; E. Keyes to J. C. Gaveny, July 7, 1900, in Keyes Papers. Mrs. Spooner was ill that spring and had returned to Madison.

When he spoke of his deep regret that you were to retire at the end of your term there went up a shout of "no" "never" from every part of the house—loud, vigorous and seemingly unanimous. The same strong expression of favor followed the reading of the committee's resolution [expressing regret at Spooner's announcement of retirement], and of Baensch's nomination of yourself to the Presidency. It was very pleasing to us who had felt that we were under a brick house and gave indubitable evidence that La Follette is No. 2 even in his own house. Don't think that this is the enthusiasm of a personal friend—I try to keep my head level though my feelings are thoroughly enlisted.[75]

Spooner, as usual, was much sought after as a campaign speaker. President McKinley personally requested him to open the campaign with a speech at Canton, Ohio, and invited Spooner and his wife to be guests at his home. Many of his colleagues begged Spooner to come into their states to aid them in their fights for re-election; even Chandler of New Hampshire and Proctor of Vermont, with whom he had violently disagreed on the floor of the Senate, solicited his help. Under the auspices of the national committee Spooner spoke in West Virginia, Kentucky, Indiana, and Illinois. Elkins wrote that his speeches in West Virginia had done a great deal of good and that many claimed that they were the best speeches ever made in the state.[76]

At first Spooner was not asked to take part in the cam-

[75] E. Coe to Spooner, August 9, 1900, in Spooner Papers. See Ralph Gordon Plumb, *Badger Politics: 1836–1930*, pp. 118–20.

[76] J. H. Manley to Spooner, June 25; R. H. Spence to Spooner, July 5; E. B. Hays to Spooner, July 7; W. Chandler to Spooner, August 29, November 1; S. B. Elkins to Spooner, September 13, November 8, 1900, in Spooner Papers; N. B. Scott to G. B. Cortelyou, August 14; W. McKinley to Spooner, October 5; Spooner to W. McKinley, October 6, 1900, in McKinley Papers. Elkins and Proctor were re-elected but Chandler was defeated.

paign in Wisconsin. But when from all parts of the state requests for the Senator as speaker poured into the headquarters of the state central committee, Chairman Bryant sent him a schedule of engagements from October 25 to election eve. The Senator closed the campaign with a speech in Milwaukee, characterized by the *Sentinel* as "Mr. Spooner at his best." In all his speeches he urged Republicans to vote for La Follette for governor since he was the party's nominee.[77] The election was an overwhelming victory for the Republican party. In light of such a landslide Spooner's friends urged him to retract his announcement of July 5 but he remained noncommittal. He still had two more years to serve in the Senate.[78]

President McKinley, after his re-election, asked Spooner to take the position of Attorney General during his second administration. Spooner regretfully declined. It was the cabinet office he would have preferred above all others but his wife did not want to live in Washington all year around and, as he wrote a friend, "I cannot live without her, and, happily for me, she cannot get on without me." [79]

It was at this time that there was talk of Spooner as the presidential nominee of the Republican party in 1904. After McKinley's emphatic statement of June 11, 1901, that he would not accept a nomination for a third term, there was considerable speculation regarding his successor. Spooner was the one most frequently mentioned, especially

77 G. E. Bryant to Spooner, October 5, 1900, in Spooner Papers; *Milwaukee Sentinel,* October 30, November 2, 1900.

78 Spooner to S. H. Clough, December 15, 1900; C. Pfister to Spooner, January 11, 1901, in Spooner Papers; H. A. Taylor to E. Keyes, December 21, 1900, April 19, 1901; E. Keyes to Spooner, February 10, 1901, in Keyes Papers.

79 *Milwaukee Sentinel,* November 18, 1900; Spooner to C. Smith, March 8, 1901, in Spooner Papers.

by newspapers in the East.[80] Even Vice-President Roosevelt was inclined to think Spooner would make an admirable President, although he preferred Elihu Root or William Howard Taft—or Theodore Roosevelt.[81] Spooner personally might have enjoyed the challenge of being President but his wife would have hated the position of first lady. Spooner believed the office of President should not be sought and declared he would never make a campaign for it. Spooner also recognized that the presidential boom for him was premature, for much could happen in four years to change the political picture.[82] Less than four months elapsed before the political situation was drastically changed by the assassination of President McKinley at the Pan-American Exposition in Buffalo and the accession to the Presidency of Theodore Roosevelt.

80 *Milwaukee Sentinel,* August 13, 21, 1901; *Washington Times,* August 12, 1901; H. Taylor to E. Keyes, March 13, 1901, in Keyes Papers. In 1896 some of Spooner's friends started to organize Spooner Republican clubs to work for his nomination for President but he immediately squashed the movement (see S. L. Perrin to Spooner, January 30; Spooner to G. W. Esterly, February 3, 1896, in Spooner Papers).

81 Henry Fowles Pringle, *The Life and Times of William Howard Taft,* II, 217.

82 Spooner to O. H. La Grange, June 14, 1901, in Spooner Papers. Spooner's daughter-in-law relates how some men were discussing the subject of the Presidency with Spooner in New Hampshire and Mrs. Spooner interrupted with: "Oh, John, NO."

9 : *Advisor on Foreign Policy (1901-1904)*

"HE [PRESIDENT ROOSEVELT] IS ANXIOUS TO BE RIGHT"*

ON SEPTEMBER 14, 1901, in a private home in Buffalo, New York, Theodore Roosevelt was sworn in as President of the United States. That orderly succession of power dramatically marked the beginning of a new era of personal and progressive politics in America. More immediately, it marked the end of an era of conservative complacency and Congressional government.

Theodore Roosevelt was the most unpredictable element ever accidentally to reach the White House. Not that he was unknown personally or politically, for he had served with credit and publicity as Civil Service Commissioner and Assistant Secretary of the Navy. But these were minor positions. He had never been a member of Congress, never held a cabinet post, never sat in the inner circle of the Republican party. The Stalwart Republicans, who had

* Spooner to O. H. Platt, October 14, 1901, in Spooner Papers.

grudgingly acquiesced in his nomination as Vice-President in Philadelphia the previous summer, had even then been alarmed at the remote possibility of his becoming President. He had always dramatized himself and his office; he had expressed startling and unorthodox opinions; when governor of New York, he had resisted dictation from "Boss" Platt. Now the Senate leaders, especially Mark Hanna, were apprehensive.

If Spooner held any opinions of the new President, he kept them to himself. Like so many of the other Republican leaders, he apparently preferred to wait and see what Roosevelt would do. He did not have long to wait, for two weeks later Spooner began to feel the soothing influence of the Roosevelt charm and personality which reassured the Old Guard.[1] By October 4 Spooner was dining at the White House, consulting and advising on the President's forthcoming message to Congress.[2] On his return home, Spooner reported to Orville H. Platt of Connecticut: "I had a long conference with the President. He will talk to you about a variety of subjects, I doubt not. Subsidy, on which don't be too brash; reciprocity, tariff revision, trusts, etc., etc. He is anxious to be right, and, of course, anxious to do right." [3]

Theodore Roosevelt proved himself a master of the art of "doing right"; in the weeks that followed, he assiduously cultivated Spooner as an entree to the Republican power in the Senate. Perhaps each saw in the other's friendship certain political advantage; perhaps they were mutually

[1] T. Roosevelt to Spooner, September 30, 1901, in Roosevelt Papers at The Library of Congress.

[2] *Milwaukee Sentinel*, October 5, 1901; T. Roosevelt to E. Root, October 5, 1901, in Roosevelt Papers.

[3] Spooner to O. H. Platt, October 14, 1901, in Spooner Papers.

attracted by personalities so dissimilar. Hardly a week went by when Spooner was in Washington that he did not receive a note from the White House, inviting him to one of the famous "stag dinners" or to stop in informally for a chat. "When you come here, *always* come straight into my room," the President directed Spooner.[4]

Spooner was then at the height of his political career. Not only was he intimate with the President but by many he was considered the leader of the Senate. He was again a member of the two important Republican caucus committees. He retained most of the same committee positions he had held in the Fifty-sixth Congress—membership on the Finance, Relations with Cuba, and Public Health and Quarantine committees and the chairmanship of the Committee on Rules. During the previous Congress he had had a sharp disagreement with Senator Hoar over a bill to limit the use of restraining orders and injunctions in labor disputes. Spooner at that time declared he would not serve on the Judiciary Committee as long as Hoar was chairman. He was therefore appointed to the Committee on Foreign Relations which, during Roosevelt's administration, was to be an especially important position.[5] It was not just his committee memberships that made Spooner such a valuable man in the Senate; it was his zeal, his tirelessness, his legal

---

4 T. Roosevelt to Spooner, November 29, December 4, 1901, January 28, 1904, in Roosevelt Papers; G. B. Cortelyou to Spooner, November 27, December 17, 1901, January 2, 11, 26, February 14, April 11, 21, May 19, 21, 29, 1902, in Spooner Papers.

5 *Congressional Record*, 57th Cong., 1st Sess. (1901–2), p. 387; Coolidge, *Platt*, p. 425; O. H. Platt to A. Beveridge, November 21, 1904, in Platt Papers. Cullom had just become chairman of that committee, edging out Lodge. Other Republican members were Frye of Maine, Foraker of Ohio, and Fairbanks of Indiana; Democrats were Morgan of Alabama, Bacon of Georgia, and Bailey of Texas.

acumen, his alertness and judgment, his combativeness and willingness to take responsibility, combined with his good nature, his modest ways, and his desire to be of assistance to his colleagues that gave him the title of "consultation doctor" of the Senate.[6]

On one major issue only did Spooner disagree with the Republican Old Guard and that was on the protective tariff. This issue threatened to split the Republican party into its component parts: agricultural and revisionist on the one hand, industrial and protectionist on the other. The fall of the Populist party had not ended the discontent in the Middle West and in the popular mind the protective tariff was hated in the same terms as railroads and Wall Street. Basically, western farmers felt that the high cost of manufactured goods (essentially eastern products) was due to the huge trusts, which fattened on excess profits guaranteed by tariffs having long ago outlived their usefulness in protecting domestic industry. The relationship of trusts to tariff was known as the "Iowa idea," and it was widely held by the liberal Republicans of the Middle West.

To accommodate the agricultural discontent and the enlightened business realization that the expansion of foreign trade could not be a one-way street, the Dingley Act had authorized the administration to negotiate reciprocity treaties, and McKinley had made serious efforts toward tariff reductions by that method. The particular promise of this mode of reduction was that it could be bargained for selectively, *quid pro quo,* without opening the question to Congressional logrolling. Speaking at the Pan-American Exposition the day before he was shot, McKinley had de-

[6] Foraker, *Notes,* II, 10; Wellman, "Spooner of Wisconsin," *Review of Reviews,* 26 (August, 1902), 168.

clared, "The period of exclusiveness is past. . . . Reciprocity treaties are in harmony with the spirit of the times, measures of retaliation are not." Vice-President Roosevelt, in a speech at Minneapolis, had echoed the same view.[7]

With the exception of Spooner, the Republican Old Guard was by no means won over to the principle of reciprocity. Allison felt that McKinley's reciprocity pronouncements had been misinterpreted by those who favored free trade. He agreed that the Senate should honor reciprocity treaties already negotiated under the Dingley Act, but he insisted that none would be ratified which did not fully recognize the principle of protection.[8] Aldrich, Hanna, and Platt opposed revision and flatly advised Roosevelt to forget about reciprocity.[9] After assuming the Presidency, Roosevelt felt the full force of pressure against tariff revision, and he began to hedge on the issue, using such ambiguous language as, "Reciprocity must be treated as the handmaiden of protection." [10] At a conference convened at Oyster Bay by Roosevelt in September, 1902, Spooner, Hanna, Aldrich, Allison, Lodge, and Henry C. Payne, the

[7] Richardson, *Messages and Papers of Presidents,* IX, 6621; *The Times* (London), October 8, 1901.

[8] James Wilson to W. B. Allison, September 28; Allison to J. Wharton (copy), November 2, 1901, in Allison Papers; Allison to T. Roosevelt, November 2, 1901, in Roosevelt Papers.

[9] Stephenson, *Aldrich,* pp. 177–80.

[10] *Congressional Record,* 57th Cong., 1st Sess., p. 84. Sporadically throughout the Fifty-seventh Congress the Committee on Foreign Relations considered the so-called "Kasson treaties" but none of them was adopted. Spooner, with Foraker and Bacon, was a member of a subcommittee to consider the constitutional issues involved in the pending reciprocity treaties. This was occasioned by contention of the House of Representatives that it should be consulted about commercial agreements. Spooner reported that the Senate's power was absolute and it could consider tariff treaties independent of the House (see *Milwaukee Sentinel,* February 20, 1902; *Washington Post,* March 13, 1902).

new Postmaster General,[11] attempted to hammer out some position on the tariff which would be acceptable to all of the conflicting regional and economic interests.[12] Spooner was disappointed with his colleagues; he thought they were unaware of how much a revision was desired in the Middle West. "I do not think the mass of the people demand an immediate and snapshot revision of the tariff," he wrote Allison, "but that they do demand that tariff schedules shall not be treated as irrevocable is certain, and I think our friends in the east are finding that there is a great deal of that feeling in the east." [13]

Impatient with inaction, Congressman Babcock of Wisconsin introduced a bill incorporating the "Iowa idea," removing the duty from products the domestic competitor of which was produced by trusts. Spooner was not in accord with this approach, stating, "That is really the Democratic scheme, which assumes that the tariff is the father, or mother, of trusts, and that the only way to take care of the offspring is to kill the father and mother." Spooner preferred a long-range solution of the tariff question by placing it in the hands of a nonpartisan commission, thereby obtaining a gradual reduction to a scientific schedule.[14]

[11] Payne finally realized his ambition and was appointed Postmaster General on January 15, 1902. It was the first change that Roosevelt made in his cabinet. It was not a fortunate appointment. Payne was repeatedly under attack and Spooner had to defend him on the floor of the Senate. See Fowler, *Cabinet Politician,* pp. 262, 273–77; *Congressional Record,* 57th Cong., 2d Sess. (1902–3), pp. 1174–87; 58th Cong., 2d Sess. (1903–4), pp. 492–98, 4561–66.

[12] Stephenson, *Aldrich,* pp. 194–95, 454; T. Roosevelt to W. B. Allison, October 9, 1902, in Allison Papers.

[13] Spooner to W. B. Allison, October 9, 1902, in Spooner Papers.

[14] J. W. Babcock to T. Roosevelt, September 12, 1902, in Roosevelt Papers; Spooner to F. Bigelow, June 14, 1901, in Spooner Papers; *Washington Post,* February 13, 1901, January 15, 1902.

Spooner's tariff proposal was supported that fall by Roosevelt in a speech at Logansport, Indiana, despite misgivings of the Old Guard.[15] Roosevelt, knowing it might mean political suicide to insist on tariff revision, never asked for legislation to implement his suggestion and Spooner, out of loyalty to the Republican party, dropped the issue for the time.

If the general issue of tariff revision was a troublesome one, the specific structure of the tariff within the new American empire was an even more involved one. Congress had attempted to have an empire and a protective tariff too, but most of the new possessions exported agricultural goods and raw materials in at least partial competition with domestic production. The conflict had been precipitated by the Supreme Court in December, 1901, in the case of the Fourteen Diamond Rings, through the pronouncement that the Dingley Tariff Act could not be applied to the Philippine Islands since they were no longer foreign territory. The ultimate disposition of the islands, the question of imperialism, and competition with domestic agriculture and industry were all involved; the temporary solution and compromise pressed by the House of Representatives was to apply 75 per cent of the Dingley rates to importations from the Philippines, and to avoid the other embarrassing complications of the problem. When the bill reached the Senate, the arch anti-imperialist Teller of Colorado dragged the skeleton from the closet by offering an amendment disclaiming any intention of per-

15 T. Roosevelt to Spooner, October 1, 1902, in Roosevelt Papers; Spooner to T. Roosevelt, September 26, 1902, in Spooner Papers; *The New York Times*, September 24, 1902.

manently annexing the Philippines. The tariff question was soon forgotten, and the battle raged on the matter of imperialism, straining the discipline of both parties.

Spooner was chosen to defend McKinley, the war, and expansion from the not necessarily genuine attacks of the Democrats and not without some misgivings of his own. On one occasion for five hours Spooner enraptured the galleries and entertained the Senate with an extemporaneous and earnest defense of American policy in the Philippines. Teller's amendment, he declared, would "raise hell in the Philippine Archipelago." The Filipinos, he said, were not yet ready to assume self-government, but Spooner took pride in our manfully shouldering the "white man's burden" to lead them to that goal. The speech was frequently interrupted by the Democrats; it was even claimed that Spooner invited the interruptions, knowing that he was at his best in the heat of parliamentary exchange. The Teller amendment was defeated and the Philippine tariff bill was passed.[16]

The Senate returned to a discussion of the Philippines on April 18 in connection with the government bill for the islands. According to Senator Lodge, the bill had been framed by himself with the aid of Spooner and Secretary of War Root. Root's biographer claims that Root whipped it into shape with the aid of Lodge and Congressman Cooper of Wisconsin, with Spooner lending a friendly

[16] *Congressional Record,* 57th Cong., 1st Sess., pp. 2020–37, 2087, 2134; Stephenson, *Aldrich,* p. 185; Walters, *Foraker,* pp. 188–89; *Washington Post,* February 22, 1902. For the benefit of his constituents the beer manufacturers Schlitz and Pabst, Spooner got some rebates of taxes on beer included in the Philippine tariff bill. See Spooner to C. Pfister, December 10, 1901; to J. Schlitz, February 6, 8, 1902, in Spooner Papers; *Congressional Record,* 57th Cong., 1st Sess., p. 1014.

hand.[17] Whatever the contents or whoever the author, the real issue was imperialism, and Spooner was expected to close the debate for the administration. The opposition complained that Spooner was always the "great disappearing gun" and expressed the wish that he might just once not occupy the floor until the minute for voting arrived.[18] Spooner, because of his size and brilliance, was given the cognomen "The Little Giant," and was hailed as "the first debater of the American Congress of our time." [19]

While the Senate was debating the Philippine government bill, Spooner was working behind the scenes, in committee and at the White House, to resolve a similar problem with imperial overtones—Cuba's economic problem.[20] The island's plight was desperate. Its prosperity depended on increased export of sugar and tobacco to the United States, which conflicted with the domestic production of the same products. The partial reciprocity existing before the Spanish-American War, during which over 75 per cent of the island's products had been sent to this country, had been terminated by the war. President McKinley, Secretary Root, and General Wood had tried to get Con-

17 Jessup, *Root*, I, 363–64; Garraty, *Lodge*, p. 208; H. C. Lodge to W. B. Allison, January 9, 1902, in Allison Papers; Spooner to W. MacVeagh, June 24, 1902, in Spooner Papers. Spooner said he drew the amendment that made the Philippine Supreme Court independent as to salary and jurisdiction of the commission. He also insisted on a bill of rights being specifically set forth in the bill.

18 *Congressional Record*, 57th Cong., 1st Sess., pp. 5547, 6102–9, 6125–42.

19 Wellman, "Spooner of Wisconsin," *Review of Reviews*, 26 (August, 1902), 169; *Washington Post*, May 30, June 1, 1902; *Milwaukee Sentinel*, June 1, 1902.

20 Spooner to J. F. Prentiss, March 8, 1902, in Spooner Papers: "The Cuban situation is the most troublesome one that I have had anything to do with since I came into public life. . . . We are all giving it the very best attention possible."

gress to grant tariff concessions to Cuba at the time of the passage of the Platt Amendment.[21] President Roosevelt had requested a tariff reduction on Cuban imports in his message to Congress, but it was not until April 18, 1902, that the legislation cleared the House, and then only after the President's personal intervention induced Representative Babcock of Wisconsin to break the log jam in the Committee on Ways and Means.[22]

Platt was chairman, and Spooner and Aldrich members, of the Committee on Relations with Cuba, to which the Cuban reciprocity bill was referred. Despite domestic repercussions, the President insisted that the bill be passed during that session in order to stabilize the Cuban economy. Spooner doubted the wisdom of projecting such a measure just before the Congressional elections, for he knew it would encounter the concerted opposition of the beet sugar and tobacco Senators. Spooner himself had received letters from his own tobacco-growing constituents, expressing their views in unmistakable terms. In an attempt to resolve the sectional conflict, the Republican members of the committee held meeting after meeting—but could come to no agreement.[23] At the request of Platt, Aldrich, and Spooner, the President held a conference at the White House, attended by those three Senators as well as Senator Foraker and General Wood. It was decided that the President should send a special message to Congress

[21] Chapman, *History of the Cuban Republic,* pp. 122, 155; E. Root to L. Wood, January 9, 19, 1901, in McKinley Papers; L. Wood to N. Aldrich, January 12, 1901, in Aldrich Papers.

[22] *Washington Post,* March 28, 1902.

[23] Spooner to G. M. Tollefson, March 10, 1902; O. H. Platt to Spooner, April 19, 22, May 7, 26, 1902, in Spooner Papers; *Washington Post,* April 20, 1902.

urging the reduction of the sugar duty by 25 per cent "on the ground of simple justice to Cuba."

The Cuban reciprocity message was sent in on June 13, but it evoked no sympathetic response in the Senate. The opposition was led by Teller, representing the Colorado beet sugar industry, who shifted the debate into a personal attack on General Wood, accusing him of using government funds for propagandizing for a lower tariff for Cuba. Spooner and Platt worked out a compromise draft, designed to prevent the sugar trust from benefiting from the tariff reductions, which was acceptable to the Republican members of the committee. But it was rejected by the Republican caucus on June 17 because of the bitter opposition of seventeen members who represented the beet sugar interests.[24] The rebuff was one not only to "The Four" but also to President Roosevelt. As Spooner observed: "The Cuban business . . . has come to a halt. . . . As it stands now the President's message is doing work among the people, and his power to make a treaty is unfettered. Possibly later the Senate could be induced to ratify one." [25]

But the "Cuban business" had not come to a halt; on the advice of Spooner and other Republican members of the Foreign Relations Committee, the administration negotiated a reciprocity treaty with Cuba. It was presented to the Senate in December, 1902, but Congress adjourned without acting on it. The President thereupon called the Senate into extra session on March 5, 1903. The Cuban Reciprocity Treaty was finally assented to but only on con-

24 T. Roosevelt to Spooner, June 10, 1902, in Roosevelt Papers; Stephenson, *Aldrich*, pp. 185–87; *Washington Post*, June 19, 20, 1902; *Congressional Record*, 57th Cong., 1st Sess., p. 6720; see Ellis, *Teller*, pp. 344–45.
25 Spooner to W. MacVeagh, June 24, 1902, in Spooner Papers.

dition that it not go into effect until an act implementing it had received the assent of both houses.[26] The President then called Congress in special session on November 9 to consider such a bill. The administration was aware of the difficulty in getting such an act passed. In an effort to smooth the way, Aldrich, Platt, Allison, and Spooner met in Allison's apartment at the Arlington Hotel on November 5, and two days later they met at the White House with the President, Secretary of the Treasury Shaw, and the leading members of the House Ways and Means Committee.[27]

The House quickly passed the bill to give effect to the convention with Cuba, but it encountered stiff opposition in the Senate. The beet sugar Senators used every conceivable dilatory tactic against it. They began by opposing reference to the Committee on Foreign Relations, ostensibly because it was a tariff measure but actually because the committee was already committed to passage. Spooner, chairman of the Rules Committee, in giving a parliamentary opinion on the question of referral, ruled that only reason and common judgment determined which class of bills went to one committee or another. Since the Cuban Reciprocity Treaty had naturally gone to the Committee on Foreign Relations, it was only proper that it should also review legislation which merely implemented the treaty. He urged prompt action on the merits of the bill in order to include the current sugar crop, and admitted that the committee had already studied the question and could

[26] N. M. Mallory to Spooner, March 10, 11, 1903; *Congressional Record,* 58th Cong., 2d Sess., Appendix, pp. 64–72.

[27] *Washington Post,* November 6, 1903; *Madison Democrat,* November 8, 1903.

quickly make a report. The motion to refer was finally adopted and the committee reported the bill on November 23.[28] Despite the President's appeals and Spooner's best efforts, the bill was still pending at the close of the special session.[29]

The special session continued to sit until the exact moment the new regular session began in December, and Spooner had another occasion to advance Cuban reciprocity by ruling that the tariff measure remained the order of the day in the new session. "What a trump Spooner is," President Roosevelt wrote Platt when he heard of the ruling. "He has done so much for me." [30] As usual, Spooner closed the debate for the Republicans, pitted against Bailey of Texas, and the issue was constitutional rather than economic or political. Spooner maintained that treaties fixing tariff duties were perfectly in accordance with the Constitution, for there was no limitation in the Constitution on the treaty-making power. In this case the issue was perfectly clear since the Senate's assent to the treaty had required implementing legislation. The bill was finally passed on December 16. The eighteen negative votes were cast by Teller of Colorado, Bard of California, and sixteen Southern Democrats.[31]

At the risk of disrupting party harmony, Spooner un-

28 *Congressional Record,* 58th Cong., 1st Sess., pp. 335, 400–412; *Washington Post,* November 22, 1903.

29 W. Loeb to Spooner, November 20, 1903, in Spooner Papers.

30 T. Roosevelt to O. H. Platt, December 9, 1903, in Platt Papers; *Congressional Record,* 58th Cong., 2d Sess., pp. 66, 72.

31 *Congressional Record,* 58th Cong., 2d Sess., p. 286, Appendix, pp. 64–72; Spooner to W. B. Devos, November 28, 1903, in Spooner Papers; *Washington Post,* December 17, 1903.

complainingly carried out the President's wishes in the Cuban reciprocity question because he basically agreed with the policy on its own merits. He was also sympathetic with the project to have the United States build and control an isthmian canal. Although he agreed with Roosevelt that the Panama route was the better one, he was a little disconcerted and dismayed by the methods used by the President to obtain his way and resented the President's attempt to dictate his actions on the Panama canal treaties.

By 1900 popular demand for a water route through the Central American isthmus had become universal. In fact, public opinion was so entranced by the canal project that it failed fully to appreciate the ramifications of the vicious struggle raging between the proponents of the competing routes. The one generally favored lay through Nicaragua, largely because it was assumed that the French company had obtained from Colombia the exclusive privilege of building a canal across the Panama isthmus. In 1899 Congress had passed an act incorporating the Maritime Canal Company to build a canal in Nicaragua financed entirely by private capital. Once accorded legal and diplomatic sanction, bills to give financial assistance to the company or to purchase its rights and privileges were introduced in every session of Congress, generally by Senator John T. Morgan of Alabama or Representative William P. Hepburn of Iowa. Despite widespread interest in both houses, none of these bills ever passed both chambers because of the varied and conflicting interests of the proponents of various canal schemes. And over them all hung the specter of the Clayton-Bulwer Treaty with Great Britain. All that had been accomplished was the passage of bills establishing commissions to investigate the practicability of canals through both Nicaragua and Panama.[32]

Spooner had consistently opposed the Nicaraguan canal projects, at first because he considered them to be in violation of the Clayton-Bulwer Treaty, which had provided that any canal that should be built should be neutral and that neither nation should ever obtain exclusive control or erect or maintain any fortifications in the vicinity of such canal.[33] When the treaty was negotiated in 1850 it had been considered a diplomatic triumph for the United States, for British influence in Central America was then greater than that of the United States. With positions reversed at the turn of the century, the treaty was an embarrassment to America's consolidation of her position as a world power. Morgan and the canal advocates preferred to ignore the treaty as a diplomatic anachronism, but Spooner insisted it was still a subsisting obligation. "We have repeatedly in the last few years so treated it by negotiating for its abrogation or modification," he pointed out. "Great Britain certainly regards it as still in force." He begged the Senate not to endanger the amicable relations with Great Britain by taking unilateral action before the obstruction of the treaty had been removed by negotiation.[34]

As early as December, 1898, Secretary of State Hay had suggested to Great Britain a modification of the Clayton-

32 Dwight C. Miner, *Fight for the Panama Route*, pp. 29, 79–84; John Ely Briggs, *William Peter Hepburn*, pp. 200–222; *Congressional Record*, 55th Cong., 3d Sess. (1898–99), pp. 100, 895–910, 2816.

33 William Malloy (comp.), *Treaties, Conventions, International Acts, Protocols, and Agreements Between the United States of America and Other Powers*, I, 660: Gerstle Mack, *The Land Divided*, pp. 184–86.

34 *Milwaukee Sentinel*, January 18, 1899; Spooner to C. F. Smith, June 8, 1900, in Spooner Papers; *Congressional Record*, 55th Cong., 3d Sess., pp. 687–95.

Bulwer Treaty, but it was not until February 5, 1900, that the Hay-Pauncefote Treaty was presented to the Senate. The treaty embodied the substance of American demands but the Senate attached so many clarifying amendments to the treaty that Great Britain refused to ratify it. Finally a second treaty, more broadly incorporating the American demands, was negotiated and presented to the Senate in November, 1901. Chauvinists expressed doubt that the treaty gave the United States military control over any canal it might construct, but Spooner assured them that the United States would have complete dominion over it at least in time of war. After a brief debate, the Senate approved the treaty on December 16, 1901, by a vote of 72 to 6.[35]

Although the diplomatic stumbling block had been removed, Spooner and the Senate Republican leaders were still lukewarm to Morgan's Nicaraguan canal bills. Spooner, for one, was convinced that the transfer of the franchise from the private company to the government would invalidate it, and he was not at all convinced that the Nicaraguan route was the best or most feasible one.[36] His attention had only recently been directed to the Panama route by an article written by Brigadier General Henry L. Abbot, U.S.A., Ret., consulting engineer of the New Panama Canal Company, which had been organized in France in 1894 to purchase and exercise the rights of

[35] Tyler Dennett, *John Hay: From Poetry to Politics,* pp. 248–63; Walters, *Foraker,* pp. 158–60; *Senate Document,* 63d Cong., 2d Sess., No. 474, pp. 1–4, 20.

[36] *Congressional Record,* 55th Cong., 3d Sess., pp. 842–50; *Washington Post,* January 18, 21, 22, 1899. See Miner, *Fight for Panama Route,* p. 30, who says that there was growing opposition to the Maritime Canal Company in Nicaragua and that President José Santos Zelaya had given notice that the company's concessions were to expire on October 9, 1899.

the old French Canal Company.[37] Spooner was also well acquainted with William Nelson Cromwell, a close asso- ciate in the Northern Pacific receivership, counsel and di- rector of the Panama Railroad Company, and since 1896 the adviser to the New Panama Canal Company. In Febru- ary, 1899, the new French company had made its first offer to sell its rights to the United States, but the purchase had been blocked by Morgan even before the administration could explore the matter. Thereafter, Cromwell concen- trated on frustrating Morgan's efforts for the Nicaraguan project, keeping alive a market for the rapidly expiring French rights. Spooner's role strongly suggests that he may have acted as Cromwell's agent, at least when he attempted to persuade the President and the Secretary of State not to appoint Rear Admiral John G. Walker and Professor Lewis Haupt to the second canal commission in 1901 on the ground that they were prejudiced in favor of Nicara- gua. Spooner's efforts failed, for the President appointed to the nine-man Isthmian Canal Commission the three members of the previous Nicaraguan Canal Commission.[38]

After several months of studying the comparative merits of the two routes, the canal commission reported on November 16, 1901, and the issue of the routes came to a head at the opening of the Fifty-seventh Congress in De- cember. In view of the exorbitant terms offered by the

37 Spooner to E. H. Abbott, November 29, 1898, December 20, 1900, in Spooner Papers. See H. L. Abbot, "The New Panama Canal," *Forum,* 26 (November, 1898), 343–53, and "The Best Isthmian Canal," *Atlantic Monthly,* 86 (December, 1900), 844–48. Mack, *Land Divided,* p. 418, says General Abbot was employed by Cromwell to write these articles.

38 Miner, *Fight for Panama Route,* pp. 75–80; W. J. Curtis to Spooner, March 10, December 23, 1899, May 18, 1900; W. N. Cromwell to Spooner, November 9, 1899; Spooner to W. J. Curtis, March 19, 1899, January 15, 1900, in Spooner Papers.

New Panama Canal Company, the commisssion recommended the Nicaraguan route. Cromwell and Philippe Bunau-Varilla, engineer of the de Lessep company and one of the organizers of the New Panama Canal Company, immediately prevailed upon the stockholders and the directors of the company to offer their rights to the United States for $40,000,000 instead of $109,141,500, which they had previously demanded in October.[39] Spooner and Hanna conferred with the members of the canal commission at Hanna's home; Spooner then saw the President, who summoned Admiral Walker, chairman of the canal commission. The result of all these conferences was a new and unanimous report from the commission in favor of the Panama route if the rights could be purchased at a reasonable figure. The President forwarded the new report to Congress on January 20, 1902.[40]

When the report arrived in the Senate, action was pending on a House bill appropriating $180 million for the construction of a canal through Nicaragua. Spooner hastily offered a substitute amendment bearing his name. By it, the President, at his discretion, was authorized to purchase for not more than $40 million the rights and property of the New Panama Canal Company and to acquire from Colombia the transit zone; failing on either count, the President was authorized to press the Nicaraguan route to completion.[41] The amendment doubtless was framed in

[39] J. G. Walker to President McKinley, August 12, 1901, in McKinley Papers; Miner, *Fight for Panama Route,* pp. 118–20; Philippe Bunau-Varilla, *Panama: The Creation, Destruction and Resurrection,* p. 212.

[40] M. Hanna to Spooner, January 3, 1902, in Spooner Papers; Pringle, *Theodore Roosevelt,* p. 314.

[41] *Congressional Record,* 57th Cong., 1st Sess., p. 7069. See Spooner to W. S. Grubb, March 23, 1904, in Spooner Papers.

consultation with the President and aimed to secure a canal by one route or the other, without further legislative delay. Cromwell later claimed credit for the amendment, but Spooner declared that he alone had devised it. That is probably true, for it was remarkably similar in import to the one he had introduced in January, 1899.[42]

The House bill and the Spooner Amendment were referred to the Interoceanic Canal Committee, on which sat Mark Hanna, one of the foremost advocates of the Panama route. When Hanna failed to sway the committee to the Spooner Amendment, he urged its passage in a minority report. Little debate took place on the measure for several months, while votes were lined up behind the scenes. On June 5 Hanna opened the campaign for the Panama route with a speech considered to have been one of the most important of his career.[43]

"When do you speak?" Cromwell asked Spooner, sending him armloads of material as well as a little flattery. The issue had probably already been decided by the time Spooner presented his speech on June 18. He rehearsed the dramatic scope of the enterprise and its economic and cultural advantages and rested the argument for his amendment purely on the ground of the report of the canal commission [44]—a report he had been instrumental in reversing. Adroit "postage stamp" lobbying by the promoters of the Panama route may have had some effect, but the passage of

42 *Congressional Record,* 55th Cong., 3d Sess., pp. 842–50; Miner, *Fight for Panama Route,* pp. 123–25, thinks the instigation came from the White House but says that Spooner was the logical choice to direct a political maneuver of this kind.

43 Bunau-Varilla, *Panama,* p. 174; Herbert David Croly, *Marcus Alonzo Hanna,* pp. 382–85.

44 W. N. Cromwell to Spooner, June 11, 1902, in Spooner Papers; *Congressional Record,* 57th Cong., 1st Sess., pp. 6981–92.

the Spooner Amendment was more probably due to mas-
sive pressure from the administration.[45] Under the act the
President was directed first to seek the property and rights
of the New Panama Canal Company, and he immediately
dispatched the Assistant Attorney General to Paris to make
a preliminary investigation. In August, Attorney General
Knox followed and urged Spooner to join him. The Senator hesitated; he thought the trip would be pleasant enough
but he had qualms about being party to an undertaking
he would subsequently be called upon to review.[46] Knox
found that the United States could acquire a good title
from the Panama company.[47]

The next task was to secure the necessary transit site
from Colombia. Spooner played a prominent part in the
negotiations of the treaty both before and after the passage
of the Spooner Amendment and with the Colombian minister, General José Vincente Concha, and with the secretary of the legation, Tomás Herran, after Concha returned
to Colombia. In fact, it was not until Spooner agreed that
a renewable lease proposition was tantamount to "per-
petual control of a strip of land," as the amendment had
specified, that the treaty was finally completed.[48] It was sub-

[45] *Congressional Record,* 57th Cong., 1st Sess., pp. 7070, 7074. In the
Spooner Papers is one of the Nicaraguan stamps sent by Bunau-Varilla to
each of the Senators a few days before the vote. It has a picture of an
erupting volcano, under which is written: "An official witness of the vol-
canic activity on the isthmus of Nicaragua."

[46] *Milwaukee Sentinel,* July 7, 1902; P. Knox to Spooner, July 22, August
2, 1902; Spooner to J. V. Quarles, August 4; to P. Knox, September 27,
1902, in Spooner Papers.

[47] Spooner to W. N. Cromwell, October 27, 1902, in Spooner Papers; T.
Roosevelt to M. Hanna, September 29, 1902, in Roosevelt Papers.

[48] Miner, *Fight for Panama Route,* pp. 126–37, 157–58; Spooner to S.
Baker, May 6, 1902; J. Hay to Spooner, July 15, December 2, 1902; W. N.
Cromwell to Spooner, November 15; Spooner to W. N. Cromwell, Novem-
ber 17, 1902, in Spooner Papers.

mitted to the Senate on January 22, 1903, but the Democrats, led by Morgan, blocked action during that session [49] so President Roosevelt called the Senate in special session immediately after adjournment. By that time Spooner had thought of several amendments he wanted. Roosevelt grumbled in a letter to Hay: "He [Spooner] is an admirable man of great intellect; but I wish that every tom cat in the path did not strike him as an unusually large and ferocious lion." Spooner was finally won over and concluded the debate for the administration with a five-hour speech. The treaty was agreed to on March 17 by a vote of 73 to 5.[50]

Although the Hay-Herran Treaty provided for $10 million and an annual rental of $250,000 for the canal zone, on sober reflection Colombia thought it nothing compared to the $40 million which the United States was prepared to pay for the paper rights of the French company. Since these rights would expire shortly, Colombia saw a chance to obtain also the sum to be paid the French company, if she stalled. Colombia's rejection of the treaty might have meant that President Roosevelt would then turn to the Nicaragua route. But he preferred the Panama route. He was well aware that the agents of the Panama Canal Company, unwilling to lose the $40 million to Colombia or the canal route to Nicaragua, were making preparations for a revolution to bring about the independence of Panama. He co-operated at least to the extent of sending a warship to prevent the landing of Colombian troops to quell the revolution. Two days after Panama declared her inde-

[49] Miner, *Fight for Panama Route,* pp. 190–96.
[50] Morison (ed.), *Letters of Theodore Roosevelt,* III, 445; *Washington Post,* March 15, 18, 1903.

pendence, the United States recognized her *de facto* government; ten days later her new minister, Philippe Bunau-Varilla, was received and negotiations for a new treaty were begun.[51]

At the President's suggestion Spooner was consulted in drafting the new treaty. The first draft was very similar to the Hay-Herran Treaty with Colombia, but Spooner thought that it could be strengthened and he prepared memoranda of suggested changes. At luncheon on November 18 Secretary Hay presented still another draft to Attorney General Knox, Secretary of War Root, and Spooner. The Senator thought it a better one than the first. That draft was ratified by Panama the following day; it was sent to the Senate on December 7.[52]

The treaty encountered bitter opposition in the Senate, not only from Democrats but from administration Senators as well. The issues were complex; they involved all the old machinations of the Panama and Nicaragua plans in addition to the role of the administration in the Panama revolution. Hay begged Spooner to prevent any amendments being added, for fear they might jeopardize the treaty in Panama, and Roosevelt remonstrated with Spooner for even considering amendments: Why did he have Hay go over the treaty line by line with him if not to avoid the necessity for amendments? Spooner hotly denied the implication that his blind commitment to the treaty had been purchased by prior consultation. When the Senator asked why he had been appealed to, the President

51 Dennett, *John Hay*, pp. 377–83; Miner, *Fight for Panama Route*, pp. 340–41; Pringle, *Roosevelt*, pp. 315–29.
52 J. Hay to Spooner, November 10, 14, 17, 1903, in Spooner Papers; Miner, *Fight for Panama Route*, pp. 375–79.

answered: "If you will treat this note as purely confidential, old man, I should say that I made the appeal to you
because it struck me you were the biggest man around."
In response to the President's plea, or flattery, Spooner prevailed upon Cullom to call a special meeting of the Committee on Foreign Relations, where Spooner presented a
cablegram from William I. Buchanan, United States Minister to Panama, predicting serious consequences if the
treaty were amended.[53]

The committee promptly reported the treaty, but it was
bitterly debated in executive session in the Senate. Spooner
defended the legality and honesty of the administration's
course. The treaty was finally consented to on February 23
by a vote of 66 to 14, not a party division. The southern
Senators voted for the treaty, seeing in the canal commercial advantages for their section greater than the political
advantages of indignation at the President's questionable
diplomacy.[54]

The treaty having been approved behind closed doors,
there followed in open session an acrimonious debate for
domestic consumption—raising the question of the President's role in Panama. Senator Morgan offered a resolution
repudiating the use of United States military and naval
forces in the area, and Senator Bacon of Georgia proposed
that the United States indemnify Colombia for our culpa-
bility in the revolution.[55] Even the authors of these resolu-

[53] J. Hay to Spooner, January 18, 19, 1904, in Spooner Papers; T. Roosevelt to Spooner, January 20, 25, 1904; Spooner to T. Roosevelt, January 23,
24, 1904, in Roosevelt Papers.

[54] *Milwaukee Sentinel,* February 11, 24, 1904; Spooner to N. Brown,
March 14; to L. M. Perley, March 21, 1904, in Spooner Papers. See Lambert, *Gorman,* pp. 303–7.

[55] *Congressional Record,* 58th Cong., 2d Sess., pp. 361, 614. A treaty com-
pensating Colombia was finally ratified in 1921.

tions did not expect them to be passed; they were just good partisan politics in an election year.

Spooner bore the main defense of the administration in the Panama imbroglio, just as in pressing the policy in the Senate he had been its whip. For two months he was in almost daily communication with the State Department, gathering information from its files. He examined all the constitutions of Colombia, searching for the constitutional justification for secession. (The right had been admitted in the 1863 document but had been omitted in a later one.) He compiled a record of American military intervention on the isthmus to protect the transit rights, and he prepared a history of the various canal bills in Congress.[56] Armed with his information, Spooner engaged in the debate with a legalistic and highly oratorical defense of the administration and himself.[57]

"By George, I congratulate myself and the country that you are in the Senate," the President wrote Spooner in gratitude for the speech. Mrs. Roosevelt also expressed her appreciation, and sent her regrets for having missed hearing it. Spooner self-effacingly congratulated her for missing

[56] W. Rockhill to Spooner, November 28, 1903; State Department to Spooner, January 18, 19, 23, 1904; Spooner to H. C. Reed, February 4, 1904, in Spooner Papers.

[57] *Congressional Record*, 58th Cong., 2d Sess., pp. 523–25, 614–24, 632–34, 711–19, 752–58, 2015–17, 2134–43; *Milwaukee Sentinel*, January 13, 14, February 19, 21, 1904. President Roosevelt's own defense in his message to Congress, January 4, 1904, and in his *Autobiography*, pp. 526–42, closely follows Spooner's argument except for the additional point of "international eminent domain." Spooner thought that point, for which John Bassett Moore was responsible, should not have been projected into the debate by the President. "There is a great deal in the old books in favor of it, and a great deal in the conduct of nations which sustained it, but in the last analysis I doubt if it will do." (See Spooner to W. J. Curtis, May 4, 1904, in Spooner Papers.)

a heavy and dreary one, intended mainly for the "school deestrict" orators of the campaign.[58]

Spooner was again called to the administration's defense in April during debate on the Panama Canal Act, providing detailed provisions for the operations of the canal and the government of the canal zone. One of the most controversial issues involved the interpretation of the third article of the Hay-Pauncefote Treaty, which stipulated: "The canal shall be free and open to the vessels of commerce and of war of all nations . . . on terms of entire equality." Spooner maintained that the language did not preclude preferential rates for American vessels engaged in coastal trade. Before the canal was opened, the question was ultimately resolved in favor of absolute equality.[59]

The Panama Canal Act of 1904 continued the government of the canal zone in the hands of the Isthmian Canal Commission, as provided initially by the Spooner Amendment. It also authorized the President, upon acquisition of the property of the New Panama Canal Company and payment to the Republic of Panama of ten million dollars, to take possession of the ten-mile-wide strip to be called the Panama Canal Zone. But the President was impatient to begin work on the project and wanted to make a token payment to Panama and take possession immediately. Aside from the diplomatic considerations, Spooner ad-

[58] T. Roosevelt to Spooner, January 14, February 19, 1904, in Roosevelt Papers; Spooner to Mrs. Roosevelt; to President Roosevelt, February 20, 1904, in Spooner Papers.

[59] *Congressional Record*, 58th Cong., 2d Sess., pp. 4798, 4856, 4858, 4860; Malloy (ed.), *Treaties, Conventions,* I, 783. In 1912–13, when President Wilson requested the repeal of preference to United States coastal vessels, Elihu Root supported him on the ground of knowing the intent of the promoters of the Panama project. It would seem that he was mistaken as to Spooner's viewpoint (see Jessup, *Root,* II, 263).

vised the President that nothing could be done until the United States formally obtained possession of the French company's rights. Toward this end Cromwell had gone to Paris to meet with the stockholders, and he cabled Spooner on April 23 that the transfer had been approved. By the end of May the United States held not only the transit and construction rights but also the title to the canal zone.[60]

The hasty course of the administration in pushing through the Panama canal project caused Spooner some painful misgivings and the rabid criticism and scandalous accusations which had been made during the debates hurt him deeply. Plaintively, he wrote Edwin H. Abbott, whose brother's article had first attracted him to the Panama route: "I thought that I was doing the country service in what I did to secure the alternative proposition, giving preference to Panama. If blundering in administration shall discredit the legislation I shall be grievously disappointed. The situation here is a peculiar one. Action, action, action, rapid, too rapid action. . . ." [61]

Roosevelt's aggressive approach to foreign affairs seemed to epitomize the new spirit of triumphant imperialism. But when his "big stick" policy brought the nation to unaccustomed brinks of international crises, Senators counseled a more cautious tack. The members of the Foreign Relations Committee kept an especially close watch on situations in which the Executive held the sole responsibility, such as in the Venezuelan crisis in the winter of 1902–3. The crisis was precipitated by President Cipriano Castro's

[60] *United States Statutes at Large,* 58th Cong., p. 429; W. N. Cromwell to Spooner, April 23, 1904, in Spooner Papers; Mack, *Land Divided,* pp. 480–81.

[61] Spooner to E. H. Abbott, March 21, April 3, 1905, in Spooner Papers.

declaration, following his revolutionary coup in 1899, that he would recognize no foreign debts incurred before 1900. The major creditor powers, Great Britain, Germany, and the United States, registered sharp protests and suggested the question be arbitrated, but Castro refused. Finally, in December, 1902, the European powers issued several ultimatums, blockaded the Venezuelan coast, and bombarded Puerto Cabello. Castro capitulated and requested arbitration, which was accepted in principle by England and Germany.

Although the action of the European powers was a threat to the spirit of the Monroe Doctrine, Theodore Roosevelt utilized the incident more firmly to establish American influence in the international balance, moving in haste to brandish the "big stick" against Germany at least, according to his own account.[62] In any event, members of the Foreign Relations Committee consulted with the President and the Senate, in secret session, discussed the matter. In retrospect, Spooner was in substantial agreement with the President. He thought that a very real threat of German aggression had been averted and arbitration forced by the intervention of the United States. A protocol was signed, mixed commissions were established to settle the claims, and the question of preferential treatment for the blockading nations was submitted to the Hague Court.[63]

[62] Joseph Bucklin Bishop, *Theodore Roosevelt and His Times,* I, 221–30. More recent accounts, e.g., Dennett, *John Hay,* pp. 389–92, and Pringle, *Theodore Roosevelt,* pp. 279–89, have challenged Roosevelt's account, and claim that he exaggerated his own role and that England was more the aggressor than Germany. For the most recent account see Howard K. Beale, *Theodore Roosevelt and the Rise of America to World Power,* pp. 395–431.

[63] Spooner to J. S. Henry, December 17; to E. R. Hicks, December 20, 1902; to W. La Meres, March 27, 1903; to G. B. Moyer, March 31, 1905, in Spooner Papers.

As Roosevelt embraced a more audacious foreign policy, Spooner grew more cautious in supporting it. He walked a tortuous line between loyalty to the administration and maintenance of senatorial independence. Although this conflict was not serious in the Alaskan boundary treaty, it does illustrate it.

The boundary line between Canada and Alaska had been a matter of dispute between the United States and England since the discovery of gold in the Klondike in 1895. Canada claimed a boundary running ten marine leagues measured from the outer shore, giving her most of the best harbors in the region. The sinuosities of the coast made it crucial whether the line were measured from outer or inner shoreline, and an Anglo-American Joint High Commission had been established in 1898 to settle this and all other disputes between the two nations.[64] The commission had accomplished nothing, and after McKinley's death its appropriation had been eliminated by the Senate.[65]

The boundary dispute continued to cloud relations with Great Britain, and Roosevelt permitted the State Department in 1903 to draft a treaty submitting the question to arbitration by six "impartial jurists of repute"—three each from the United States and the British Empire. Arbitration treaties were never popular in the Senate, and the

[64] Spooner had been asked by President McKinley to become a member of this Anglo-American Joint High Commission in July, 1898, but he had declined the honor on account of health and pressure of other burdens although he thought the work would have been very congenial. See Spooner to W. McKinley, July 9, 1898, in Spooner Papers.

[65] Callahan, *American Foreign Policy in Canadian Relations,* pp. 465-89. In 1903 there was talk of reviving the commission, primarily to take up the issue of Canadian reciprocity. See Spooner to H. G. Mitchell, April 1; E. Hale to Spooner, August 14, 1903, in Spooner Papers.

President was forced to use his personal influence to secure consent. As part of the price for ratification, the word "arbitral" was stricken out of the phrase "arbitral tribunal," and also the Senators were confidentially told the names of the American members of the commission: Senator Lodge, former Senator George Turner of Washington, and Secretary Root. Of the three, only Root might fairly be considered an impartial jurist. Lodge was commonly know to be an ardent American expansionist; some feared that Turner might be pro-Canadian, as he had been retained by the Canadian Pacific Railway as its local representative in the State of Washington. In reply to a protest from the president of the Great Northern Railroad, Spooner pointed out that Roosevelt was aware of Turner's Canadian connections, and that if he had any bias, it was in favor of the United States.[66] Spooner was asked to serve as American counsel for the commission at the suggestion of Ambassador Joseph H. Choate; reluctantly he refused, for personal reasons, for he felt the United States case was "a strong and just one." [67] Law and evidence did strongly support the American argument, and one of the British members of the commission voted with the Americans to sustain their position.

The conflict between the Executive and the Senate, between Spooner and President Roosevelt, reached a climax on the issue of the arbitration treaties. In this case Spooner was consulted even before any treaties were negotiated. He

[66] Beale, *Theodore Roosevelt,* pp. 117–19; J. J. Hill to Spooner, February 23; Spooner to J. J. Hill, March 26; to T. Burke, March 24; to E. Hallam, March 27, 1903, in Spooner Papers. See Garraty, *Lodge,* chap. 14.

[67] Spooner to T. Roosevelt, March 7, 1903, in Spooner Papers; Edward Sanford Martin, *Life of Joseph Hodges Choate as Gathered Chiefly from His Letters,* II, 221.

had been asked to confer with a Thomas Barclay, of London, who had been instrumental in bringing about a treaty between England and France providing for the submission of disputes of a certain character to the Permanent Court of Arbitration, established at The Hague by the Conference of 1899. This treaty became the model for the arbitration treaties which Secretary Hay negotiated with Great Britain, France, Germany, Portugal, Switzerland, and Italy.[68]

The Senate Foreign Relations Committee, fearing the encroachment of the Executive,[69] proposed an amendment whereby each agreement to arbitrate (as provided in Article II) must be submitted to the Senate before arbitration could take place. President Roosevelt was furious and remonstrated with Spooner in a long, verbose, and very repetitious letter. He concluded: "I in no way question the right of the Senate to amend a treaty; but when amendments turn a treaty into a sham then it is both the right and duty of the President to say so and refuse to go farther with the treaty." [70] Both sides were unyielding. In defiance of a directive from the Executive, the treaties with amendments were passed by the Senate; President Roosevelt then refused to ratify them. Of "The Four," only Platt supported the President.[71]

* *

[68] S. Cullom to Spooner, November 12, 1903; J. Hay to Spooner, March 11, 1904, in Spooner Papers.
[69] Bishop, *Theodore Roosevelt*, I, 435–37; Foraker, *Notes of a Busy Life*, II, 426–27.
[70] T. Roosevelt to Spooner, January 6, 1905, in Roosevelt Papers.
[71] William Roscoe Thayer, *Life and Letters of John Hay*, II, 292–93; Walters, *Foraker*, pp. 228–29; S. Cullom to Spooner, February 6, 1905, in Spooner Papers; O. H. Platt to J. E. Heaton, February 14, 16, 1905, in Platt Papers.

By virtue of his standing with the administration, Spooner was privileged to participate in the more glittering and social aspects of foreign affairs as practiced in Washington. The Spooners did almost no formal entertaining, although their rented house at 1800 F Street, Mrs. Spooner's favorite of all their homes in Washington, had sufficient facilities to have done so. They were, however, often guests at the homes of other Senators and cabinet members, at foreign embassies, and at the White House.

Entertainment at the White House during the Roosevelt regime was much more formal and frequent than in McKinley's term, for Theodore Roosevelt considered that one of the accouterments of the nation's new international influence was an official social life. The season opened with the President's New Year's Day reception, which Washington society attended en masse. The Spooners seldom attended this event, preferring to await their invitations to one of the subsequent and more exclusive receptions. Social status in Washington was determined by the particular White House reception to which one was invited and by which door one entered. The diplomatic reception was the first, most colorful, and most desirable one of the year, and to be invited to stand behind the ropes with the President in the receiving line was to be elevated to the first rank of official society. Mrs. Spooner described the reception of 1904: "The Dip. recept. was very large, but as we go in the private entrance, we weren't crowded.—The line was Prest. Mrs. R. then Mrs. Root, Mrs. Hay & Shaw, Knox, Payne, Hitchcock, Miss Hilton, & Cortelyou.—We were behind the line with many many others. . . . We remained an hour & then left."

In sharp contrast with the informality and conviviality

of the White House stag dinners, Roosevelt insisted on regal pomp and protocol at his diplomatic dinners. He expected to be treated like European royalty. On one such occasion when the guests were conducted to the East Room, Mrs. Spooner was surprised to find no chairs. Everyone was expected to stand in the presence of the President.

The protocol established at the White House was naturally reflected on all levels of Washington officialdom, and deviations from it horrified those whose relative status was endangered. Who should escort whom to the table and who should sit where were questions of protocol as important to some as policy decisions in a new world power. Mrs. Spooner became quite sensitive on the matter of precedence, even if she did err at times in its application. She once noted in her diary what she thought to be a serious infraction at a dinner at the Chinese embassy. "To our utter disgust, Mrs. Cortelyou (Sec. of Commerce) tail end of Cab—was at the right of minister while Mrs. Aldrich & Cullom were there as well as we. . . . We all were degoutee." According to the rules of precedence, cabinet members did rank above senators. The real significance was that the Spooners did command a place in diplomatic society far beyond his membership on the Foreign Relations Committee. At one of these dinners Mrs. Spooner was seated at the right of the President. She later described him in her diary:

I think the Prest. is a most fascinating man to hear talk, so dead in earnest, so full of information & wit, & humor. In his place, it is hard to be quite sincere, tho' it is his nature I am sure & under normal conditions, he is sincere, I believe. I am not sure however that he is quite truthful, the politician seems to be inbred—tho' he is so fond of books & simple living—in his *woods*—not in civilization. I fancy—he puts on the "togs" that go with the world, flesh & the devil.[72]

During Roosevelt's first administration Spooner, for the most part, supported the President's foreign policy. Although Roosevelt was launching the United States as a world power, he was still wielding his "big stick" comparatively cautiously. In later years, looking back on this period, he seems to have somewhat exaggerated the role he played at that time, especially in the Venezuela imbroglio and the Panama revolution.

Spooner, throughout this period, tried to help the President realize his ambitions, albeit he might be a little worried at Roosevelt's impetuousness. His legal advice was usually sought at the time a treaty was being negotiated, his influence implored to get it through, and his oratorical ability called on to defend the President when attacked. Spooner's disposition was such, and his admiration of the President so great, that he usually did as Roosevelt wished. However, he felt that the Republican Senate, as an independent branch of the treaty-making power, could differ from a Republican President, and that it would not be a good thing for the republic if it did not sometimes do so.

During this period the conflict between Spooner and Roosevelt over the role of the Senate in foreign policy gradually evolved, reaching its climax on the issue of the arbitration treaties just at the end of the first administration. Spooner was zealous in defending the Senate's role in advising and consenting to treaties. He resented the idea

[72] Annie Spooner, Diaries, 1903–4; see Foraker, *I Would Live It Again*, pp. 192, 209; Charles Hurd, *Washington Cavalcade*, pp. 134, 137, 164.

that if he were consulted in the negotiation of a treaty, then he was bound to support it unconditionally. He took exception to the notion that the Executive could follow a treaty into the Senate. He defended the right of the Senate to add amendments to treaties. On the other hand, President Roosevelt, by the end of his first administration, was beginning to fume at the Senate's desire to exercise a major part in foreign affairs. He felt it wholly incompetent to take such a part. Roosevelt was to become even more incensed at the actions of the upper house during his second administration.

10 : *Leader of the Stalwarts Against La Follette (1902-1904)*

"I HAVE NO TASTE OR TOLERANCE FOR POLITICS"*

"MR. SPOONER'S USEFULNESS as a public man, and its recognition by the country at large, ought to arouse the pride of the State of Wisconsin in so worthy a Senator. His term is about to expire, and the whole country hopes he may be reelected; but the Republicans of Wisconsin have been sharply divided over certain State issues," commented the editor of the *Review of Reviews*.[1] The Republican party in Wisconsin was badly split into the Half-Breeds, followers of La Follette, and the Stalwarts. During the campaign of 1902 the latter were referred to as the Eleventh-Story League, for after the adjournment of the legislature in 1901, fifty-nine members of the assembly and senate, in protest against Governor La Follette's attempt to dictate to the legislature, had organized the Republican

---

* Spooner to O. H. Platt, June 2, 1904, in Spooner Papers.
[1] *Review of Reviews*, 26 (August, 1902), 147.

League of Wisconsin, and had leased the eleventh floor of the Herman Building in Milwaukee for their head-quarters.[2]

Although it had been customary to renominate a governor for a second term, the Stalwart leaders decided not to support Governor La Follette, and selected as their candidate state senator John M. Whitehead.[3] The Governor, incensed not only because of this personal affront but also because his primary measure had been defeated by the Stalwart-controlled senate,[4] retaliated with covert opposition to Spooner's re-election to the Senate. The senior Senator was still so popular, even among La Follette's own followers, that the Governor did not dare attack him openly but hoped to bring about his defeat by indirection.

2 Plumb, *Badger Politics*, pp. 124–27.

3 C. Pfister to Spooner, January 11, 1901, in Spooner Papers. E. Keyes thought he was a weak candidate (see E. Keyes to Spooner, January 8, February 6, 1902, *ibid.*) and Hod Taylor thought La Follette should be renominated for it was best to keep the party united (see H. Taylor to Spooner, May 23, 1901, *ibid.*).

4 *1902-Voter's Handbook. The Truth About the Governor, the Legislature, Taxation and Primary Election*, pp. 81–91; Lovejoy, *La Follette and the Direct Primary*, pp. 55–68. The Stevens bill, providing for primary nominations, passed the assembly but was defeated in the senate (13 to 20). The Hagemeister bill, which provided that the direct primary principles might be applied in any county that voted to adopt the system, was passed but vetoed by La Follette. The Governor asked Representative Cooper to use his influence to help get the Stevens bill passed but he refused (see R. La Follette to H. A. Cooper, February 16; Cooper to La Follette, February 27, 1901, in La Follette Papers). Spooner was accused by the Governor of helping defeat his program; this Spooner denied (Spooner to J. Hicks, November 8, 1902, in Spooner Papers): "I sedulously refused to do so, directly or indirectly, and I inspired nothing of opposition, either on primary election or taxation, although pressed to do so by some friends, and sought to be inveigled into doing it by some enemies. I have always considered it the duty of a United States Senator to keep his hands off of local legislation. A man in that position has enough to do to attend to his own duty, and, moreover, I have always felt that the people needed no assistance from him in running the State government."

He succeeded in getting defeated by the Republican state convention a resolution endorsing Spooner unconditionally and got adopted instead the following one:

We especially commend the official career of Hon. John C. Spooner. . . . We again express our regret for his announced determination not to serve the state another term in the senate and should he now find it possible to reconsider this decision and express his willingness to stand as a candidate in harmony with the sentiments, and in support of the platform principles here adopted by Wisconsin Republicans in state convention, and for the election of a legislature favorable to their enactment into law, his decision would meet the general approval of Republicans everywhere.[5]

The platform included planks favoring the direct primary and taxation reform; La Follette was sure Spooner would not accept these conditions.

The Governor's scheme boomeranged. Spooner clubs were formed throughout the state. In spite of La Follette's strenuous campaigning, district after district, as they nominated their legislative representatives, unconditionally endorsed Spooner's re-election. By the beginning of September, ten out of the twelve senators nominated and thirty-six (including those of Dane County) out of forty-five assemblymen had been so pledged.[6] Finally even the state central committee capitulated and, by unanimous

[5] *Milwaukee Sentinel,* July 17, 1902. The candidate for Spooner's place was Isaac Stephenson, who early in 1901 had tried to purchase the *Sentinel* for the La Follette wing but Charles Pfister had bought it instead (see H. C. Payne to Spooner, February 7; Spooner to H. C. Payne, February 11, 1901, in Spooner Papers). Stephenson then had established the *Free Press* (see Stephenson, *Recollections,* pp. 218–19).

[6] *Milwaukee Sentinel,* July 29, August 5, 10, 21, 29, September 7, 12, 14, 16, 18, 1902.

resolution, begged Spooner to take the stump to prevent the defeat of the party. By this invitation they practically repudiated the platform.[7]

Up to this time Spooner had kept silent. He had ignored the resolution and had not even declared whether he was a candidate for re-election. He had sedulously remained away from Wisconsin. Stalwart leaders became worried; even Willet Spooner and the Senator's secretary thought he ought to come home pretty quick and campaign and let the people know where he stood.[8] Even when Spooner finally returned to Wisconsin late in September, he re mained only a week and then left for French Lick, Indiana, to rejuvenate himself by taking the waters there. Finally, in the middle of October he consented to enter the campaign, not under the auspices of the state central committee but under the direction of the Congressional campaign committee. He was scheduled for twenty-two meetings, two in each Congressional district. In the campaign he not only paid tribute to President Roosevelt but appealed for the election of the entire Republican state ticket.[9]

Governor La Follette, however, refused to yield. When, as he finished a speech in Appleton, he was asked the direct question if he was for the unconditional re-election of Senator Spooner, he replied that he was for the success of the principles of the Republican party and "the day and hour that Senator Spooner raises his voice for the prin-

[7] Spooner to J. Hicks, November 8; to F. T. Tucker, September 27; to G. Bryant, October 9, 1902, in Spooner Papers.

[8] Willet Spooner to H. Reed, September 16; H. Reed to Willet Spooner, September 17, 1902, *ibid.*

[9] Spooner to H. C. Lodge, November 7, 1902, *ibid.; Milwaukee Sentinel*, September 21, 1902.

ciples of the Republican party, as laid down in the state platform, I will raise my voice for his re-election to the United States Senate." [10] Many of his friends criticized his stand; one wrote that since nine-tenths of the legislative conventions had declared in favor of the unconditional re-election of Spooner, that was tantamount to a platform declaration, and it was his duty to support that platform as it was Spooner's duty to support the state ticket.[11]

The election was a great triumph for the Republicans; they elected 10 Congressmen, the whole state ticket, and 107 members of the legislature. Of these, 83 had been instructed to vote for Spooner's re-election and many others had pledged themselves in speeches or by letter. Spooner, thereupon, announced on December 10 that if he were elected, he would feel himself bound to accept.[12] A joint caucus was held on January 14 and on the first roll call Spooner received 104 votes, while one was cast for Judge Webb; his nomination was then made unanimous. At the official election on January 27, Spooner received 103 votes, while Neal Brown received 26. Because of the entreaties of his friends, Spooner had come from Washington to accept the election in person. He described his reception:

The performance out at Madison was one in the highest degree delightful to me. The vote was unanimous, and the ovation which was given me was beyond description. Gov. La Follette was present. He came forward and said, "I congratulate you, Senator Spooner," to which I replied, "I thank you, Gov. La Follette." It took but a second, was formally polite,

10 La Follette, *La Follette,* I, 154–55; Spooner to J. Hicks, November 7, 1902, in Spooner Papers.

11 H. Colman to La Follette, October 28, 1902, in La Follette Papers.

12 *Milwaukee Sentinel,* December 10, 1902; Spooner to O. H. Platt, November 7; to R. A. Alger, November 8, 1902, in Spooner Papers.

doubtless the most disagreeable thing he ever had to do. . . . The honor, as it came to me, was wonderfully fine. . . . It was unparalleled, and I am grateful to the party, and to the splendid individual support and devotion which I received.[13]

The Stalwarts continued to try to block the adoption of La Follette's progressive program but became less and less successful. Under the leadership of Senator Whitehead they added an amendment to the primary bill, passed in March, 1903, so that it would not go into effect until submitted to a referendum of the people at the next general election, that is, in November, 1904. The amendment had been drawn up by Spooner although he had conspicuously remained away from Wisconsin while the fight for its adoption was taking place.[14] Concerning the primary law, Spooner wrote an old friend:

I am utterly opposed to such a primary law as Mr. La Follette would wish. . . . I think, as you do, that it would make him boss. I do not believe in bosses, and especially I do not believe in such bosses as Mr. La Follette. I think a primary election law as he wants it would destroy the party machinery, which is necessary in order to fight the political enemy of the party, and would build up a lot of personal machines, would make every man a self-seeker, would degrade politics by turning candidacies into bitter personal wrangles and quarrels, etc. I do not see

[13] Spooner to R. R. Frazier, March 25, 1903, in Spooner Papers; *Milwaukee Sentinel*, January 15, 28, 1903.

[14] Spooner to P. L. Spooner, February 7; Willet to Spooner, March 20; C. Pfister to Spooner, March 21; H. Reed to Spooner, March 26, 1903, in Spooner Papers; R. M. La Follette to C. F. Ilsey; to E. W. Krick (copy), March 17, 1903, in La Follette Papers, intimates that Spooner used federal patronage to corrupt the press and to buy votes against the bill. See Lovejoy, *La Follette and the Direct Primary*, pp. 80–81, who says instigation for Spooner's amendment came from the White House but the Spooner Papers give no evidence of this.

how under such a scheme that the office would be likely to seek the man.[15]

Spooner liked to think the office always sought him.

The Stalwarts decided again to oppose the renomination of Governor La Follette. Congressman Babcock, an experienced political manager, for he had been chairman of the Republican Congressional campaign committee for ten years, took charge of the Stalwart campaign. He had broken with the Half-Breeds and his own future was at stake since his return to Congress was being vigorously contested.[16] Spooner had a conference with Babcock in October, 1903, and they decided to put up as their candidate for the gubernatorial nomination Judge Emil Baensch, once lieutenant governor. Philip Spooner, the Senator's brother, became his personal campaign manager. The entrance into the race of former Congressman Samuel A. Cook complicated the situation.[17]

Both factions were aware that this election was the decisive one. In 1900 the Stalwarts had surrendered; in 1902 the election resulted in a draw, with La Follette winning the governorship and Spooner the senatorship. Relations between the two, however, had become increasingly bitter. It was now a fight to the finish. If La Follette won, Spooner would be out of public life at the end of his next term, if not before then. If the Stalwarts won, La Follette and his progressive program would vanish from the political scene.

15 Spooner to S. M. Booth, March 28, 1903, in Spooner Papers.

16 J. Babcock to Spooner, August 5, September 20, 1903; J. V. Quarles to Spooner, August 17, 31, 1903, *ibid.; Milwaukee Sentinel,* February 10, 1904.

17 Annie Spooner, Diary, October 3, 27, 1903; E. Keyes to Spooner, November 15, December 17, 1903, January 9, 1904; Spooner to S. Cook, March 21, 1904, in Spooner Papers.

Each group was determined to annihilate the other and neither was scrupulous about the methods used.

The state central committee, controlled by Governor La Follette, decided that there would be only one convention in 1904; the spring convention, which selected delegates-at-large to the national convention, should also nominate the state officials. This was unprecedented in the Wisconsin Republican party and was considered a political trick to weaken the Stalwart group. Spooner questioned its legality, holding that it was not within the authority of the committee to call a convention to nominate state officers and at the same time to deal with a national issue.[18] When time and time again La Follette had failed to get himself or his candidate nominated, he had charged that the party "bosses" had bought the delegates. Now the Stalwarts accused La Follette of using not only money but also state employees to put over his renomination. Most ubiquitous were the game wardens who, it was said, spent their time not searching for violators of the game laws but ferreting out voters.[19]

The fight for delegates was a desperate one. While La Follette had his state machine, the Stalwarts used the federal officeholders. Senator Quarles, whose own seat was in jeopardy, visited party workers throughout the state to rally them to greater efforts—"to make it a battle royal," he said. "They [party workers] are simply waiting for their trusted leader to draw his sword," he wrote Spooner, urg-

[18] Spooner to E. Keyes, December 1, 1903; E. Keyes to Spooner, November 15, 1903, March 13, 1904; E. Coe to Spooner, December 21, 1903, *ibid.*

[19] E. Keyes to Spooner, March 13, 1904; J. V. Quarles to Spooner, May 7, 1904; Spooner to O. H. Platt, June 2, 1904, *ibid.;* La Follette, *La Follette,* I, 117, 127.

ing him to take over command of the party.[20] It was not until just before the meeting of the convention, however, that Spooner left Washington to take personal charge of the Stalwart campaign. He did so reluctantly, as he had "no taste or tolerance for politics in detail, or for factional leadership." His friend Platt, however, thought it was the only thing for him to do. He wrote:

> The Wisconsin matter is quite ugly, but if it has really brought Spooner to the front to take charge of the situation, it may have improved conditions rather than to have complicated them. The trouble out there has largely been that there was no one to organize and direct the anti-La Follette sentiment. Spooner has been anti-La Follette, but rather wanted to stand out at one side and let others be responsible for the Stalwart organization and effort. If he now takes hold of it I think he can down La Follette.[21]

Governor La Follette made his usual tour of the county fairs that spring to arouse the people to action. He claimed the contest was one between the people and the railroads; the "question is whether the railroads shall control the people or the people control them," he said. He urged individuals to attend the local caucuses, pointing out that the absence of one individual from a caucus might mean the loss of a ward and the loss of a ward might be the loss of an assembly district. He was accused of using Democrats and Socialists to control Republican caucuses. Caucus and convention meetings were exciting; victory was obtained by small margins—so small that sometimes a second meet-

20 J. V. Quarles to Spooner, August 10, 17, 31, 1903, May 7, 1904, in Spooner Papers.
21 Spooner to O. H. Platt, June 2, 1904, in Spooner Papers; O. H. Platt to J. Kean, May 23, 1904, in Platt Papers.

ing was held. This usually meant two delegations.[22] There was considerable confusion. Many delegates did not have correctly certified credentials, that is, ones signed by the chairman and secretary of the county committee. Fully one-tenth of the seats were contested. As the time for the convention drew near, both sides claimed they had enough duly certified delegates to control the convention. But the organization of the convention was in the hands of the La Follette-dominated committee. The day before the convention convened, the state central committee, composed of sixteen La Follette men and six Stalwarts, met to make up the roll of delegates. They decided to seat fifty-nine and a half administration men and forty-three and a half Stalwarts.[23]

The state convention met on May 18 in Madison, for La Follette in 1902 had shifted the state conventions from Milwaukee to the capital. This one was held in the gymnasium of the University of Wisconsin. A double line of husky football players, prison guards, game wardens, and other state employees were stationed at all the entrances to inspect the credentials of those entering the building. The delegates were admitted only in single file into the

22 La Follette, *La Follette*, I, 170–73; A. W. Sanborn to La Follette, May 9, 1904, in La Follette Papers. See also carbons of letters to various political leaders, e.g., to J. C. Kerwin, May 1; to F. W. Rahn, May 2, 1904, in La Follette Papers.

23 *Madison Democrat,* May 15, 1904; *Milwaukee Sentinel,* May 18, 1904. See La Follette Papers for tabulation of delegates, divided into uncontested with correctly certified credentials, those with imperfect credentials, and contested delegates. This tabulation gave La Follette 480⅓ and Stalwarts 423⅔ in the first category. Totals were 571⅓ to 493⅔. See also J. M. Olin to M. Jeffries, May 31, 1904, in Olin Papers at State Historical Society of Wisconsin. His investigation showed that 74 did not have duly accredited credentials and of those with credentials, Stalwarts had 513 and La Follette had 478.

convention area, which had been surrounded by barbed wire to separate the delegates from the spectators. Three huge gridiron heroes were stationed behind Marvin L. Rosenberry, Stalwart member of the state central committee. The chairman of the committee, General George E. Bryant, announced that Irving L. Lenroot, speaker of the assembly, had been selected temporary chairman. When the majority report of the committee, seating the La Follette delegates, was presented, Rosenberry moved that a minority report seating Stalwart delegates be substituted for it. The chairman ruled that those holding certificates of election from the state central committee should be allowed to vote except on their own eligibility. This was the crucial moment; if Lenroot's ruling were upheld by the delegates, then the majority report would be accepted and the nominations made as planned. Almost breathlessly the convention awaited the roll call; the ruling was upheld by a vote of 574⅚ to 485⅙ and the majority report adopted. Then 350 delegates, those supporting Baensch for the gubernatorial nomination, walked out. The "Gym Convention" then nominated La Follette for governor and selected as delegates-at-large to the national convention, La Follette, Isaac Stephenson, J. H. Stout, a state senator, and W. D. Connor, a wealthy businessman who had recently joined the La Follette movement.[24]

The Stalwarts, 567 in number, for they had been joined by the Cook delegates led by former Attorney General E. R. Hicks, met at nine that evening in the Fuller Opera

[24] La Follette, *La Follette*, I, 150, 174–77; *Milwaukee Sentinel*, May 19, 20, 1904. Before the convention met it was reported that La Follette men had tried to conciliate the opposition by promising to elect Spooner and Quarles as delegates-at-large but they declined (see *New York Tribune*, May 19, 1904).

House and organized, selecting Malcolm Jeffries as presiding officer. The next morning, with a notable group present, consisting of two United States Senators, two former governors (Scofield and Upham), and Congressman Babcock, the convention proceeded to the business of the meeting. Judge Baensch announced his withdrawal as a candidate for the governorship and Samuel A. Cook was nominated for that position by acclamation. The convention then selected as delegates-at-large, Spooner, Quarles, Babcock, and Baensch. Spooner, in a stirring speech, called on the Stalwarts to fight. He said:

I have deplored the absolutism which has characterized the last few years' administration. I have supported the party, though at times it meant a supreme test of party loyalty. The crisis was inevitable. I hoped that it might be averted in a way compatible with the rights of the people. But when men are deprived of a *prime facie* right, not by a convention of their peers, but by a committee controlled in the interest of personal ambition, then manly honesty demands justice. I am here today to indorse your action. I cast my fortunes, and I am without political ambitions, with you to the end.[25]

The next engagement in the battle between the Stalwarts and Half-Breeds took place in the national capital. Spooner, in a personal call, and Babcock and Quarles, in long letters, explained to President Roosevelt their side of the controversy.[26] A delegation composed of W. D. Connor,

[25] *New York Tribune,* May 20, 1904; Barton, *La Follette,* pp. 362–64.
[26] J. Babcock to T. Roosevelt, May 25; J. V. Quarles to T. Roosevelt, May 21, 1904, in Roosevelt Papers; Morison (ed.), *Letters of Theodore Roosevelt,* IV, 805. Roosevelt wrote W. E. Cramer on May 27, 1904, that he saw Spooner the day before and that the latter said he should not interfere on one side or the other.

C. C. Gittings, W. Houser, Wisconsin secretary of state, H. P. Myrick, editor of the *Milwaukee Free Press,* and I. L. Lenroot presented the case of the La Follette delegation. The President advised them to see Senator Aldrich and Postmaster General Payne. The former, according to Lenroot, received them very coldly.[27] Payne was in a difficult position; he had always been associated with the Stalwarts but he was a member of President Roosevelt's cabinet and was, because of the death of Mark Hanna, chairman of the Republican National Committee. Although he favored the Stalwarts, he remained aloof from the contest.[28]

An attempt was made to get the two groups to agree to the seating of both delegations with half a vote each. In that way the dispute could be kept off the floor of the convention and the presidential ticket, which both groups supported, would not be endangered. The chief advocate of this plan was former Senator Chandler, the Washington representative of the Half-Breeds. "He is a pestiferous and meddlesome man, who knows, as you know, nothing about the situation in Wisconsin. Because he was beaten [in 1900] by the Boston & Maine in New Hampshire he thinks every demagogue who shouts anti-railroad is a statesman, and every man who opposes him, no matter upon what grounds, is a corporationist," Spooner wrote Payne.[29] The Stalwarts absolutely refused to consider an equal division, and the Half-Breeds, although not quite so obstinate, did not favor it. Chandler continued his efforts to bring about a compromise, trying to persuade Aldrich and Lodge that

27 I. Stephenson to T. Roosevelt (copy), May 26; C. C. Gittings to R. M. La Follette, June 4, 1904, in La Follette Papers; interview with Lenroot, March 25, 1947.

28 H. Taylor to Spooner, May 21, June 4, 1904, in Spooner Papers.

29 Spooner to H. C. Payne, July 4, 1904, *ibid.*

this was the best solution. He maintained that the chief issue was between government by the people and government by railroad corporations. Lodge replied that the attitude of the two groups as to state laws had nothing to do with the question; that only the methods used to seize control of the state convention concerned the national committee. Chandler tried to convince Roosevelt that he should intervene and insist on a division of the votes of the delegates-at-large but the President refused to take any action.[30]

No decision had been made when the national committee held its meeting on June 17 to decide on the credentials of the delegates. With Payne absenting himself, the committee listened to Gilbert Roe and H. C. Chynoweth present the case for the Half-Breeds and John M. Olin and Malcolm Jeffries for the Stalwarts. Four and a half hours were consumed in the presentation of the case but the committee took only one minute to come to a decision —to throw out the delegation headed by Governor La Follette and seat the one headed by Spooner.[31]

The Stalwart delegation from Wisconsin had established itself in ten bedrooms and a club room at the Hotel Auditorium. On June 20 the delegation met to select their members for the various committees. Payne was re-elected to the national committee, Quarles was elected chairman of the delegation, and Spooner was made a member of the

[30] W. E. Chandler to N. Aldrich, June 2, 4; to W. Houser; to I. Lenroot, June 5; to H. C. Lodge, June 5; to T. Roosevelt, June 15, 1904; H. C. Lodge to W. Chandler, June 8; W. Houser to W. Chandler, June 8; I. Lenroot to W. Chandler, June 10, 1904, in Chandler Papers.

[31] J. M. Olin to M. Jeffries, May 20; to J. Whitehead, May 31, 1904, in Olin Papers; Mark A. De Wolfe Howe, *George von Lengerke Meyer: His Life and Public Services,* p. 92.

resolutions committee.[32] Lodge, chairman of the latter committee, had expressed his desire that Spooner be on his committee and in May they had met with President Roosevelt and prepared the planks to be included in the platform.[33]

On June 21 Postmaster General Payne, as chairman of the national committee, called the convention to order and Elihu Root was elected temporary chairman and delivered the keynote address. On that day also the committee on credentials considered the Wisconsin case. The La Follette group merely filed a statement to the effect: "We do not . . . consider this an unprejudiced committee. . . . We therefore decline to present our case, preferring to submit it to the people of Wisconsin at the election in November." The committee unanimously concurred with the national committee and recommended the placing of the Stalwart delegates on the permanent roll. The report was adopted by the convention with only one dissenting vote. The Wisconsin case was the only exciting thing at the convention; President Roosevelt was nominated by acclamation and Senator Charles W. Fairbanks was given second place on the ticket.[34]

President Roosevelt was disgruntled over the split in the Republican ranks in Wisconsin; he thought it unfair of the Stalwarts to pick the year he was running for President to bolt La Follette.[35] However, he continued to rely on

[32] H. C. Payne to Spooner, June 2, 18, 1904, in Spooner Papers; *Milwaukee Sentinel*, June 21, 22, 1904.

[33] H. C. Lodge to Spooner, May 11, 1904, in Spooner Papers; *Milwaukee Sentinel*, May 5, 1904.

[34] *Official Proceedings of the Thirteenth Republican National Convention, 1904*, pp. 44, 76–77; *Washington Post*, June 22, 1904.

[35] Henry Cabot Lodge, *Selections from the Correspondence of Theodore Roosevelt and Henry Cabot Lodge, 1884–1918*, II, 91.

Spooner and urged him to come and see him either in
Washington or at Oyster Bay as soon as he could, as there
were several matters about which he wanted his advice. He
also sent him, for his criticism, a draft of his letter of acceptance. Spooner read it carefully several times. It is a
"powerful paper," he wrote. With that compliment, he
included a thirteen-page memorandum containing not
only suggestions of changes in phraseology but also some
new proposals. To this the President replied: "Next to
Root it is you who have given me the best suggestions for
changes in my letter. The bulk of the changes you suggest
I have adopted." [36]

The Spooners went to the northern New Hampshire
farm they had purchased the previous year but the summer was spoiled by politics, Mrs. Spooner complained.[37]
The Senator spent his vacation studying Wisconsin election laws, Wisconsin Supreme Court decisions on them,
election laws of other states, and the statements filed by
Olin and Lenroot before the Republican National Committee. He was gathering material for the preparation of a
brief for a case which the Stalwarts planned to present to
the Wisconsin Supreme Court. They were going to request
an injunction to restrain the secretary of state from placing
the La Follette ticket on the official ballot under the regular Republican designation.[38] The La Follette group

[36] T. Roosevelt to Spooner, July 30, 31, August 26, 1904; Spooner to T.
Roosevelt, August 22, 1904, in Roosevelt Papers.

[37] Annie Spooner, Diary, August 3, 1904. At the time they bought the
farm a story was circulated through the Associated Press that Spooner had
bought a great game preserve of 100,000 acres. Spooner was irritated, as he
was bombarded by salesmen and applicants for positions as game super-
intendents (see Spooner to W. A. Van Brunt, June 3; to O. A. Ellis, June
17, 1903, in Spooner Papers).

[38] Spooner to H. Reed, July 8; to H. C. Payne, July 4, 1904; G. G. Hill
to Spooner, July 18, 1904, in Spooner Papers.

claimed that the secretary of state had to place on the ballot the names certified by the state central committee, in this case the committee which had conducted the "Gym Convention." That committee met on September 12 and, as was to be expected, declared in favor of the nominees of that convention.[39]

Spooner returned to Wisconsin early in September to help prepare the argument. He put his faith in the court but John M. Olin thought the Stalwarts should merely announce they were the regular Republican party and fight La Follette on the stump. Olin had been retained by the Stalwarts to present the oral argument before the court, as Spooner thought it would be unseemly for him to do so since he was a United States Senator. Spooner did, however, consult with the lawyers about the case and spent the whole night before the hearing writing arguments on various points. His den was in a state of confusion when he finished; paper and cigar stubs were scattered all over the floor.[40] The Stalwarts had three arguments: First, that the convention which nominated Samuel A. Cook as governor was the regular one, as it had been recognized by the national committee; second, that the state law said candidates were to be certified by officers of the convention but did not specify the state central committee; third, that the decision as to which convention was the regular one was a judicial matter, and that the old state central committee was disqualified from acting judicially because it was being asked to decide on the regularity and validity of its own

39 Barton, *La Follette*, pp. 402–5.
40 J. Olin to H. McGillan, May 20; to T. W. Goldin, July 18, August 8; to J. W. Babcock, July 27, August 31, September 5, 1904, in Olin Papers; Spooner to J. A. Humbird, September 26, 1904, in Spooner Papers.

acts and also because some members on the committee were financially interested.[41]

Although the arguments were presented on September 16–17, it was October 5 before the decision was rendered. The court by a three-to-one decision, with Justice Siebecker abstaining, decided that according to the statutes of Wisconsin, the state central committee had the power to certify which was the regular convention and that any bias or interest of its members did not disqualify it. The jurists went on to say that the decision of the national committee was not entitled to recognition by the secretary of state because the statute gave the state central committee exclusive jurisdiction. Since the state committee had decided that the nominations headed by Governor La Follette were entitled to the use of the name Republican party, the secretary of state should act accordingly. The court concluded:

What the real right of the matter in dispute might be found to be, were this court permitted to disregard the decision of the special tribunal and investigate and determine the merits of the controversy from that standpoint, it has no right to decide or suggest. Duly constituted authority having spoken within its jurisdiction, it must be conclusively presumed here to have spoken rightly.[42]

The night the decision was announced Spooner was scheduled to speak in Milwaukee. Never before had he been put in such an embarrassing position, for he had always prided himself on his party regularity and here he was speaking on behalf of a bolting ticket. He announced at

[41] J. M. Olin to Spooner, August 24; Spooner to J. Olin, August 29, 1904, in Spooner Papers.
[42] 122 Wis. 534 (*State ex rel. Cook & Others* v. *Houser, Secretary of State*).

the meeting that the Stalwarts would remain in the race since the court had given no opinion on the merits of the case. Privately he advised the withdrawal of the state ticket for fear that a campaign for it might endanger the national ticket and defeat many Stalwart candidates for the state legislature. His advice was not followed. Cook, however, withdrew from the gubernatorial race but former Governor Scofield consented to be a sacrificial candidate.[43]

Spooner announced that he was going to retire from the campaign. He explained that it would be impossible for him to make speeches for the national ticket and for members of Congress without at the same time disclosing his opposition to the state ticket. Never again, he declared, would he ask the Republicans of Wisconsin to vote for La Follette.[44]

The national committee immediately recognized the La Follette ticket. Shortly after the decision was announced, the vice-presidential nominee, Senator Fairbanks, and other prominent Republicans were sent into Wisconsin with instructions to couple the name of La Follette with that of Roosevelt. Babcock, chairman of the Congressional campaign committee, was told he should give no aid to the Stalwart state committee as it was the bolting one. If he were not reasonable, everything concerning Wisconsin should be taken out of his hands, the President directed the chairman of the national committee, George B. Cortelyou.[45]

[43] Spooner to E. M. Rogers, October 14; to W. H. Phipps, October 15, 1904, in Spooner Papers; *New York Tribune,* October 6, 1904.

[44] Spooner to H. Kohlsaat, to R. Alger, to H. C. Putnam, October 14, 1904, in Spooner Papers. He did make one speech for the national ticket just before the election (see *Madison Democrat,* November 6, 1904).

[45] T. Roosevelt to G. B. Cortelyou, October 6, 1904, in Roosevelt Papers; *The Nation,* October 13, 27, 1904.

October brought one blow after another to Spooner. The decision of the supreme court adverse to the Stalwarts and President Roosevelt's support of La Follette was followed by the death of Henry C. Payne, Spooner's old friend and political associate, and then *McClure's Magazine* came out with the Lincoln Steffens article. Spooner knew that Steffens was writing an article about Wisconsin to be included in a series entitled "Enemies of the Republic." Some time during the summer Steffens had left a card at Spooner's hotel in New York City, asking for an interview with him; he said he had an introduction from Loeb, President Roosevelt's secretary. The Senator had ignored the request and had had no communication with Steffens. Postmaster General Payne had heard from the President that Steffens had been to Wisconsin and that "his article was strongly commendatory of La Follette and his efforts for reform and purer politics and very condemnatory of Spooner and Payne, etc. etc. . . . Judging by the previous articles written by Steffens and which have appeared in McClures—we may expect a nasty screed," he had written Spooner.[46]

Steffens' article, appearing in a reputable monthly magazine, purported to be an unbiased one. The author claimed that he had gone to Wisconsin prejudiced against Governor La Follette, but that after an exhaustive study he had become convinced that the Stalwarts were the "Enemies of the Republic." The article began with La Follette's race for the office of district attorney against the wishes of the local bosses, Elisha W. Keyes and Philip L. Spooner.

[46] Annie Spooner, Diary, October 9, 1904; L. Steffens to Spooner, n.d.; H. C. Payne to Spooner, August 19, 1904; Spooner to J. Whitehead, September 29, 1904, in Spooner Papers.

It told how he had fought against the lumber and railroad interests which had purchased seats in the Senate for Sawyer and Spooner, and asserted that the latter represented in the national legislature not the people of Wisconsin but the "interests." It concluded with the defeat of the Stalwarts in 1900. The article was one long paean of praise for La Follette.[47]

The Stalwarts claimed that the article was just a piece of political propaganda designed to be the culminating blow in the campaign against them. The time of its appearance and the fact that free copies seem to have been widely distributed throughout the state would bear out their contention. La Follette had spent a week conferring with Steffens and during the summer had been in close touch with him, furnishing him with material adverse to Spooner and the Stalwarts. He had been confident that the tone of the article would be "right" and that it would appear during the last month of the campaign to settle things in their favor.[48] The *Milwaukee Sentinel,* commenting on the article, asserted: "A more brazen, disreputable prostitution of the power of the press has never been recorded in this country." It declared Steffens had neglected all documentary evidence and had written La Follette's story as La Follette had wanted it written. Spooner, during the summer, had been asked by *Collier's* and *Harper's* to write an article about Wisconsin but he had refused. He finally did give a

47 Lincoln Steffens, "Enemies of the Republic: Wisconsin," *McClure's Magazine,* 23 (October, 1904), 564–79.
48 La Follette to A. R. Hall, July 26; to G. E. Roe, July 27; to L. Steffens, November 14, 1904, in La Follette Papers; W. E. Howe to Spooner, September 25; H. O. Fairchild to Spooner, October 3, 1904, in Spooner Papers; W. E. Chandler to W. Houser, September 23, 1904; W. Houser to W. Chandler, September 28, 1904, in Chandler Papers.

statement to the *Milwaukee Sentinel*. He declared the article had not touched the real merits of the controversy in the Wisconsin Republican party, that it was nothing but a partisan brief for Governor La Follette. Most of his declaration was a denial of the charge that Sawyer and Stephenson had purchased the Senate seat for him in 1885.[49] Steffens had cited as his source for that accusation a conversation with Isaac Stephenson himself. After the appearance of the article Stephenson was purported to have said that the story was not true and, when asked why he did not say so publicly, replied: "That would hurt La Follette, and I want to help him; it would help Spooner, and I hate him." Finally after the election, much to Spooner's satisfaction, Stephenson made a public retraction in the *Milwaukee Free Press*. He said he had never told Steffens the story that appeared in the article concerning a conversation between himself and Sawyer about spending $52,000 to purchase the Senate seat for Spooner in 1885. He also stated that although he had contributed a large sum to the party campaign fund, it had not been given for the purpose of electing Spooner Senator, for it was not until after the election that he had known he was a candidate for that position.[50]

The election of 1904 resulted in an overwhelming victory for the Republicans; President Roosevelt received a plurality of over 155,000 and Governor La Follette of over 50,000; Scofield received only 12,000 votes. Besides giving

[49] *Milwaukee Sentinel*, September 23, October 3, 1904; *Collier's* to Spooner, September 2; *Harper's* to Spooner, September 6, 1904, in Spooner Papers.

[50] Spooner to F. W. von Cotzhausen, December 25, 1904; P. L. Spooner to J. Spooner, December 2, 1904, in Spooner Papers; *Milwaukee Sentinel*, December 2, 3, 1904.

La Follette control of the state government, the election resulted in the establishment of the first mandatory state-
wide direct primary in the United States, for in the refer-
• endum on that issue almost 62 per cent of the votes were
cast in favor of its adoption.[51]

Republican control of the state legislature ensured the
election of a Republican to the United States Senate but
it was also quite evident that Quarles had little chance of
being re-elected. There were three avowed candidates besides Quarles: Representatives John J. Esch and Henry A.
Cooper, and Judge Charles T. Webb.[52] Isaac Stephenson,
as usual, hoped he would be elected and thought he had
the support of Governor La Follette. Yet there were rumors that La Follette had accepted the nomination for the
governorship not because he wanted a third term but because it would put him in a good position to receive the
senatorship.[53] Spooner wrote his brother Philip: "I intend
to do everything I can for Quarles, and I desire him above
all others, of course, but I am extremely anxious that
neither La Follette nor Cooper should be sent to the Senate while I am here. On questions of patronage it would
be simply disgusting." [54]

Just before the Republican caucus meeting it was rumored, and evidence seems to support it, that an agreement
had been made whereby the men supporting Esch and
Cooper would, on the first ballot, give their votes to Gov-

51 Lovejoy, *La Follette and Direct Primary,* pp. 90–91; *New York Tribune Almanac, 1905,* p. 377.

52 *Milwaukee Sentinel,* November 2, 9, 22, 29, 30, December 2, 23, 1904.

53 J. V. Quarles to Spooner, August 31, 1903, December 30, 1904, January 18, 1905; Spooner to J. V. Quarles, May 2, 1904, in Spooner Papers; *Milwaukee Sentinel,* October 12, December 8, 1904.

54 Spooner to P. L. Spooner, December 9, 1904, in Spooner Papers.

ernor La Follette as a compliment. He would then decline the nomination and the real balloting would take place.[55] The caucus was called to order by Chairman Connor on January 23, and on the first ballot votes were cast as follows: La Follette, 65; Quarles, 26; Webb, 10; Esch, 4; and Connor, 2. Instead of declining, La Follette accepted the nomination, which was confirmed by his election by the legislature the following day. He announced that he would remain in Wisconsin to see that his legislative program was carried through and would not assume the senatorship until January, 1906.[56]

The galleries looked on with amusement when Spooner, on January 4, 1906, escorted Robert M. La Follette to the Vice-President's desk to take the oath of office as United States Senator. The Half-Breeds had expected Spooner to snub the junior Senator when he arrived. Instead, Spooner met him at the door, introduced him to several of his associates, and invited him to sit down by him. "I always intended to do about it what would be in accord with the traditions of the Senate, due to the State which has honored me, and due to myself as a gentleman," Spooner wrote his brother Philip.[57]

La Follette was very disgruntled when he compared his position in the Senate with that of his colleague. Spooner was chairman of the Committee on Rules and a member of

55 J. V. Quarles to Spooner, January 9, 19, 25, 1905; E. Keyes to Spooner, January 25, 1905, in Spooner Papers; *Milwaukee Sentinel*, January 20, 1905.
56 *Milwaukee Sentinel*, January 24, 25, 26, 1905; La Follette, *La Follette*, I, 187–89.
57 *Milwaukee Sentinel*, January 5, 1906; Willet to Spooner, January 6; Spooner to P. L. Spooner, January 9, 1906, in Spooner Papers; see La Follette, *La Follette*, I, 199–200.

the committees on Finance, Foreign Relations, Judiciary, Public Health, and Revolutionary Claims. The first four were the most important committees in the Senate. La Follette had wanted to be on the Committee on Interstate Commerce; instead, he had been given positions on the committees on the Census, Civil Service and Retrenchment, Claims, Immigration, Indian Affairs, Pensions, and the chairmanship of the Committee to Investigate Conditions of the Potomac River Front.[58] He had been warned, he said, that a hole had been prepared for him by the reactionary Senators so that Spooner could claim that Wisconsin had "one Senator and a vacancy." Spooner had been a member of the caucus committee, which assigned committee positions, as well as a member of the one which allotted offices. La Follette might think he was badly treated, but in reality his committee positions and his office were far better than those Spooner received when he first entered the Senate.[59]

"What a brutal thing it was to send La Follette here in his place, brutal to Joe and brutal to me. It is worse to me than Joe, I think," Spooner wrote former Senator Quarles's brother after a particularly bitter battle over patronage.[60] To quarrel with his colleague over this issue was a new experience for Spooner. When Sawyer was in the Senate Spooner had usually deferred to his wishes, for he disliked that part of the senatorial job. Besides, they had been in accord as to the control of the Republican party in Wisconsin, as had Spooner and Quarles. La Follette and

[58] *Congressional Record,* 59th Cong., 1st Sess. (1905–6), pp. 537, 683; La Follette, *Autobiography,* p. 375.

[59] Stephenson, *Aldrich,* p. 265; *Milwaukee Sentinel,* December 23, 1905; W. B. Allison to Spooner, December 7, 1905, in Spooner Papers.

[60] Spooner to Charles Quarles, June 12, 1906, in Spooner Papers.

Spooner, however, were not likely to agree on any recommendation, for each was trying to strengthen his faction of the party. Even before La Follette took his seat, he had complained that Spooner was trying to pension off leading Stalwarts by getting them positions in the Roosevelt administration. He especially criticized the appointment of A. L. Sanborn, Spooner's former law partner, as federal judge of the Western District.[61]

The first clash between Senators Spooner and La Follette regarding distribution of patronage came over the nomination of Dr. Amos Parker Wilder to succeed General Edward S. Bragg as consul general at Hong Kong. It was an appointment over which Spooner himself was not enthusiastic. It had been promoted by Secretary of War Taft, Albert Shaw, editor of the *Review of Reviews,* President Nicholas Murray Butler of Columbia University, and other educators. At President Roosevelt's request, Spooner had recommended the appointment but he was about the only Wisconsin resident to endorse it. Wilder was not popular in the Badger State, not even with the Stalwarts.[62] He was editor of the *Wisconsin State Journal,* a Stalwart paper that had recently been sold by Horace Taylor to Wilder. The latter, according to Spooner, had not made a success of it "either from the party or a financial standpoint." [63] Appointment to the consul generalship, however, would enable Wilder to keep control of the

61 La Follette to H. A. Cooper, December 23, 1904, February 22, 1905; to R. L. Jones, January 6, 1905, in La Follette Papers; Spooner to A. L. Sanborn, December 22, 1904; to T. Roosevelt, January 5, 1905, in Spooner Papers.

62 *Milwaukee Sentinel,* January 24, 1906; *The Nation,* February 8, 1906; T. Roosevelt to Spooner, March 14, 1905, in Roosevelt Papers; Spooner to O. H. Fethers, January 29, 1906, in Spooner Papers.

63 Spooner to P. L. Spooner, January 9, 1905, in Spooner Papers.

paper, which might otherwise fall into the hands of La Follette or Stephenson.[64] When the junior Senator gave notice he was going to oppose the confirmation of the appointment because Wilder had filled the *Wisconsin State Journal* with constant abuse of him, with charges of crimes and of using offices to purchase legislators' votes for measures, Spooner prepared for "a nasty fight." To offset the plea made by La Follette that the appointment was "personally offensive" to him—a claim that usually won over the full support of Senators, a practice called "senatorial courtesy"—Spooner got copies of La Follette's speeches in which he had attacked the Senate and individual Senators. Spooner won this first round; Wilder's appointment was confirmed by the Senate.[65]

Spooner and La Follette could not even agree on the division of the districts in Wisconsin. It was customary for a Senator to nominate the judge, attorney, marshal, and Indian and pension agents in the federal judicial district in which he lived. Sawyer and Quarles, therefore, had made the recommendations for the positions in the eastern district and Spooner in the western. Spooner and La Follette, however, both lived in Madison so residence could not be the basis for division. The eastern district had the larger number of offices to fill, so both Senators wanted it. For several months all appointments were held up. Not being able to come to any agreement themselves, the two Senators presented the problem to President Roosevelt. The latter decided that since in the past Spooner had suggested the nominations for appointments in the western

[64] Spooner to W. C. Cowling, February 19, 1906, *ibid.*

[65] Spooner to A. P. Wilder, February 23, March 4; to E. Keyes, March 5, 1906, *ibid; Congressional Record*, 59th Cong., 1st Sess., pp. 1825, 3460.

district, he should continue to do so and La Follette could make the recommendations for the eastern.[66] Spooner was not particularly upset about this decision for it gave him the opportunity to reappoint some of his friends who undoubtedly would have lost their jobs if La Follette had been awarded that district.[67]

The two Senators had also disagreed over postmasterships. According to custom, Senators made the recommendations only in those Congressional districts represented by a member of the opposition party, and in their home towns. There was only one Democratic district—the sixth—and both Senators wanted to be responsible for Fond du Lac County. La Follette suggested they cast lots, but Spooner refused and insisted that President Roosevelt decide. This time the decision was in Spooner's favor; he kept the same counties he had when Quarles was his colleague.[68] The situation was also complicated because Spooner and La Follette claimed the same home town. Spooner recommended the reappointment of Keyes. La Follette considered this "personally offensive" to him. Spooner, however, assured Keyes that everything would be all right for he had, before La Follette came to the Senate, explained the whole situation to Postmaster General Cortelyou and he had promised that Keyes would be retained. He admitted that there was a chance that the appointment might be overruled by President Roosevelt; one could

66 Spooner to M. C. Phillips, December 19, 1900; to A. Stewart, June 5, 1906, in Spooner Papers; T. Roosevelt to Spooner; to R. M. La Follette, June 29, 1906, in Roosevelt Papers.

67 Willet Spooner to J. Spooner, January 28; Spooner to J. G. Clark, June 12; to S. W. Campbell, June 13, 1906, in Spooner Papers.

68 Spooner to V. Warner, September 29, 1906, *ibid.;* La Follette to W. B. Ninahan, January 13; to C. R. Boardman, February 2, 1906, in La Follette Papers; *Milwaukee Sentinel,* February 2, 1906.

never be absolutely sure what the President would do. The appointment was made in April, 1906, and confirmed without protest.[69]

La Follette even interfered in postmaster appointments in districts represented by Republicans.[70] "This is the first time I have ever known a Senator to intervene to overturn the recommendation of a Member of Congress of a candidate for postmaster in the latter's district," Spooner alleged. Since before the time of Lincoln it had been a precedent that the Representative should control appointments in his district. Yet La Follette asked for the withdrawal of the name of the man recommended by Congressman Minor and appointed by Roosevelt as postmaster at Marinette. He had done so at the demand of Isaac Stephenson. The latter should be recognized, La Follette said, for he had done so much great work for the Republican party over a period of forty years and Congressman Minor was not a Republican for he had openly bolted the state ticket in the last election. When Spooner learned that the name had been withdrawn, he felt it was necessary that he take a hand in the fight. It was a very bitter one. La Follette told the President he would rather give up all the rest of the patronage than to lose in this Marinette case. Spooner and other Stalwarts felt that if they did not win in this contest, it would mean a great loss of prestige for them and would lead to La Follette's attempting to set up a full dictatorship over Wisconsin ap-

[69] Spooner to E. Keyes, February 5, March 8, 1906, in Spooner Papers; *Congressional Record,* 59th Cong., 1st Sess., pp. 4949, 5147.

[70] For a fight over the Milwaukee postmastership see *Milwaukee Sentinel,* March 3, 8, 1906; Spooner to C. Pfister, January 22; to G. P. Stickney, June 6, 1906, in Spooner Papers; La Follette to A. J. Reid, March 7; to C. A. Sercomb, March 9, 1906, in La Follette Papers.

pointments. Spooner had three conferences with the President and the appointment was even made a matter of cabinet discussion. The case was finally decided against La Follette; the President declared there was no justification for upsetting the precedent of accepting the recommendation of the congressman from that district.[71]

These patronage fights increased Spooner's dislike of La Follette. "The man . . . has such overwhelming qualities of malice, conceit, effrontery, impudence and general cussedness that I dare not trust myself to write of him lest I might seem to abuse him," he wrote a friend. Spooner not only distrusted La Follette but he believed the reforms advocated by him would destroy the very foundations of the American democratic system. He did not think La Follette was sincere, thought his progressive program was merely a trick on his part to gain power. He was sure that if the people had the facts, their sound second judgment would overthrow the movement and the right principles would in the end triumph.[72]

Spooner hoped that some progress might be made toward the overthrow of La Follette in the 1906 election. That year in Wisconsin there was held the first state-wide

[71] I. Stephenson to La Follette, May 8, June 2, 3, 1906; La Follette to L. S. Patrick, April 23; to T. Roosevelt, June 16, 1906, in La Follette Papers; Spooner to H. P. Bird, June 4; to Willet, June 11; to E. Keyes, June 18, 1906, in Spooner Papers; T. Roosevelt to R. La Follette, June 29, 30, 1906, in Roosevelt Papers. Stephenson in his May 8 letter reminded La Follette that he had put a quarter of a million dollars into the *Milwaukee Free Press*.

[72] Spooner to G. W. Burnell, June 12; to Willet, June 11, 1906, in Spooner Papers. Lenroot, in an interview on March 25, 1947, compared Spooner's abhorrence of La Follette to that of many people today toward Communists.

primary to nominate the men who would run in the general election. James O. Davidson, acting governor, was a candidate for the office he was occupying. He had expected La Follette's support, for it had been at his solicitation that he had consented to run for the office of lieutenant governor, which paid only $1,200, instead of being a candidate for re-election to the treasuryship, a $5,000 job. La Follette, however, even before he resigned the governorship, had persuaded Irving Lenroot to be a candidate. Lenroot, against his better judgment, had agreed and had begun his campaign as soon as La Follette took office as Senator.[73] The Spooners in Wisconsin, the Senator's brother Philip and the Senator's son Willet, decided to support Davidson. The Senator at first did not think much of the acting governor and had written Willet: "He is as limp as a wet rag. I judge he would be utterly spineless if it were not for the influence of his wife. When he shall have been elected, if he is, La Follette with a pass or two over his empty head, will probably own him." Philip, however, was certain that Davidson was on the square and that La Follette would never be able to touch him again.[74]

The campaign was a bitter one and a queer one, with the Stalwarts allied with the independent Half-Breeds against La Follette and his candidate. Since only about one-fifth of the new alignment consisted of Half-Breeds, the Stalwarts expected to be back in control of the party if Davidson won. La Follette stumped the state for Lenroot and opposed the re-election of Congressmen Babcock, Stafford,

[73] Haugen, "Reminiscences," *Wisconsin Magazine of History*, 12 (March, 1929), 275, 278; La Follette to I. Lenroot, January 5, 1906, in La Follette Papers.

[74] Spooner to Willet, June 11; Willet to Spooner, August 14, 23, 1906, in Spooner Papers.

and Otjen.[75] Spooner, in conformity with his belief that federal officials should not meddle in a contest between candidates for a nomination within the party, remained in New Hampshire throughout the campaign.[76]

The primaries were held in September. At the polls the voters received several ballots, one for each party. The voter used whichever one he chose, discarding those of the other parties; thus Democrats could vote in Republican contests. Davidson had been afraid of this Democratic vote, but his fears had been needless for he won almost a two-to-one victory over Lenroot. In accordance with the primary law, the men nominated at the primaries for state offices and for senate and assembly were to meet at the capital to draw up a platform for the party and to select a state central committee.[77] They met in Madison on September 25–26. William D. Connor was elected chairman of the state central committee. He had broken with La Follette and had supported Davidson for the gubernatorial nomination; he had been nominated for the lieutenant governorship. Connor had the reputation of being an excellent organizer and it was said that La Follette hated him even more than he did Spooner.[78] The new chairman, however, was intent on building up his own party organization rather than being controlled by the Stalwarts. Not until near the end of the campaign were Stalwart leaders asked to take the stump. During the last week before the election Spooner made several speeches in the state advocating the election

[75] La Follette to I. Stephenson, June 23, 1906, in La Follette Papers; La Follette, *La Follette*, I, 213.

[76] Spooner to J. Luchsinger, June 6, 1906, in Spooner Papers.

[77] Raney, *Wisconsin*, pp. 289–90.

[78] E. Keyes to Spooner, June 3; Willet to Spooner, August 14; Annie Spooner to J. Spooner, September 26, 1906, in Spooner Papers.

of all those nominated at the primaries on the Republican ticket.[79] This was the last time Spooner campaigned in Wisconsin; for over thirty years he had stumped the state in almost every campaign for the success of the Republican party.

The election of 1904 had marked the end of an era in Wisconsin politics. For a quarter of a century the Republican party had been dominated by Sawyer, Payne, and Spooner, men of wealth with broad business interests and a big stake in the survival of the existing American capitalistic system. To maintain it the Republican party should be kept in control, they believed. To do that it was essential that party unity be preserved. It seemed to Spooner that La Follette threatened not only to destroy the existing economic system but also the party to which throughout his life Spooner had been devoted. Spooner explained to a friend: "It is not a struggle for leadership, power or patronage among the Republicans with whom I am acting, but is a struggle to prevent the disintegration and Bryanization of the Republican party in Wisconsin." He thought that before long there would be a realignment of parties— that the Solid South would be broken and conservative Democrats would ally with conservative Republicans to form a party in opposition to the "socialists, populists, the social democrats, the radicals of the democracy and the radicals of the republican party." [80] Half a century later the same prophecy is being made by many political leaders.

79 Spooner to O. Fethers, October 16; to C. D. Booth, November 9, 1906; O. Fethers to Spooner, October 12, 1906, in Spooner Papers; Davidson and the state ticket were elected by a plurality of 80,000. Nine Republican congressmen were elected but Babcock was defeated.

80 Spooner to G. A. Benham, July 1; to J. Hicks, November 11, 1904, in Spooner Papers.

11 : *Last Session in Congress (1905-1907)*

"THE TIDAL WAVE OF POPULISM . . . SEEMS TO BE BUBBLING OVER IN THE WHITE HOUSE YARD"*

S P O O N E R F E L T that President Roosevelt was gravitating toward the progressive political and economic philosophy and was "drifting away from the doctrines and principles of the Fathers." He wrote to a friend: "The line of demarcation which they drew in the Constitution between the three co-ordinate and independent branches of the Government is constantly invaded." [1] Roosevelt was developing a theory of Executive leadership, a belief that the President was the steward of the people and should do all he could for the benefit of the rank and file. He insisted the President was not bound to carry on merely those functions specified in the Constitution but that the Executive power was limited only by the restrictions and prohibi-

* Spooner to E. Keyes, December 25, 1904, in Spooner Papers.
[1] Spooner to A. S. Batchellor, June 18, 1906, in Spooner Papers.

tions mentioned in the document.[2] During his first administration Roosevelt had made a name for himself as an
independent Executive with his trust-busting program and
his unprecedented interference in the coal strike. Spooner
at the time thought his intervention, when he called the
representatives of labor and management to a conference,
a mistake as entirely beyond federal jurisdiction—"a dangerous experiment." [3] Yet when the question of an appropriation to pay the expenses of the Anthracite Coal Strike
Commission, selected by Roosevelt to help settle the strike,
came up in the Senate, Spooner vindicated the President.
What legal subtleties he used to explain the actions of
President Roosevelt! When he called the conference he
was not acting in his official capacity, said Spooner, but as
a representative of the people, who were vitally interested
in the outcome of the strike. When he selected a commission to study the dispute he had merely invited certain
men to act as arbitrators, for only Congress had the power
to establish commissions. Whether or not the congressmen
were taken in by these legal ramifications, they voted the
appropriation.[4] The setting up of extralegal commissions
was a favorite device used by Roosevelt to accomplish his
aims, especially those for which he had no specific grant of
power. When the work was finished, he then requested

[2] Theodore Roosevelt, *Autobiography,* pp. 371–72.

[3] Spooner to W. B. Allison, October 9, 1902, in Spooner Papers; Pringle,
Roosevelt, pp. 264–78; Jessup, *Root,* I, 272–77. *The Times* (London), October 17, 1902, said: "We are witnessing not merely the ending of a coal
strike, but the definite entry of a powerful government upon a novel
sphere of operation."

[4] *Congressional Record,* 57th Cong., 2d Sess., pp. 222–25; Spooner to
O. W. Mosher, January 15; to S. E. Haislip, January 17; to L. E. Riblet,
March 26, 1903, in Spooner Papers. Spooner also got anthracite coal put
on the free list to help alleviate the coal famine caused by the strike.

of Congress an appropriation to publish the report or to implement the findings.

During his second administration Roosevelt took the initiative in developing a legislative program. He admitted that in theory the President had no legislative power but maintained that, as the representative of all the people, he was obligated to see that the right laws were passed. This he could do, constitutionally, by means of his messages to Congress and his veto, or threat of veto.[5]

Spooner disagreed with President Roosevelt on most of the domestic issues that came up before the Fifty-ninth Congress. Spooner was primarily a lawyer, well-versed in history and economics but as adjuncts to his study of law. He revered the Constitution as a document and thought it was the bulwark of the rights of the people. The courts were the instruments to protect these rights and an attack on the judiciary was to him anarchism. It was a government of law, not of men, that he believed in. He deplored "the tidal wave of populism" which he saw sweeping eastward to Washington and the "geyser" of which "seems to be bubbling over in the White House yard." He hated to see Roosevelt tending toward a belief in complete popular sovereignty—of absolute majority rule with few constitutional restrictions—with very few judicial limitations on the executive and legislative branches of the government, with the encroachment of the federal government into the realm of state activities.[6]

The ascendancy of President Roosevelt as a legislative leader and the declining influence of the Old Guard in the

[5] Wilfred E. Binkley, *President and Congress*, pp. 192–94.
[6] Spooner to E. Keyes, December 25, 1904; to H. Baker, June 14, 1906, in Spooner Papers.

Senate is clearly indicated in the Fifty-ninth Congress. In this same Congress "The Four" split on many issues. This division was frequently on geographical lines, the representatives of the agrarian Middle West opposed to those of the commercial and industrial East. Consequently, Spooner and Allison opposed the merchant marine subsidy bills. Senator Hanna, until his death, had sponsored them and President Roosevelt, in his first message to Congress, had recommended consideration of a bill to give subsidies to the American merchant marine. Spooner had helped prevent the passage of any such subsidy measures in the Fifty-sixth, Fifty-seventh, and Fifty-eighth Congresses.[7] In the Fifty-ninth Congress Spooner again spoke against the merchant marine subsidy bill then sponsored by Frye of Maine and Gallinger of New Hampshire. Subsidies for an American merchant marine, if they really produced cheaper transportation for American products and would benefit the people as a whole, would be all right, he stated, but this bill would benefit only the East, in fact, only a few corporations. The framers of the bill pay much attention to the builders of ships, Spooner declared, but little to the men who navigate them. He believed that a large percentage of the navigating crew should be trained seamen. All his amendments, introduced to make the bill accord more with his views, were voted down and the bill was

---

[7] Hanna had expected Spooner to help him get the bill passed. E. H. Gary, of the Federal Steel Company, and the Morgan bankers also tried to enlist his support for the bill, but the more Spooner studied it, the more convinced he became that it was one of the most vicious measures he had encountered. See M. Hanna to Spooner, November 10, 1900; E. Gary to Spooner, February 6, 1901; Spooner to E. Gary, March 9; to R. Bunn, February 14; to E. Baensch, February 18; to E. A. Thompson, March 8, 1901; to S. H. Hawkins, May 1, 1902, *ibid.*

passed by the Senate with only five Republicans voting against it. Spooner and La Follette voted in the negative.[8]

President Roosevelt, in his annual message at the opening of the Fifty-ninth Congress, recommended the passage of a law to regulate interstate commerce in misbranded and adulterated foods, drinks, and drugs. Spooner thought Congress had the authority under the interstate commerce clause to protect the people from poisonous foods and drugs. He believed, however, that in general the states could deal with that problem more effectively than the federal government and that Congress was passing too many laws paternalistic in character. In case there were a federal law, he wanted it to provide for co-operation between the national officers and the state authorities, as had been done in the Public Health and Marine Hospital Act, which he had gotten passed in the Fifty-seventh Congress.[9]

[8] *Congressional Record,* 59th Cong., 1st Sess. (1905–6), pp. 800, 1820–22, 1875–76, 2476–83, 2532–39; *Milwaukee Sentinel,* February 15, 1906. On the final vote Allison voted "aye." The La Follette Seamen's Act of 1915 incorporated many of the points suggested by Spooner at this time.

[9] *Congressional Record,* 58th Cong., 3d Sess., pp. 3754, 3854–55; Spooner to W. H. Gordon, March 31, 1905; to J. Wolfenden, June 18, 1906, in Spooner Papers. Spooner, in the Fifty-fifth Congress, had introduced two bills—one to establish a national public health commission and one to regulate quarantine. They were supported by city and state boards of health but opposed by the Marine Hospital Service. He had himself put on the Committee on Public Health and Quarantine in the Fifty-sixth Congress and remained on that committee during the rest of his term in the Senate. With the aid of A. H. Doty, of the Quarantine Station on Staten Island, and U. O. B. Wingate, of the Wisconsin State Board of Health, who put on a vigorous campaign in support of the bills, he had been able to get through a compromise measure which became a law on July 1, 1902 (see 57th Cong., *Statutes-at-Large,* pp. 712–14). In the Fifty-ninth Congress, because of Spooner's efforts, a bill to enlarge its power over quarantine was passed. It was done very quickly because of the fear of the spread of yellow fever from Cuba. There are a great number of letters to and from Spooner on this whole subject from 1898 to 1906.

During that Congress also he had helped get passed a new oleomargarine bill, amending the one of 1886. This bill made imitation dairy products subject to the laws of the state or territory into which they were transported, and levied a tax of ten cents (previous tax was two cents) a pound on such products when colored in imitation of butter. The National Dairy Union, headed by former Governor Hoard, had been formed to lobby for the passage of this bill. The bitterness between Spooner and Hoard that had arisen during the election of 1890 was forgotten as they co-operated to obtain passage of this bill to protect Wisconsin's dairy interests. Opposed to the bill were the labor organizations; they deluged Spooner with resolutions (form ones) of protest.[10] Also opposed to the bill were the Democrats, especially the representatives of the cottonseed oil states. Spooner had enlisted the support of the Swifts, owners of the Chicago meat packing firm, had gotten Quarles on the Committee on Agriculture, which had charge of the oleo bill,[11] and made the closing speech on the bill. He discussed oleomargarine itself, declared it was simply hog fat even when colored and was not innocuous, for a member of his family had been made ill by it. He dragged in the trust issue by pointing out that the manufacture of cottonseed oil was controlled by two organizations, while over five million farmers were in the business of making butter. As he had in 1886, he defended the constitutionality of the bill and declared that without a federal law it was almost impossible for the states that had laws

10 *Milwaukee Sentinel,* March 8, 1900; Spooner to W. D. Hoard, February 21, 1901, in Spooner Papers.

11 L. F. Swift to Spooner, April 27; C. Knight to Spooner, December 18, 1901; Spooner to C. Knight, December 18, 1901, in Spooner Papers.

regulating the sale of oleomargarine (there were thirty-two of them) to enforce their laws. "The Four" divided on this issue, Aldrich voting against the bill.[12]

Since the subject matter of pure food had been so exhaustively explored in the Senate during the debate on the oleomargarine bill, the sponsors of the pure food and drug bill thought their measure could be passed in short order. They appealed to Spooner and Allison to let it be brought up for action during the Fifty-seventh Congress. They pointed out that it had been "carefully drawn so as to avoid any opposition from the strict constructionists on the Constitution, or from those who jealously guard the police powers of the state. It deals only with misbranding and adulterations, while the articles affected are subjects of interstate commerce." [13] The bill, however, was blocked by the statehood bill during that Congress. When it came into the Senate in the Fifty-eighth Congress, the House bill, which required the labeling of all products in interstate commerce, was amended so that nothing was left but the enacting clause. The Senate bill prohibited the introduction into any state or territory of adulterated or misbranded articles of food and drugs, and provided fine and imprisonment for anyone who shipped or delivered such an article. As can be seen, this bill differed from the oleomargarine bill in that it provided for federal enforcement rather than making the products subject to state regulation. Spooner spoke against the bill, declared it had not

12 *Congressional Record,* 57th Cong., 1st Sess., pp. 3190, 3505–13, 3601–6, 3614; *Washington Post,* April 3, 1902; Spooner to W. D. Hoard, March 8, April 3, 1902, in Spooner Papers. The act was declared constitutional in *McCray* v. *United States* (195 U. S. 271).

13 P. M. McCumber to Spooner, April 14, 1902; P. M. McCumber to W. B. Allison, April 7, 1902, in Spooner Papers.

been prepared with much care or with much appreciation of what its practical effect would be, and said it was literally full of traps for the unwary so that some corner grocer might be punished for unknowingly selling adulterated food. He insisted that the words "willfully" and "knowingly" be inserted in several places, and a guarantee of the purity of the product by the manufacturer of the article be placed in a conspicuous place on the article. The bill failed to pass during the Fifty-eighth Congress and Spooner, Platt, and Aldrich (a onetime grocer) were largely responsible for its defeat.[14]

When a pure food and drug bill was brought up early in 1906, most of the objections made by Spooner had been obviated. The word "knowingly" had been inserted and the retail dealer was further protected by a provision whereby he would not be convicted if he had a guarantee from the manufacturer or wholesaler that the articles were not misbranded or adulterated. By this time the public had become aroused to the need for such a law. The *Ladies' Home Journal* and *Collier's* ran articles exposing frauds in patent medicines, and the American Medical Association urged citizens to write their congressmen to vote for the bill. The bill finally passed the Senate with only four negative votes; Platt, alone of "The Four," voted for the bill, while the others did not vote. That and the meat inspection bill, which helped the passage of the former bill by the House, were revolutionary in that they marked the first major excursion of the federal government into the

14 *Congressional Record*, 58th Cong., 3d Sess., pp. 126–29, 196–99, 3754, 3854–55; Stephenson, *Aldrich,* p. 233; Briggs, *Hepburn,* p. 281. See G. G. Pabst to Spooner, April 21, 1904, for protest against the bill; Spooner to A. J. Aikens, March 21, 1904, in Spooner Papers, in answer to protest of a druggist.

field of protection of the health of the citizens, thereby encroaching on the police power of the states.[15]

The third measure on which Spooner differed from the administration was the joint statehood bill. The supporters of the bill, led by Beveridge, chairman of the Committee on Territories, knew that Spooner favored the admission of Oklahoma and Indian Territory as one state and that he had many times denounced the practice of making omnibus bills for the admission of states. They were, however, quite disconcerted when he made such a violent attack on the Senate amendment providing for the admission of New Mexico and Arizona as one state, which the committee had added to the House bill enabling Oklahoma. Spooner declared it was a shame to hold up the admission of the latter state, which had been ready for two years and would have been admitted at the end of the Fifty-eighth Congress if it had not been for a disagreement among the conferees of the two Houses. Arizona and New Mexico were not ready for statehood, he claimed; the former region had neither sufficient population nor wealth, and much of the population of New Mexico could not speak English or understand American legal institutions. Beveridge maintained that the opposition to the admission of Arizona and New Mexico as a state came from cattlemen, business corporations, and railroad companies, who enjoyed comparative freedom from taxation under a territorial government.

15 Stephenson, *Aldrich*, pp. 464–65; *Congressional Record*, 59th Cong., 1st Sess., pp. 895–96, 1130–33, 1218–20, 2730–36, 2773; Swisher, *American Constitutional Development*, p. 511. The conference committee cut out the word "knowingly" but kept the guarantee. Allison and Spooner were paired; Allison said he would have voted "aye," but Spooner did not say. For a discussion of the measure see Louis Filler, *Crusaders for American Liberalism*, chap. 12.

Spooner taunted Beveridge with the fact that when he returned from his junket to the southwest in the fall of 1903, he had reported that the people of that region were not yet ready for statehood. He also reminded the Indiana Senator that a promise had been made to Arizona in 1863 that it would be admitted as a separate state.[16]

Senator Foraker also opposed the administration bill but for an entirely different reason. After Quay's death he had taken the lead in advocating the admission of Arizona and New Mexico as separate states.[17] Since that seemed impossible at this time, he introduced an amendment providing for a referendum in the two territories on the question of joint statehood. The bill for joint statehood would not go into effect unless a majority of the electors in each territory, voting separately, agreed to it.[18] Beveridge tried his best to prevent Spooner from joining the Arizona camp, but in a speech, very denunciatory of the administration's position, he came out in support of the Foraker amendment. He did so because he wanted the bill passed so that

[16] *Congressional Record,* 59th Cong., 1st Sess., pp. 105, 3455–59, 3575; A. Beveridge to Spooner, September 7, 1903, in Spooner Papers. Pabst, the Wisconsin brewer, had protested Spooner's vote in favor of the Oklahoma bill in the Fifty-eighth Congress because it prohibited the manufacture and sale of intoxicating liquors for twenty-one years after its admission (see Spooner to G. Pabst, March 15, 1905, *ibid.*); *Congressional Record,* 58th Cong., 3d Sess., pp. 1974, 1986).

[17] Quay's insistence on the passage of his bill, admitting Oklahoma, Arizona, and New Mexico as states, had blocked most domestic legislation during the second session of the Fifty-seventh Congress. He had been opposed by the Old Guard, led by Aldrich. See Bowers, *Beveridge,* pp. 182–84; Stephenson, *Aldrich,* pp. 209–11; Ellis, *Teller,* pp. 375–77.

[18] Foraker, *Notes of a Busy Life,* II, 184–89; Walters, *Foraker,* pp. 225–27; Bowers, *Beveridge,* pp. 216–18, 233–35; *Congressional Record,* 59th Cong., 1st Sess., p. 3591. During the debate Elkins ridiculed Spooner for trying to prevent the passage of the statehood bill; he compared it to an attempt of a donkey to hide an elephant.

Oklahoma could be admitted into the Union and he was quite sure that Arizona would defeat the proposition for joint statehood.[19] When chided for his position, Spooner answered: "The administration was, of course, very strongly for the two states, but I could not see my way clear to support it. I am so constituted that I cannot surrender myself to the blind leadership of anybody. I never have done so, and I never intend to do so." [20]

On the issue of railroad regulation Spooner took a quite independent position; he was in agreement with neither President Roosevelt nor Aldrich and other members of the Old Guard. Spooner favored new railroad legislation, even the regulation of rates; in that he was in accord with Roosevelt but he differed with him on the status of the courts. The conservative Senators (Aldrich, Lodge, Elkins, and Foraker) were opposed to any rate regulation by the Interstate Commerce Commission.[21] When, therefore, Aldrich prepared to fight Roosevelt on the Hepburn bill, he did not select Spooner to be his floor leader, as he had done so many times before during the past eight years. He chose Senator Knox of Pennsylvania, Roosevelt's former Attorney General, who had successfully prosecuted the Northern Securities Company. When shortly after that decision

19 *Milwaukee Sentinel,* March 8, 1906; *Washington Post,* March 9, 1906, a cartoon showing Spooner going into the Arizona camp and Beveridge trying to prevent him. Allison voted "nay" and Aldrich was recorded as not voting. Arizona voted overwhelmingly against joint statehood.

20 Spooner to J. B. Gilfillan, June 11, 1906, in Spooner Papers.

21 S. Elkins to N. Aldrich, October 11, 1905, in Aldrich Papers; Stephenson, *Aldrich,* p. 303; Walters, *Foraker,* p. 217; Schriftgiesser, *Gentleman from Massachusetts,* p. 216. See John M. Blum, "Theodore Roosevelt and the Hepburn Act: Toward an Orderly System of Control," in Morison (ed.), *Letters of Theodore Roosevelt,* VI, 1558–71.

Knox had entered the Senate, Aldrich had opposed his appointment to the Judiciary Committee, not sure that Knox could be trusted for safe and conservative views. The Rhode Island Senator had insisted on Spooner's appointment instead.[22] Now the situation was reversed; Spooner was considered too radical to lead the opposition to railroad rate legislation. Not that anyone would ever call Spooner a radical; he would not even be called a liberal. He merely represented a little of the discontent of the Middle West at the economic dominance of eastern capitalists.

The Middle West was the center of the agitation for railroad rate legislation in the early twentieth century, just as in the 1870's it had been the focal point of the Granger movement, which had led indirectly to the passage of the Interstate Commerce Act in 1887. The Supreme Court in 1896 had declared that the Interstate Commerce Commission had no power to fix rates. For ten years it had been assumed that the commission had the power, when rates were found to be unreasonable, to prescribe alternative rates.[23] In 1899 the Milwaukee Chamber of Commerce had appointed a special committee to promote changes in the Interstate Commerce Act and to restore to the commission the power to fix railroad rates. The committee had several conferences both in Milwaukee and Washington with the members of Congress from the Milwaukee district and with the Wisconsin Senators. In 1900 they urged Spooner to try to have Quarles appointed a member of the Senate Interstate Commerce Committee but it was not until the

22 N. Aldrich to O. H. Platt, November 19, 1904, in Platt Papers.
23 Swisher, *American Constitutional Development*, p. 419; 162 U. S. 196 (*Cincinnati, New Orleans and Texas Pacific Railroad Co. v. Interstate Commerce Commission*).

beginning of the Fifty-eighth Congress that Quarles received that position.[24] With the aid of the committee of the Chamber of Commerce, headed by E. P. Bacon, chairman of the National Shippers Organization, Senator Quarles and Representative Cooper of Wisconsin prepared a bill enlarging the powers of the Interstate Commerce Commission, giving it the power to fix freight rates and also providing machinery for appeal to the courts. This bill they introduced in Congress in the spring of 1903.[25]

The only railroad bill which passed that year, however, was the so-called Elkins Act, strengthening the provision of the Interstate Commerce Act dealing with personal discriminations. This act made the corporations receiving rebates as responsible as the railroads giving them. Spooner had considerable to do with the passage of this bill. He was not a member of the Senate Interstate Commerce Committee but he helped iron out difficulties between committee members, especially between Elkins and Aldrich. Then, through his position on the steering committee, Spooner obtained right of way for its passage. The bill was reported out with the proviso that no debatable amendment that might endanger its passage could be offered, and the bill was passed without a dissenting vote in the Senate just before the end of the Fifty-seventh Congress. Later, railroad owners were so pleased with the act that they claimed credit for its framing and passage.[26]

24 Spooner to E. P. Bacon, November 22, 1899; to R. Eliot, July 9, 1900; E. P. Bacon to Spooner, November 7, 1899, April 5, August 15, 1900; R. Eliot to Spooner, June 11, 1900, in Spooner Papers.
25 *The Nation*, December 15, 1904; *Washington Post*, December 7, 1904; Ripley, *Railroads: Rates and Regulations*, p. 494.
26 Spooner to E. P. Bacon, February 15, 17, March 6; to C. Paine, March 27, 1903; R. Eliot to Spooner, March 31, 1903, in Spooner Papers. See Lambert, *Elkins*, pp. 261–65.

Considerable impetus to railroad legislation was given by President Roosevelt's message to Congress in December, 1904. This was his first message after his triumphant election; he was giving notice that he was going to be a legislative leader as well as a strong Executive. The section on railroad regulation startled the conservatives. He said:

> I do believe that, as a fair security to shippers, the Commission should be vested with the power, where a given rate has been challenged and after full hearing found to be unreasonable, to decide, subject to judicial review, what shall be a reasonable rate to take its place; the ruling of the Commission to take effect immediately, and to obtain unless and until it is reversed by the court of review.[27]

Roosevelt did not recommend giving the commission the general power to fix rates; almost no one except radicals such as La Follette went that far.[28] The significant part of the message was the recommendation that the ruling of the commission should take effect immediately.

As a result of this message many bills for railroad regulation were introduced in both houses of Congress. At Quarles's request, for he was in Wisconsin fighting des-

[27] *Congressional Record,* 58th Cong., 3d Sess., p. 13; Pringle, *Roosevelt,* p. 418.

[28] La Follette, *La Follette,* I, 202–8. La Follette suggested that the Interstate Commerce Commission have power to fix rates that should be based on the capitalization valuation. Bailey of Texas suggested rates based on the actual value of the railroads (see Sam Hanna Acheson, *Joe Bailey: The Last Democrat,* p. 187). See Spooner to J. Luchsinger, June 6, 1906, in Spooner Papers: "Your point that the Commission should not be given the power to originate rates is sound as the eternal hills. That power is not given them. We did not either put the business of the country on a mileage basis, as some desired, nor did we turn over to the Commission the fixing of differentials, which would give them a power which never ought to be vested in any body of men."

perately for re-election, Spooner introduced Quarles's amended bill in January, 1905.[29] Wires, letters, and postal cards from shippers and bankers, expressing their opposition to rate regulation, poured in on Spooner. A great many were form protests, indicating that the railroad companies had launched a big campaign against such legislation. Spooner replied that he himself was in favor of a new law regulating transportation.[30] Instead of the Cooper-Quarles measure, the House passed a bill, framed by Esch of Wisconsin and Townsend of Michigan, embodying in general the ideas expressed by Roosevelt in his message. At the same time the House sent that bill to the Senate, it also sent a resolution for the impeachment of Charles Swayne, judge of the District Court of Florida. His trial occupied the attention of the Senate from February 13 to 27, and there was not time during the short session to take up the railroad measure; the sponsors claimed the bill had been deliberately blocked by the Old Guard.[31]

The Senate Interstate Commerce Committee held hearings during the summer of 1905. Stephen Elkins of West Virginia, railroad owner and official, had replaced Cullom as chairman of the committee in 1901. The latter, well versed on the subject of railroad regulation and favorable to it, had given up that chairmanship because he felt the committee had been stacked against him. Spooner was

29 J. V. Quarles to Spooner, January 16, 1905; Spooner to J. V. Quarles, January 25, 1905, in Spooner Papers; *Milwaukee Sentinel,* December 15, 17, 1904; Briggs, *Hepburn,* pp. 249, 251.

30 E. Keyes to Spooner, January 9, 1904; W. C. Banks to Spooner, February 21, 1905; Spooner to J. O'Neil, January 23, 1905, in Spooner Papers. The box dated February, 1905, containing letters to Spooner, is almost full of communications opposing railroad rate legislation.

31 Spooner to R. Eliot, March 21, 1905, *ibid.;* Acheson, *Bailey,* p. 185; Stephenson, *Aldrich,* p. 257.

asked to appear before the committee to give it the benefit of his judgment and advice.[32] Although he was well acquainted with the legal aspects, Spooner felt he did not know enough about the practical details of railway operation and he consulted J. W. Midgley, manager of the Railroad Clearing House Bureau. In one letter he wrote: "The subject is a complicated one to me, although it does not seem complicated to very many men who never have had anything whatever to do with railroads or with legal questions, and this class seems to be in the saddles just at this time on the subject." Throughout the summer Spooner studied the subject; he pored over a multitude of pamphlets, state laws, and the hearings of the Interstate Commerce Commission.[33] It was that diligence, that zeal to master a subject, that made Spooner such a valuable public servant.

President Roosevelt, in his message to Congress on December 5, 1905, declared that some competent administrative body should have the power to decide upon a case being brought before it, whether the rates were reasonable, and if unreasonable, "to prescribe . . . the maximum reasonable rate . . . this decision to go into effect within a reasonable time and to obtain from thence onward subject to review by the court." This was a more conservative recommendation than the one in his 1904 message; it did not specify the Interstate Commerce Commission, and instead of saying the ruling should go into effect immedi-

32 Cullom, *Fifty Years*, p. 329; *Milwaukee Sentinel*, April 16, 1905; Spooner to A. C. Wells, March 13, 1905; S. Elkins to Spooner, April 1, 1905, in Spooner Papers.

33 Spooner to J. W. Midgley, December 16, 1905, January 15, 1906; H. Reed to Spooner, July 6, 1905; J. W. Midgley to Spooner, December 7, 1905, March 8, May 26, June 18, 1906, in Spooner Papers.

ately, it stated "within a reasonable time." The 1905 message, however, spelled out in much more detail than his previous one Roosevelt's views on government regulation of railroads.[34]

A bill sponsored by Representative Hepburn, chairman of the House Committee on Interstate Commerce, passed the House in short order by an overwhelming vote (346 to 7). The Old Guard knew it would encounter opposition in the Senate. The measure incorporated the suggestions in the President's message regarding regulation of rates and specified they should go into effect within thirty days and be observed by the roads "unless the same shall be . . . suspended or set aside by a court of competent jurisdiction." That phrase was ambiguous and the bill was badly drawn and unconstitutional, Spooner thought.[35]

The bill was referred to the Senate Committee on Interstate Commerce, where it encountered great opposition. Elkins and Aldrich were wholly opposed to it (the former had framed a bill of his own). Cullom, who favored the Hepburn bill, was ill and recuperating in Florida. Spooner and Allison, although not members of the committee, tried to adjust the differences, for they thought it was of the utmost importance that the committee report out a bill that would unite Republicans on this subject.[36] Allison's protégé, Jonathan Dolliver, member of the committee, wanted to sponsor the bill but Aldrich deliberately ignored him, and, much to the surprise of everyone, the bill was put into

34 *Congressional Record,* 59th Cong., 1st Sess., pp. 92–93.
35 Briggs, *Hepburn,* pp. 254–55; Spooner to J. Luchsinger, June 6, 1906, in Spooner Papers.
36 S. Elkins to N. Aldrich, October 11, 1905; W. B. Allison to N. Aldrich, October 19, 1905, in Aldrich Papers; *Milwaukee Sentinel,* February 17, 1906. See Lambert, *Elkins,* pp. 266–79.

the hands of Benjamin Tillman of South Carolina, a Democrat.

Tillman had never directed a bill through Congress and knew nothing about railroad legislation. He was also not on speaking terms with President Roosevelt, having sworn, at the time his invitation to the dinner for Prince Henry was withdrawn, that he would never enter the White House as long as it was occupied by Roosevelt. Tillman was outmaneuvered by the Old Guard at every point—in parliamentary strategy, in debate, in marshaling of votes; finally he was repudiated by the President. Aldrich was the one mainly responsible for his defeat and Senator Knox was his chief lieutenant.[37]

Spooner brought up the reserves. He engaged in battle the legal light of the Democrats, Joseph W. Bailey, the real minority leader because the titular head, Gorman of Maryland, was ill. The Texas Senator presented an amendment that prohibited circuit courts from issuing injunctions to restrain enforcement of orders of the commission before the court passed on their reasonableness. That is unconstitutional, declared Spooner; it would deprive railroad companies of the preventive relief afforded by equity law. Injunctions are an essential part of equity jurisprudence, he said; the Constitution specifically states that the judicial power of the courts should extend to all cases of law and equity. For hours he discussed the origin, history, and benefits of equity law. Tillman of South Carolina interrupted. He could see no sense to all this legal discussion.

[37] Spooner to J. E. Bruce, June 4, 1906: "The giving of the rate bill into the hands of Mr. Tillman was a surprise, I think, to everybody. It came out of a conflict in the committee between certain Republicans, the outgrowth of differences, ambitions and cross purposes, upon which it is useless to dilate." See Stephenson, *Aldrich*, pp. 284, 291–96.

He himself was a "cornfield lawyer" and he thought it was about time the Supreme Court squared its decisions with cornfield common sense. If it ever did that, retorted Spooner, then the people will need a new court. The next time Tillman interrupted, Spooner refused to yield. He complained that for years he had been yielding half his time to the South Carolina Senator and that he could not give a comprehensible legal argument when interrupted continually.

Spooner explained his views on railroad rate-making. He believed Congress had the power to give the commission the authority to fix maximum rates. The Supreme Court had never ruled on that (only that the Interstate Commerce Act had not given the commission that authority) and it could not rule on it until Congress enacted legislation which involved it. He thought it was time that Congress enacted such legislation. The rates set by the commission, after it had overturned as unreasonable rates fixed by the carriers, are limited by Amendment V of the Constitution, which says no one may "be deprived of life, liberty, or property, without due process of law." It would be the presumption that the rates set by the commission were reasonable and it would be up to the carriers to prove they were unreasonable. The carrier, however, is entitled to receive for the service rendered just compensation at the time it is rendered. In order to do that he must have the right to obtain an injunction to suspend the rate until the court had passed on the reasonableness. Thus Spooner, in a masterly and exhaustive exposition, which lasted sixteen hours, described broad judicial review.[38]

[38] *Congressional Record,* 59th Cong., 1st Sess., pp. 4115–22, 4156–64, 5296–98, 5887–98, 5945–53; *Milwaukee Sentinel,* March 23, April 24, 27, 28,

Broad court review was insisted on by Aldrich, Knox, Spooner, and other conservative Senators. Tillman and Bailey upheld narrow court review, that is, that the courts could act only if a given rate were so low as to be confiscatory of railroad property or extortionate to shippers or if the commission had exceeded its powers. For almost two months they debated this issue. Their speeches may have interested other lawyers but it is doubtful if they swayed many votes. Both sides claimed they had the support of President Roosevelt. He was keeping close watch on all the plays but had not shown his hand. He called into conference, on March 31, five Republican Senators who were sympathetic to railroad regulation; Allison, the conciliator, was invited but Spooner was not. At that conference he seemed to favor an amendment (the so-called Long amendment) providing for narrow court review. On the same day Roosevelt set out to line up the support of the Democratic Senators. Since neither Tillman nor Bailey were on speaking terms with the President, former Senator Chandler acted as go-between. The latter reported that the President agreed with them on the issue of narrow court review and a limitation of the injunction. On April 15 Tillman, Chandler, and Bailey met with Attorney General Moody and drew up an amendment incorporating these ideas; this Tillman presented to the Senate on May 3.[39]

1906. After Tillman's description of himself it is interesting to read his letter to Spooner, April 7, 1906, in Spooner Papers: "You mentioned some days ago a valuable new law book calling it as I recollect: 'Judicial Interpretations of Words and Phrases.' Will you please give me the exact title and tell me where I can buy it cheapest?"

[39] Acheson, *Bailey*, pp. 189–95; Walters, *Foraker*, pp. 215–44; Richardson, *Chandler*, pp. 661–67; Francis Butler Simkins, *Pitchfork Ben Tillman: South Carolinian*, pp. 429–30.

The next day President Roosevelt, in a press interview, announced that he was in favor of the "Allison amendment" rather than the one presented by Tillman. The "Allison amendment" was quite verbose and a little confusing but it left up to the courts the power to decide the extent of their power to review rates. It also included a provision that the rates established by the commission could be set aside by injunction if it were found that the order was beyond the authority of the commission or in violation of the constitutional rights of the carriers.[40] Roosevelt's endorsement ensured its passage. The President had repudiated the Democratic alliance. To some it seemed as if he had capitulated to the reactionaries, for Aldrich accepted the "Allison amendment." In reality, it was not a victory for the Old Guard as they preferred no regulation of railroad rates; it was a triumph for the Middle Western Senators who favored regulation but wanted it to be constitutional.[41]

Tillman, understandably enough, was furious at what he called Roosevelt's betrayal. In a carefully written speech, delivered in a manner calm for him, he related the negotiations that had taken place between Roosevelt and Chandler. He told how the President had said he had "come to

[40] Sage, *Allison*, pp. 302–5; Stephenson, *Aldrich*, p. 310, says Aldrich framed the Allison amendment and had made it purposely vague so narrow court review people could claim they had won. Conservatives were willing to take their chances with the Supreme Court. The court subsequently upheld narrow court review (see *Interstate Commerce Commission* v. *Illinois Central Railroad in 1910*, 215 U.S. 452).

[41] Acheson, *Bailey*, pp. 199–202. The Democratic caucus on April 18 failed to support Bailey, so it was obvious that Tillman could not deliver enough Democratic votes to pass the measure. Bailey claims that Senator Crane of Massachusetts told Roosevelt that if he could get the Republicans to help pass the bill, it would be considered a Republican bill, but that he would get no credit for it if it were passed by Democratic votes alone.

complete disagreement with the Republican leaders of the Senate, especially the lawyers, who were trying to injure or defeat the bill by ingenious constitutional interpretations, and in this connection he named Senators Knox, Spooner and Foraker." The three named held a hurried conference and called in Lodge, close friend of the President. He rushed to the nearest telephone. He returned and reported that the President had called the statement a "deliberate and unqualified falsehood." He asserted he had not even mentioned Foraker and that Spooner's name had been mentioned only when he expressed cordial approval of his amendment.[42]

This amendment of the Wisconsin Senator provided for the impounding of excess charges in freight transportation. In effect, this would mean that the rate set by the commission would be in operation immediately. The railroad would be required to put into escrow the difference between the old and new rates. If the court upheld the commission's rate, the money would go to the shippers. One of the great merits of this proposition was that it would deter the railroads from instituting dilatory and unreasonable lawsuits. Railroad companies would not want to have large sums of money tied up in escrow. This amendment had been under discussion for a couple of months and had the approval of the Attorney General and the Interstate Commerce Commission. The amendment was not formally offered in the Senate until May 10, which was after the "Allison amendment" had been presented to the Senate. Spooner did not push his proposition, for some of the Republican leaders thought it was an amendment to the ju-

[42] Richardson, *Chandler*, pp. 667–72; Acheson, *Bailey*, pp. 202–7; Lodge, *Roosevelt-Lodge Correspondence*, II, 217–18.

dicial review provision and therefore "violated the tacit understanding upon which the majority of the Senate got together on the rate bill." Spooner felt it would have greatly improved the bill but he did not want to be the cause of delaying the passage of the measure. The Hepburn bill with the "Allison amendment" passed the Senate on May 18 by a vote of 71 to 3 (Foraker and the two Senators from Alabama voted "no").[43]

During the fight over judicial review and the exchange of insults between the President and Bailey and Tillman, Spooner had not lost sight of other important phases of railroad regulation. He, with the help of Midgley, had been working on an amendment that would separate railroads from the coal business. He felt one of the worst evils was "the manner in which the great railway companies handle the coal situation, to fill the coffers of favorites, ruin independent operators, limit the output, and enable themselves to fix the selling price." The bill as adopted had a provision that prohibited railroad companies from carrying over their lines things owned by them except those used for their own carrying business. This was the famous commodities clause, one of the important sections of the act.[44]

The granting of passes by railroads, especially to government officials, was another evil of which Spooner was very much aware and which he had long despised. He, however,

[43] *Milwaukee Sentinel*, May 3, 11, 1906; *Congressional Record*, 59th Cong., 1st Sess., p. 7088; Spooner to G. Schroeder, June 11, 1906, in Spooner Papers; Morison (ed.), *Letters of Theodore Roosevelt*, V, 173–74, 210, 274.

[44] Spooner to J. W. Midgley, January 15, March 3, 1906; to L. W. Bowers, June 16, 1906; J. W. Midgley to Spooner, May 26, 1906, in Spooner Papers; *Congressional Record*, 59th Cong., 1st Sess., p. 6459. Bailey and Elkins also claim credit for this clause (see Acheson, *Bailey*, pp. 208–9; Lambert, *Elkins*, p. 280).

opposed the Culberson amendment, for it forbade the granting of passes to anyone. He thought there were certain groups of people to whom passes might be granted— especially railway employees, for passes were practically a part of their compensation. This exception was opposed by the railroad lobby in Washington, but after a considerable fight Spooner succeeded in getting included in the act provisions allowing the granting of passes to railroad employees and their families and to former Union soldiers and sailors going to and from homes for disabled veterans.[45]

Spooner entered the debate on two other features of the conference report. He expressed disapproval that the amendment forbidding Jim Crow cars had been eliminated. He defended a ten-thousand-dollar salary for members of the Interstate Commerce Commission although, as Senator Bacon pointed out, it was more than the Vice-President and circuit judges received. Spooner stated that since fees paid by corporations were very large, the salary of the commissioners should be high enough to secure the services of outstanding men, for the commission would possess great power and would have to deal with very complex problems.[46] During the discussion Spooner declared that he himself had not received a dollar from any railroad company for twenty-two years and also while in the Senate he had not practiced for any corporation except to bring to a close a few cases that were almost finished when he became Senator. Spooner's son wrote Reed that Hill of the *New York Tribune* had arranged to have this portion of the

[45] *Congressional Record,* 59th Cong., 1st Sess., pp. 6669–70, 6948, 7921, 9112–14; Spooner to M. Sherman, June 16; to C. F. Merrill, June 18, 1906, in Spooner Papers.

[46] *Congressional Record,* 59th Cong., 1st Sess., pp. 7855–56, 7989–90; Spooner to J. Nimme, June 11, 1906, in Spooner Papers.

speech widely distributed "so that Father's denial of any connection *ever* while in the Senate, with any trust or railroad company, will go all over the country." [47] This was to be an answer to the article on Spooner that had just appeared in *Cosmopolitan Magazine.*

This was the second time that Spooner had been attacked by the muckrakers. The term "muckraker" had just been coined by President Roosevelt when, at the Gridiron dinner on March 17, 1906, he had compared the sensational writers in *McClure's, Cosmopolitan,* and *American* magazines to the man in *Pilgrim's Progress* who was so busy raking up dirt that he could not look up to receive the celestial crown. He declared these men who had been hired by the "yellow magazines" to write articles attacking "bad men with exaggeration or for things they have not done" and even attacking good men, had hindered the work of those who were earnestly striving to improve conditions. The *Cosmopolitan* series entitled "The Treason of the Senate," by David Graham Phillips, it is thought, was responsible for Roosevelt's indignation. Phillips had written several muckraking novels. In 1906 he agreed, for a large sum of money, to write a series of articles exposing the federal government. There had been articles exposing corruption in local and state governments, the most outstanding of them being written by Lincoln Steffens. The latter had gone to Washington to do some articles on Congress but they were not sensational enough so they had not been published. It was up to Phillips, therefore, to dig up as much dirt as he could on the Senators.[48]

[47] Philip Spooner to H. Reed, May 15, 1906, in Spooner Papers; *Congressional Record,* 59th Cong., 1st Sess., p. 7997.

[48] Cornelius Regier, *The Era of the Muckrakers,* pp. 1, 110; Bishop, *Theodore Roosevelt,* II, 10–11.

The series had begun in the March issue. An introductory sentence, declaring that Senators were not elected by the people but by the "interests," set the tone. The first issue had blasted Senators Chauncey Depew and Thomas C. Platt of New York. The April issue was devoted to the organizer of this "treason of the Senate," Nelson W. Aldrich, and the May one to his left arm, the Democratic leader Arthur P. Gorman. The next issue dealt with their chief spokesmen, the men who strike the keynote, Spooner and Bailey. Phillips entitled his article on the Wisconsin Senator: "Chief Spokesman of 'the Merger,' " and in a diagram of the Senate chamber showed Spooner's "coigne of vantage as the mouthpiece of special privilege"—his seat in the second row on the center aisle. He sketched Spooner's rise and repeated the story Steffens had used in 1904, that Spooner's Senate seat had been purchased by Sawyer and Stephenson—Phillips ignoring the fact that Stephenson had publicly retracted the story. He attacked not only Spooner's private career as a railway attorney and attorney for the receivers of the Northern Pacific but also claimed that in the Senate he was always representing the interests of the corporation rather than the people. He concluded:

Wisconsin—Spooner's "home folks"—have long known him, through and through. His oratory has been admired, listened to and applauded—and that is all. . . . Further, everybody at Washington has long known Spooner as thoroughly as Wisconsin and his friends in the Wall Street district know him. Yet the country at large has looked on him as an almost ideal Senator. He has been put forward by the leaders of his party, by the leaders of the other party, by his fellow-Senators, by the entire "merger," as an ideal Senator and as typical of the Senate.[49]

[49] Phillips, "The Treason of the Senate," *Cosmopolitan Magazine,* 40 (March, 1906), 488; 41 (June, 1906), 123-32.

Spooner thought a good deal of the inspiration for the assault on him came from the progressives in Wisconsin, especially since La Follette's picture with a complimentary caption was published in the article attacking him. Spooner refused to sue *Cosmopolitan* for libel; he suspected the owners of the magazine were hoping for a suit by a man of prominence, since that would increase their sales. He also refused to present a detailed answer to the article on the floor of the Senate, as was done by Senator Bailey, for he felt he needed no such defense there.[50]

Spooner, although he deplored the President's deviations from the Constitution, almost always succumbed to the force of Roosevelt's personality. He might go to the White House in a towering state of rage toward the President, but he would come out subdued although not necessarily convinced that Roosevelt was right.[51] Then he would enter the Senate and defend the President and his policies. Just as he had earned the sobriquet of defender of the President when McKinley was in the White House, so during his last five years as Senator, he vindicated Roosevelt whenever he was under attack in Congress.

He upheld Roosevelt's aggressive foreign policy against the onslaughts of the Democrats although he did not wholly approve of the President's actions. In 1902 Roosevelt may have used the Monroe Doctrine to insist on arbitration of claims against the Venezuelan government; in 1904 there is no doubt he used it as the basis for the United States government acting as "an international police power," taking over the collection of the customs of

[50] Spooner to J. M. Olin, June 18, 1906, in Spooner Papers; Acheson, *Bailey*, p. 215.
[51] Stephenson, *Aldrich*, p. 203.

the Dominican Republic and supervising the payment of that country's public debt. Spooner did not believe the President had the right to declare that a foreign country could not forcibly collect debts owed it. Great Britain and other countries had always claimed that right and the Hague Court, in giving preference to the blockading nations in the Venezuela case, had put a premium on that method. He thought the Monroe Doctrine had no relationship to the collection of debts unless a nation attempted to acquire territory, and that in any case enforcement of the doctrine rested with Congress, the war-making body, not with the Executive.[52]

But in spite of his disapproval of the policy, Spooner could not sit silent and allow the President to be criticized by the Democrats. The first occasion arose in connection with a resolution by Bacon of Georgia, asking what the President had been doing in Santo Domingo during the last two years, for Bacon had seen a newspaper item reporting that an American fiscal agent was in charge of the customhouses there. The adoption of such a resolution would be tantamount to a vote of lack of confidence and Spooner begged the members of the Foreign Relations Committee not to condemn the President without evidence. The resolution was pigeonholed.[53]

During the next session of Congress, Teller introduced a resolution directing the Secretary of State to send to the

[52] *Congressional Record*, 58th Cong., 3d Sess., p. 19; Spooner to G. B. Moyer, March 31, 1905, in Spooner Papers. It is interesting to note that Spooner's point of view on the Roosevelt corollary to the Monroe Doctrine is the one taken by the State Department in its official memorandum (so-called Clark memorandum) issued in 1930.

[53] *Milwaukee Sentinel*, January 26, 1905; Stephenson, *Aldrich*, pp. 259–60.

Senate copies of all correspondence relating to Dominican affairs. Spooner objected and pointed out that the Senate did not pass resolutions "directing" the Secretary of State, as that cabinet officer was on a different basis than other cabinet members, for he merely performed duties imposed by the President. The Senator from Colorado, declaring that he always bowed to any suggestion of the Senator from Wisconsin on questions of parliamentary procedure, modified it to read "request the President," but that resolution was also pigeonholed.[54]

Several times Spooner had to rebuke Senator Tillman; the wielder of the pitchfork accused Roosevelt of "trickery." That is "a nasty and undignified word" to apply to the President of the United States, the Wisconsin Senator retorted. "The Senator from Wisconsin is a very adroit antagonist in a law court, and he is a supple acrobat in playing with words," replied Tillman. At one point in the debate the exchange of epithets between the two Senators became so caustic that the Vice-President had to reprove them. That was not the first time that had happened. Most of Spooner's speech, however, dealt with the constitutional prerogatives of the Senate and the President as to treaty making. He pointed out that the President had full power of negotiating treaties and, for that matter, he did not have to ratify a treaty even though the Senate had approved it.[55]

Because of the opposition his Executive action had aroused, President Roosevelt had negotiated a treaty with the Dominican Republic. It provided that customs duties

[54] *Congressional Record,* 59th Cong., 1st Sess., pp. 22–23; *Milwaukee Sentinel,* March 15, 1905.
[55] *Congressional Record,* 59th Cong., 1st Sess., pp. 433–36, 1417–31; *Washington Post,* December 16, 24, 1905.

should be collected under supervision of the United States and that 55 per cent of the money collected should be put into a special fund for the liquidation of the debt.[56] Pending action by the Senate on the treaty, which might be long delayed judging from the attitude of the Democrats, President Morales of the Dominican Republic suggested a modus vivendi incorporating the principles of the treaty. Before adopting this proposal, Roosevelt consulted Spooner, Foraker, Lodge, and Knox. They all agreed that some action was necessary. Concerning this conference the President wrote Secretary of State Hay: "Rather to my horror Taft genially chaffed them about going back on their principles as to the 'usurpation of the executive.' But they evidently took the view that it was not a time to be over particular about trifles." [57]

Roosevelt called on Spooner time and time again to use his influence to obtain the Senate's assent to the treaty. He sent T. C. Dawson, United States Minister to the Dominican Republic, who had made the original arrangement for United States supervision of customs, to visit Spooner at his farm in New Hampshire. The President wrote Spooner long letters urging him not to allow any amendments to be added to the treaty which might "unnecessarily wound Dominican national pride and susceptibilities." [58] He even conceded to Spooner in his objection to the use of the Monroe Doctrine as the basis for his interference, and in

[56] *Papers Relating to Foreign Relations, 1905*, p. 334; T. Roosevelt to Spooner, February 24, 1905, in Roosevelt Papers. The treaty had been submitted to the Senate on February 15, 1905.

[57] Bishop, *Theodore Roosevelt*, I, 432–33; *Papers Relating to Foreign Relations, 1905*, p. 361; Morison (ed.), *Letters of Theodore Roosevelt*, IV, 1150.

[58] T. C. Dawson to Spooner, July 11, 1905, in Spooner Papers; T. Roosevelt to Spooner, July 7, 1905, in Roosevelt Papers.

his State of the Union message of December, 1905, of which the part on Santo Domingo was taken from a memorandum written by Spooner, urged consent to the treaty on the basis that the republic had appealed to the United States for help.[59] Spooner did as Roosevelt requested but he was not able to get the Senate's assent to the treaty. The Democrats used the caucus to line up their men so as to make approval of the treaty impossible. Finally, after the treaty had been before the Senate for over a year, Elihu Root, who had become Secretary of State after the death of John Hay, in consultation with Spooner, Lodge, and Foraker, worked out another plan. It was decided to separate the adjustment of the debt from the collection of customs; the United States would be responsible only for the latter and the adjustment of the debt would be taken care of by an American banking house. The Senate finally consented to this treaty in February, 1907.[60]

Although Roosevelt in his second message had repudiated the Monroe Doctrine as the basis for his interference, this intervention in the affairs of the Dominican Republic has always been known as the Roosevelt corollary to the Monroe Doctrine. In reality, the extent of the intervention was moderate, consisting only of the collection of customs under the supervision of the United States and of certain limitations on the fiscal policies of the Dominican Republic. Yet it was to form a precedent for a very aggressive

[59] T. Roosevelt to Spooner, October 16, 1905, in Roosevelt Papers; E. Root to Spooner, November 3, 1905; Spooner to T. Roosevelt, October 13, 1905, in Spooner Papers; *Congressional Record,* 59th Cong., 1st Sess., p. 98.

[60] Spooner to S. Cullom, February 5; H. C. Lodge to Spooner, February 4; E. Root to Spooner, March 16, 1906; J. H. Hollander to Spooner, January 14, 1907, in Spooner Papers; Jessup, *Elihu Root,* I, 541–49; Dana G. Munro, *The United States and the Caribbean Area,* pp. 106–12.

policy of the United States in the Caribbean, one which was to lead to so much resentment against "Yankee imperialism."

On the same day that Spooner gave his masterly vindication of the President's actions in the Western Hemisphere, he also defended Roosevelt's conduct in regard to other crises in the world, especially in the Moroccan affair. The status of that region had been agreed upon at a conference in Madrid in 1880. This agreement, to which the United States had been a party, had provided for the protection of foreigners and most-favored-nation treatment. In 1905 France, with the acquiescence of Great Britain, attempted to extend her influence in North Africa. Germany tried to block her action; the German ambassador in Washington suggested to President Roosevelt that he might be the peacemaker and help Morocco resist the encroachment of France. The President, delighted at the opportunity of playing a part in international politics, arranged a conference of the interested nations in Algeciras, Spain, in January, 1906. He selected as representatives of the United States, Henry White, ambassador to Italy, and S. R. Gummere, consul general at Morocco.[61]

It was to the sending of delegates that the Senate objected. Bacon offered a resolution stating: "That interference with or participation in any controversy between European governments relating to European international questions is a violation of the well-settled, well-defined policy of this Government, which has been recognized and observed for more than a century past." Spooner promptly objected; he declared it was improper for such a resolution

[61] Pringle, *Theodore Roosevelt*, pp. 387–97; Bishop, *Theodore Roosevelt*, I, 467–505; Jessup, *Elihu Root*, II, 56–60.

to be introduced and debated in open legislative session as it was purely an Executive matter, and he declared that if the United States had not sent representatives, the conference would not have been held and war might have resulted. He added: "I am in favor of the United States attending any conference to which it is invited by European nations which involves in any degree our interest— first, to look after our interests, and second, to use the kindly offices and the influence and power of the United States to prevent war between foreign governments at friendship with us." [62]

Not satisfied with defending the President's actions in the Caribbean and North Africa, Spooner also paid tribute to Roosevelt for his interference in the Far East, for hitting on the psychological moment for successful intervention to bring to an end the terrible war between Russia and Japan.[63] The President wrote Spooner: "That was a magnificent speech of yours. I congratulate you upon it and thank you for it." [64] *The Nation* declared that the President could hardly act quicker than his apologist Spooner could think up legal subtleties and historical allusions to defend him.[65]

Not only did Spooner defend the President against the assaults of the Democrats but also against attacks by members of his own party. There was an undercurrent of unrest in Congress. President Roosevelt's assumption of Executive power and legislative leadership had irritated many of the Old Guard who viewed with alarm the encroachment

[62] *Congressional Record,* 59th Cong., 1st Sess., pp. 1075, 1421-23, 2139-48.
[63] *Congressional Record,* 59th Cong., 1st Sess., p. 1423.
[64] T. Roosevelt to Spooner, January 24, 1906, in Roosevelt Papers.
[65] *The Nation,* April 28, 1904, February 1, 1906.

of the federal government on the functions of the states and interference with their economic interests. On the other hand, a group in the Republican party—and its influence in Congress was increasing—felt President Roosevelt compromised too much with the conservatives. They disagreed with his belief that half a loaf was better than none. Spooner was the President's defender against all his enemies.

Spooner's first engagement, as the President's champion against one of the Old Guard, was with Senator Foraker of Ohio, one of the early endorsers of Roosevelt's nomination for President in 1904. Since Roosevelt had become "His Excellency" rather than "His Accidency" and had asserted himself as the Executive, Foraker had attacked many of his policies.[66] On the opening day of the second session of the Fifty-ninth Congress, Foraker introduced a resolution proposing that the Secretary of War be directed to furnish complete information to the Senate about the Brownsville case. During the summer some Negro troops stationed at Fort Brown, Texas, had been accused by the citizens of Brownsville of shooting up the town. Investigations had been unsuccessful in turning up any proof against any individual or group of individuals. No one in the regiment would admit his guilt, so the investigators had recommended that the three companies of Negro troops be discharged. Immediately after the Congressional election Roosevelt had ordered the men dishonorably discharged and forever barred from re-enlisting and from employment in any civil capacity in the federal government.[67]

[66] Foraker, *Notes of a Busy Life,* II, 109–11, 203.
[67] Pringle, *Theodore Roosevelt,* pp. 458–64; Walters, *Foraker,* pp. 232–47; Foraker, *Notes of a Busy Life,* II, chap. 41.

President Roosevelt answered Foraker's resolution with a vitriolic message on the Brownsville case. The Ohio Senator replied, questioning the President's authority to discharge the soldiers. Debate continued throughout December and into January. The press speculated as to what position Spooner would take, whether he would rise to defend the President.[68] The very day that Foraker brought up the issue in the Senate, President Roosevelt had sent for Spooner. Shortly thereafter the Wisconsin Senator began to receive from Secretary of War Taft batches and batches of material on the Brownsville case—reports, affidavits, testimony, and other evidence.[69] On January 14 President Roosevelt sent another message to the Senate, much more temperate than the December one. In it he announced that he had revoked the order barring the soldiers from government employment. It was generally rumored that Spooner had insisted on that if he were going to speak on behalf of the President.

Immediately after the message was read Spooner began his defense. He spoke for an hour and the next day continued his speech before crowded galleries and a full Senate. First he assailed the Senator from South Carolina for his attitude toward the Negro and lynching. He then devoted the rest of his speech to the legal aspects. This is a country of law, he asserted, and no federal official can be above the Constitution. If the President has exceeded his power, then it is the responsibility of the House to bring impeachment proceedings, he said, but the Senate had no right to act in a legislative manner about an Executive

68 *Washington Post,* December 27, 1906.
69 W. Loeb to Spooner, December 6, 1906; W. H. Taft to Spooner, December 22, 1906, January 4, 5, 1907, in Spooner Papers.

action. Citing many Supreme Court decisions, he showed that the President had the power as Commander-in-Chief to discharge the soldiers and stated that he thought Roosevelt had acted in the people's interest and for the good of the Army. He acknowledged, however, that no lawyer could have defended that portion of the President's order of dismissal in which he forever barred the discharged men from entering the civil service of the government, and he expressed gratification because that part of the order had been revoked.[70]

The night of the speech Mrs. Spooner wrote in her diary:

John spoke 4 hrs.—A great speech—all say.—When we got to the Tafts' dinner Mr. Taft couldn't get over his delight over it. After the Prest. and Mrs. R. we were the next guests of honor. —John was the hero of the hour—& I came in for a share. We had to stay late because the Pres. always does & I had on my handsomest *Altman* dress—wh. nearly crushed me being so tight, so I got easily fatigued.[71]

No policy of President Roosevelt's was more under attack than his conservation policy. Aroused to the need of preserving the country's natural resources, Roosevelt had, at the instigation of Gifford Pinchot, established the United States Forest Service in 1905 and had put Pinchot at its head. Roosevelt had then, by Executive action, withdrawn millions of acres of public land from entry, to be used for forest reserves. Senators from the western states,

[70] *Congressional Record,* 59th Cong., 2d Sess. (1906–7), pp. 1084–88, 1130–41; *Washington Post,* January 16, 21, 1907. Aldrich, Spooner, Lodge, Knox, and Crane, after several conferences, agreed on a compromise resolution which did not include the question of the President's authority. It was passed. The March, 1908, report of the committee investigating the Brownsville affair upheld the President.

[71] Annie Spooner, Diary, January 15, 1907.

where these reserves were established, were alarmed and during this second session attacked the Forest Service. They opposed the appropriation of half a million dollars for the protection of forests. Spooner several times came to the defense of Pinchot and the Forest Service, saying it was one of the best services under the government and ought to have the money so it could be expanded. He declared that Wisconsin would be much better off if there had been a forest reserve program when all the northern part of the state was covered with valuable timber, for now it was almost barren land.[72] So spoke Spooner, who, during his early career as a railroad lawyer and investor in timberlands, had been responsible in part for despoiling large tracts of virgin forest!

Besides conservation of timberlands, the question of the preservation of the country's mineral resources was raised by President Roosevelt. Both Wisconsin Senators were interested in this issue: La Follette, as a member of the Indian Affairs Committee, for Indian lands were rich in coal, and Spooner, as the leading member of the Judiciary Committee and Roosevelt's consultant on constitutional questions. Just before the end of the long session of the Fifty-ninth Congress, La Follette suggested to the President that he withdraw from entry, by Executive order, coal and asphalt lands, just as he had withdrawn forest lands. Attorney General Moody, however, advised the President that such action would be unconstitutional unless Congress authorized it as it had authorized the withdrawal of forest lands in 1891. La Follette then offered a

---

[72] *Congressional Record,* 59th Cong., 2d Sess., pp. 3296–99, 3516–17, 3526, 3531; E. A. Hitchcock to Spooner, January 9, February 23, 1907, in Spooner Papers. See Roosevelt, *Autobiography,* chap. 11.

joint resolution authorizing such action but it was not passed. During the summer President Roosevelt withdrew millions of acres of coal lands but it was questionable how long he could continue this policy after Congress had a chance to act.[73]

The President, therefore, was anxious that some action on mineral lands be taken by Congress during that short session. A proposed bill, prepared by Charles D. Walcott, director of the Geological Survey, had been sent to Spooner to be introduced.[74] Meanwhile La Follette had prepared a very comprehensive bill providing for reserving all coal lands in the public domain; they were never to be sold but operated under lease. He had consulted with Walcott, Attorney General Moody, and President Roosevelt. He thought the President was thoroughly in accord with him and at the time he introduced his bill he intimated that it was an administration measure. The following day Roosevelt wrote La Follette that he was afraid his bill would cause too much opposition and that it would be better to push the bill framed by Director Walcott; this bill would leave to the Secretary of the Interior discretion in certain matters that La Follette's bill fixed by law. The President said he might prefer La Follette's bill but

[73] F. E. Leupp to Spooner, December 26, 1906, in Spooner Papers; La Follette, *La Follette,* I, 209–11; memorandum of telephone call from La Follette, January 22, 1907, in Roosevelt Papers. Considerable discussion of this issue of coal lands took place during the debate on the dissolution of the Five Civilized Tribes in Indian Territory. At that time Spooner proposed that the United States should always hold these lands in trust and only lease them on nonassignable leases (see *Congressional Record,* 59th Cong., 1st Sess., pp. 3269–75, 4389, 4395, 6051–55; La Follette, *Autobiography,* pp. 377–79).

[74] *Congressional Record,* 59th Cong., 2d Sess., p. 3531; T. Roosevelt to Spooner, January 11, 1907, in Roosevelt Papers; W. Loeb to Spooner, January 13, 1907, in Spooner Papers.

thought it essential to get some measure passed that would embody the principle of leasing coal, lignite, oil, and natural gas in public lands without regard to surface rights. He feared that if some legislation were not secured, he would have to return to entry the coal lands he had withdrawn. He asked La Follette not to push his own bill but to help get passed the milder measure. La Follette was furious at what he considered to be the President's "kerflop"; he criticized him for preferring half a loaf and refused to co-operate. No legislation was passed during that session and two-thirds of the coal lands were returned to entry.[75]

Another Senator who, like La Follette, thought he had the support of the President for his pet project—a federal child labor law—was Albert Beveridge of Indiana. Instead, the President endorsed Lodge's bill regulating child labor in factories in the District of Columbia—where there were practically no factories. Beveridge went ahead with plans to push his bill in spite of the President's disapproval.[76] He was summoned to the White House; Spooner was asked to be present when Roosevelt reprimanded the Indiana Senator. Beveridge persisted in his course, so Spooner took up the cudgels for the President in the Senate. When Beveridge in a long speech in the Senate described child labor conditions, Spooner interrupted and asked the Indiana Senator if he thought he was more sincere in his concern over child labor than the rest of his colleagues. "Yes, I think a good deal more earnest," Beveridge replied. "I doubt the Senator's accuracy," Spooner re-

[75] La Follette, *Autobiography*, pp. 380–90; T. Roosevelt to R. M. La Follette, January 23, February 5, 19, 1907, in Roosevelt Papers; E. Keyes to Spooner, January 25; R. S. Ryan to Spooner, March 2, 1907, in Spooner Papers. In 1910 such a law was passed.

[76] Bowers, *Beveridge*, pp. 245–47, 250–55.

torted. "I suppose there is no one in this Chamber who is not opposed to child labor. It is withering—that is a good word for it—the mental and physical faculties of the young, who are to be the governing body of this country." He admitted that many states had not dealt adequately with the subject but he did not think Congress had the power to pass a child labor law. Congress had the power to regulate interstate commerce but not to prohibit or destroy; it might prohibit the transportation of lottery tickets, for example, for they were articles of commerce, but in the case of child labor it was not the article that was being regulated but the manufacturing of the article.[77] No federal child labor law was passed during that session. Instead, there was passed Spooner's bill to incorporate the National Child Labor Committee, an organization sponsored by Felix Adler, Florence Kelley, Lillian Wald, Paul Warburg, and others. Its object was to investigate conditions of employment of children, to promote state legislation restricting child labor, and to see that the laws on the statute books of the states were enforced.[78]

Ten years had passed since Spooner began his second period of service in the Senate. Not only had the membership changed but its position in the government; at that time it had been the most powerful organ of the federal government, but by 1907 it was subordinate to the Executive, for the President formulated and directed the policies

[77] *Milwaukee Sentinel,* January 5, 1907; *Congressional Record,* 59th Cong., 2d Sess., pp. 1803, 1811–12, 1873–77. See 247 U.S. 251 (*Hammer v. Dagenhart*), in which the child labor law of 1916 was declared unconstitutional on the same basis that Spooner used in his argument.

[78] *Congressional Record,* 59th Cong., 1st Sess., p. 8461; 2d Sess., pp. 517, 1623, 2519.

of government. Leadership in Congress was also changing. Younger and more progressive congressmen, whose economic philosophies and interpretation of the Constitution differed widely from the former leaders', were clamoring for control and were making some headway. Most of the leaders with whom Spooner had begun his senatorial career were gone. The cabal of "The Four" had disintegrated. Platt of Connecticut, with whom Spooner had probably worked the closest and whom he regarded as "a man of great experience, faithfulness and ability," had died two years before. Allison was in poor health and had not returned to Washington in 1907. He was one of Spooner's best friends; they represented neighboring states and sat next to each other in the Senate. Spooner considered him "of greater public importance than any other man in the Legislative Department of the Government." He had often been called the dictator of the Senate because he had for years been chairman of the Republican caucus.[79]

Aldrich was still the leader of the Old Guard in the Senate. Spooner, although he admired him, had never been as intimate with the Rhode Island Senator as he had with Allison and Platt. They had often had little differences of opinion, in private or in committee, but during this last Congress Spooner and Aldrich openly disagreed on several matters; most of these concerned the issue of government aid—to railroads, the merchant marine, and industry.[80] Each Senator represented the economic interests of his section of the country. Therefore, during this Congress

[79] Spooner to A. O. Bacon, April 12, 1905; to F. E. Allison, February 20; to W. B. Allison, September 29, 1906, in Spooner Papers.

[80] Stephenson, *Aldrich,* pp. 203, 320; *Congressional Record,* 59th Cong., 2d Sess., pp. 2645–48.

Spooner discovered that La Follette and he were occasionally in agreement opposing Aldrich. Spooner was astonished the first time La Follette voted the same as he did on an issue. "Sometimes he is right, you see," he wrote a friend.[81] Spooner disagreed entirely with La Follette's program of "direct democracy" and thought he tended toward socialism. But they both represented the agrarian Middle West as opposed to the industrial East. In contrast to Aldrich, both approved of some federal government regulation, although Spooner favored it only when state regulation was inadequate or ineffective. Both Wisconsin Senators opposed government subsidies (of which Aldrich approved) to the merchant marine and to industry in the form of a high protective tariff.

In fact, what was to be one of the major platforms of the Progressive party—a nonpartisan, scientific tariff commission—had been suggested by Spooner as early as 1897. Spooner had continued to favor tariff revision but had said little publicly because Aldrich, Allison, and Platt had been vehemently opposed to the issue being raised. They had prevented President Roosevelt from including that subject in his message to Congress in December, 1904, so he had stressed railroad regulation instead. At that time the London *Times* ran a short item stating that although three of the four who ruled the Senate showed no signs of giving up their hostility to tariff revision, courageous Spooner had announced he had some ideas for the solution of the tariff problem.[82] Now at the very end of the Fifty-ninth Congress

[81] Spooner to G. W. Burnell, June 6, 1906, in Spooner Papers.

[82] *The Times,* December 5, 1904; W. B. Allison to T. Roosevelt, November 11, 1905, in Roosevelt Papers; O. H. Platt to T. Roosevelt, November 21, 1904; W. B. Allison to N. Aldrich, November 21; N. Aldrich to O. H. Platt, November 23, 1904, in Platt Papers.

Spooner again brought up the issue. He was arguing with Aldrich over an item in the army appropriation bill and suddenly he announced: "I have thought for some years that the tariff ought to be revised." The statement seemed almost to be dragged into the debate. It had not been done inadvertently, however, for he repeated it.[83] There was considerable speculation on why Spooner raised the tariff issue at this time. He knew there was no chance of anything being accomplished by this Congress. Maybe it was a last gesture of independence of Aldrich. Perhaps he wished to disconcert the progressives of Wisconsin, for their platform contained planks favoring tariff revision and a scientific tariff commission.

Spooner certainly accomplished the latter. The Half-Breeds in Wisconsin were extremely discomfited when they received reports of Spooner's utterances in the Senate. "There are lots of goats who think you did it for political purposes which, of course, under the circumstances, is a very foolish idea," Willet wrote his father. Both factions in the Wisconsin legislature prepared resolutions on the subject. Neither group was willing that the other should receive credit for sponsoring such a popular issue, so two resolutions were passed, one declaring for an immediate revision of the tariff and the other memorializing the President to call a special session of Congress for that purpose.[84]

At the time Spooner brought up the tariff issue in the Senate he had already sent his resignation to Governor Davidson. Announcement of it had been delayed until

[83] *Congressional Record,* 59th Cong., 2d Sess., p. 2695; *Milwaukee Sentinel,* February 12, 1907.

[84] Willet to Spooner, December 5, 1905, February 14, 1907; J. Whitehead to Spooner, February 21, 1907, in Spooner Papers. See the cartoon in the *Washington Post,* February 27, 1907.

Philip Spooner could ascertain the political situation in Wisconsin in hopes that the Stalwarts might be able to control the selection of Spooner's successor. On the evening of March 3 Spooner told the newspapers of his resignation. "In Madison, all is confusion—the Legislature over John's unexpected resignation—it is amusing," Mrs. Spooner wrote gloatingly in her diary. "He *never* could have 'hit' it at a better time for the dismay of La f. & the rest of John's enemies." Concerning its reception in Washington, she wrote: "It gradually got about & Senators kept coming to ask 'what *is* this I hear' & many cried—never was such a sensation. This mornings papers are full of it & such great things they say." [85]

On March 4, 1907, the *Washington Post* carried the following tribute to Spooner for his senatorial services:

The resignation of Senator Spooner, of Wisconsin, from the seat he has held with such signal honor and ability for sixteen years is news that will be received with the keenest regret by those who are best aware of the nature of his services to the country.

In some respects the ablest member of the Senate, Mr. Spooner has not only rendered distinguished service by the exercise of his consummate legal ability but he has earned the gratitude of the country for his industry, watchfulness, and independence. He has attacked wrong wherever he has found it, whether in his own party or in the opposition. His conspicuous gifts of oratory and his prominence in constitutional arguments have tended to obscure the steady, thankless work he has performed in perfecting legislation and killing off foolish or otherwise objectionable measures.

[85] Philip L. Spooner to J. Spooner, February 1, 18; J. O. Davidson to Spooner, February 5; Spooner to Willet, February 2, 1907, in Spooner Papers; Annie Spooner, Diary, February 4, March 4, 5, 1907. There were so many candidates for Spooner's Senate seat that the Republican caucus was in a deadlock for four weeks. Finally, on May 17, Isaac Stephenson was elected.

12 : *Corporation Lawyer in New York City (1907-1919)*

"FREE FROM THE RESTRICTIONS OF PUBLIC LIFE"*

Mrs. Spooner left Washington on March 7, 1907, but the Senator remained for ten days, "clearing the decks and preparing to break camp for good." He had decided to live in New York City, but he wrote a friend:

My plans are not definite. I have, as you will understand, some sense of dislocation and bewilderment, but I begin to feel like a boy out of school.

I can understand fully the anxiety expressed in your letter as to the future, but I assure you, my good friend, you need have none. I have already refused what under ordinary circumstances would be tempting proffers of professional employment. I have gone out without a client, or the promise of a client. I shall be glad to be free from the restrictions of public life.[1]

---

* Spooner to E. H. Abbott, March 16, 1907, in Spooner Papers.
[1] Spooner to M. E. Hoyt; to E. H. Abbott, March 16, 1907, in Spooner Papers.

A few months later Secretary of State Root asked Spooner to act as chief counsel for the United States in the Northeastern fisheries arbitration. This problem of the Newfoundland and Labrador fisheries had been a troublesome one ever since the United States received its independence. When Spooner was a member of the Senate in 1888, the Chamberlain-Bayard Treaty had been rejected and a modus vivendi had been agreed on. Under this temporary arrangement American vessels had been given certain port privileges on payment of a license fee of a dollar and a half per ton. This agreement had been renewed every year and had been quite satisfactory until 1905, when Newfoundland passed some local laws discriminating against foreign vessels. Root maintained that Newfoundland had no power to prescribe regulations for fishermen from the United States. He thought, however, that England and the United States might work out some rules satisfactory to both governments. A new modus vivendi was arranged in July, 1907, at which time Sir Edward Grey indicated that England would be willing to arbitrate the whole fisheries dispute. Secretary Root, asking Spooner to present the United States case, wrote: "You will have competent and well informed assistants, and you will be asked to contribute nothing to the cause except the trifling and unimportant incidents of brains, eloquence, skill, wisdom, force of character, and a controlling personality." [2] Three weeks went by before Secretary Root received a reply; Mrs. Spooner had misplaced the letter in the confusion of moving. Spooner decided to refuse the honor although he was pleased by the compliment of being asked, and especially

[2] Jessup, *Elihu Root*, II, 83–99; Callahan, *American Foreign Policy in Canadian Relations*, pp. 376–78, 518–22.

to have the request come from one whom he admired as much as he did Secretary Root.[3]

For a while after he left the Senate Spooner kept in touch with some of his old Washington friends, especially Root and Taft. He was particularly fond of Taft, and Taft had a deep regard for him, and whenever he was in New York City, even between trains, he tried to have a visit with Spooner.[4] In June, 1908, they were together at the Yale commencement exercises. Spooner, in an address before the Yale Law School Alumni Association, emphasized, as he did so often, the necessity of maintaining separation of powers between the executive, legislative, and judicial branches of the government as defined in the Constitution. Intimating that the incumbent in the White House had not done so, he declared that in his opinion the "next President of the United States would be a lawyer who knew the constitutional limitations of each branch." As he finished speaking, Taft walked in; he had just been nominated for the Presidency by the Republican National Convention. At the graduation ceremonies the next day, the honorary degree of doctor of laws was conferred on Spooner. Concerning it, President Roosevelt said: "I do wish . . . that Hadley of Yale had not chosen this particular time, when Taft was a great feature at the Yale commencement, to confer degrees on J. Pierpont Morgan and

[3] Spooner to E. Root, November 11, 1907, in Root Papers at The Library of Congress. When the treaty was finally signed in January, 1909, Secretary Root became the senior counsel representing the United States in the arbitration at The Hague.

[4] Spooner to E. Root, July 11, 1908, *ibid.;* Spooner to A. P. Wilder, March 16, 1907, in Spooner Papers; W. H. Taft to H. W. Taft, May 15; to Spooner, July 1, 1907, November 5, 1908, November 12, 1913, in Taft Papers at The Library of Congress.

Spooner. . . . Still, I cannot help believing we are going to pull Taft through all right." [5]

During the presidential campaign Spooner made several speeches indicating his distrust of many of the Rooseveltian policies in spite of the fact that Taft was running on that platform. In December he spoke at a dinner given by the Ohio State Society in honor of the President-elect. Again Spooner criticized Roosevelt for deviating from the Constitution in many of his policies. Taft, who spoke after Spooner, made no reference to the latter's speech. Oscar Straus, Secretary of Commerce and Labor, thought Spooner was trying to drive a wedge between Taft and Roosevelt.[6]

When Taft was elected President it was generally expected that Spooner would become a member of his cabinet, probably Secretary of State. Some thought it would not be a wise appointment in light of Spooner's public attacks on President Roosevelt's policies. There is no evidence that Spooner was asked to become a member of the cabinet and it is extremely doubtful that he would have accepted had he been asked. He was anxious to make money, and was making it, and he was enjoying his new home in New York.[7]

The Spooners had finally found an apartment that suited them, in the Osborne, 205 West 57th Street, overlooking

[5] *The New York Times,* June 23, 25, 1908. Spooner had received an honorary doctorate from the University of Wisconsin in 1894. Pringle, *Theodore Roosevelt,* p. 503.

[6] Oscar S. Straus Papers. Brief Personal Records as Secretary of Commerce and Labor, Reel 8, pp. 260–61. (Microfilm at Columbia University.) Courtesy of Dr. Naomi Wiener Cohen.

[7] *New York Tribune,* December 13, 1908; W. F. Small to W. H. Taft, December 2, 1908; W. H. Taft to W. F. Small, December 3, 1908, in Taft Papers; W. A. Day to P. Knox, December 22, 1908, January 5, 1909, in Knox Papers.

Central Park. It was a large duplex apartment for which they paid $541.67 a month. Philip, the youngest son, lived with them. He had come to New York the year before to study art and music. To be with him was one of the reasons the Spooners moved to the metropolis. Memphis and Lizzie, a Negro couple, took care of the household. Spooner had a study back of the kitchen where he could, if he wished, work all night. It was furnished simply, with an oak flat-top desk, a mounted elk's head, and on the floor a white polar bear rug given him by a client. It was crowded with books; he kept there his duplicate set of *United States Reports,* some European court records, several encyclopedias, a compilation of myths and legends and one of words and phrases. Several collections of the classics, forty-five volumes of "the best" literature, a set of the works of John Muir, the "American Statesmen" series, Prescott's works, the writings of Alexander Hamilton, John Jay, and Benjamin Franklin, and Von Holst's and Bancroft's histories of the United States made up the rest of his library.

The Spooners lived a quiet life. When they first arrived in New York, the Pinchots, Carnegies, Rockefellers, Cromwells, and others entertained them. Mrs. Spooner, however, disliked entertaining so they soon withdrew from the social whirl. Her chief delight was the opera, which during the season they attended frequently. After the development of the motion picture they often had an early dinner and then were driven to one of the new movie houses on Broadway.

Spooner was more gregarious. Almost every morning he rode horseback in Central Park, sometimes with George W. Wickersham, sometimes with his young granddaughter. After a hearty breakfast he was driven downtown in his

Packard to his law office. Often on his way home he stopped off at the Century Club, 7 West 43d Street, for a short visit with some of his old friends.[8] He continued his interest in Psi U, a fraternity of which he had been made an honorary member when his sons had been initiated into it at the University of Wisconsin. He had been president of the Washington chapter in 1905 when the annual banquet had been given in honor of Secretary Taft.[9] He was also a trustee of the Carnegie Institution of Washington, which he considered one of the noblest foundations the steel millionaire had created. He had been chosen by Carnegie in 1902, when the institution was established, but had been too busy to give it much attention until he was free from the burdens of public life.[10]

Spooner had opened his law office at 32 Liberty Street. A newspaper correspondent said that he obtained the cream of the legal business and many of Elihu Root's former clients. In 1910 Joseph P. Cotton, Jr., of the Cravath firm, joined him in a partnership. He, like Spooner, was of New England ancestry. He had been educated at Harvard University and immediately after his graduation from the law school in 1900 had entered the office of Paul Cravath. He had become a partner of that firm in 1907 and achieved prominence not only as a trial lawyer but also in the field of corporation finance. The historian of the

8 Annie Spooner, Diary, March 7–April 14, 1907; Surrogates Court, County of New York, Decree, June 21, 1921; reminiscences of granddaughter Dorothy Spooner.

9 Annie Spooner, Diary, April 12, 1907; Psi U notices of meetings, December 30, 1904, March 18, 1905, in Spooner Papers.

10 Spooner to A. Carnegie, January 29, 1902, March 15, 1907; to W. G. Walker, April 1, 1902, in Spooner Papers.

Cravath firm said of his partnership with Spooner: "While Spooner doubtless gave the new firm maturity and prestige, Cotton was its vibrant force and shortly became its better-known partner." At the time they formed the partnership, Joseph Cotton was only thirty-five while the former Senator was sixty-seven.[11]

A few years later Spooner persuaded Charles to join the firm. It was against the better judgment of his eldest son that he left his law practice in Seattle, where he had since 1906 been a partner in the firm of Bogle, Hardin, and Spooner, and where he had been prominent in civic affairs and musical circles. By 1915 the firm, then at 14 Wall Street, consisted of John C. Spooner, Joseph P. Cotton, Jr., Charles P. Spooner, and George S. Franklin, with A. Perry Osborn and George H. Savage as junior partners. The London *Times* wrote of Spooner:

For the last decade of his life he had offices in the Lower Broadway district of New York City, where he immersed himself in the intricacies of "American corporation law." His picturesque figure and long curly locks were familiar throughout the district. He figured in many important law cases and was always ready to serve the interests of his clients by settlements out of court.[12]

One of Spooner's first clients after his retirement from the Senate was the State of West Virginia, in a suit brought against her by Virginia. When West Virginia seceded from Virginia in 1861, she had agreed to assume an equitable proportion of the existing public debt. The two states had

[11] Barry, *Forty Years in Washington*, p. 139; Robert T. Swaine, *The Cravath Firm and Its Predecessors, 1819–1948*, II, 13–15; *New York City Directory*, 1909, 1911.

[12] *New York City Directory*, 1916; *The Times*, June 12, 1919.

not been able to come to any agreement as to the amount owed by West Virginia, so finally in 1906 Virginia had begun a suit against her in the Supreme Court. At that time it was said that Spooner had been offered a retainer of thirty thousand dollars by West Virginia but had refused it because it would interfere with his duties as Senator. When the case was finally argued in the Supreme Court in the spring of 1908, Spooner appeared with the attorney general of the state and several other notable lawyers. The decision, handed down on May 4, declared that the agreement made by the two states in 1861 was a compact binding on both and that Virginia, whether or not her government at that time was a lawful one, had been recognized as a restored state when her representatives had been admitted to Congress. The amount of the public debt and the proportion that West Virginia should assume was referred to a special master for determination.

A final argument was made before the Supreme Court in January, 1911. On behalf of West Virginia, Spooner first defended her secession from Virginia at the time when troops of the latter state were being used against the United States. He devoted the rest of his argument to the method to be used in dividing the debt. He cited many decisions of foreign courts and in international law to support his contention that it should be divided on the basis of the value of taxable property. He also contended that his client should not be charged interest from 1861, since it had been the fault of Virginia that no settlement had yet been reached. The court, with Justice Holmes handing down the decision, declared that West Virginia's proportion of the principal was about seven million dollars and expressed the hope that as far as interest was concerned, there would be forbearance on both sides. West Virginia not only objected to the settlement but also questioned whether the United States Supreme Court could carry out a decision against "a sovereign State." (Not until 1939 were the final payments made.) [13]

One of the most famous cases in which Spooner appeared before the Supreme Court was that of *Harriman* v. *Interstate Commerce Commission*. Edward H. Harriman had by degrees obtained control of many of the railroad systems in the West. He had started out with the Illinois Central and then he, with Jacob Schiff, of Kuhn, Loeb and Company, had reorganized and rebuilt the Union Pacific, which had become bankrupt during the panic of 1893. After the death of Collis P. Huntington in 1900, he had gained control of the Southern Pacific system, which included railroads in California, the Central Pacific, which connected with the Union Pacific at Ogden, Utah, and roads linking California with Kansas City and New Orleans. He had then entered into a contest with James J. Hill and J. P. Morgan for control of the Northern Pacific.[14]

In that struggle Spooner had favored Harriman. When he was counsel for the receivers of the Northern Pacific, he had opposed the proposal that that road be associated with Hill's Great Northern and in 1897 he had expressed deep concern over Hill's increasing control over the Northern Pacific, a control that had finally resulted in the resignation from the presidency of his old friend E. W. Winter.[15]

13 209 U. S. 514 (*Commonwealth of Virginia* v. *State of West Virginia*); 220 U. S. 1; Charles Henry Ambler, *West Virginia: The Mountain State*, pp. 449–52, 528–29; James Morton Callahan, *Semi-Centennial History of West Virginia*, pp. 252–55.

14 John Moody, *Railroad Builders*, pp. 193–210.

15 Spooner to E. W. Winter, May 15, 1897, in Spooner Papers.

In 1901 Hill and Harriman had fought it out on the floor of the New York Stock Exchange; the result had been a draw. Instead of continuing the struggle, there had been formed the Northern Securities Company, a holding company, to take over the Northern Pacific, the Great Northern, and the Chicago, Burlington and Quincy.

It was the Northern Securities Company that President Roosevelt had used to initiate his trust-busting campaign. Without consulting anyone, he had authorized Attorney General Knox to bring suit in Minnesota for the dissolution of the company.[16] At that time Harriman had asked Spooner to appear on his behalf at St. Paul as he had applied for intervention in the government suit. Spooner had refused not only because he had been consulted by Knox about the case but also because, since it was a government case, it might sometime bear a relationship to some legislation on which he as Senator might have to act. Decisions in favor of the government had been handed down both by the lower court (April 9, 1903) and by the Supreme Court (March 14, 1904).[17]

After the dissolution of the Northern Securities Company, Harriman had sold his Northern Pacific stock at a good profit and had invested in the Chicago and Alton, the Atchison, Topeka and Santa Fe, the Baltimore and Ohio, and some lines in the New York Central System. The Interstate Commerce Commission, investigating railroad consolidations, called on Harriman to testify before the

16 Pringle, *Theodore Roosevelt,* pp. 251–64.
17 Spooner to L. S. Smith, March 15; to H. H. Porter, April 24, 1904, in Spooner Papers. See 193 U. S. 197 (*Northern Securities Co.* v. *United States*).

commission as to his railroad stock purchases. On advice of counsel he refused to answer. The commission then obtained a decree from the Circuit Court for the Southern District of New York ordering him to answer all questions except those relating to the purchase of Union and Southern Pacific stock in 1906. From that order he appealed to the Supreme Court.[18]

John C. Spooner represented Harriman in that court on November 3–4, 1908, as he had in the lower court. He argued that the Interstate Commerce Commission had been given only specified administrative duties by act of Congress and that its power to investigate extended only to the duties imposed on common carriers and practices and duties forbidden them. The commission, he claimed, had nothing to do with other acts of the carriers and Congress had not conferred on that body all inquisitorial powers of Congress with respect to interstate commerce. The commission was represented by Frank B. Kellogg, with a brief on its behalf filed by Henry L. Stimson (both men later held the office of Secretary of State). They asserted that the commission did have all the powers of a Congressional committee of inquiry since its object was also to discover abuses in order to recommend additional legislation to Congress. Justice Holmes presented the opinion of the Court, which was a five-to-three decision (Justices Day, Harlan, and McKenna dissenting). He accepted Spooner's argument. He declared that the commission had been set up to enforce only those regulations that Congress had imposed and that therefore the body could require testimony from witnesses only in

18 157 Federal Reporter 432 (*Interstate Commerce Commission* v. *Harriman et al.*).

connection with complaints for violations of the act. The order of the Circuit Court was reversed.[19]

President Roosevelt was not satisfied with the decision and he did not like Harriman. The railroad man had been trying to gain political as well as financial power in New York State and by 1904 had considered himself the boss of the Republican machine in the state. This had irritated Roosevelt, and when Harriman had stated in a public letter that he had raised large sums in the campaign at the request of the President, the break had become complete. Harriman's biographer claims that the Interstate Commerce Commission's investigation had been definitely hostile to Harriman.[20] After its decision proved adverse to the commission, the President directed the Attorney General to bring suit to dissolve the connection of the Union Pacific with other railroads. The suit was brought in Utah but before the trial was completed Harriman died. The Supreme Court, when the case reached it in 1912, declared that since the Union Pacific held 46 per cent of the stock of the Southern Pacific, it was an illegal combination under the Sherman Anti-Trust Act and it ordered the combination dissolved. How this could be done without injuring innocent stockholders was a problem. Spooner and other lawyers, representing the Union Pacific, suggested the sale or distribution, as a dividend, of the Southern Pacific shares to shareholders of the Union Pacific. They contended that the distribution of the stock among so many stockholders would conclude the combination. The Court,

[19] 211 U. S. 407 (*Harriman* v. *Interstate Commerce Commission*). See Swaine, *Cravath Firm,* II, 21–23; David Bryn-Jones, *Frank B. Kellogg,* pp. 47–59.

[20] George Kennan, *E. H. Harriman,* II, 228–304; Pringle, *Theodore Roosevelt,* pp. 450–54.

however, rejected the plan, saying that the large stockholders might be able to acquire the shares of the small stockholders. Finally a plan was worked out between the Cravath firm, representing the Union Pacific, and James C. McReynolds, the new Democratic Attorney General. The Union Pacific was directed to give over to the Pennsylvania Railroad Company some of its shares in the Southern Pacific in exchange for shares of the Baltimore and Ohio that it held. The remaining holdings of the Southern Pacific were sold to shareholders of the Union Pacific.[21]

Another trust case of Spooner's was a suit by the United States against the Hamburg-American steamship line. That company had entered into an agreement with other steamship companies (North German Lloyd, International Mercantile Marine, Cunard, Holland-America, and Canadian Pacific) to regulate transportation of third-class and steerage passengers. The United States government claimed that this Atlantic Conference, as the association was called, was a violation of the Sherman Act since it had obtained a virtual monopoly of the steerage traffic. The following charges were made: First, that these steamship companies undersold their competitors; second, that the agents of these lines were forbidden to handle tickets of non-Conference lines; and third, that the steamship companies also arranged the immigrants' railroad transportation.

Spooner, lawyer for the Hamburg-American line, maintained that it was impossible to apply to a sea traffic concern the same standards as were applied to a railroad or other land enterprises. He entered into a long discussion

21 Moody, *Railroad Builders*, pp. 193–201; Swaine, *The Cravath Firm*, II, 26–27; 188 Federal Reporter 102; 226 U. S. 61, 470 (*United States* v. *Union Pacific*).

of the history of the passage of the Interstate Commerce Act and the Sherman Anti-Trust Act, about which he was well informed since he had been a member of the Senate at the time of their passage. He contended that these steamship agreements were reasonable, were not in undue restraint of trade, and had, in fact, resulted in more regularity of sailings and accommodations, protected steerage passengers against fraud, and maintained reasonable rates.[22] By the time the special expediting court handed down its decision in 1915 that the Sherman Act did apply to foreign commerce, the Atlantic Conference had been broken up. Because of World War I, the Hamburg-American line had ceased operations. The steamship company gave Spooner a note for fifty thousand dollars, to be paid three months after the resumption of regular service. At the time of Spooner's death this note had not been paid, but on February 23, 1921, the Alien Property Custodian paid the full amount of the note.[23]

Spooner appeared in several other cases concerning the Sherman Anti-Trust Act. In most of these he supported a narrow interpretation of the act. In one case he maintained that the purchase of futures was not illegal, for the Sherman Act was not an instrument to curb the profits of an individual. The court, however, declared that an attempt to corner the cotton market was an illegal combination in restraint of trade, since its object had been to control and enhance the price of cotton and that therefore it had af-

[22] *The New York Times,* April 1, 18, May 3, 5, 1914; Brief, *United States v. Hamburg-Amerikanische Packetfahrt-Actiengesellschaft, and Others.* District Court of United States. In Equity; United States District Court, New York, Docket, Equity, IX:201.

[23] Surrogates Court, County of New York, Decree, June 21, 1921, accounting rendered by Farmers' Loan and Trust Company.

fected interstate commerce.[24] In another case Spooner denounced the criminal penalties provided for in the Sherman Act. He said that he had always disapproved of them, since the aim of the act was to punish conspiracies on a common-law basis. In this case his viewpoint was accepted by the court.[25] In one case, however, Spooner tried to obtain a broader interpretation of the act. He contended that the system whereby a company holding a patent required licensees to join with other licensees in a combination or pool to control prices and output was in violation of the Sherman Act. The court, however, declared that, although the patented articles were a monopoly, they were not articles of trade or commerce in the meaning of the act because, since they were patented, they were not articles in connection with which people were entitled to freedom of trade.[26]

At the time of the discussion of new antitrust legislation early in President Wilson's administration, Spooner made several addresses on the subject. He defended the Sherman Anti-Trust Act but declared the law had been singularly misconstrued from the time of its passage until the Supreme Court in 1911 brought in the "rule of reason" in the Standard Oil and American Tobacco cases. He, however, attacked the pending measures regulating business, commonly called the "five brothers." "Five brothers—I call them five pups," he said. "If they are made into law, what will be the situation? The business of the United States—

24 226 U. S. 526 (*United States* v. *Patten*).

25 219 U. S. 587 (*Edmund S. Nash* v. *United States*); 229 U. S. 374 (*Nash* v. *United States*). See also 172 Federal Reporter 455 and 186 Federal Reporter 592 (*United States* v. *American Naval Stores*).

26 154 Federal Reporter 358; 207 U. S. 589; 210 U. S. 439 (*Rubber Tire Wheel Company* v. *Milwaukee Rubber Works Co.*).

yours and everybody elses'—will be in a strait jacket." [27]

The firm of Spooner and Cotton also participated in many receivership controversies. When firms got into financial difficulties, as many did during the panics of 1907 and 1912, and had to petition to be declared bankrupt, committees of bondholders and stockholders hired law firms to represent their interests during the receivership proceedings and the subsequent reorganization transactions. Spooner was retained as counsel in many such suits, and in several bankruptcy cases he appeared as attorney presenting the argument before the United States Supreme Court. [28]

One of the most complicated of the bankruptcy cases with which the firm of Spooner and Cotton was connected was that of the New York City transit lines. These companies had been in financial difficulties for many years, and finally in 1907 the Metropolitan Street Railway Company, which controlled the surface lines in Manhattan and the Bronx, and the New York City Railway Company, which operated the surface lines for the Metropolitan, went into receivership in the federal courts. Spooner represented the Guaranty Trust Company when it petitioned the Supreme Court to prevent the Metropolitan Street Railway Company from issuing receiver certificates, but the petition was denied. He was also retained by one of the bondholders' committees to represent their interests in the financial arrangements which paved the way for the reorganization of

27 *The New York Times,* February 12, July 17, 1914.
28 220 U.S. 616 (*Guaranty Trust Co.* v. *Chicago Railways Co.*); 225 U.S. 112 (*Bigelow* v. *Old Dominion Copper Mining and Smelting Co.*); 225 U.S. 714 (*Frank T. Wells* v. *United States*); 230 U.S. 36 (*Ex parte American Steel Barrel Co.*); Swaine, *Cravath Firm,* II, 169–75, 180–84, 191–92.

the transit companies. After three years, during which the surface lines were in financial chaos, the properties were reorganized and the New York City Railway Company took over the old Metropolitan lines and the Third Avenue Railroad Company.[29]

In 1909 a candidate for mayor, William J. Gaynor, began a campaign for a city-owned subway, the "Triborough," to compete with the Interborough and the Brooklyn Rapid Transit companies. Alarmed by this threat of competition, the old companies offered to build not only extensions but also new lines. After a great many conferences with the Public Service Commission and the new transit committee of the Board of Estimate, dual contracts were drawn up and signed, whereby the existing companies and the city would finance the construction of the lines and the two companies would finance the buying of the equipment. In order to finance their $40-million share of the project, the Brooklyn Rapid Transit Company sold notes of their company to bankers.[30] The firm of Spooner and Cotton was retained to take care of the legal aspects involved in the financial arrangements with Kuhn, Loeb and Company. For these professional services they received $35,000. Several years later, in 1916, when a joint legislative committee was investigating the Public Service Commission, the chairman noticed this item and wanted to know who Spooner and Cotton were that they should receive $35,000. In the final report he criticized the large sums that had been paid to lawyers working for corporations other

29 161 Federal Reporter 787, 163 Federal Reporter 243, 165 Federal Reporter 455, 166 Federal Reporter 569 (*Guaranty Trust Co.* v. *Metropolitan Street Railway Co.*); Swaine, *Cravath Firm*, II, 45, 62–63.

30 Louis Heaton Pink, *Gaynor*, pp. 196–98; James Blaine Walker, *Fifty Years of Rapid Transit*, pp. 211, 220, 229–31.

than the Brooklyn Rapid Transit, and especially the fact that their fees had been charged by the transit company to "Construction B" account.[31]

After the United States entered World War I, Joseph P. Cotton withdrew from the firm. He had assisted G. W. Goethals in establishing the United States Shipping Board in 1916, and in 1917 he became head of the meat division in the United States Food Administration, established by Herbert Hoover. The law firm of Spooner and Spooner continued with its offices at 14 Wall Street.[32] After 1914 John C. Spooner did not appear in person to argue any cases before the United States Supreme Court although he sometimes presented briefs. His last brief filed in that court concerned the Sixteenth Amendment. The case was argued by Charles P. Spooner. The Spooners maintained that the income tax could not be applied to income derived from an export business because the Constitution forbade an export tax and a tax on income was a tax on the source from which the income was derived. Justice Van Devanter held, however, that the income tax was a general tax and affected exports only remotely. This case was argued in December, 1917, just a year and a half before John C. Spooner's death.[33]

By 1914 Spooner's very active and intensive career had begun to undermine his health, and the experience of being caught in Europe when war broke out hastened his

[31] *The New York Times,* June 20, 24, 1916; New York Legislature, *Report of Joint Legislative Committee Appointed to Investigate the Public Service Commission,* V, 1140; VI, 618.

[32] Swaine, *Cravath Firm,* II, 13–15; *New York City Directory,* 1918.

[33] 247 U.S. 165 (*W. E. Peck* v. *John Z. Lowe, collector*). See also 217 U.S. 423 (*Heike* v. *United States*), an interesting case about "bar immunity"; and 234 U.S. 423 (*Johnson* v. *Gearlds*), about sale of liquor to Indians.

decline. Spooner, his wife, and Philip had sailed on the *Mauretania* on July 7, 1914. He was soon identified as "Senator" Spooner, his wife noted in her diary. As usual, they stayed at hotels patronized by Americans, ate American food, attended the opera and concerts, and went shopping. They spent most of their time in northern Italy and Switzerland, where the climate seemed to make Spooner feel better, although Mrs. Spooner blamed his indisposition on the fact that he ate too much and would not stick to his diet. On August 1 Mrs. Spooner, for the first time, seemed to be aware of the crisis in European affairs and noted: "John is worrying over the Servian-Austrian war for fear we can't get home, or that being here in Italy, he can't get his letter of credit honored. The Milan Bank already is closed to foreign letters of credit." The next day she wrote: "Great excitement over war between Austria & Servia, actual fighting going on & Americans anxious to get home, or in England. Probably Phil can't go to Mozart Festival at Salzburg in Austria. Some Americans say the Hamburg Am has taken off the large steas. probably French too—the concierge here has been called off to serve in this army." On August 4 she wrote of how her husband and son had gone to Como from Lugano, where they were staying, to see about getting money on their letter of credit. They did succeed in getting sixty dollars by paying a premium on it and the Spooners started for Lucerne. Mrs. Spooner was evidently less alarmed than her husband; she seemed to find it rather exciting and wrote: "Soldiers everywhere. Found good rooms at Lucernefhof—very tired. Big Am. meeting tonight to consider what to do.—No trains outside of Switzerland. . . . Was wakened at 6 by drums beating. We looked out & saw soldiers. . . . England has declared war on Germany—the rumor is. I can't be sorry to be in it, in a measure—it is so exciting." They had to stay in Lucerne for two weeks since there seemed to be no way of getting out of the country. The Swiss people, she remarked, were as anxious that they leave as they were to go, on account of the food supply. They finally received assurances that they could have passage on the Cunard line if they could get to England before September 1. On August 20 they were able to leave Switzerland, and although the journey was anything but pleasant ("went on for two hrs. or so, then stopped, changed cars, waited an hour or two, nothing happened," Mrs. Spooner noted), they arrived in Paris three days later and succeeded in reaching London in time to sail on the *Laconia* to New York on August 29.[34]

Spooner's health continued to decline although he was still active until May, 1919, when *The New York Times* noted that he had suffered a nervous breakdown. Almost every day the paper reported his condition until he died on June 11. No service was held in New York; his body was taken to Madison for burial in Forest Hills Cemetery.[35] At the funeral, held in the First Baptist Church, the minister read one of Spooner's favorite poems, Tennyson's "Crossing the Bar." The local chapter of the G.A.R. attended in a body and the Knights Templar formed an escort of honor. Spooner had joined the Masons when he was in the army and in November, 1904, had taken the higher degrees, but he had never been active in the Masonic Order.[36]

[34] Annie Spooner, Diary, July 7–August 25, 1914.
[35] *The New York Times*, May 22, 23, 24, 25, 26, 27, June 12, 1919.
[36] *Madison Democrat*, June 12, 13, 15, 1919; Annie Spooner, Diary, November 14, 1904.

John Coit Spooner had succeeded in his desire to make money after his retirement from public life. He had not only been able to provide his family with the comforts of life as well as many luxuries but he also left an estate of over $350,000. He had already divided his real estate among his sons so the remaining property was in stocks and bonds, personal effects, insurance policies, and cash. Since his "fortune" had always been a matter of public comment during his political career, it is interesting to note that his money was invested in bonds of Anaconda Copper, Canadian Northern Railroad, Locomotive & Machine Company of Montreal, Wilson and Company, Wisconsin Central Railroad, and United States government bonds. He also had one thousand shares of stock of the Atchison, Topeka and Santa Fe Railroad and one hundred shares of Geneva Cutlery. He had $100,000 in life insurance and a large cash balance at the Guaranty Trust Company. He left all this property to the Farmers' Loan and Trust Company to be used to set up a trust fund for the support of his wife. She was to receive $1,000 a month (later raised to $1,200) and at her death the fund was to be divided among her sons.[37]

At the time of his death Spooner was recognized by the metropolitan papers both of this country and England as one of the outstanding statesmen in United States history. *The New York Times,* giving a sketch of his life, wrote:

It has been said of Senator Spooner's record in the National Legislature that it probably has never been surpassed in the magnitude of its labors, their practical efficiency and the historical importance of their results. Elihu Root, Secretary of

[37] New York County, Surrogates Court, Record of Will, Liber 1087:278; accounting decree, June 21, 1921.

State when Senator Spooner resigned in 1907, two years before his term was up, remarked, discussing his work: "Our history shows a succession of a few able men, men of great force of character, and devotion to the public service, who have been prominent in molding the legislative policy of the country. Mr. Spooner belongs to this succession." The Wisconsin Senator, however, was known as a practical and constructive statesman rather than as an oracle of political principles. He was interested in the details of legislation and many times he suggested the compromise upon which the Senate would agree or give final touches to an important bill. . . . It is said that there are today more "Spooner amendments" and "Spooner compromises" of large importance on the statutes than one could count.[38]

That was the contemporary estimate. What is the verdict of history? Today, less than half a century later, Spooner is almost forgotten. Even in Wisconsin his career has been practically erased from the pages of its history. If he is mentioned at all, he is presented merely as a tool of the "interests"—the picture of him drawn by the muckrakers and the progressive wing of the Republican party. Just as the latter group, led by Spooner's colleague La Follette, was intent on reform and radically changing the economic and political order, so Spooner was devoted to preserving what he considered the essential features of the American system. Spooner could never be, like La Follette, a rebel; he was always a conservative, but not a reactionary or a cowardly conservative, as he called the mossbacks. He worshiped the Constitution and subscribed to the philosophy of the "gospel of wealth." Individual liberty and freedom

[38] *The New York Times,* June 11, 12, 1919. See also *The Times* (London), June 12, 1919, *New York Tribune,* June 11, 1919; *Milwaukee Sentinel,* June 12, 1919.

were for him the keystones of American democracy. He believed that individuals also had responsibilities—to provide for their own families and to help those less fortunate than themselves; these should never be functions of the government. He recognized that by the end of the nineteenth century capitalism, unbridled, had brought about some injustices and inequities. He worked to remedy some of these defects and favored enough governmental regulation to ensure fair play, but he did not want any fundamental changes made in the existing system. He had no understanding of the progressive program and naïvely thought that the people in the long run would repudiate the movement toward centralization and paternalism.

Spooner was first and throughout his adult life a lawyer. Even when he was a child, the two men he most admired were lawyers. His training as a youth was toward that goal. He thought as a lawyer; he was not introspective or philosophical; nor was he an original thinker. He had a brilliant mind, an amazingly retentive memory, and an ability to discern legal loopholes. He had a tremendous capacity for hard work, an ability to work under pressure and give complete absorption to the task at hand. For that reason he was not able to continue his private law practice after he became United States Senator.

When he entered public life he was a faithful public servant. It was a considerable financial sacrifice for him to give up his profession, but when he entered the Senate, he made that career his only one and gave to the public his entire loyalty. He frequently referred to his constituents as his clients; yet in reality it was the American people rather than just the residents of Wisconsin whom he represented. He was little interested in local legislation.

In the Senate he approached legislative problems as lawyers approach cases. First he carefully studied all questions, working hard to understand the ramifications of the wide variety of issues with which he was confronted. He had no respect for his colleagues who had snap solutions for problems about which they knew nothing. Having mastered a subject, he then tried to make a bill perfect from the legal standpoint, to be sure it was in accord with the Constitution. As one person said, he seemed to be the Senate's "Court for the Correction of Errors." [39] A modest man, he did not care who received credit for a measure, just so it was a good one and constitutional. When a bill was ready, he worked out the strategy to obtain its acceptance and, as an expert parliamentary tactician, he was familiar with all possible loopholes in the rules which would facilitate passage. The amendments for which he is best known, those to which he gave his name, were significant not for the subject matter but for the method by which the desired objective was obtained. Finally, he presented the argument extemporaneously, brilliantly, and persuasively. "He is concededly the greatest parliamentary debater of his day," William Howard Taft said of him, "and really deserves the title, so much misapplied, of a great constitutional lawyer." [40]

While Senator, Spooner's relationship to Presidents Harrison, McKinley, and Roosevelt was like that of counselor to client. He might not like certain features of their policies and advise changes in them; he might disagree with them in private; but never while in the Senate did he publicly attack a Republican President or any of his policies.

39 E. Keyes to Spooner, March 31, 1906, in Spooner Papers.
40 *Washington Post*, March 4, 1907.

He defended their policies at the bar of the Senate or, for that matter, at the bar of public opinion. For that reason, John Coit Spooner may be recorded in history as "defender of Presidents."

Bibliographical Notes

.

I. Manuscripts

This biography is based primarily on the papers of John Coit Spooner on deposit at The Library of Congress. It is a very large collection, consisting of over 135 filing boxes of letters received and 108 letterpress copybooks of letters sent by Spooner. They cover the period from 1866 to 1907. Mrs. Spooner's diaries, although fragmentary, for she kept them quite irregularly, provide glimpses of their family life from 1885 to 1914. They are in the possession of the family.

The Theodore Roosevelt correspondence in The Library of Congress was the next most valuable source; these papers are indispensable for a study of Spooner when he was at the height of his political career. There are very few of the Spooner letters in *The Letters of Theodore Roosevelt,* the collection edited by Elting E. Morison *et al.*

Of less importance were the Benjamin Harrison, the William McKinley, and the Grover Cleveland Papers, also in The Library of Congress. The papers of Spooner's contemporaries deposited there contain some letters to and from Spooner; they were of more value for the information they gave about problems with which Spooner was concerned. The following were the most useful: Nelson W. Aldrich, William E. Chandler, William M. Evarts, Walter Q. Gresham, Philander C. Knox, Louis Michener, Elihu Root, John Sherman, and William Howard Taft Papers.

In the Historical, Memorial, and Art Department of Iowa, Des Moines, Iowa, is the large collection of papers of William Boyd Allison, consisting mainly of letters to him. They were a disappointment. Of more value, especially for the years from 1903 to 1905, were the papers of Orville H. Platt, at the Connecticut State Library, Hartford, Connecticut. Of some use also were the letters of Levi P. Morton, in the New York Public Library, and of George von Lengerke Meyer, in the Massachusetts Historical Society, Boston, Massachusetts.

The Wisconsin State Historical Society, Madison, Wisconsin, has many collections which are indispensable for a study of Spooner. For his university career there are the records of the Hesperian Society, both the Bill of Exercises and the Book of Minutes. Very enlightening are the papers of Elisha W. Keyes, a large collection of letters to him and forty-one letterpress copybooks. The papers of Lucius Fairchild, John Hazelton, John M. Olin, Jeremiah Rusk, Andrew J. Turner, and William F. Vilas throw light on certain phases of Spooner's career. The Robert M. La Follette Papers, recently opened for research, were a great disappointment. Willett S. Main's diaries give interesting details about Spooner's courtship, his early legal career, and his election to the Senate in 1885. In the University of Wisconsin archives are the Minutes of the Board of Regents. This was the only source of information on Spooner's service as a regent of the university.

The record of Spooner's will and an accounting by the Farmers' Loan and Trust Company are in the New York County Surrogates Court. In the archives of the United States District Court (New York Docket, Equity), Federal Court Building, are lists of some of the cases for which Spooner was lawyer after 1907.

II. Documents

For Spooner's university career the catalogues of the University of Wisconsin, 1860–1864, contributed some information. The *Roster of Wisconsin Volunteers. War of Rebellion, 1861–1865* (Madison, 1866, 2 vols.) and United States War Department, *War of the Rebellion: Official Records of the Union and Confederate Armies* (Washington, 1880–1901, 4th ser.) were used to obtain information about his military service. The *Wisconsin Blue Book*, 1867–1870, the *Wisconsin Assembly Journal, 1872,* and the *Wisconsin Session Laws, 1872,* gave information about the political positions Spooner held from 1867 to 1872.

For his career in the United States Senate the following records of the United States Congress were invaluable:

Congressional Record and *Statutes-at-Large,* 49th through 51st
    Congresses, 55th through 59th Congresses
Senate Documents: 55th Congress, 3d Session, No. 62
                56th Congress, 1st Session, No. 188

57th Congress, 1st Session, Nos. 54, 182, 331, 357
58th Congress, 2d Session, No. 222
63d Congress, 2d Session, No. 474
Senate Executive Documents: 53d Congress, 2d Session, Nos. 81, 120
Senate Executive Journals, 49th through 51st Congresses, 55th through 59th Congresses
Senate Reports: 50th Congress, 1st Session, No. 2373
55th Congress, 2d Session, No. 681
56th Congress, 1st Session, Nos. 249, 1337
57th Congress, 1st Session, No. 783

For information about the problems with which Spooner was confronted when he was a member of the Senate, the following were consulted:

Malloy, William M. (comp.), *Treaties, Conventions, International Acts, Protocols, and Agreements Between the United States of America and Other Powers.* 4 vols. Washington, D. C., 1910.
Richardson, James D. (ed.), *A Compilation of the Messages and Papers of the Presidents.* 10 vols. Washington, D. C., 1910.
United States State Department. *Papers Relating to the Foreign Relations of the United States,* 1898, 1905. Washington, D. C., 1901, 1906.

Spooner's career as a lawyer was traced through:

Federal Reporter. Cases Argued and Determined in the Circuit and District Courts of the United States. Vols. 6, 10, 20, 27, 46–54, 58–72, 154–88.
Reports of Cases Argued and Determined in the Circuit Courts of the United States for the Seventh Circuit. 17 vols. Cincinnati and Chicago, 1840–1884. Vols. 7–11.
United States Department of the Interior. *Decisions of the Department of the Interior Relating to Public Lands.* Vol. 5.

United States Supreme Court Reports. Vols. 88–247.
Wisconsin Assembly Journal for the years 1870–1885, 1891,
    1893, 1897, 1899, 1901.
Wisconsin Supreme Court Reports. Vols. 23–95.

Information on Spooner's political activities was found
in:

*Official Proceedings of the Ninth Republican National Con-
    vention, 1888* (Minneapolis, 1903).
*Official Proceedings of the Tenth Republican National Con-
    vention, 1892* (Minneapolis, 1892).
*Official Proceedings of the Thirteenth Republican National
    Convention, 1904* (Minneapolis, 1904).
*1902-Voters Handbook. The Truth About the Governor, the
    Legislature, Taxation and Primary Election* (Milwaukee,
    1902).

Spooner's various residences were traced through:

Boyd, William. *Boyd's Directory of the District of Columbia,*
    Washington, D. C., 1886–1891, 1897–1907.
———. *Boyd's Directory of New York City,* 1908–1919.
Madison, Wisconsin, Directory, 1866. Madison, Wis., B. W.
    Luchow, 1866.

III. Newspapers and periodicals

The most valuable source is the *Milwaukee Sentinel,* 1880–
1907. This was the outstanding Republican paper in Wisconsin. It tended to be independent in factional quarrels
in the party but usually was friendly to Spooner. From
1882 to 1896 it was edited by Horace Rublee, for whose
son Spooner twice obtained a consulship. In 1901 it was
acquired by Charles F. Pfister, boss of the Stalwart wing of

the Wisconsin Republican party. Other Wisconsin papers of value were the *Hudson Star and Times,* 1870–1885, published during this period by Spooner's close friend Horace A. Taylor; the *Madison Daily Democrat,* 1880–1907, an independent Democratic paper; the *Wisconsin State Journal* (Madison), owned by David Atwood (1864–1867), Horace Taylor (1890–1901), and Amos P. Wilder (1901–1906).

The following out-of-state papers were consulted:

Chicago Inter-Ocean (1884–1885), for Spooner's election to the Senate; *Nantucket Inquirer and Mirror* (1887–1888), for Spooner summer activities; and *Railway Age* (Chicago, 1893–1897), for Northern Pacific receivership.

For Spooner's public career the following were useful:

The Nation (New York, 1880–1907); *New York Morning Herald* (1880–1896); *The New York Times* (1912–1919); *New York Daily Tribune* (1900–1908); *Review of Reviews* (New York, 1890–1907); *The Times* (London), (1900–1905, 1910–1919); and *Washington Post* (1896–1907).

IV. Biographical sketches other than those in newspapers and periodicals

There was no biography of John Coit Spooner available, but brief biographical sketches were found in the following:

Appleton's Cyclopedia of American Biography, 1899.
Congressional Biographical Directory.
Dictionary of American Biography, 17:465–66.
National Cyclopedia of American Biography, Vol. 16.

Nelke, D. I. *The Columbian Biographical Dictionary and Portrait Gallery of the Representative Men of the United States. Wisconsin Volume.* Chicago, Lewis Publishing Company, 1895, pp. 126–43.
Who's Who in America, for the years 1899, 1918–19.

Information concerning Spooner's ancestry and family are found in:

Chapman, Frederick William. *The Coit Family.* Hartford, Conn., Lockwood and Brainard, 1874.
Reports of Cases Argued and Determined in the Supreme Court of the State of Wisconsin, 72:xxvii–xxxvii (1888). Biographical sketch of Philip L. Spooner.
Spooner, Thomas. *Records of William Spooner of Plymouth, Mass. and His Descendants.* Cincinnati, Press of F. W. Freeman, 1883.
Wisconsin Blue Book, 1882. Biographical sketch of Philip L. Spooner, Jr.

V. Memoirs and biographies of Spooner's contemporaries

Most of the following give little information concerning Spooner himself but they do throw considerable light on the problems with which Spooner was concerned.

Acheson, Sam Hanna. *Joe Bailey: The Last Democrat.* New York, Macmillan, 1932.
Adler, Selig. *Senatorial Career of George Franklin Edmunds, 1866–1891.* Urbana, University of Illinois Press, 1934.
Barrows, Chester L. *William M. Evarts.* Chapel Hill, University of North Carolina Press, 1941.
Beale, Howard K. *Theodore Roosevelt and the Rise of America to World Power.* Baltimore, The Johns Hopkins Press, 1956.

Bishop, Joseph Bucklin. *Theodore Roosevelt and His Times. Shown in His Own Letters.* 2 vols. New York, Charles Scribner's Sons, 1920.

Bolles, Blair. *Tyrant from Illinois.* New York, Norton, 1951.

Bowers, Claude G. *Beveridge and the Progressive Era.* Boston, Houghton Mifflin, 1932.

Briggs, John Ely. *William Peter Hepburn.* Iowa City, State Historical Society of Iowa, 1919.

Bryn-Jones, David. *Frank B. Kellogg: A Biography.* New York, G. P. Putnam's Sons, 1937.

Busbey, L. White. *Uncle Joe Cannon.* New York, Henry Holt, 1927.

Casson, Henry. *"Uncle Jerry": Life of General Jeremiah M. Rusk.* Madison, Wis., J. W. Hill, 1895.

Chandler, Julius Converse. *Annals of the Fortieth.* n.d., n.p.

Conkling, Alfred R. *The Life and Letters of Roscoe Conkling.* New York, C. L. Webster, 1889.

Connelley, William Elsey. *Ingalls of Kansas: A Character Study.* Topeka, Kan., published by the author, 1909.

Coolidge, Louis A. *An Old Fashioned Senator: Orville H. Platt of Connecticut,* New York, G. P. Putnam's Sons, 1910.

Cortissoz, Royal. *The Life of Whitelaw Reid.* 2 vols. New York, Charles Scribner's Sons, 1921.

Croly, Herbert David. *Marcus Alonzo Hanna: His Life and Work.* New York, Macmillan, 1912.

Cullom, Shelby. *Fifty Years of Public Service: Personal Recollections of Shelby M. Cullom.* Chicago, A. C. McClurg, 1911.

Current, Richard Nelson. *Pine Logs and Politics: A Life of Philetus Sawyer, 1816–1900,* Madison, Wisconsin State Historical Society, 1949.

Dawes, Charles G. *A Journal of the McKinley Years.* Chicago, Lakeside Press, 1950.

Dawson, Thomas Fulton. *Life and Character of Edward Oliver Wolcott.* 2 vols. New York, Knickerbocker Press, 1911.

Dennett, Tyler. *John Hay: From Poetry to Politics.* New York, Dodd, Mead, 1933.

Depew, Chauncey M. *My Memories of Eighty Years.* New York, Charles Scribner's Sons, 1922.

Doan, Edward N. *The La Follettes and the Wisconsin Idea.* New York, Rinehart, 1947.

Dunn, Arthur Wallace. *From Harrison to Harding: A Personal Narrative, Covering a Third of a Century.* 2 vols. New York, G. P. Putnam's Sons, 1922.

Dyer, Brainerd. *The Public Career of William M. Evarts.* Berkeley, University of California Press, 1933.

Ellis, Elmer. *Henry Moore Teller.* Caldwell, Idaho, The Caxton Printers, 1941.

Foraker, Joseph Benson. *Notes of a Busy Life.* 2 vols. Cincinnati, Stewart and Kidd, 1917.

Foraker, Julia B. *I Would Live It Again: Memories of a Vivid Life.* New York, Harper & Bros., 1932.

Garraty, John A. *Henry Cabot Lodge: A Biography.* New York, Alfred A. Knopf, 1953.

Gillett, Frederick H. *George Frisbie Hoar.* Boston, Houghton Mifflin, 1934.

Gompers, Samuel. *Seventy Years of Life and Labor: An Autobiography.* 2 vols. New York, E. P. Dutton & Co., 1925.

Gresham, Matilda. *The Life of Walter Quintin Gresham.* 2 vols. Chicago, Rand McNally & Co., 1919.

High, James Lambert. *The Great Chancellor and Other Papers.* Chicago, Callaghan & Co., 1900.

Hoar, George Frisbie. *Autobiography of Seventy Years.* 2 vols. New York, Charles Scribner's Sons, 1905.

Howe, Mark A. De Wolfe. *George von Lengerke Meyer: His Life and Public Services.* New York, Dodd, Mead, 1920.

Jessup, Philip C. *Elihu Root.* 2 vols. New York, Dodd, Mead, 1938.

Kennan, George. *E. H. Harriman: A Biography.* 2 vols. Boston, Houghton Mifflin, 1922.

La Follette, Belle Case, and Fola La Follette. *Robert M. La Follette.* 2 vols. New York, Macmillan, 1953.

La Follette, Robert M. *La Follette's Autobiography: A Personal Narrative of Political Experience.* Madison, Wis., R. M. La Follette Company, 1913.

Lambert, John R., Jr. *Arthur Pue Gorman.* Baton Rouge, Louisiana State University Press, 1953.

Lambert, Oscar Doane. *Stephen Benton Elkins.* Pittsburgh, University of Pittsburgh Press, 1955.

Lodge, Henry Cabot. *Selections from the Correspondence of Theodore Roosevelt and Henry Cabot Lodge, 1884–1918.* 2 vols. New York, Charles Scribner's Sons, 1925.

Longworth, Alice. *Crowded Hours.* New York, Charles Scribner's Sons, 1933.

McCall, Samuel Walker. *Life of Thomas Brackett Reed.* Boston, Houghton Mifflin, 1914.

McElroy, Robert McNutt. *Grover Cleveland.* 2 vols. New York, Harper & Bros., 1923.

———. *Levi Parsons Morton: Banker, Diplomat, and Statesman.* New York, G. P. Putnam's Sons, 1930.

Martin, Edward Sanford. *Life of Joseph Hodges Choate as Gathered Chiefly from His Letters.* 2 vols. New York, Charles Scribner's Sons, 1921.

Mason, Alpheus Thomas. *Brandeis: A Free Man's Life.* New York, Viking, 1946.

Mayes, Edward. *Lucius Q. C. Lamar, 1825–1893.* Nashville, Banbee & Smith, 1896.

Merrill, Horace S. *William Freeman Vilas.* Madison, Wisconsin State Historical Society, 1954.

Morison, Elting E., John M. Blum and John J. Buckley (editors). *The Letters of Theodore Roosevelt.* 8 vols. Cambridge, Mass., Harvard University Press, 1951–1954.

Muzzey, David S. *James G. Blaine: A Political Idol of Other Days.* New York, Dodd, Mead, 1934.

Nevins, Allan. *Grover Cleveland: A Study in Courage.* New York, Dodd, Mead, 1932.

Olcott, Charles S. *Life of William McKinley.* 2 vols. Boston, Houghton Mifflin, 1916.

Orcutt, William Dana. *Burrows of Michigan and the Republican Party: A Biography and a History.* 2 vols. New York, Longmans, Green, 1917.

Parker, William Belmont. *The Life and Public Services of Justin Smith Morrill.* Boston, Houghton Mifflin, 1924.

Pink, Louis Heaton. *Gaynor, the Tammany Mayor Who Swallowed the Tiger: Lawyer, Judge, Philosopher.* New York, International Press, 1931.

Platt, Thomas Collier. *The Autobiography of Thomas Collier Platt.* New York, B. W. Dodge & Co., 1910.

Pringle, Henry Fowles. *The Life and Times of William Howard Taft.* 2 vols. New York, Farrar & Rinehart, 1939.

———. *Theodore Roosevelt: A Biography.* New York, Harcourt, Brace, 1931.

Richardson, Leon Burr. *William E. Chandler: Republican.* New York, Dodd, Mead, 1940.

Robinson, William Alexander. *Thomas B. Reed: Parliamentarian.* New York, Dodd, Mead, 1930.

Roosevelt, Theodore. *An Autobiography.* New York, Macmillan, 1914.

Sage, Leland L. *William Boyd Allison.* Iowa City, State Historical Society of Iowa, 1956.

Schriftgiesser, Karl. *The Gentleman from Massachusetts: Henry Cabot Lodge.* Boston, Atlantic Monthly Press, 1944.

Sherman, John. *Recollections of Forty Years in House, Senate, and Cabinet.* 2 vols. Chicago, The Werner Co., 1895.

Simkins, Francis Butler. *Pitchfork Ben Tillman: South Carolinian.* Baton Rouge, Louisiana State University Press, 1944.

Stealey, Orlando O. *Twenty Years in the Press Gallery.* New York, Publishers Printing Co., 1906.

Stephenson, Isaac. *Recollections of a Long Life, 1829–1915.* Chicago, R. R. Donnelley & Sons, 1915.

Stephenson, Nathaniel Wright. *Nelson W. Aldrich: A Leader in American Politics.* New York, Charles Scribner's Sons, 1930.

Swaine, Robert T. *The Cravath Firm and Its Predecessors, 1819–1948.* 2 vols. New York, Ad Press, Ltd., 1948.

Thayer, William Roscoe. *Life and Letters of John Hay.* 2 vols. Boston, Houghton Mifflin, 1915.

Thompson, E. Bruce. *Matthew Hale Carpenter: Webster of the West.* Madison, Wisconsin State Historical Society, 1954.

Walters, Everett. *Joseph Benson Foraker: An Uncompromising Republican*. Columbus, Ohio History Press, 1948.
Wight, William Ward. *Henry Clay Payne*. Milwaukee, Burdick & Allen, 1907.

VI. Special studies important for an understanding of the problems with which Spooner was concerned

Bailey, Thomas A. *A Diplomatic History of the American People*. 4th ed. New York, Appleton-Century-Crofts, 1950.
Bemis, Samuel Flagg. *A Diplomatic History of the United States*. 2d ed. New York, Henry Holt, 1950.
Binkley, Wilfred E. *President and Congress*. New York, Alfred A. Knopf, 1947.
Buck, Solon. *The Agrarian Crusade: A Chronicle of the Farmer in Politics*. New Haven, Conn., Yale University Press, 1921.
Bunau-Varilla, Philippe. *Panama: The Creation, Destruction and Resurrection*. New York, McBride, Nast & Co., 1920.
Butterfield, Consul Willshire. *History of the University of Wisconsin, from Its First Organization to 1879*. Madison, University Press Co., 1879.
Callahan, James Morton. *American Foreign Policy in Canadian Relations*. New York, Macmillan, 1937.
Carey, John W. *Organization and History of the Chicago, Milwaukee and St. Paul Railway Company*. Chicago, Press of Cramer Aikens & Cramer, 1892.
Casey, Robert J., and W. A. S. Douglas. *Pioneer Railroad*. New York, McGraw-Hill, 1948.
Chadwick, French Ensor. *The Relations of the United States and Spain: Diplomacy*. New York, Charles Scribner's Sons, 1909.
Chapman, Charles E. *A History of the Cuban Republic*. New York, Macmillan, 1927.
Curti, Merle, and Vernon Carstensen. *The University of Wisconsin: A History, 1848–1925*. 2 vols. Madison, University of Wisconsin Press, 1949.

Daggett, Stuart. *Railroad Reorganization.* Cambridge, Mass., Harvard Economic Studies, No. 4, 1908.

Elliott, Charles Burke. *The Philippines.* 2 vols. Indianapolis, Bobbs-Merrill, 1916.

Filler, Louis. *Crusaders for American Liberalism.* New York, Harcourt, Brace, 1939.

Fish, Carl Russell. *The Civil Service and Patronage.* Cambridge, Mass., Harvard University Press, 1920.

Forbes, W. Cameron. *The Philippine Islands.* 2 vols. Boston, Houghton Mifflin, 1928.

Foster, John W. *American Diplomacy in the Orient.* Boston, Houghton Mifflin, 1903.

Fowler, Dorothy Ganfield. *The Cabinet Politician: The Postmasters General, 1829–1909.* New York, Columbia University Press, 1943.

Freis, Robert F. *Empire in Pine.* Madison, Wisconsin State Historical Society, 1951.

Gabriel, Ralph Henry. *The Course of American Democratic Thought.* New York, Ronald Press Co., 1940.

Gates, Paul Wallace. *The Wisconsin Pine Lands of Cornell University.* Ithaca, N. Y., Cornell University Press, 1943.

Glasson, William Henry. *History of Military Pension Legislation in the United States.* New York, Columbia University Press, 1900.

Haney, Louis H. *A Congressional History of Railways in the United States.* Madison, University of Wisconsin Bulletin, No. 342, 1910.

Hotchkiss, George W. *History of the Lumber and Forest Industry of the Northwest.* Chicago, G. W. Hotchkiss & Co., 1898.

Knoles, George Harmon. *The Presidential Campaign and Election of 1892.* Stanford, Calif., Stanford University Press, 1942.

Larson, Agnes. *History of the White Pine Industry in Minnesota.* Minneapolis, University of Minnesota Press, 1949.

Lombardi, John. *Labor Voice in the Cabinet.* New York, Columbia University Press, 1942.

Lovejoy, Allen Fraser. *La Follette and the Establishment of the Direct Primary in Wisconsin: 1890–1904.* New Haven, Conn., Yale University Press, 1941.

Mack, Gerstle. *The Land Divided: A History of the Panama Canal and Other Isthmian Canal Projects.* New York, Alfred A. Knopf, 1944.

McMurry, Donald L. *Coxey's Army: A Study of the Industrial Army Movement of 1894.* Boston, Little, Brown, 1929.

Merrill, Horace Samuel. *Bourbon Democracy of the Middle West: 1865–1896.* Baton Rouge, Louisiana State University Press, 1953.

Millis, Walter. *The Martial Spirit.* Boston, Houghton Mifflin, 1931.

Miner, Dwight Carroll. *The Fight for the Panama Route: The Story of the Spooner Act and the Hay-Herran Treaty.* New York, Columbia University Press, 1940.

Moody, John. *The Railroad Builders.* New Haven, Conn., Yale University Press, 1919.

Munro, Dana G. *The United States and the Caribbean Area.* Boston, World Peace Foundation, 1934.

Pratt, Julius W. *Expansionists of 1898.* Baltimore, The Johns Hopkins Press, 1936.

Regier, Cornelius. *The Era of the Muckrakers.* Chapel Hill, University of North Carolina Press, 1932.

Riegel, Robert Edgar. *Story of the Western Railroads.* New York, Macmillan, 1926.

Ripley, William Z. *Railroads: Finance and Organization.* New York, Longmans, Green, 1927.

———. *Railroads: Rates and Regulations.* New York, Longmans, Green, 1924.

Stanwood, Edward. *A History of the Presidency.* Boston, Houghton Mifflin, 1898.

Stennett, William H. *Yesterday and To-Day: A History of the Chicago and Northwestern Railroad System.* Chicago, Chicago and Northwestern Railroad Co., 1905.

Swisher, Carl Brent. *American Constitutional Development.* Boston, Houghton Mifflin, 1954.

Tarbell, Ida M. *The Tariff in Our Times.* New York, Macmillan, 1911.

Walker, James Blaine. *Fifty Years of Rapid Transit.* New York, Law Printing Co., 1918.

Willison, George F. *Saints and Strangers, Being the Lives of the Pilgrim Fathers and Their Families.* New York, Reynal & Hitchcock, 1945.

Wittke, Carl Frederick. *We Who Built America.* New York, Prentice-Hall, 1940.

VII. Local histories that throw light on aspects of Spooner's career

Ambler, Charles Henry. *West Virginia: The Mountain State.* New York, Prentice-Hall, 1940.

Barry, David S. *Forty Years in Washington.* Boston, Little, Brown, 1924.

Barton, Albert O. *La Follette's Winning of Wisconsin: 1894–1904.* Madison, Wis., n.p., 1922.

Callahan, James Morton. *Semi-Centennial History of West Virginia.* Morgantown, W. Va., Semi-Centennial Commission, 1913.

Folsom, William H. C. *Fifty Years in the Northwest.* St. Paul, Pioneer Press, 1888.

History of Dearborn and Ohio Counties, Indiana. Chicago, F. E. Weakley and Co., 1885.

Hurd, Charles. *Washington Cavalcade.* New York, E. P. Dutton, 1948.

Lockwood, Mary Smith. *Yesterdays in Washington.* 2 vols. Roslyn, N. Y., Commonwealth Co., 1915.

Love, William De Loss. *Wisconsin in the War of the Rebellion.* Chicago, n.p., 1866.

Merk, Frederick. *Economic History of Wisconsin During the Civil War Decade.* Madison, Wisconsin State Historical Society, 1916.

Plumb, Ralph Gordon. *Badger Politics: 1836–1930.* Manitowoc, Wis., Brandt Printing & Binding Co., 1930.

Quiner, Edwin B. *The Military History of Wisconsin.* Chicago, n.p., 1866.

Raney, William Francis. *Wisconsin: A Story of Progress.* New York, Prentice-Hall, 1940.
Usher, Ellis B. *Wisconsin, Its Story and Biography: 1848–1913.* 8 vols. Chicago, Lewis Publishing Co., 1914.
Works Progress Administration, Wisconsin. *A Guide to the Badger State.* New York, Duell, Sloan & Pearce, 1941.

VIII. Articles of interest to a student of Spooner's career

Beatty, Arthur, and E. A. Birge. "University of Wisconsin and Its President," *Wisconsin Alumnus,* 1940–1943.
Bogart, Ernest Ludlow. "Alpheus Beede Stickney," *Dictionary of American Biography,* ed. Dumas Malone. New York, 1935, 18:15–16.
Daland, Robert T. "Enactment of the Potter Law," *Wisconsin Magazine of History,* 33 (September, 1949), 45–54.
Dexter, Morton. "Members of the Pilgrim Company in Leyden," *Proceedings of the Massachusetts Historical Society,* (April, 1903), pp. 167–84.
Dozer, Donald Marquand. "Benjamin Harrison and the Presidential Campaign of 1892," *American Historical Review,* 54 (October, 1948), 49–78.
Durant, Edward W. "Lumbering and Steamboating on the St. Croix River," *Collections of the Minnesota Historical Society,* 10 (February, 1905), 645–75.
Ellis, David Maldwyn. "The Forfeiture of Railroad Land Grants, 1867–1894," *Mississippi Valley Historical Review,* 33 (June, 1946), 27–60.
Fowler, Dorothy Ganfield. "Congressional Dictation of Local Appointments," *Journal of Politics,* 7 (February, 1945), 25–57.
Ganfield, Dorothy. "Influence of Wisconsin on Federal Politics." Unpublished doctoral dissertation, University of Wisconsin, 1928.
Glover, Wilbur H. "The Agricultural College Crisis of 1885," *Wisconsin Magazine of History,* 32 (September, 1948), 17–25.

Halsell, Willie D. "The Appointment of L. Q. C. Lamar to the Supreme Court," *Mississippi Valley Historical Review,* 28 (December, 1941), 399–413.

Hantke, Richard W. "Elisha W. Keyes, the Bismarck of Western Politics," *Wisconsin Magazine of History,* 31 (September, 1947), 29–42.

Haugen, Nils P. "Pioneer and Political Reminiscences," *Wisconsin Magazine of History,* 11 (March, 1928), 269–300; (June, 1928), 395–436; 12 (September, 1928), 41–58.

Hayes, Clara Lyon. "William Penn Lyon," *Wisconsin Magazine of History,* 9 (March, 1926), 260–80.

Kellogg, Louise P. "The Bennett Law in Wisconsin," *Wisconsin Magazine of History,* 2 (September, 1918), 3–25.

Miller, Willis H. "John Comstock: Banker," *Wisconsin Magazine of History,* 22 (December, 1948), 168–76.

Mood, Fulmer. "Frederick Jackson Turner and the Chicago *Inter-Ocean,* 1885," *Wisconsin Magazine of History,* 35 (Spring, 1952), 189–94, 210–17.

Paxson, Frederic L. "Roswell Pettibone Flower," *Dictionary of American Biography,* 16:479–80.

Phillips, David Graham. "The Treason of the Senate," *Cosmopolitan Magazine,* March–June, 1906.

Reid, Harvey. "Diary of Harvey Reid," *Wisconsin Magazine of History,* 1 (September, 1917), 35–64.

Sanborn, John D. "The Supreme Court of Wisconsin in the Eighties," *Wisconsin Magazine of History,* 15 (September, 1931), 19–20.

Steffens, Lincoln. "Enemies of the Republic: Wisconsin," *McClure's Magazine,* 23 (October, 1904), 564–79.

Sumner, William A. "William Dempster Hoard," *Dictionary of American Biography,* 9:90.

Volwiler, Arthur T. "Tariff Strategy and Propaganda in the United States, 1887–1888," *American Historical Review,* 36 (October, 1930), 76–96.

Wellborn, Fred. "The Influence of the Silver Republican Senators, 1889–1891," *Mississippi Valley Historical Review,* 14 (March, 1928), 462–80.

Wellman, Walter. "Spooner of Wisconsin: A Sketch of the Present Leader of the Senate," *Review of Reviews,* 26 (August, 1902), 167–70.

Whyte, William F. "The Bennett Law Campaign," *Wisconsin Magazine of History,* 10 (June, 1927), 364–90.

Williams, Helen J., and Harry Williams. "Wisconsin Republicans and Reconstruction," *Wisconsin Magazine of History,* 23 (September, 1939), 17–39.

Index